Court House, Martinsburg, Berkeley County.

ALER'S HISTORY
—OF—
MARTINSBURG AND BERKELEY CO., W. VA.

Aler's History of
MARTINSBURG
AND
BERKELEY COUNTY
WEST VIRGINIA

From the Origin of the Indians, Embracing Their Settlement, Wars and Depredations, to the First White Settlement of the Valley; also Including the Wars between the Settlers and Their Mode and Manner of Living. Besides a Variety of Valuable Information, Consisting of the Past and Present History of the County, Including a Complete Sketch of the Late Wars, Strikes, Early Residents, Organizations, etc., Accompanied by Personal Sketches and Interesting Facts of the Present Day

BY

F. Vernon Aler

HERITAGE BOOKS
2008

HERITAGE BOOKS
AN IMPRINT OF HERITAGE BOOKS, INC.

Books, CDs, and more—Worldwide

For our listing of thousands of titles see our website
at
www.HeritageBooks.com

A Facsimile Reprint
Published 2008 by
HERITAGE BOOKS, INC.
Publishing Division
100 Railroad Ave. #104
Westminster, Maryland 21157

Copyright © 1888 F. Vernon Aler

Originally printed for the author by
The Mail Publishing Company
Hagerstown, Maryland

— Publisher's Notice —
In reprints such as this, it is often not possible to remove blemishes from the original. We feel the contents of this book warrant its reissue despite these blemishes and hope you will agree and read it with pleasure.

International Standard Book Numbers
Paperbound: 978-1-58549-979-3
Clothbound: 978-0-7884-7746-1

Entered according to Act of Congress, in the year 1888, by
F. VERNON ALER,
in the Office of the Librarian of Congress, at Washington.

All Rights Reserved.

PREFACE.

In idle wishes fools supinely stay.
Be there a will, then wisdom finds a way.
—BURNS.

IN presenting this work to the public I feel that a great responsibility has been undertaken. It may, no doubt, meet with the harsh criticism of many; but as a consolation I feel satisfied that nothing but facts have been stated, and that every reader interested in the growth, prosperity and history of Berkeley County will appreciate this honest attempt. I have ventured this work on the market, feeling confident that the interested class—the people that have labored for our City and County—the ones that owe and feel a debt of gratitude to their forefathers for the present stage of their existence and welfare of the County—will sustain me in my efforts.

The present generation, now enjoying the benefits of this soil, perhaps, have a very small conception as to the manner in which it was settled, cultivated and reared to its present state of prosperity. Perhaps many may doubt the credibility of these chapters, but I would ask a perusal and careful examination of early history, and by information from our old citizens, you will find my collections have not fallen far short of facts. Several attempts, in various ways, have been made to give a history and reminiscence of our County; but as yet none had been published full and complete, until the introduction of this work. It will be found to contain from the origin of the Indian and White Settlers, and their early warfares, to the present day, accompanied by a complete history of both Martinsburg and Berkeley County.

Preface.

For days, weeks and months, and at times into the mid-hour of night, constant and laborious work has been a theme and pleasure, to dive into the torn and rusty pages of an old Court docket—some half-printed histories, published over half a century ago—or some old newspapers upon which ink was almost invisible, and then to scan the hand-writing of years gone by, that one would hardly recognize as the English language.

To the following gentlemen, Berkeley's most able and respected citizens, I owe a debt of gratitude for their assistance in the work of publishing this small history: Senator C. J. Faulkner, C. W. Doll, Esq., James M. Vanmetre, Esq., Capt. Wm. Hoke, Hon. E. B. Faulkner, J. W. Curtis, Esq., and Stuart W. Walker, Esq., who acted at times as my critic and rendered valuable assistance. Considerable information has been taken from a small history of the valley published by Samuel Kercheval in 1833.

I look around me and see the young of both sexes with hearts bounding high with hope, forms elastic with health and eyes bright with the enjoyment of life, and then the thought of the rude settlements, life and civilization of our fore-parents touches the tenderest chord. To tell them of how they performed the journey of life, hand in hand, interrupted now and then by the savage warfare, and after all lived in harmonious companionship, I have published this work. It has been with me an honest and earnest task, in the object of which I am sure you will feel interested. I only hope that you will find little to criticise and nothing to condemn, in the nature and style of the means by which I have sought to accomplish it. Then I shall feel that my undertaking has been crowned with success by a non-condemnatory people in a worthy and honest purpose.

Yours very truly,

F. VERNON ALER.

CONTENTS.

	PAGE.
Introductory	15

CHAPTER I.
Origin of the Indian Settlements. The different Tribes. Their Wars, Customs, Habits, etc ... 25

CHAPTER II.
First Settlements of the Valley. Locations, Land Titles, Dwellings, etc ... 32

CHAPTER III.
The Indian Warfare. Forts Established, etc. The Wars between the Settlers and Indians, and the manner in which they carried on their Barbarism ... 38

CHAPTER IV.
Houses, Furniture, Diet and Dress of the early Settlers. Interesting and amusing Scenes of centuries back of our Foreparents ... 47

CHAPTER V.
Northern Neck of Virginia. Berkeley County laid off. The Land Grants, etc., from Lord Fairfax's time to the establishment of the County ... 54

CHAPTER VI.
Martinsburg established. The Lots laid off by the first Commissioned Sheriff. Sale of Lots, with terms to purchasers ... 61

CHAPTER VII.
Report of Hon. C. J. Faulkner on Adjustment of the Boundary Line between Virginia and Maryland ... 67

CHAPTER VIII.
Historical Sketches of the early Inhabitants, etc., by the late Hon. Charles James Faulkner ... 87

CHAPTER IX.
Slavery—Mode and Manner of Punishment—Freedom ... 200

CHAPTER X.
The late War of the Rebellion. The different Companies of Berkeley County, Federal and Confederate, with full Names, Happenings, etc ... 209

CHAPTER XI.
Historical Reminiscence of Martinsburg from 1835 until the year 1861, by John W. Curtis ... 249

Contents.

CHAPTER XII.
Commencing and ending of Strikes. A full and complete detail of the Happenings, Incidents, etc.. 300

CHAPTER XIII.
Life of the late Hon. Charles James Faulkner, by Col. Frank A. Burr. 314

CHAPTER XIV.
The Churches—Organization and present Condition 343

CHAPTER XV.
Berkeley County in 1810. Topographical Description. Natural Curiosities. Mineralogy and Lithology. Inhabitants, Towns, Manufactories, etc 366

CHAPTER XVI.
Present situation of the Town and County—Journalism in the County—County Court and Officials—Martinsburg Schools—Home Organizations, Lodges, etc 377

CHAPTER XVII.
Personal Sketches of the Enterprising Public and Professional Men of the present day... 397

CHAPTER XVIII.
Biography of Martinsburg's Business Men..................................... 412

INTRODUCTORY.

THE Indian origin and settlements contained in the following chapters will be found to embrace every particular trait and detail so familiar to the race. Berkeley County, without doubt, will be found to be among the most historic pages of the world's history. For centuries its soils were inhabited by the most barbarous races, whom, it seems, carried out the habits and customs of ages past to their fullest extent. From what particular part of the old world the aboriginals found their way to this continent is a question which has given rise to much disquisition among philosophical and learned historians. However, it appears to be a settled opinion that America first received its inhabitants from Asia, and in Mr. Snowden's History of America many able and ingenious arguments are advanced in support of this opinion. This is a matter, however, familiar to our people of the present day, and to describe the customs of the old world, from whence they originated, will perhaps, prove of interest to the reader. Mr. Snowden states:

"The custom of scalping was a barbarism in use with the Scythians, who carried about them at all times this savage mark of triumph. A little image found among the Kalmucs, of a Tartarian diety mounted on a horse and sitting on a human skin, with scalps pendant from the breast, fully illustrates the custom of the ancient Scythians, as described by the Greek historian. The ferocity of this race to their prisoners extended to the remotest part of Asia. The Kamtschatkans, even at the time of their discovery by the Russians, put their prisoners to death by the most lingering and excruciating torments. A race of the Scythians were named Anthropophagi, from their feeding on human flesh. The people of Nootka Sound still make a repast on their fellow creatures. The savages of North America have been known to throw the mangled limbs of their prisoners into the horrible caldron and devour them with the same relish as those of a quadruped."

These usages were continued for centuries, and have been described by many as of a horrid experience. Among the aboriginal Americans these practices are said to be in full force at the present day.

FIRST SETTLEMENT OF VIRGINIA.

After giving the foregoing brief sketch of the probable origin of the Indians in America, it is deemed an important part of this work to give a brief history of the first settlement of Virginia, and the laws then in force, which will not be unacceptable to the general reader. The author, having access to the large law libraries of Faulkner & Walker, has been enabled to gain much valuable information, and would refer the reader wishing to make a deeper research, to Hening's Statutes at Large, vol. 1, page 57.

Charters to two separate companies called the "London and Plymouth Companies," for settling colonies in Virginia, were granted by James I, King of England, on the 10th day of April, 1606. On the 20th of December, 1606, Capt. Christopher Newport was sent to Virginia by the London Company with a colony of one hundred and five persons, and instructions to settle on the island of Roanoke, now in North Carolina. However, by stress of weather, they were driven North of their destination, and entered Chesapeake Bay. From here they ascended what they called the James River, and on a beautiful peninsula commenced the settlement of Jamestown about May, 1607. This was the first permanent settlement in

Introductory.

the country. King James granted several subsequent charters to the company for the better ordering and government of the colony, "and in the year 1619 the first legislative council was convened at Jamestown, then called 'James City.'" The following is the commission to Sir Francis Wyatt, the first Governor under that ordinance and constitution, to call a meeting of the General Assembly:

"*The Treasurer and Company's Commission to Sir Francis Wyatt, Governor, and Council*, which said Council are to assist the Governor in the administration of justice, to advance Christianity among Indians, to erect the colony in obedience to his majesty and in maintaining the people in justice and christian conversation, and strengthening them against enemies. The said Governor, Council and two burgesses out of every town, hundred or plantation, to be chosen by the inhabitants, to make up a General Assembly, who are to decide all matters by the greater number of voices; but the Governor is to have a negative voice, to have power to make orders and acts necessary wherein they are to initiate the policy of the form of government, laws, customs, manner of trial and other administration of justice used in England, as the company are required by their letters patent. No law to continue or be of force till ratified by a quarter court to be held in England and returned under seal. After the colony is well framed and settled, no order of quarter court in England shall bind till ratified by the General Assembly."

"Dated 24th July, 1621."

"*Instructions to Governor Wyatt.*"

"By instructions dated 24th July, 1621: To keep up religion of the Church of England as near as may be; to be obedient to the King and do justice after the form of the laws of England, and not to injure the natives; and to forget old quarrels now buried.

"To be industrious and suppress drunkenness, gaming

and excess in deaths ; not to permit any but the Council and heads of hundreds to wear gold in their cloaths or to wear silk till they make it themselves.

"Not to offend any foreign princes; to punish piracies ; to build fortresses and block-houses at the mouths of the rivers.

"To use means to convert the heathens, viz., to converse with some ; each town to teach some children fit for the college intended to be built.

"After Sir George Yeardley has gathered the present year's crop, he is to deliver to Sir Francis Wyatt the hundred tenants belonging to Governor's place ; Yeardley's government to expire the 18th November next, and then Wyatt to be published Governor; to swear the Council.

"George Sandis appointed treasurer, and he is to put in execution all orders or court about staple commodities ; to whom is allotted fifteen hundred acres and fifty tenants ; to the marshall, Sir William Newce, the same ; to the company's deputy the same; to the physician five hundred acres and twenty tenants, and the same to the secretary.

"To review the commissions to Sir George Yeardley, Governor, and the Council, dated 18th November, 1618, for dividing the colony into cities, boroughs, &c., and to observe all former instructions (a copy whereof was sent) if they did not contradict the present ; and all orders of court (made in England.)

"To make a catalogue of the people in every plantation, and their conditions ; and of deaths, marriages and christenings.

"To take care of dead persons' estates for the right owners ; and keep a list of all cattle, and cause the secretary to return copies of the premises once a year.

"To take care of every plantation upon the death of their chief ; not to plant above one hundred pounds of tobacco per head ; to sow great quantities of corn for their own use, and to support the multitudes to be sent yearly; to inclose lands; to keep cows, swine, poultry, &c., and particularly kyne, which are not to be killed yet.

"Next to corn, plant mulberry trees and make silk, and take care of the Frenchman and others sent about that work; to try silk grass; to plant abundance of vines and take care of the vignerors sent.

"To put prentices to trades, and not let them forsake their trades for planting tobacco or any such useless commodity.

"To take care of the Dutch sent to build saw-mills, and seat them at the falls that they may bring their timber by the current of the water.

"To build saw-mills and block-houses in every plantation.

"That all contracts in England or Virginia be performed, and the breaches punished according to justice.

"Tenants not to be enticed away; to take care of those sent about an iron work, and especially Mr. John Berkeley, that they don't miscarry again, this being the greatest hope and expectation of the colonies.

"To make salt, pitch, tar, soap, ashes, &c., so often recommended and for which materials had been sent; to make oyl of walnuts and employ apothecaries in distilling lees of beer and searching after minerals, dyes, gums and drugs, &c., and send small quantities home.

"To make small quantity of tobacco, and that very good; that the houses appointed for the reception of new-comers and public storehouses be built, kept clean, &c.; to send the state of affairs quarterly and a duplicate next shipping.

"To take care of Capt. Wm. Norton and certain Italians sent to set up a glass house.

"A copy of the treatise of the plantation business and excellent observances made by a gentleman of capacity is sent to lie among the records, and recommended to the councillors to study.

"Mr William Clayborne, a surveyor, sent to survey the planters' lands and make a map of the country.

"Chief officers that have tenants reprimanded for taking fees, but require that the clerks have fees set for passes, warrants, copies of orders, &c.

"Governor and Council to appoint proper times for administration of justice, and provide for the entertainment of the Council during their session, to be together one whole month about state affairs and lawsuits; to record plaints of consequence; to keep a register of the acts of quarter sessions and send home copies.

"If a Governor dies, the major part of Council to choose one of themselves within fourteen days, but if voices be divided the Lieutenant Governor shall have the place, and next the marshall, next the treasurer, and one of the two deputies next.

"Governor and chief officers not to let out their tenants as usual.

"The Governor only to summon the Council and sign warrants and execute, or give authority to execute Council orders, except in cases that do belong to the marshall, treasurer, deputies, &c.

"The Governor to have absolute authority to determine and punish all neglects and contempts of authority except the Council, who are to be tried at the quarter sessions and censured. Governor to have but the casting voice in Council or court, but in the Assembly a negative voice.

"That care be taken that there be no engrossing commodity or forestalling the market.

"All servants to fare alike in the colony, and their punishment for any offences is to serve the colony in public works.

"To see that the Earl of Pembroke's thirty thousand acres be very good.

"To make discoveries along the coast and find a fishery between James River and Cape Cod.

"As to raising staple commodities, the chief officers ought to set examples and to aim at the establishment of the colony.

"And lastly, not to let ships stay long, and to freight them with walnut and any less valuable commodity.

The Governor administered the following oath to the Council:

"You shall swear to be a true and faithful servant
"unto the king's majesty, as one of his Council for Vir-
"ginia. You shall in all things to be moved, treated,
"and debated in that Council concerning Virginia or
"any the territories of America, between the degrees of
"thirty-four and forty-five from the equinoctial line
"northward, or the trades thereof, faithfully and truly
"declare your mind and opinion, according to your heart
"and conscience; and shall keep secret all matters com-
"mitted and revealed to you concerning the same, and
"that shall be treated secretly in that Council, or this
"Council of Virginia, or the more part of them, publi-
"cation shall not be made thereof; and of all matters of
"great importance, or difficulty, before you resolve
"thereupon, you shall make his majesty's Privy Coun-
"cil acquainted therewith, and follow their direction
"therein. You shall to your uttermost bear faith and
"allegiance to the King's majesty, his heirs, and lawful
"successors, and shall assist and defend all jurisdictions,
"preheminences, and authorities granted unto his ma-
"jesty and annext unto the crown against all foreign
"princes, persons, prelates or potentates whatsoever, be
"it by act of parliament or otherwise; and generally,
"in all things, you shall do as a faithful and true ser-
"vant and subject ought to do. So help you God and
"the holy contents of this book."

The foregoing instructions were drawn up by the Council, and it appears, were intended as the general principles for the government of the colony. They go far to prove that hopes were entertained that the Indians were disposed to be at peace, and evidences an amicable state of feeling towards the natives. Unfortunately their hopes were blasted, for lo! in less than one year after, this state of peace and tranquility was changed into one of devastation, blood and mourning. On the 22nd of March, 1622, the Indians committed the most bloody massacre on the colonists recorded in the annals of our country. This year has been stated by historians as the American revolution, and was remarkable for massacres of the colonists by the Indians, which were executed with the utmost subtility, and without any regard to age, sex or dignity.

In 1623, the following year, the Colonial General Assembly, by statute, directed "that the 22nd day of March be yearly solemnized as holliday," to commemorate the escape of the colony from entire extirpation. These bloody massacres produced, on the part of the whites, a most deadly and irreconcilable hatred toward the natives, and accordingly, we find that a long continued and unabating state of hostility was kept up. At the legislative session of 1623, laws were enacted in relation to a defense against the savages. About one hundred years later the Indians were driven east of the Blue Ridge Mountains, and scattered over the surrounding country, hence, their origin on Berkeley soil.

The foregoing extracts are considered sufficient to enable the reader to form some opinion of the spirit, character and customs of the early settlers of our country; particularly as it relates to their sufferings and difficulties with the Indian tribes, and goes far to prove their origin in our country and the veracity of the contents of this book.

Some may ask, of what interest are the extracts from Hening's Statutes at Large? In return I would ask, who would place confidence in my work without it was based

Introductory.

on a reliable foundation? The extracts, after given a study and careful consideration, will prove of much interest and enable the reader to form a quaint idea of the origin and introduction of our laws, customs, religion, habits, manufactures, etc., of the present day in our country and county.

Prior to the Independence of the United States, the popular branch of Virginia Colonial Legislation was known as "The House of Burgesses." It enacted its laws under the provincial charter granted by the English government, to whom its allegiance was due. The "House of Burgesses," by its enactments from time to time laid off the territory into counties, as the interests of its increasing population demanded.

At a session of the legislature, Frederick and Augusta were laid off about the year 1738, and included all the vast region of country west of the Blue Ridge mountain. Previous to that time the county of Orange included all the territory west of the mountains, and was taken from Spotsylvania in 1734, which had previously crossed the mountain and took in considerable part of what is now known as Page County. Spotsylvania was laid off in 1720, and was reduced by the laying off of Frederick in 1738. The first court of justice was held in this county in 1743. The county of Hampshire was next taken from Frederick and Augusta in 1753. The first court held in this county was in December 1757. Berkeley and Dunmore were taken from Frederick in 1772, and in 1777 the name of Dunmore was altered to Shenandoah.

I deem it a particular and interesting part of this work to give the dates of the establishment of these counties, as the following chapters in various ways relate to them. It will be noticed that Berkeley was among the earliest, and many incidents happened on its soil, before the laying off of other counties. It included all that territory composing Jefferson County from 1772 until 1801, a period of nearly thirty years. Martinsburg was laid off in the month of October, 1778, by Adam Stephen, Esq., and consisted of one hundred and thirty acres. In October, 1786, Charlestown (then in the county of Berkeley and now the seat of justice for the county of Jefferson) was established. It consisted of eighty acres, and was laid off by Charles Washington, a brother of the illustrious George Washington. He laid off his own land into lots and streets, and in honor of his act the town bears his christian name to the present day. In the month of October, 1787, Middletown, (now called Gerardstown,) in the county of Berkeley, was established, with one hundred lots laid off by Wm. Gerard. Darkesville, also in Berkeley County, was laid off in October, 1791. The establishment of these towns are among the earliest of the valley.

CHAPTER I.

ORIGIN OF THE INDIAN SETTLEMENTS.

FROM ancient history it appears that this entire portion of country (Berkeley County) was inhabited by various tribes of Indians. From the best evidence obtained from deep researches, we find the settlement of this valley and present county was commenced in the year 1732. Long and bloody wars were carried on by contending tribes of Indians known as the Delaware and Catawba tribes. They were engaged in these wars at the time the valley was first known by the white people, and continued for years after the county was numerously inhabited by white settlers.

The two great branches of the Potomac and Shenandoah rivers seem to have been the favorite places of residence of the Indians. Along these streams are to be found numerous signs and relics at the present day. In the bank of the river, a short distance below the forks, human skeletons and articles of curious workmanship are constantly being unearthed. Indian mounds are scattered over the entire county, and it is no unusual occurrence to hear that Indian pipes, tomahawks, axes, utensils, etc., are being yet found. Their cups and pots were made of a mixture of clay and shells, and though the workmanship was rude, yet they were strong in texture. There are many other places on all our water courses, to wit, Cedar Creek, Stony Creek and Opequon, as well as the larger water courses, that exhibit evidences of ancient Indian settlements.

This portion of the country was inhabited chiefly by a tribe known as the Tuscarora Indians, their place of residence being on Tuscarora Creek, from which the creek derived its name. Along this stream are a number of Indian graves now marked, while many have been plowed down. Skeletons and bones of unusual size have been turned up by the plow. It appears to the author that no reflecting man can view so many burying places broken up—their bones torn up with the plow—reduced to dust and scattered to the winds—without feeling some degree of melancholy regret. It is to be lamented for another reason. If those mounds and places of burial had been permitted to remain undisturbed, they would have stood as lasting monuments in the history of our country. Many of them were doubtless the work of ages, and future generations would have contemplated them with great interest and curiosity. But these memorials are rapidly disappearing, and the time, perhaps, will come when not a trace of them will remain.

It is in no way wonderful that this unfortunate race of people reluctantly yielded, and with all their force resisted the intrusion made upon their rightful and just possessions by people who were strangers to them from a foreign country. But, perhaps, this was the fiat of Heaven. In the creation of this globe God probably intended it should sustain the greatest possible number of his creatures. And as the human family, in a state of civil life, increases with more rapidity than a people in a state of nature or savage life, the law of force has been generally resorted to, and the weaker compelled to give way to the stronger. It is a fact undeniable that the greater portion of our country has been obtained by the law of force. However, as a matter of consoling reflection, there are some exceptions to this arbitrary rule. Several respectable individuals of the Quaker society thought it unjust to take possession of these lands, and adopted measures to effect some way of compensating the Indians for their just rights. Upon inquiry no particular tribe could be found that claimed a priority over the soil. It was considered by the various tribes a com-

Origin of the Indian Settlements. 27

mon hunting ground, and neither claimed authority to sell.

To confirm the authenticity of this statement it is deemed proper to publish the following letter, written by Thomas Chaulkley to a monthly meeting that was held on Opequon on the 21st of May,* 1738, and is a strong evidence. The following is from the original copy:

"VIRGINIA, AT JOHN CHEAGLES, 21st May, 1738.
"*To Friends of the Monthly Meeting at Opequon*:

Dear friends who inhabit Shenandoah and Opequon: Having a concern for your welfare and prosperity, both now and hereafter, and also the prosperity of your children, I had a desire to see you, but being in years and heavy, and much spent and fatigued with my long journeyings in Virginia and Carolina, makes it seem too hard for me to perform a visit in person to you, wherefore I take this way of writing to discharge my mind of what lies weighty thereon; and

"First. I desire that you be careful (being far and back inhabitants) to keep a friendly correspondence with the native Indians, giving them no occasion of offense, they being a cruel and merciless enemy, where they think they are wronged or defrauded of their rights, as woeful experience hath taught in Carolina, Virginia and Maryland, and especially in New England, etc.; and

"Second. As nature hath given them and their forefathers the possession of this continent of America (or this wilderness) they had a material right thereto in justice and equity; and no people, according to the law of nature and justice and our own principle, which is according to the glorious gospel of our dear and holy Jesus Christ, ought to take away or settle on other men's lands or rights without consent, or purchasing the same by agreement of parties concerned; which I suppose in your case is not yet done.

"Thirdly. Therefore my counsel and christian advice

---

*The people of that day numbered the month.

to you is, my dear friends, that the most reputable among you do with speed endeavor to agree with and purchase your lands of the native Indians or inhabitants. Take example of our worthy and honorable late proprietor, William Penn, who by his wise and religious care in that relation hath settled a lasting peace and commerce with the natives, and through his prudent management therein hath been instrumental to plant in peace one of the most flourishing provinces in the world.

"Fourthly. Who would run the risk of the lives of their wives and children for the sparing a little cost and pains? I am concerned to lay these things before you, under an uncommon exercise of mind, that your new and flourishing little settlement may not be laid waste, and (if the providence of the Almighty doth not intervene,) some of the blood of yourselves, wives or children be shed or spilt on the ground.

"Fifthly. Consider you are in the province of Virginia, holding what rights you have under that government, and the Virginians have made an agreement with the natives to go as far as the mountains and no further; and you are over and beyond the mountains, therefore out of that agreement, by which you lie open to the insults and incursions of the Southern Indians, who have destroyed many of the inhabitants of Carolina and Virginia, and even now have destroyed more on the like occasion. The English going beyond the bounds of their agreement, eleven of them were killed by the Indians while we were traveling in Virginia.

"Sixthly. If you believe yourselves to be within the bounds of William Penn's patent from King Charles the Second, which will be hard for you to prove, you being far southward of his line, yet if done that will be no consideration with the Indians without a purchase from them, except you will go about to convince them by fire and sword, contrary to our principles; and if that were done they would ever be implacable enemies and the land could never be enjoyed in peace.

"Seventhly. Please to note that in Pennsylvania no new settlements are made without an agreement with the natives, as witness Lancaster County, lately settled, though that is far within the grant of William Penn's patent from King Charles the Second; wherefore you lie open to the insurrections of the Northern as well as Southern Indians; and

"Lastly. Thus having shown my good will to you and to your new settlement, that you might sit every one under your own shady tree where none might make you afraid, and that you might prosper naturally and spiritually, you and your children; and having a little eased my mind of that weight and concern (in some measure) that lay upon me, I at present desist and subscribe myself, in the love of our Holy Lord Jesus Christ, your real friend, T. C."

This good man proves, through his most excellent letter, that Quakers were among our earliest settlers, and that they were early disposed to do justice to the natives of the country. It is highly probable that the white people might have obtained possession of the soil gradually without so much loss of blood if they had first adopted and adhered to this humane and just policy of purchasing the Indians' lands.

Historians and records give considerable evidence of proof that repeated purchases were made, covering the lower portion of the county, while records show that nearly all of the upper portion was purchased. Tradition relates that several tracts of land were purchased by Quakers, near what is now known as Apple-Pie Ridge, and that the Indians were never known to disturb them while residing on the land so purchased.

It, however, affords matter of curious speculation and interesting reflection to the inquiring mind, to notice in this chapter several of the wars that took place in and near this county. That nations are frequently urged to war and devastation by the restless and turbulent disposition so common to mankind, particularly among their leaders, is a question of little doubt. The glory and renown (falsely so termed) of great achievements in war, is probably one principal cause of the wars frequently carried on by people in a state of *nature*.

We have already stated the Indians that inhabited this portion of the country were known as the Delawares and Catawba tribe. Tradition relates that these two tribes of Indians exterminated a tribe called the Senedos that resided on the Shenandoah River, near this county. An aged Indian frequently visited the settlers, and on one occasion informed an old settler, Benjamin Allen, that these "tribes of Indians had killed his whole nation, with the exception of himself and one youth; that this bloody slaughter took place when he (the Indian) was a small boy." From the tradition it is probable the affair took place some time shortly after the middle of the seventeenth century. Tradition also relates that an old Indian visited Mayor Andrew Keyser's grandfather, of Pennsylvania, and asked for something to eat, appearing to be much agitated. After refreshing himself he was asked what disturbed him. He replied, "The Southern Indians—Delawares and Catawbas—have killed my whole nation." History states that evident signs of the truth of this tradition are yet to be seen—that near the place of residence of the Senedos, on the north fork of the Shenandoah River, an Indian mound, when first seen, was 18 or 20 feet high, but is now ploughed down.

The Delawares were afterward in constant wars with the Catawbas, and at times inflicted the most cruel punishments. The former, we are told, was a much larger and stronger tribe than the latter, and tortured the Catawbas to death with all the wonted barbarity and cruelty peculiar to the savage character.

A party of Delaware Indians, as tradition relates,

crossed the Potomac near Oldtown, in Maryland, with a female Catawba prisoner. A short distance from this place occurred a very remarkable instance of their sacrifices. They cruelly murdered their prisoner and moved on. The next day several of them returned and cut off the soles of her feet in order to prevent her from pursuing and haunting them on the march.

This great tribe made the last sacrifice of their Catawba prisoners, near Pennsylvania. A number of prisoners were slowly tortured to death, and during their protracted and cruel sufferings their tormentors used the most insulting language, tantalizing and threatening them with the terrible vengeance of their nation as long as they could speak.

This bloody tragedy soon reached the ears of the Governor of Pennsylvania, and he at once commanded and required all the authorities, both civil and military, to interpose and prohibit a repetition of such acts of barbarity and cruelty.

CHAPTER II.
FIRST SETTLEMENTS OF THE VALLEY.

IN the year 1732, Joist Hite with his family, and his sons-in-law, viz: George Bowman, Jacob Chrisman and Paul Froman, with their families; Robert McKay, Robert Green, William Duff, Peter Stephens, and several others, making sixteen families in all, removed from Pennsylvania, cutting their road from York and crossing the Cohongoruton* about two miles above Harper's Ferry. Hite settled on the Opequon. Peter Stephens and several others settled at Stephensburg and founded the town. The several families settled in the same neighborhood, adjoining each other, where they could find wood and water most convenient. The most authentic information, handed down from one generation to another, leads us to believe that Hite and his party of immigrants were the first settlers west of the Blue Ridge.

John and Isaac Vanmetre next obtained a warrant from Governor Gooch for locating 40,000 acres of land, in the year 1730. They sold or transferred part of their warrant to Joist Hite; and from this warrant emanated several of Hite's grants. Of the titles to the lands on which Hite settled, with several other tracts in the neighborhood of Stephensburg, the originals are founded on this warrant. In 1734 Richard Morgan obtained a grant for a tract of land in the immediate neighborhood of Shepherdstown. The first settlers on this tract numbered about twenty-five.

Tradition relates that a man by the name of John Howard, and his son, previous to the first settlement of our

---

*Cohongoruton is the ancient Indian name of the Potomac, from its junction with the river Shenandoah to the Alleghaney Mountains.

First Settlements of the Valley. 33

valley, made explorations and discovered the charming South Branch Valley. They crossed the Alleghaney mountains, and on the Ohio killed a very large buffalo, which they skinned, and stretching his hide over ribs of wood made a kind of boat. In this frail bark they descended the Ohio and Mississippi to New Orleans, where the French apprehended them as suspicious characters, and made them prisoners. However, they were discharged, from whence they crossed over to England. Lord Fairfax,* living in England at the time, heard of Mr. Howard's arrival, and sought an interview with him. Mr. Howard gave him a description of the fertility and immense value of the South Branch, which determined his lordship to secure it at once in manors. Notwithstanding the selfish monopoly on the part of Lord Fairfax, numerous tenants were induced, by the great fertility and value of the country, to take leases, settle and improve the lands. At an early period many immigrants settled on Capon, (anciently called Cacaphon, which is said to be the Indian name); also on Lost river. Along Back Creek, Cedar Creek, and Opequon, pretty numerous settlements were made. The two great branches of the upper forks of the Shenandoah were among our earliest settlements. Surveys were made on a warrant along the Opequon, north of Winchester, to Apple-Pie Ridge, by an enterprising Quaker, named Ross. Numerous immigrants of the Quaker profession removed from Pennsylvania, and as early as the year 1738 held regular monthly meetings on Opequon. The west side of the Shenandoah below the forks were first settled by overseers and slaves. Another survey was granted, which lies immediately below the above lines, running a considerable distance into the county of Jefferson. The greater portion of the country between North mountain and the Shenandoah River, at the first settling of the

---

*The reader should note Lord Fairfax, as considerable mention is made in the following chapters.

valley was one vast prairie, and afforded the finest possible pasturage for wild animals. The country bounded in the larger kinds of game, such as the buffalo, elk, deer, bear, panther, wild-cat, wolf, fox, beaver, otter, and all other kinds of animals, wild fowl, etc., common to forest countries, were abundant.

The country, now the county of Shenandoah, between the Fort and North Mountains was also settled very early. The settlements through the valley progressed without interruption for about twenty-three years. The Indians suddenly disappeared in the year 1754, and crossed the Alleghaney mountains. Settlers west of the Alleghaney moved into their midst and invited them to move off. The Indians did not object to the Pennsylvanians settling the country, from the fact of William Penn's treatment toward them. They believed all Penn's men to be honest, virtuous, humane and benevolent; but fatal experience taught them quite a different lesson, and they soon found Pennsylvanians were little better than others. The natives held in utter abhorrence the Virginians, whom they designated as "Long Knife," and were literally opposed to their settling in the valley. Tradition informs us of the fact, that the Indians and white people resided in the same neighborhood for several years after the first settlement, and that the Indians were friendly and peaceable. During this period many good, substantial dwelling houses had been erected, and the settlements were in a flourishing condition.

Some years previous to the first settlement of the valley, a man by the name of John Vanmetre, from New York, discovered the fine country on the Wappatomaka, (the ancient Indian name of the South Branch of the Potomac.) He was a kind of wandering Indian trader, and became well acquainted with the Delawares. A company was formed among them, and under his command marched to the South for the purpose of invading the Catawbas. However, the Catawbas had anticipated them and encountered and defeated them with immense slaughter. When Mr. Vanmetre returned to New York, he advised his sons, that if they ever migrated to Virginia, to secure a part of the South Branch bottom. He described it as "The Trough," and the finest body of land he had ever seen. One of his sons, Isaac Vanmetre, who was about to migrate, took his father's advice, and about the year 1736 or 1737, settled in Virginia. Mr. Vanmetre returned to New Jersey shortly afterward, and in 1740 came back, only to find other settlers on his place. He went back to New Jersey again, and in 1744 returned with his family to make a permanent settlement. In the meantime a large number had settled in the neighborhood, and already much progress could be noted.

Maj. Isaac Hite once stated, "that numerous parties of Indians in passing his grandfather's house on Opequon, would call, and that but one instance of theft was ever committed." The Indians charge the white people with teaching them the knowledge of theft and other vices. After the chiefs had received information of a theft search was made until the article found, and the one in possession of it was punished severely. These facts go far to show their high sense of honesty and summary justice. An educated old Cherokee chief in a conversation with Col. Barrett, one of the commissioners for running the boundary line of Indian lands in 1815–16, remarked:

"That before their fathers were acquainted with the whites, the red people needed but little, and that little the Great Spirit gave them, the forest supplying them with food and raiment; that before their fathers were acquainted with the white people, they never got drunk, because they had nothing to make them drunk, and never committed theft because they had no temptation to do so. It was true that when parties were out hunting, and one party was unsuccessful, and found the game of the more successful party hung up, if they needed provision they took it ; and this was not stealing—it was the law and custom of the tribes. Red people never swore, because they had no words to express an oath. The red people meet once a year, at the feast of new corn, extinguish all their fires and kindle up a new one, the smoke of which ascends to the Great Spirit as a greateful sacrifice. Now what better is your religion than ours? The white people have taught us to get drunk, steal, lie, cheat and swear, and with a knowledge of these vices they uphold them ; therefore, we are injured by acquaintance with them."

To say the least of this untutored old man, his opinion, religion excepted, was well founded and conveys a severe rebuke upon those who boast of superior advantages of the lights of education and a knowledge of the religion of God. From this digression let us again turn our attention to the early settlers.

In 1763 many of them were giving their time and attention to rearing large herds of horses, cattle, hogs, etc. Some of them became expert, hardy and adventurous hunters, and depended chiefly for support and money-making on the sale of skins and furs. Considerable attention was given to the culture of the pea vine, which grew abundantly fat in the summer season. The Hites, Frys, Vanmetres and others raised vast stocks of horses, cattle and hogs in those days, upon which Lord Fairfax highly commented at times.

The majority of our first immigrants were principally from Pennsylvania, composed of native Germans or German extraction. A number, however, were direct from Germany, and several from Maryland, New Jersey and New York. These immigrants brought with them the religion, customs and habits of their ancestors. They constituted three religious sects, viz: Lutherans, Menonists and Calvanists, with a few Tunkers, and were very strict in their worship.

Land was the object which invited the greater number of these people to cross the mountain ; for as the saying then was, "it was to be had here for the taking up." Building a cabin and raising a crop of grain, however small, of any kind, entitled the occupant to four hundred acres of land, and a pre-emption right to one thousand acres more adjoining, to be secured by a land office warrant. This right was to take effect if there happened to be so much vacant land, or any part thereof, adjoining the tract secured by the settlement right. There was, at an early period of our settlements, an inferior kind of land title, denominated a "tomahawk right," which was made by deadening a few trees near the head of a spring, and marking the bark of some one or more of them with the initials of the name of the person who made the improvement. These rights were often bought and sold. Those who wished to make settlements on their favorite tracts of land, bought up the tomahawk improvements, rather than enter into quarrels with those who made them. Other improvers of the land with a view to actual settlement, and who happened to be stout veteran fellows, took a very different course from that of purchasing these rights. When annoyed by the claimants under the tomahawk rights, they deliberately cut a few good hickories, and gave them what was called in those days "a laced jacket," or a sound whipping.

The buildings occupied a low situation, and the tops of the surrounding hills were the boundaries of the tracts to which the family mansion belonged. Our forefathers were fond of farms of this description, and believed that they were attended with the convenience, "that everything comes to the house down hill."

CHAPTER III.
THE INDIAN WARFARE.

ABOUT the year 1756 this whole frontier was left exposed to the incursions of the Indians and French, who had returned to this neighborhood after the defeat of General Braddock by the French and Indians combined. In the spring of the year a party of fifty or more Indians, with a French captain at their head, crossed the Alleghany Mountains, committing on the white settlers every act of barbarous war. Capt. Jeremiah Smith, living in what is now known as Frederick County, raised a party of twenty men and marched out to meet the savages. At the head of Capon River he fell in with them, when a fierce and bloody battle was fought. Smith killed the captain with his own hand. After having killed five other Indians and wounding a number, the savages gave way and fled. Only two of Smith's men were killed. On searching the body of the Frenchman a commission and written instructions were found in his possession to meet another party of about 50 Indians at Fort Frederick*, to attack the fort, destroy it, and blow up the magazine. Fortunately, the other party of Indians were encountered low down on the North Branch of the Capon River by Capt. Joshua Lewis, with a party of 18 men, when one Indian was killed and the others broke and ran off. Previous to the defeat of this party they had committed considerable destruction of the property of the white settlers, and took a Mrs. Horner and a girl about 13 years of age prisoners. Mrs. Horner was the mother of seven or eight children, and never returned to her family.

---

*Fort Frederick is situated about 12 miles from Martinsburg, in Maryland.

The girl, Sarah Gibbons, was a prisoner 8 or 9 years before she returned home.

These Indians dispersed into small parties, and carried the work of death and desolation into several neighborhoods, in the counties now Berkeley, Frederick and Shenandoah. About 18 or 20 of them crossed the North Mountain at Mill's Gap, in the county of Berkeley, killed a man by the name of Kelly, and several of his family. This massacre occurred about one mile from Gerardstown. The Indians then passed on to the present site of Martinsburg. About two miles from the latter place a stockade was built, and known as the John Evans fort, in which the neighboring people generally took shelter. (The land on which this fort stands is now situated south of our town, and owned by a Mr. Fryatt.) A small party of Indians attacked the dwelling house of a Mr. Evans, a brother to the owner of the fort; but being beaten off they went in pursuit of a reinforcement. In their absence, Mr. Evans and his family made their escape to the fort. The Indians returned and fired the house, which was situated three miles south of town, near the Big Spring. These Indians took a female prisoner on the same day, at John Strode's house. A boy by the name of Hackney, on his way to the fort, met and advised her not to go to the house, as Strode's entire family had gone to the fort,.and the Indians had possession of the house. She disregarded the advice of the boy, went to the house, was seized by the Indians and made a prisoner. The boy went back to the fort and told what had happened; but the men had all turned out to bury Kelly, and went in pursuit of the Indians, leaving nobody to defend the fort but the women and children. Mrs. Evans armed herself, and called on all the women, who had firmness enough to aim, to join her; and such as were too timid she ordered to run bullets. She then made a boy beat "to arms" on a drum. The Indians became much alarmed at this, and after firing Strode's house made a hasty retreat, when they discovered the party of white men just mentioned and fired upon them, to no effect. The latter finding the Indians too strong for them, retreated to the fort.

After a captivity of three years, the girl spoken of as being made a prisoner, returned to her home. Mrs. Evans is the great-grandmother of our worthy and estimable citizen, Mr. James M. Vanmetre, now living a short distance south of town, and other brothers scattered. Tillitson Evans, six brothers, and many others of her great-grand children are living at the present day.

The Indians, from thence, passed on to Opequon, and the next morning attacked Neally's fort, massacred most of the people, and took a number of prisoners, among whom were a Mr. Cohoon and wife, and a family of small children. Mrs. Cohoon being unable to travel fast enough, her husband was forced ahead, in order to murder her. Cohoon, however, heard her screams, and that night made his escape.

The Indians proceeded as far as the vicinity of Fort Pleasant* with several prisoners, and then divided themselves into two parties, in order to watch the fort. At a late hour in the night, Mrs. Neff, a prisoner, escaped to the fort and informed the inmates of the Indians whereabouts. On the following day another party joined the fort, and on the next morning sixteen men, well mounted and armed, left the fort with a view to attack the Indians, who were soon discovered by their camp fires. The whites separated in two parties, intending to close in upon the Indians, but however were discovered by the latter, who were alarmed by the barking of a dog. The Indians cautiously moved off between the two parties of white men unobserved, and taking a position between them and their horses, opened a most destructive fire. The whites stood their ground with great firmness and

---

*Fort Pleasant was a strong stockade with block houses, erected on the lands formerly owned by Isaac Vanmetre, on the South Branch of the Potomac.

bravery, and a desperate and bloody conflict ensued. Seven of the whites were killed and four wounded. Three Indians fell in this conflict and several were seriously wounded. The men of the fort were compelled to retreat, and their horses were secured by the victors. Just before this action commenced, Mr. Vanmetre, an old man, mounted his horse, rode upon a high ridge, and witnessed the battle. He returned with all speed to the fort and gave notice of the defeat. He was killed by the Indians in 1757.

Near about this year a Mr. Williams resided on Patterson's Creek. Hearing of the approach of the Indians he repaired with his neighbors to Fort Pleasant for security, a distance of nine miles. After remaining here a few days, supposing their houses might be revisited with safety, Mr. W., with seven others, crossed the mountain for that purpose. On reaching the creek they separated and Mr. Williams went to his farm alone. Having tied his horse to a bush he commenced salting his cattle, when seven Indians stepped between him and his horse and demanded a surrender. His only answer was a ball from his rifle that laid one of their number low to the ground. The Indians then retreated to the house, and barricading the doors began firing through the windows. Mr. Williams hid behind a hominy block in a corner, from which he fired at his assailants through the cracks of the building, as opportunity offered. In this way he killed five out of the seven. The remaining two would not give up their prey, but resolved to proceed more cautiously, and going to the least exposed side of the house, one was raised upon the shoulders of the other to an opening in the logs some distance above the level of Mr. Williams, who consequently did not observe their manœuvre, and in this way the Indian shot him. His body was instantly taken, cut in quarters and hung to the four corners of the building. His head was stuck upon a fence stake in front of the door.

In the year 1757, a numerous body of Indians crossed the Alleghany, and, as usual, divided themselves into small parties, hovering about the different forts, and committing many acts of murder and destruction to property. Near about the year 1758, a party of about 50 Indians and 4 Frenchmen penetrated into the neighborhood of Mill Creek, now in this county. This was a pretty thickly settled neighborhood, and among other houses, George Painter had erected a large log one, with a commodious cellar. On the alarm being given, the neighboring people took refuge in this house. Late in the afternoon they were attacked. Mr. Painter attempted to fly, but had three balls shot through his body and fell dead. The others surrendered, and the Indians then dragged the dead body back to the house, threw it in, plundered the house, and set fire to it. While the house was in flames, consuming the body of Mr. Painter, they forced from the arms of their mothers four infant children, hung them up in trees, shot them in savage sport, and left them hanging. They then set fire to a stable, containing a parcel of sheep and calves, thus cruelly and wantonly torturing to death the inoffensive dumb animals. The Indians then made a hasty retreat, taking with them about 48 prisoners. After six days' travel they reached their villages west of the Alleghany mountains. A council was held and determined upon to sacrifice their helpless prisoner, Jacob Fisher, a lad 12 or 13 years old, who was, with his parents and other children, taken captives. They first ordered the boy to collect a quantity of dry wood. The poor little fellow shuddered, burst into tears, and told his father they intended to burn him. "I hope not," said his father, and advised him to obey. When he had collected a sufficient quantity of wood to answer their purpose, they cleared and smoothed a ring around a sapling, to which they tied him by one hand, then formed a trail of wood around the tree and set it on fire. The poor boy was then compelled to run around in this ring of fire until his rope wound him up to the sapling, and then back until he came in contact with the flame, whilst his infernal tormentors were drinking, singing, and dancing around him with a horrid joy. This was continued for several hours, during which time the savages became beastly drunk, and as they fell prostrate to the ground, the squaws would keep up the fire. With long, sharp poles, prepared for the purpose, they would pierce the body of their victim when he flagged, until the poor, helpless boy, fell and expired with the most excruciating torments. The family were compelled to be witnesses of the heart-rending tragedy.

These outrages of the Indians drove many of the white settlers below the Blue Ridge, and broke up the settlements through this locality. About the year 1758 there were two white men who disguised themselves in the habit of Indians, and appeared in the neighborhood of the present site of Martinsburg. Supposed to be Indian's they were pursued and killed, and it was no uncommon thing for scoundrels and rascals to act in this manner. Their object was to frighten people to leave their homes, that they might rob and plunder them of their valuable articles. At Hedge's fort, on the present road from Martinsburg to Bath, west of Back Creek, a man was killed while watching the spring. In the years 1773-74, numerous conflicts and bloody battles occurred between the whites and Indians. About the 1st of May, 1774, during Gov. Dunmore's reign, the whites were growing in strength, and in large numbers commenced war on the savages with marked effect.

MASSACRE AT FORT NEALLY IN 1756—ROMANTIC STORY OF ISABELLA STOCKTON, OF BERKELEY COUNTY.

[Extract from an historical address delivered by the late Hon. Charles J. Faulkner, at the University of West Virginia, in June, 1875:]

"There is one incident connected with the early history of the county in which I reside which may possibly prove interesting to the fairer portion of my audience. It rests upon authentic evidence. I spoke of the massacre of Neally Fort, on the Opequon Creek, in the county of Berkeley. It was about daylight, on the 17th of September, 1756, that a roving band of Indians surprised that little fort and murdered and scalped all they found in it. On their return from this bloody work they passed the house of Wm. Stockton, east of the North Mountain, who, about one hour before their arrival, unconscious of danger, had gone with his wife about two miles distant to perform the last duties to a dying neighbor, leaving their children at home. The Indians seized two of these children, George, a boy of fourteen years, and Isabella, a girl then ten years of age, and carried them off as captives to the north. George, who was a youth of remarkable energy and spirit, after a captivity of three years, made his escape and returned to his home in Berkeley County, with his feelings deeply embittered against the Indians and their allies, the French. Isabella Stockton, after being with them something upwards of a month, was sold by them to a wealthy Canadian trader, who took her to his home near Montreal, and being touched by the artless manners and prepossessing qualities of the child, bestowed, with his wife, every care on her education and training which the condition of the country then permitted. At sixteen years of age she had developed into a girl of extraordinary beauty and attractions. At this time there arrived from France a nephew of the trader of the name of Jean Baptiste Plata, a young man highly educated and of the noblest and most chivalric traits of character Living in the same house with Isabella, a mutual attachment soon sprang up between them, and in about one year he made known to his uncle his purpose to ask her hand in marriage. The uncle approved his purpose, and the young man opened the subject to Isabella. She told him that she could not disguise from him her deep attachment to him, but she felt compelled to disclose to him what she had never before breathed to any human being—something of her early history. When but ten years of age she had been torn as a captive from her parents by the Indians, and had been sold to his uncle. The images of her dear father and mother had been continually present to her mind from that day to this. Her dreams had kept their faces and features as fresh and vivid in her memory as if she had seen them every day, and she did not feel that she could, with satisfaction to herself, change her relations in life until she had once more revisited her home in Virginia, and if her parents were still alive, to ask their consent to the proposed marriage. The young Frenchman promptly offered to take her to her parents, not for a moment doubting that they would cordially ratify his union with their daughter. He accordingly procured the necessary horses from his uncle, and they started on their long and perilous journey. They arrived safely in the county of Berkeley, and he delivered her into the embraces of her astonished and delighted parents. For a few days all was gladness and joy. But as soon as it was communicated to them that the young Frenchman was engaged to and desired their daughter in marriage, then all the animosity of the persecuted settler sprang up in their bosoms. A Frenchman at that day was more hateful to a West Virginia backwoodsman than even a Shawnee Indian, for they regarded them as the instigators and fomenters of all the cold-blooded murders and barbarities which had drenched their settlements in blood. His proposal of marriage was rejected; he was even ordered to leave the house, but he lingered long enough in the neighborhood to mature an arrangement with Isabella by which he might effect her escape and both return to Canada. Availing himself of the opportunity when the father and George were absent on a hunt across the North Mountain, the two lovers started upon their journey northward. The day after their departure the father and son returned, when the enraged father, discovering the flight, gave his orders to the fiery and impetuous George to go immediately in pursuit and "to bring Isabella back, dead or alive, for he would rather see her a corpse than hear of her marriage with a Frenchman." Meanwhile the fugitives had crossed the Potomac; they had forded the Juniata, and they had reached the west bank of the Susquehanna, in the county now called Lycoming, in Pennsylvania, where they were detained by a sudden rise in the waters of that river. Here the furious and maddened George, whose temper had not been improved by a three year's servitude among the Indians, overtook the astonished lovers. The scene that followed was as brief as it was bloody. He demanded the return of his sister. She refused to go back. Her lover interposed, and in two minutes the brave and chivalrous Frenchman lay a bleeding corpse in the arms of the agonized Isabella. History does not inform us what disposition was made of the dead body of Jean Baptiste Plata, but the lovely Isabella, crushed in all her earthly affections, was brought almost a raving maniac to her father's house. Ten years elapsed before her mind recovered its accustomed tone and vigor, when she married a gentleman of the name of Wm. McCleery, and they removed from Berkeley to Morgantown."

However, for quite a lengthy period afterward the Indians continued hostile and bitter in their depredations. Powerful armies of the whites were raised, and have at last succeeded in almost terminating Indian existence.

CHAPTER IV.
HOUSES, FURNITURE, DIET AND DRESS OF THE EARLY SETTLERS.

A CORRECT and detailed view of the origin and mode of living, and their progress from one condition or point of wealth, science and civilization, to another, is always highly interesting, even when received through the dusky medium of history. But when this retrospect of things past and gone is drawn from the recollections and experiences of old and venerable citizens, and handed down to the rising generation, the impressions it makes on the heart are of the most vivid, deep and lasting kind. The municipal, as well as ecclesiastical institutions of society, whether good or bad, in consequence of their long continued use, give a corresponding cast to the public character of society, whose conduct they direct, and the more so because in the lapse of time the observance of them becomes a matter of conscience.

The settlement of a new country in the immediate neighborhood of an old one, is not attended with much difficulty, because supplies can be readily obtained from the latter; but the settlement of a country very remote from any cultivated region, is a very different thing; because at the outset, food, raiment, and the implements of husbandry, are obtained only in small supplies and with great difficulty. The task of making new establishments in a remote wilderness, in time of profound peace, is sufficiently difficult; but when, in addition to all the unavoidable hardships attendant on this business, those resulting from an extensive and furious warfare with savages are superadded; toil, privations and sufferings, are then carried to the full extent of the capacity of men to endure them. Such was the wretched condition of our forefathers in making their settlements here, and to all their difficulties and privations, the Indian war was a weigh'y addition.

The following history of the poverty, labors, sufferings, manners and customs, of our forefathers, will appear like a collection of "tales of olden times," without any garnish of language to spoil the original portraits, by giving them shades of coloring which they did not possess.

A spot was selected on a piece of land for their habitation, and a day appointed for commencing the work of building their cabin. The fatigue party consisted of choppers, whose business it was to fell the trees and cut them off at proper lengths—a man with his team for hauling them to the place and arranging them—and a carpenter, if he might be called such, whose business it was to search the woods for a proper tree for making clapboards for the roof. The materials for the cabin were mostly prepared on the first day, and sometimes the foundation laid in the evening; the second day was allotted for the raising. In the morning of the next day the neighbors collected for the raising. The first thing to be done was the election of four corner men, whose business it was to notch and place the logs, the rest of the company furnishing them with the timbers. In the meantime the boards and puncheons were collected for the floor and roof, so that by the time the cabin was a few rounds high, the sleepers and floor began to be laid. Openings were afterward made for the door, windows and chimney. The roof was formed by making the end logs shorter until a single log formed the comb of the roof. On these logs the clapboards were placed and lapped over each considerable distance, which were held in their proper places by logs being placed upon them.

The Germans were more uniform in the building of their cabins, and their barn was usually the best building on the farm. Their dwelling houses were seldom raised more than a single story, with a large cellar underneath. In the upper floor garners for holding grain were very common. A piazza was a very common appendage, in which their saddles, bridles and very frequently the wagon or plow harness were hung up.

In the above has been given a description of the dwellings of the early settlers, and to make mention of the furniture, diet and dress used in those days may probably prove of interest. The furniture for the table for several years after the settlement of this locality consisted of a few pewter dishes, plates and spoons, but mostly of wooden bowls, trenchers and noggins. If the latter were scarce, gourds and hard-shelled squashes made up the deficiency. The iron pots, knives and forks were brought from the east side of the mountains, along with the salt and iron, on pack-horses. The table was generally fixed in one corner of the stove room, with permanent benches on one side. Their beds were filled with straw or chaff, with a fine feather-bed for the covering.

These articles of furniture corresponded very well with the articles of diet on which they were employed. Hog and hominy were proverbial for the dish of which they were the component parts. Johnny cake and pone were, at the outset of the settlement of the country, the only forms of bread in use for breakfast and dinner. At supper milk and mush were the standard dish. When milk was not plenty, which was often the case, owing to the scarcity of cattle or the want of proper pasture for them, the substantial dish of hominy had to supply the place of them. Mush was frequently eaten with sweetened water, molasses, bear's oil, or the gravy of fried meat. Every family cultivated an acre or more, which they called "truck patches," and raised a variety of vegetables. The natural result of this kind of rural life was to produce a hardy and vigorous race of people. It was this race of people who had to meet and breast the various Indian wars and the storms of the revolution.

On the frontiers, and particularly amongst those who were much in the habit of hunting, and going on scouts and campaigns, the dress of the men, resembled partly that of the Indian and the civilized nations. The hunting skirt was universally worn. This was a kind of loose frock, reaching about half way down, with large sleeves and a belt. This skirt was generally made of linsey, sometimes of coarse linen, and a few of dressed deer skins. A pair of moccasins answered for the feet much better than shoes, and were made of dressed deer skin. In the latter years of the Indian war the young men became enamored of the Indian dress, and adopted it almost entirely.

The reader will, naturally, desire a sketch of the dress adopted by the women; and the younger minds will more especially desire an idea of the weddings of those days. A description of the ceremony adopted will, doubtless, prove very interesting, in which will be described also the women's dress:

For a long time after the first settlement of this locality, the inhabitants in general married very young. There was no distinction of rank and very little of fortune. On these accounts the first impressions of love resulted in marriage, and a family establishment cost nothing more than a little labor. The practice of celebrating the marriage at the house of the bride began at an early period, and it should seem with great propriety. She was also given the choice to make the selection as to who should perform the ceremony. In those days a wedding engaged the attention of a whole neighborhood, and both old and young engaged in the frolic with eager anticipation. This is not to be wondered at, when it is told that a wedding was almost the only gathering which was not accompanied with the labor of reaping, log-rolling, building a cabin, or planning some scout or campaign.

Houses, Furniture, &c., of the Early Settlers. 51

On the morning of the wedding day, the groom and his attendants assembled at the house of his father, for the purpose of reaching the mansion of his bride by noon, which was the usual time for celebrating the nuptials, and which for certain must take place before dinner. Let the reader imagine an assemblage of people, without a store, tailor or mantuamaker, within an hundred miles, and an assemblage of horses, without a blacksmith or saddler within an equal distance. The gentlemen dressed in shoepacks, moccasins, leather breeches, leggins, and linsey hunting shirts, all homemade. The ladies dressed in linsey petticoats and linsey or linen bed-gowns, coarse shoes, stockings, handkerchiefs, and buckskin gloves, if any; if there were any buckles, rings, buttons or ruffles, they were relics of old times, family pieces from parents or grand-parents. The horses were caparisoned with old saddles, bridles or halters, and pack-saddles, with a bag or blanket thrown over them—a rope or string as often constituted the girth as a piece of leather.

The march, in double file, was often interrupted by the narrowness and obstructions of the horse paths, as they were called, for there were no roads. These difficulties were often increased, sometimes by the good, and sometimes by the ill will of neighbors; by felling trees and tying grape vines across the way. Sometimes an ambuscade was formed by the wayside, and an unexpected discharge of several guns took place, so as to cover the wedding company with smoke. Let the reader imagine the scene that followed this discharge—the sudden spring of the horses, the shrieks of the girls, and the chivalric bustle of their partners to save them from falling. Sometimes, in spite of all that could be done to prevent it, some were thrown to the ground; if a wrist, elbow, or ankle happened to be sprained, it was tied with a handkerchief, and little more was thought or said about it.

Another ceremony commonly took place before the party reached their destination. When the party were within about a mile of the bride's house, two young men would single out to run for the bottle; the worse the path, the more logs, bush and deep hollows, the better, as these obstacles afforded an opportunity for the greater display of intrepidity and horsemanship. The English fox chase, in point of danger to the riders and their horses, was nothing to this race for the bottle. The start was announced by an Indian yell, when logs, bush, mudholes, hill and glen, were speedily passed by the rival ponies. The bottle was always filled for the occasion, and there was no need of judges. The first that reached the door was handed the prize, and returned in triumph announcing his victory over his rival by a shrill whoop. The bottle was given the groom and his attendants at the head of the troop, and then to each pair in succession, to the rear of the line. After giving each a dram, he placed the bottle in his bosom and took his station in the company. The ceremony preceded the dinner, which was a substantial backwoods feast of beef, pork, fowls and sometimes venison and bear meat, with plenty of cabbage, potatoes and other vegetables.

After dinner dancing commenced with four handed reels or square sets and jigs, and generally lasted until the next morning. About 9 or 10 o'clock a deputation of the young ladies stole off the bride and put her to bed. This would be unnoticed by the hilarious crowd, and as soon as discovered a deputation of young men in like manner would steal off the groom and place him snugly by the side of his bride. The dance still continued, and when seats happened to be scarce, which was often the case, every young man, when not engaged in the dance, was obliged to offer his lap as a seat for one of the girls, which was sure to be accepted. During the hilarity the newly married couple were not forgotten. Late in the night one would remind the company that the new couple stood in need of refreshments. The bottle was then called "Black Betty," which was sent up the ladder, generally accompanied by a quantity of beef, bread, pork and cabbage sufficient to afford a good meal for half a dozen hungry men. During the festivity "Black Betty" was called out, and in taking a dram they would say, "Here's health to the groom, not forgetting myself, and here's to the bride, thumping luck and big children."

Being in perpetual hostility with the Indians, big children were considered of much importance, and this expression was thought to be of a very proper and friendly wish. It often happened that some neighbors or relations, not being asked to the wedding, took offense, and as a mode of revenge they adopted the plan of cutting off the manes, foretops and tails of the horses of the wedding company. The feasting and dancing often lasted several days, and on their return the race for "Black Betty" was the same as before. After these ceremonies several days rest were required before they could return to their ordinary labors.

Some of my readers may doubt the veracity of this statement, but I would state, that in presenting this book to the public, I have tried to give the facts as correctly as possible. This extract has been sketched from an old history published in 1833, and is vouched for by several very old citizens You may ask why this unpleasant portrait of our forefathers has been presented? In turn I would ask why are you pleased with the histories of the blood and carnage of battles, and delighted with the fictions of poetry and the novel romance? It is a true state of society and manners which are fast vanishing from the memory of man, depicted with a view to give the young people of to-day a knowledge of the advantage of civilization.

CHAPTER V.
NORTHERN NECK OF VIRGINIA.

CHARLES II, King of England, granted to the ancestors of the late Lord Fairfax all the lands lying between the head-waters of the Rappahannock and Potomac to Chesapeake bay. This immense grant included the territory now comprising the counties of Lancaster, Northumberland, Richmond, Westmoreland, Stafford, King George, Prince William, Fairfax, Loudon, Fauquier, Culpeper, Madison, Page, Shenandoah, Hardy, Hampshire, Morgan, Berkeley, Jefferson and Frederick. It is said that the first grant to the ancestors of Fairfax was only intended to include the territory in the Northern Neck, east of the Blue Ridge; but after Faixfax discovered that the Potomac river headed in the Alleghaney mountains, he returned to England, and instituted his petition in the Court of King's Bench for extending his grant into the Alleghaney mountains, so as to include the territory composing the present counties of Page, Shenandoah, Hardy, Hampshire, Morgan, Berkeley, Jefferson and Frederick. A compromise took place between Fairfax and the Crown, but previous to the institution of Fairfax's suit, several individuals had obtained grants for large bodies of land west of the Blue Ridge, from the colonial government of Virginia. In the compromise it was expressly stipulated that the holders of lands, under what were then called the King's grants, were to be quieted in their right of possession.

Joist Hite and his partners had obtained grants for a large body. Fairfax, under the pretext that Hite and others had not complied with the terms of their grants, took it upon himself to grant away large quantities of these lands to other individuals. This high handed proceeding on the part of his Lordship, produced a law suit, which Hite and his partners instituted in the year 1736, and in the year 1786 it was decided. The plaintiffs received a large amount of money for the rents and profits, and a considerable quantity of land.

In the year 1736 Fairfax entered a caveat against Hite and his partners, alleging that the lands claimed by them were within the bounds of the Northern Neck, and consequently his property. This was the beginning of the controversy, and led to the suit instituted by the latter. However, all the parties died before the suit was decided. The immense Fairfax estate has passed out of the hands of Fairfax's heirs. The lands, (as observed in a preceding chapter,) were granted by Fairfax in fee simple to his tenants, subject to an annual rent of two shillings sterling per hundred acres, which in the aggregate amounted to a very large sum. To this Fairfax added and required the payment of ten shillings sterling on each fifty acres (what he termed composition money,) and which was paid on issuing the grant. In the year 1742 he opened his office in the county of Fairfax for granting out land. A few years after he removed to the county of Frederick, and settled at what he called "Greenway-Court," about 12 or 14 miles south-east of the present Winchester, where he kept his land office during his life. He died in the autumn of 1781, very soon after the surrender of Cornwallis. It is stated that when he heard of the capture of Cornwallis, he called his servant to assist him to bed, saying, "It is time for me to die." He never left his bed again until consigned to the tomb. He had, prior to his death, made a donation to the Episcopal society of a lot of land, upon which a large stone building was erected as a place of public worship. To the church was attached a large burial ground, in which his remains were interred.

In the year 1785 the legislature of Virginia passed an

act in which, among other provisions, (in relation to the Northern Neck,) is the following :

"*And be it further enacted*, That the landholders within the said district of the Northern Neck shall be forever hereafter exonerated and discharged from composition and quitrents, any law, custom or usage to the contrary notwithstanding." This action of the State freed the people from a vexatious and troublesome taxation. Fairfax's representatives soon sold out their interest in his private estate in this country, and it is believed there is no part of this vast landed estate remaining in the hands of any branch of the Fairfax family. Chief Justice Marshall, the late Raleigh Colston, Esq., and the late Gen. Henry Lee, purchased the right of Fairfax's legatees—who were then in England—to what is called the Manor of Leeds, which contained about 150,000 acres; South Branch Manor, 55,000 acres; Patterson's Creek Manor, 9,000 acres, and various other tracts of land of immense value, the most of which had been leased out for long terms of lives.

This profligate manner of granting away lands in immense bodies was unquestionably founded in the most unwise and unjust policy. Such are the blessings of kingly governments. It tended more to tie and bind down the speedy settlement and improvement of the country, instead of advancing its interests for a more rapid development. But, alas, the disgusting, high-sounding title of "My Lord" is no longer applied to poor, frail humanity.

It appears that Lord Fairfax, among others, was an attentive officer in the time of the Indian wars. He had more at stake and the command of greater funds than any other individual of his day, therefore it behooved him to be active. The Indian hostilities retarded the settlement of his large domain, and of course lessened his revenue. It is said that he was remarkable for his eccentricities and singularity of disposition and character, and that he had an insatiable passion for hoarding up English gold. He never married, and of course left no child to inherit his vast estate. All his property, or the greater portion of it, was devised to his nephew in England, the Rev. Denny Martin, on condition that he would apply to the Parliament of Britain for an act to authorize him to take the name of Lord Fairfax. This was done, and Denny Lord Fairfax, like his uncle, never marrying, he devised the estate to Gen. Philip Martin, who, never marrying and dying without issue, devised the estate to two old maiden sisters, who sold it to Messrs. Marshall, Colston and Lee.

It is proper, before the subject of Lord Fairfax's grant is dismissed, to inform the reader that a few years after the war of the revolution an attempt was made to confiscate all that part of his landed estate devised to his nephew, Denny Martin, (after Denny Lord Fairfax.) But Messrs. Marshall, Colston and Lee having purchased the estate, a compromise took place between them and the State Government. The sale of the estate of Lord Fairfax by his legatees in England, and the devise and sale of the real estate of the late Col. T. B. Martin, is the last of the history of the Fairfax interest in the Northern Neck, a territory comprising about one-fourth of the whole of the present limits of Virginia.

BERKELEY COUNTY LAID OFF.

The two counties of Frederick and Augusta were laid off at the session of the Colonial Legislature in the year 1738, and included all the vast region of country west of the Blue Ridge. Previous to that time the County of Orange included all the territory west of the mountains. Orange was taken from Spotsylvania in the year 1734, the latter having previously crossed the Blue Ridge and took in a considerable part of what is now the County of Page. Previous to laying off the County of Orange the territory west of the Blue Ridge, except the small part which lay in Spotsylvania, does not appear to have been included in any county.

Thus it appears that a little more than one hundred years ago Spotsylvania was a frontier county, and that the vast region west of the Blue Ridge, with its millions of people, has been settled and improved from an entire wilderness. The country for more than a thousand miles to the west has been, within this short period, rescued from a state of natural barbarism, and is now the seat of the fine arts and sciences, of countless millions of wealth and the abode of freedom, both religious and political. Judging from the past, what an immense prospect opens itself to our view for the future. Within the last half century this great portion of country has poured out thousands of emigrants, who have contributed towards peopling the North, East, South and West, and immigrations still continue.

It has been already stated that Frederick County was laid off in the year 1738. Berkeley was taken from Frederick in the year 1772. The first Sheriff was Adam Stephen, who was constituted and appointed by a commission from the Governor for Berkeley County on the 18th day of April, 1772. A number of justices were appointed for the county, and their commission for their appointment is herewith given, as taken from the original copy now on file in the Clerk's Office, which doubtless will prove of interest to the reader:

"*Berkeley County, s. s.*

"Be it remembered that at the house of Edward Beeson, the Nineteenth Day of May, Anno Domini 1772, a Commission of the Peace and a Commission of Oyer and Terminer from his excellency Lord Dunmore dated the 17th Day of April in the year aforesaid directed to Ralph Wormley, Jacob Hite, Van Swearengen, Thomas Rutherford, Adam Stephen, John Heavill, Thomas Swearengen, Samuel Washington, James Hourse, William Little, Robert Stephen, John Briscoe, Hugh Lyle, James

Strode, William Morgan, Robert Stogdon, James Seaton, Robert Carter Willis, and Thomas Robinson, Gentlemen and also Dedimus's for administering Oaths, directed to the same Persons or any two of them ; where produced and read, whereupon the said Van Swearengen, having first taken the usual oaths to his Majesty's Person & Government repeated and subscribed the Test taken, the Oaths of a Justice of the Peace, of a Justice of the County Court in Chancery & of a Justice of Oyer and Terminer, which were administered to him by the said James House & William Little, he the said Van Swearengen, then administered the same oaths unto Thomas Swearengen, Samuel Washington, James Hourse, William Morgan, William Little, James Strode, Robert Stephen, Robert Stogdon, Robert Carter Willis, & James Seaton, who severally took the same & Repeated & Subscribed the Test: *Court Proclaimed*, at a court held for Berkeley County the 19th Day of May, 1772. Present:

Van Swearengen,	*James Strode,*
Thos. Swearengen,	*Robert Stephen,*
Samuel Washington,	*Robert Stogdon,*
James Hourse,	*Robert C. Willis,*
William Morgan,	*and*
William Little,	*James Seaton,*

Gent. Justices.

William Drew was the first clerk of the Court, and was appointed by a commission from Thomas Nelson, Esq. James Theith, John Magill, George Brent, George Johnston, Philip Pendleton and Alexander White were the first attorneys licensed to practice law in the court of the colony. Alexander White was appointed the first deputy attorney for this county under commission of the Attorney General of the colony. In those days when courts of law were resorted to as a means of justice, it was to be had at but little trouble, and the offender was dealt with in the most strict and hurried manner. In looking over the first court docket of this county the author could surprise the people of the present generation were he to make mention of the most cruel manner in which punishments were inflicted. Slavery was then carried out in its true sense, regardless of nature or humanity. Again, it is much of a curiosity to see the manner in which the proceedings were conducted.

CHAPTER VI.
MARTINSBURG ESTABLISHED.

MARTINSBURG was established in the month of October, 1778, and was named after Col. T. B. Martin, of whom mention has been made in the previous chapter as the last holder of the estate of this portion of country prior to its being laid off. The following is an extract from the law at the time our present city was established:

"Whereas it hath been represented to this present General Assembly that Adam Stephen, Esq., hath lately laid off one hundred and thirty acres of land in the county of Berkeley, where the Court House now stands, in lots and streets for a town, etc.; Be it enacted, etc., that the said one hundred and thirty acres of land laid out into lots and streets, agreeable to a plan and survey thereof made containing the number of two hundred and sixty-nine lots, as by the said plan and survey, relation thereunto being had, may more fully appear, be and the same is hereby vested in James McAlister, Joseph Mitchell, Anthony Noble, James Strode, Robert Carter Willis, William Patterson and Philip Pendleton, gentlemen, trustees, and shall be established a town by the name of Martinsburg."

Tradition relates an animated contest that took place between Sheriff Adam Stephen and Jacob Hite, Esq., in relation to fixing the seat of justice for this county and by which the latter lost his life. It may probably prove interesting to the reader:

Hite contended for the location thereof on his own land at what is now called Leetown, in the county of Jefferson. Stephen advocated Martinsburg, and prevailed upon it until Hite became so disgusted and dissatisfied that he sold out his fine estate and removed to the frontier of South Carolina. His removal proved fatal, for he had not long settled in that State before the Indians murdered him and several of his family in the most shocking and barbarous manner. It is said that the evening before this bloody massacre took place, an Indian squaw who was much attached to Mrs. Hite, called on her and warned her of the intended plot, and advised her to remove with her little children to a place of safety. Mrs. Hite immediately communicated the intelligence to her husband. He would not believe the information, observing "the Indians were too much attached to him to do him any injury." The next morning, however, when it was fatally too late to escape, a party of Indians, armed and painted in their usual war dress, called on Hite and told him they were determined to kill him. It was in vain that he pleaded his friendship for them and the many services he had rendered their nation. Their full purpose was fixed and nothing could appease them but his blood and that of his innocent, unoffending and helpless wife and children. They commenced their barbarous work by the most cruel tortures, cutting him to pieces, a joint at a time, and while he was thus in the most violent agonies they barbarously murdered his wife and several of her little offspring. After they had dispatched Mr. Hite, his wife and several of the children, they took two of his daughters, not quite grown, and all of his slaves as prisoners. They also carried off what plunder they choose, and their booty was considerable. Mr. Hite kept a large store and dealt largely with the Creek and Cherokee tribes. It was afterward stated that a man by the name of Parish, who was an intimate friend of and went to Carolina with Hite, grew jealous of the latter's popularity with the Indians, and instigated the savages to commit the murder.

On the 20th day of August, 1779, on motion of Adam

Stephen, Sheriff, the plat for Martinsburg was ordered to be recorded, with terms to purchasers, as follows: "The purchasers of any of the lots in the above town is to build on the purchased lot a good dwelling house, to be at least twenty feet long and sixteen feet wide, with stone or brick chimney to same, in two years from the time of purchase, and, on failure, the lot to return to the proprietor."

The first court was held in the dwelling house of Edward Beeson, situated on the land now owned by Mr. A. J. Thomas, at the north end of the city. The building was a rude log house and consisted of one story and a half. The first Court House erected was built of stone, (and a very odd looking one at that,) and located where the present fine structure now stands. The first jail was a log building, erected in the middle of the Square, with the Market House attached to the rear end. The first church built west of the Blue Ridge Mountain is the one standing at the present day on Tuscarora, about two miles from the city. The Falling Waters church was the next. A number of the buildings, solidly constructed of stone and of early date, are yet standing at an age of over one hundred and fifty years, and presenting an air of defiance to the ravages of time. From their present state there is but little doubt that they will perhaps stand the trials and tribulations of the world for centuries to come.

Among the early settlers a number of old commissions were issued by prominent Governors and Lieutenant Governors of Virginia, appointing sheriffs, justices and overseers of the poor, dated from the expulsion of George, Earl of Dunmore, his Majesty's Lieutenant Governor of the colony of Virginia, and Vice-Admiral of the same, in 1772 to the Governorship of Henry A. Wise in 1859. There are two papers signed by Patrick Henry, the young orator who rebelled against the British Ministry and stirred within the breast of the American people an independence that led to deeds of valor. These were dated "Council Chamber, Williamsburg, Dec. 9th, 1776." The next was signed by Thos. Jefferson, who afterward became President, and as an example for model simplicity but few after Presidents have ever attained to. This paper bears an impression of the first wax seal of the Virginia Commonwealth. Benjamin Harrison was the signer of two commissions. Beverly Randolph (1788,) James Wood (1793,) and Robert Brooks (1799,) also sent commissions. Among the number are the well-known signatures of Jno. Tyler, who succeeded Harrison as President, and James Monroe, also afterward President. Among the signatures of the Governors discernible were the names of Geo. W. Smith, James Barbour, James P. Preston, Lieutenant Governor Peter V. Daniels, Lieutenant Governor Tate, John Randolph, Henry A. Wise, (Virginia's war Governor,) Tillitson Tozewell and James McDowell. Among the men were statesmen and patriots whose noble traits are revered by many of the Virginia people. Many pages of American history have been scattered broadcast containing their acts of heroism and manliness.

Among the early residents were three noted generals of the revolutionary war—Horatio Gates, Alexander Stephen and Charles Lee. As an evidence of the well-known eccentricity of the former, is the following extract from his will, copied from the original, and on file in the office of the County Clerk :

"I desire, most earnestly, that I may not be buried in any church or church yard, or within a mile of any Presbyterian or Anabaptist meeting-house ; for, since I have resided in this county, I have kept so much bad company when living that I do not *chuse* to continue it when dead. I recommend my soul to the creator of all worlds and all creatures, who must, from his visible attributes, be indifferent to their modes of worship or creeds whether Christians, Mohammedans or Jews ; whether

Martinsburg Established. 65

more or less absurd ; as a weak mortal can no more be answerable for his persuasions, notions or even scepticism in religion, than for the color of his skin."

The will was presented to the Berkeley County Court for record April 15th, 1783, in his own hand-writing. Another extract is taken from the County Court records under date of November 20th, 1776 :

"Proclamation being made for the trial of a negro man belonging to General Horatio Gates, committed to the goal of this county, and for breaking open the cellar of the said General Gates and feloniously taking from thence a chest of money and clothes ; who being brought to the bar and it being demanded of him whether he was guilty of the offense wherewith he stands charged, or not guilty, he says he is guilty. It is, therefore, the judgment of the Court that he be remanded back to the goal from whence he came, and there to continue till the third Friday in December next ; then from thence to be taken and hanged by the neck till he is dead. It is the opinion of the said Court that the said slave is worth seventy pounds."

MAJOR GENERAL ALEXANDER STEPHEN.

Each one of these noted Generals was cashiered. Alexander Stephen for becoming drunk and neglecting to bring his troops forward to the support of the balance of the army at the battle of Monmouth. His remains lie buried upon the premises of the late Hon. C. J. Faulkner, on the south edge of town. A monument was commenced to his memory, but was advanced no further than the placing of three broad stones. It was supposed that the other portion was used to a more appropriate purpose.

MAJOR GENERAL CHARLES LEE.

Gen. Lee was at one time a rival of Gen. Geo. Washington, and an aspirant for the position of Commander-in-Chief of the army, and while the latter modestly urged upon Congress to relieve him from the responsibility and appoint some one whom he imagined could more creditably fill the position, the former, by intrigue and with importunity, sought and failed to obtain it. This led Gen. Lee to entertain feelings of envy and hatred toward Gen. Washington, much to the latter's regret, who did his utmost to dispel them. Gen. Lee at this time lived about ten miles from Martinsburg, in a long, low house, the back room of which was his bed-room, the next the dining-room, then the kitchen, in which his slaves and dogs remained, and in front was a sort of sitting or reception room. Gen. Washington at one time, with the intention of trying to regain the good will of Gen. Lee, wrote to him informing him that, trusting that it would be agreeable, he would do himself the honor of dining with him on the following day. Upon his arrival, however, he found the house closed, and fastened to the front door was this message: "No bread or bacon cooked to-day." There wasn't much of the boasted hospitality of the dominion exhibited by this, but it is excusable from the fact that General Lee came from England and had not been a resident of the Commonwealth long enough to become addicted to the habits of the people.

The three heroes—Gates, Stephen and Lee—were in the habit of frequently meeting at the residence of the latter, in the summer and fall of 1782, and crack jokes, drink wine and compare notes of their army experience. Upon one occasion, after a lengthy sitting and free indulgence in the spirits, which were ardent, General Lee obtained the floor and remarked: "The County of Berkeley is indeed to be congratulated. She can claim as citizens three noted Major Generals of the revolutionary war. You, Stephen, distinguished yourself by getting drunk when you should have remained sober, and was cashiered for advancing when you should have been retreating, while your humble servant covered himself with glory and laurels and was cashiered for retreating when he should have been advancing."

CHAPTER VII.
REPORT OF HON. C. J. FAULKNER ON ADJUSTMENT OF THE BOUNDARY LINE BETWEEN VIRGINIA AND MARYLAND.

THE State of Maryland, in 1832, set up a claim to a considerable tract of territory on the north-west border of Virginia, including a part of the Northern Neck. It was then the late Hon. Charles James Faulkner distinguished himself, and won the respect and esteem of his people. Maryland pushed the claim with much earnestness, and the Executive of the State in appointing a commission to collect and embody the necessary testimony, on behalf of Virginia, selected Mr. Faulkner. This gentleman, in taking up this interesting question, worked with an untiring zeal and energy, and on the 6th day of November, 1832, made a most able report on "the settlement and adjustment of the western boundary of Maryland." The author deems it of sufficient interest to every Berkeley citizen, to insert in this work the report in full. It is as follows, from the original copy:

"*Report of Charles James Faulkner relative to the Boundary line between Virginia and Maryland*:

MARTINSBURG, Nov. 6, 1832.

SIR:—In execution of a commission addressed to me by your Excellency, and made out in pursuance of a joint resolution of the General Assembly of this State, of the 20th of March last, I have directed my attention to the collection of such testimony as the lapse of time and the nature of the inquiry have enabled me to procure touching "the settlement and adjustment of the western boundary of Maryland." The division line which now separates the two States on the west, and which has heretofore been considered as fixed by positive adjudication and long acquaintance, commences at a point where the *Fairfax stone* is planted, at the head spring of the Potomac River, and runs thence due north to the Pennsylvania line. This is the boundary by which Virginia has held for near a century ; it is the line by which she held in 1786, when the compact made by the Virginia and Maryland Commissioners was solemnly ratified by the legislative authorities of the two States.

An effort is now made by the General Assembly of Maryland, to enlarge her territory by the establishment of a different division line. We have not been informed which fork of the South Branch she will elect as the new boundary, but the proposed line is to run from *one* of the forks of the South Branch thence due north to the Pennsylvania *terminus*. It is needless to say that the substitution of the latter line, no matter at which fork it may commence, would cause an important diminution in the already diminished territorial area of this State. It would deprive us of large portions of the counties of Hampshire, Hardy, Pendleton, Randolph and Preston, amounting in all to almost half a million of acres—a section of the Commonwealth which, from the quality of its soil, and the character of its population, might well excite the cupidity of a government resting her claims upon a less substantial basis than a stale and groundless pretension of more than a century's antiquity. Although my instructions have directed my attention more particularly to the collection and preservation of the evidence of such living witnesses "as might be able to testify to any facts or circumstances in relation to the settlement and adjustment of the western boundary," I have consumed but a very inconsiderable portion of my time in any labor or inquiry of that sort, for who indeed, now living, could testify to any "facts or circumstances" which occurred nearly a century ago? And if such individuals were now living, why waste time in taking depositions as to those "facts," in proof of which the most ample and authentic testimony was taken in 1736, as the basis of a royal adjudication? I have consequently deemed it of more importance to procure the original documents where possible; if not, authentic copies of such papers as would serve to exhibit a connected view of the origin, progress and termination of that controversy with the Crown, which resulted, after the most accurate and laborious surveys, in the ascertainment of those very "facts and circumstances" which are now sought to be made again the subjects of discussion and inquiry. In this pursuit I have succeeded far beyond what I had any ground for anticipation; and from the almost forgotten rubbish of past years, have been enabled to draw forth documents and papers whose interest may survive the occasion which redeemed them from destruction.

To enable your Excellency to form a just conception of the weight and importance of the evidence herewith accompanying this report, I beg leave to submit with it a succinct statement of the question in issue between the governments of Virginia and Maryland, with some observations showing the relevancy of the evidence to the question thus presented.

The territory of Maryland granted by Charles I, to Lord Baltimore, in June, 1632, was described in the grant as "that region bounded by a line drawn from Watkins's point on Chesapeake Bay to the ocean on the east; thence to that part of the estuary of Delaware on the north which lieth under the 40th degree, where New England is terminated; thence in a right line by the degree aforesaid, *to the meridian of the foundation of the Potomac;* thence following its course by its farther bank to its confluence." (*Marshall's Life of Washington, vol.* 1, *ch. II, pp.* 78—81, 1*st edition.*)

It is plain that the western boundary of this grant was

the meridian of the fountain of the Potomac, from the point where it cut the 40th degree of north latitude to the fountain of the river; and that the extent of the grant depended upon the question, what stream was the Potomac? So that the question now in controversy grows immediately out of the grant. The territory granted to Lord Baltimore was undoubtedly within the chartered limits of Virginia: (*See* 1*st Charter of April*, 1606, *sec.* 4, *and the* 2*d Charter of May*, 1609, *sec.* 6; 1*st Hen. Stat. at Large, pp.* 58—88.) And Marshall says that the grant "was the first example of the dismemberment of a colony, and the creation of a new one within its limits, by the mere act of the Crown;" and that the planters of Virginia presented a petition against it, "which was heard before the privy council (of England) in July, 1633, when it was declared that Lord Baltimore should retain his patent, and the petitioners their remedy at law. To this remedy they never thought proper to resort."

Whether there be any record of this proceeding extant, I have never been able to learn. The civil war in England broke out about ten years after, and perhaps the journals of the proceedings of the privy council were destroyed. Subsequently to this, we are informed by Graham, the planters, "fortified by the opinion of eminent lawyers whom they consulted, and who scrupled not to assure them that the ancient patents of Virginia still remained in force, and that *the grant of Maryland, as derogatory to them, was utterly void*, they presented an application to the Parliament, complaining of the unjust invasion which their privileges had undergone." (*Graham's History, vol.* 2, *p.* 12.) But as the Parliaments of those days were but the obsequious ministers of the Crown, that application, it is presumed, likewise shared the fate of their former petition to the privy council.

The present claim of Maryland, then, must be founded

on the supposition that the stream which *we* call the Potomac was *not;* and that the stream now called the South Branch of the Potomac, *was* in fact *the* Potomac intended in the grant to Lord Baltimore. I have never been informed which fork of the South Branch she claims as the Potomac (for there is a North and a South fork of the South Branch); neither have I been able to learn what is the evidence, or the kind of evidence, on which she relies to ascertain that the stream which is *now* called the *South Branch* of the Potomac, but which *at the date of the grant to Lord Baltimore* was not known at all, and when known, known for many years only as the *Wappacomo*, was *the* Potomac intended by Lord Baltimore's grant. For this important geographical fact I refer to the numerous early maps of the chartered limits of Virginia and Maryland, some of which are to be seen in the public libraries of Washington and Richmond.

The question, which stream was the Potomac? is simply a question which of them, if either, bore the name. The name is matter of general reputation. If there be anything which depends wholly upon general acceptation which ought and must be settled by prescription it is this question which of these rivers was and is *the* Potomac? The accompanying papers, it is believed, will ascertain this fact to the satisfaction of every impartial inquirer.

In the twenty-first year of Charles II. a grant was made to Lord Hopton and others of what is called the *Northern Neck* of Virginia, which was sold by the other patentees to Lord Culpeper, and confirmed to him by letters patent in the fourth year of James II. This grant carried with it nothing but the right of soil and the incidents of ownership, for it was expressly subjected to the jurisdiction of the government of Virginia. Of this earlier patent I believe there is no copy in Virginia. The *original* charter from James II. to Lord Culpeper accompanies this report, marked No. 1. They are both recited in the colonial statute of 1736, (1 *Rev. Code, ch.* 89.) The tract of country thereby granted was "all that entire tract, territory and parcel of land lying and being in America and bounded by and within the heads of the rivers Tappahannock *alias* Rappahannock, and Quiriough *alias* Potomac rivers, the course of the said rivers as they are commonly called and known by the inhabitants and description of their parts and Chesapeake Bay."

As early as 1729, in consequence of the eagerness with which lands were sought on the Potomac and its tributary streams, and from the difficulties growing out of conflicting grants from Lord Fairfax and the Crown, the boundaries of the Northern Neck proprietary became a subject which attracted deep and earnest attention. At this time the Potomac had been but little explored, and although the stream itself above its confluence with the Shenandoah was known as the Cohongoroota, or Upper Potomac, it had never been made the subject of any very accurate surveys and examinations, nor had it yet been settled by any competent authority which of its several tributaries was entitled to be regarded as the main or pricipal branch of the river. It became important, therefore, to remove all further doubt upon that question.

In June 1729, the Lieutenant Governor of Virginia addressed a communication to the Lords commissioners of trade and plantation affairs, in which he solicits their attention to the ambiguity of the Lord proprietor's charter growing out of the fact that there were several streams which might be claimed as the head springs of Potomac River, among which he enumerates the Shenandoah, and expresses his determination "to refuse the suspension of granting of patents, until the case should be fairly stated and determined according to the genuine construction of the proprietor's charter." This was followed by a petition to the King in council, agreed to by the house of burgesses of Virginia, in June 1730, in which it is set forth, among other matters of complaint, "that the head springs of the Rappahannock and Potomac are not yet known to any of your Majesty's subjects;" that much inconvenience had resulted to grantees therefrom, and praying the adoption of such measures as might lead to its ascertainment to the satisfaction of all parties interested.

Lord Fairfax, who, by his marriage with the only daughter of Lord Culpeper, had now succeeded to the proprietorship of the Northern Neck, feeling it likewise due to *his* grantees to have the question relieved from all further difficulty, preferred his petition to the King in 1733, praying that his majesty would be pleased to order a commission to issue, for running out, marking and ascertaining the bounds of his patent, according to the true intent and meaning of his charter. An order to this effect was accordingly directed by the King; and three commissioners were appointed on behalf of the Crown, and the same number on behalf of Lord Fairfax. The duty which devolved upon them was to ascertain by actual examination and survey, the true fountains of the Rappahannock and Potomac Rivers. To enable them more perfectly to discharge the important trust confided to them, they were authorized to summon persons before them, to take depositions and affidavits, to search papers and employ surveyors, chain-carriers, markers, and other necessary attendants. The commissioners convened in Fredericksburg, on the 26th of September, 1736, and proceeded to discharge their duties, by taking depositions, appointing surveyors, and making every needful and requisite preparation for the survey. They commenced their journey of observation and survey on the 12th day of October, 1736, and finished it on the 14th of December, of the same year; on which day they discovered what they marked and reported to be the first fountain of the Potomac River. Separate reports were made by the commissioners, which reports, with all the accompanying documents, papers, surveys, plans, &c., were, on the 21st of December, 1738, referred to the council for plantation affairs. That board, after hearing counsel, made a report on the 6th day of April, in which they state, "that having examined into the several reports, returns, plans and other papers transmitted to them by the commissioners appointed on behalf of the Crown, as likewise of Lord Fairfax, and having been attended by counsel on behalf of your Majesty, as likewise of Lord Fairfax, and having heard all that they had to offer thereupon, and the question being concerning that boundary which ought to be drawn from the first head or spring of the river Rappahannock to the first head or spring of the river Potomac, the committee do agree humbly to report to your Majesty as their opinion, that within the words and meaning of the letters patent, granted by King James II, bearing date the 27th day of September, in the fourth year of his reign, the said boundary ought to begin at the first spring of the South Branch of the river Rappahannock, and that the said boundary be from thence drawn in a straight line northwest *to the place in the Alleghany Mountains where that part of the Potomac River, which is now called Cohongoroota, first rises.*" The Cohongoroota is known to be the stream which the Maryland writers term the *North Branch* of the Potomac, but which is recognized in Virginia, and described on all the maps and surveys which I have ever yet seen, as the *Potomac River*, from its first fountain, where the Fairfax stone is located, to its confluence with the Shenandoah; there being, properly speaking, no such stream as the North Branch of the Potomac. This report of the council for plantation affairs was submitted to the King in council on the 11th of April, 1745, and fully confirmed by him, and further order made, directing the appointment of commissioners to run and work the dividing line agreeably to his decision thus made. Commissioners were accordingly appointed, who, having provided themselves with surveyors, chain-carriers, markers, &c., commenced their journey on the 18th of September, 1746. On the 17th of October, they planted the *Fairfax stone* at the spot which had been described and marked by the preceding commissioners as the true head spring of the Potomac River, and which has continued to be regarded, from that period to the present time, as the southern point of the western boundary between Maryland and Virginia. A joint report of these proceedings was made by the commissioners to the King, accompanied with their field notes; which report was received and ordered to be filed away among the records of his Majesty's privy council. Thus terminated, after a lapse of sixteen years, a proceeding which had for its object, among other matters, the ascertainment of the *first fountain of the Potomac River*, and which resulted in the establishment of that "fact" by a tribunal of competent jurisdiction. This decision has now been acquiesced in for near a century; and all the topographical description and sketches of the country have been made to conform to it. I say *acquiesced in*, for it is impossible to regard the varying, fluctuating legislation of Maryland upon the subject, at one session of her General Assembly *recognizing* the line as now established, (*see compact of* 1785, *session Acts of* 1803, 1818 *and others*,) at another authorizing the appointment of commissioners to adjust the boundary, as a grave resistance of its conclusions, or such a *continual claim*, as under the usage of international law would bar an application of the principles of *usucaption* and *prescription*. (*See Vattel, p.* 251. *Grotius, lib.* 2, *cap.* 4. *Wolfus. Jus. Nat. par.* 3.)

Jurisdiction in all cases relating to boundaries between provinces, the dominion and proprietary government, is by the common law of England exclusively vested in the *King and council* (1 *Ves. sen p.* 447.) And notwithstanding it may be a question of boundary between the

Crown and a Lord proprietor of a province, (such as that between Lord Fairfax and the Crown,) the King is the only judge, and is presumed to act with entire impartiality and justice in reference to all persons concerned, as well as those who are parties to the proceeding before him, as others not parties who may yet be interested in the adjustment. (*Vesey, ib.*) Such is the theory and practice of the English Constitution; and although it may not accord precisely with our improved conceptions of juridicial practice, it is nevertheless the law which must now govern and control the legal aspect of the present territorial dispute between Virginia and Maryland.

It does not appear by the accompanying papers, that Charles Lord Baltimore, the then proprietor of Maryland, deputed an agent to attend *upon his part in the examination and survey of the Potomac River.* It is possible he conceived his interests sufficiently protected in the aspect which the controversy had then assumed between Lord Fairfax and the Crown. Certain it is, that it nowhere appears that he ever considered himself aggrieved by the result of that adjustment. That his government was fully apprised of what was in progress, can scarcely admit of a rational doubt. For it is impossible to conceive that a controversy so deeply affecting not only the interests of Lord Baltimore, but all who were concerned in the purchase of land in that section of the country, and conducted with so much solemnity and notoriety, could have extended through a period of sixteen years, without attracting the attention of the government of Maryland—a government ever jealous because ever doubtful of the original tenure by which her charter was held. But had Lord Baltimore even considered himself aggrieved by the result of that settlement, it is difficult now to conceive upon what ground he would have excepted to its justice or questioned its validity. Could he have said that the *information* upon which the decision was founded was imperfect? Or that the proceedings of the commissioners were characterized by haste, favoritism or fraud? This the proceeding of that board still preserved, would contradict For never was there an examination conducted with more deliberation, prosecuted with more labor, or scrutinized with a more jealous and anxious vigilance. Could he have shown that some other stream *ought* to have been fixed upon as the true head spring of the Potomac? This, it is believed, is impossible, for although it may be true that the south branch is a longer stream, it nevertheless wants those more important characteristics which were then considered by the commissioners and have been subsequently regarded by esteemed geographers as essential in distinguishing a tributary from the main branch of a river. (*See Flint's Geography, vol. 2, p.* 88.) Lastly, would he have questioned the *authority* of the Crown to settle the boundaries of Lord Fairfax's charter without having previously made him a *party* to the proceeding? I have before shown the futility of such an idea. Besides, this would have been at once to question the authority under which he held his own grant, for Baltimore held by virtue of an arbitrary act of the second Charles. His grant was manifestly made in violation of the chartered rights of Virginia, and carried into effect not only without the acquiescence, but against the solemn and repeated remonstrances of her government. Was Virginia consulted in the "dismemberment" of her territory? Was she made a party to that proceeding by which, "for the first time in colonial history, one new province was created within the chartered limits of another by the mere act of the Crown?" But the fact is that Charles Lord Baltimore, *who lived for six years* after the adjustment of this question, never did contest the propriety of the boundary as settled by the commissioners, but from all that remains of his views and proceedings, fully acquiesced in its accuracy and justice. (*See treaty with the Six Nations of Indians at Lancaster in June*, 1744.)

The first evidence of dissatisfaction with the boundary as established, which the researches of the Maryland writers have enabled them to exhibit, are certain instructions from Frederick Lord of Baltimore, (successor of Charles) to Governor Sharp, which were presented by the latter to his council, in August 1753. I have not been able to procure a copy of those instructions, but a recent historian of Maryland, and an ingenious advocate of her present claim, referring to them, says. "His instructions were predicated upon the supposition that the survey might possibly have been made *with the knowledge and concurrence of his predecessor*, and hence he denies the *power* of the latter to enter into *any arrangement* as to the *boundaries*, which could extend *beyond his life estate*, or conclude those in remainder." (*M'Mahon's History of Maryland, p.* 53.)

What were the precise limitation of those *conveyances* made by the proprietors of Maryland, and under which Frederick Lord Baltimore denies the power of his predecessor to enter into any arrangement as to the boundaries, which could extend beyond his life estate, I am not able to say—my utmost researches having failed to furnish me with a copy of them—but they were so far satisfactory to his Lordship's legal conceptions, as to induce him to resist even the execution of a decree pronounced by Lord Hardwicke, in 1750, (1 *Ves. sen. pp.* 444—46) upon a written compact as to boundaries, which had been executed by his predecessor and the Penns, in 1732. To enforce submission to that decree, the Penns filed a bill of reviver in 1754, and after an ineffectual struggle of six years, Lord Baltimore was compelled with a bad grace to submit, and abide by the *arrangement* as to the boundaries which had been made by his predecessor. To this circumstance, in all probability, was Lord Fairfax indebted for his exemption from the further demands of the proprietor of Maryland. For Lord Frederick, no ways averse to litigation, had by this time doubtless become satisfied that the *power* of his predecessor did not extend beyond his life estate, and might even *conclude those in remainder*. Be that as it may, however, certain it is that the records of Maryland are silent upon the subject of this pretension, from September 1753, until ten years subsequent to the compact between Virginia and Maryland in 1785.

An opinion prevails among some of our most distinguished jurists, resting solely upon traditionary information, that about 1761, Frederick Lord Baltimore presented a petition to the king and council, praying a revision of the adjustment made in 1745, which petition was rejected, or after a short time abandoned, as hopeless. If there ever was such a proceeding, I can find nothing concerning it in the archives of Virginia.

Be that as it may, it is certain that ever since 1745 Lord Fairfax claimed and held, and the commonwealth of Virginia constantly to this day has claimed and held by the Cohongoroota, that is by the northern branch, as *the* Potomac; and whatever Lord Baltimore or his heirs, and the State of Maryland may have *claimed*, she has *held* by the same boundary. There was no reason why Lord Fairfax, being in actual possession, should have controverted the claim of Lord Baltimore, or Maryland. If Lord Baltimore or Maryland, ever controverted the boundary, the question must, and either has been decided against them, or it must have been abandoned as hopeless. If they never controverted it, the omission to do so, can only be accounted for, upon the supposition that they know it to be hopeless. If Maryland ever asserted the claim—seriously asserted it, I mean—it must have been before the revolution, or at least during it, when we all know, she was jealous enough of the extended territory of Virginia. *The claim must have had its origin before the compact between the two states, of March* 1785, (*See* 1 *Rev. Code, ch.* 18.) We then held by the same boundary by which we now hold; we held to what *we* called and now call the Potomac; she then held to what *we* call the Potomac. Is it possible to doubt that this is *the* Potomac recognized by the *compact?* That compact is now 47 years old.

I have diligently inquired whether, as the Potomac above the confluence of the Shenandoah was called the Cohongoroota, the stream now called the south branch of the Potomac ever had any peculiar name independently of its relation to the Potomac—I mean, of course, any peculiar name known to and established among the English settlers—for it is well known it bore the Indian name of Wappacomo. I never could learn that it was known by any other name but that which it yet bears, the south branch of the Potomac. Now that very name of itself sufficiently evinces that it was regarded as a *tributary* stream of another river, and that river the Potomac, and that the river of which the south branch was the tributary, was regarded as the main stream.

But let us for a moment concede that the decision of the King in council was not absolutely conclusive of the present question; let us concede that the long acquiescence of Maryland in that adjustment has not precluded a further discussion of its merits; let us even suppose the compact of 1785 thrown out of view, with all the subsequent recognitions of the present boundary by the legislative acts of that State, and the question between the two streams now for the first time presented as an original question of preference ; what are the facts upon which Maryland would rely to show that any other stream than the one now bearing the name is entitled to be regarded as the main branch of the Potomac? It were idle to say that the south branch is the Potomac because the south branch is a longer or even larger stream than the north branch, which Virginia claims to hold by. According to that sort of reasoning the Missouri, above its confluence with the Mississippi, is the Mississippi, being beyond comparison the longer and larger stream. The claim of the south branch, then, would rest solely upon *its greater length*. In opposition to this it might be said that the Cohongoroota is more frequently navigable, that it has a larger volume of water—*that the valley of the south branch is, in the grand scale of conformation, secondary to that of the Potomac—that the south branch has not the general direction of that river, which it joins nearly at right angles—that the valley of the Potomac is wider than that of the south branch, as is also the river broader than the other.* And lastly, that the course of the river and the direction of the valley are the same above and below the junction of the south branch. (*See letters accompanying this report, No.* 26.) These considerations have been deemed sufficient to establish the title of "the father of waters" to the name which he has so long borne. (*See History and Geography of Western States, vol.* 2, *Missouri.*) And as they exist in an equal extent, so should they equally confirm the pre-eminence which the Cohongoroota has now for near a century so proudly and peacefully enjoyed.

The claim of Maryland to the territory in question is by no means so reasonable as the claim of the great Frederick of Prussia to Silesia, which that prince asserted and maintained, but which he tells us himself he never would have thought of asserting if his father had not left him an overflowing treasury and a powerful army.

With this brief historical retrospect, presented as explanatory of the accompanying testimony, I will now lay before your excellency, in chronological order, a list of the documents and papers referred to in my preceding observations.

No. 1. Is the original grant from King James II to Thomas Lord Culpeper, made on the 27th September, in the fourth year of his reign.

No. 2. Copy of a letter from Mayor Gooch, Lieutenant Governor of Virginia, to the lord's commissioners for trade and plantations, dated at Williamsburg, June 29th, 1729.

No. 3. Petition to the King in council in relation to the Northern Neck grants and their boundaries, agreed to by the house of burgesses June 30th, 1730.

No. 4. The petition of Thomas Lord Fairfax to his Majesty in council, preferred in 1733, setting forth his grants from the crown, and that there had been divers disputes between the Governor and Council in Virginia and the petitioner, and his agent, Robert Carter, Esq., touching the boundaries of the petitioner's said tract of land, and praying that his Majesty would be pleased to order a commission to issue for running out, marking and ascertaining the bounds of the petitioner's said tract of land.

No. 5. A copy of an order of his Majesty in his privy council bearing date 29th of November, 1733, directing William Gooch, Esq., Lieutenant Governor of Virginia, to appoint three or more commissioners, (not exceeding five,) who in conjunction with a like number to be named and deputed by the said Lord Fairfax, are to survey and settle the marks and boundaries of the said district of land, agreeably to the terms of the patent under which the Lord Fairfax claims.

No. 6. Copy of the commission from Lieutenant Governor Gooch to *William Byrd*, of Westover; *John Robinson*, of Piscataway, and *John Grymes*, of Brandon, appointing them commissioners on behalf of his Majesty, with full power, authority, &c., &c.

[I have not been able to meet with a copy of the commission of Lord Fairfax to his commissioners—they were *William Beverly*, *William Fairfax* and *Charles Carter*. It appears by the accompanying report of their proceedings that "his lordship's commissioners delivered to the King's commissioners an attested copy of their commission," which having been found upon examination more

Boundary Line. 83

restricted in its authority than that of the commissioners of the Crown, gave rise to some little difficulty which was subsequently adjusted.]

No. 7. Copy of the instructions on behalf of the right honorable Lord Fairfax to his commissioners.

No. 8. Minutes of the proceedings of the commissioners appointed on the part of his Majesty and the right honorable Thomas Lord Fairfax, from their first meeting at Fredericksburg, September 25th, 1736.

No. 9. Original correspondence between the commissioners during the years 1736 and 1737, in reference to the examination and survey of the Potomac River.

No. 10. The original field notes of the survey of the Potomac River, from the mouth of the Shenandoah to the head spring of said Potomac River, by Mr. Benjamin Winslow.

No. 11. The original plat of the survey of the Potomac River.

No. 12. Original letter from John Savage, one of the surveyors, dated January 17, 1737, stating the grounds upon which the commissioners had decided in favor of the Cohongoroota over the Wappacomo as the main branch of the Potomac. The former, he says, is both wider and deeper than the latter.

No. 13. Letter from Charles Carter, Esq., dated January 20, 1737, exhibiting the result of a comparative examination of the north and south branches of the Potomac. The north branch at its mouth, he says, is twenty-three poles wide, the South branch sixteen, &c.

No. 14. A printed map of the Northern Neck of Virginia, situate betwixt the rivers Potomac and Rappahannock, drawn in the year 1737, by William Mayo, one of the King's surveyors, according to his actual survey in the preceding year.

No. 15. A printed map of the courses of the rivers Rappahannock and Potomac, in Virginia, as surveyed according to order in 1736 and 1737, (supposed to be by Lord Fairfax's surveyors.)

No. 16. A copy of a separate report of the commissioners appointed on behalf of the Crown. [I have met with no copy of the separate report of Lord Fairfax's commissioners.]

No. 17. Copy of Lord Fairfax's observations upon and exceptions to the report of the commissioners of the Crown.

No. 18. Copy of the report and opinion of the right honorable the lords of the committee of council for plantation affairs, dated 6th April, 1745.

No. 19. The decision of his Majesty in council, made on the 11th of April, 1745, confirming the report of the council for plantation affairs, and further ordering the Lieutenant Governor of Virginia to nominate three or more persons (not exceeding five) who, in conjunction with a like number to be named and deputed by Lord Fairfax, are to run and mark out the boundary and dividing line, according to his decision thus made.

No. 20. The original commission from Thomas Lord Fairfax to the honorable Wm. Fairfax, Charles Carter and William Beverly, Esqs., dated 11th of June, 1745.

[Col. Joshua Fry, Col. Lunsford Lomax and Maj. Peter Hedgeman, were appointed commissioners on the part of the Crown.]

No. 21. Original agreement entered into by the commissioners preparatory to their examination of the Potomac River.

No. 22. The original journal of the journey of the commissioners, surveyors, &c., from the head spring of the Potomac in 1745. [This is a curious and valuable document, and gives the only authentic narrative now extant of the planting of the Fairfax stone.]

No. 23. The joint report of the commissioners appointed as well on the part of the Crown as of Lord Fairfax in obedience to his Majesty's order of 11th April, 1745.

No. 24. A manuscript map of the head spring of the Potomac River, executed by Col. George Mercer of the regiment commanded in 1756 by Gen. Washington.

No. 25. Copy of an act of the General Assembly of Maryland passed February 19th, 1819, authorizing the appointment of commissioners on the part of that State, to meet such commissioners as may be appointed for the same purpose by the Commonwealth of Virginia to settle and adjust, by mutual compact between the two governments, the western limits of that State and the Commonwealth of Virginia, *to commence at the most western source of the north branch of the Potomac River, and to run a due north course thence to the Pennsylvania line.*

No. 26. Letters from intelligent and well-informed individuals residing in the country watered by the Potomac and its branches, addressed to the undersigned, stating important geographical facts bearing upon the present controversy.

There are other papers in my possion not listed nor referable to any particular head, yet growing out of and illustrating the controversy between Lord Fairfax and the Crown; these are also herewith transmitted.

There are other documents again not at all connected with my present duties, which chance has thrown in my way, worthy of preservation in the archives of the State. Such, for example, as the original "*plan of the line between Virginia and North Carolina, which was run in the year* 1728, *in the spring and fall, from the sea to Peters's Creek, by the Hon. Wm. Byrd, Wm. Dandridge and Richard Fitzwilliams, Esqrs., commissioners, and Mr. Alex'r Irwine and Mr. Wm. Mayo, surveyors, and from Peters's Creek to Steep Rock Creek, was continued in the fall of the year,* 1749, *by Joshua Fry and Peter Jefferson.*"

Such documents, should it accord with the views of your excellency, might be deposited with "the Virginia Historical and Philosophical Society," an institution of recent origin, yet founded upon the most expanded views of public utility, and which is seeking by its patriotic appeals to individual liberality, to wrest from the ravages of time the fast-perishing records and memorials of our early history and institutions.

With sentiments of regard, I am, very respectfully, your obedient servant,

CHARLES. JAS. FAULKNER.

To JOHN FLOYD, Esq., *Governor of Virginia.*

The controversy between the two States pended for some time after Mr. Faulkner's report, and in addition to Col. John B. D. Smith, of Frederick, and John S. Gallaher, Esq., of Jefferson, were appointed commissioners on the part of Virginia.

CHAPTER VIII.

HISTORICAL PEN SKETCHES OF THE EARLY RESIDENTS OF BERKELEY COUNTY, WITH HAPPENINGS, Etc.

BY THE LATE HON. CHAS. JAMES FAULKNER.

THESE papers were prepared and written over fifteen years ago, and like nearly all of Mr. Faulkner's writings, relate in some manner to Berkeley County. Among the papers, the author found one package marked "Memorabilia"—or things to be remembered. Mr. Faulkner prepared these sketches to accompany the "Berkeley Centennial Celebration," but the pamphlet was never published.

HORATIO GATES,

A Major General in the army of the United States. He was a native of England. He was with Braddock at the time of his defeat, 1755, and was shot through the body. He then purchased an estate in Berkeley County, Virginia, where he resided until the commencement of the American war in 1775, when he was appointed by Congress Adjutant General, with the rank of Brigadier General. The success which attended his arms in the capture of Burgoyne in October, 1777, filled America with joy. Congress passed a vote of thanks, and ordered a medal of gold to be presented to him by the President. August 16th, 1780, he was defeated by Cornwallis at Camden. He was superceded by General Greene, but in 1782 restored to his command. After peace, he retired to his farm, called "Traveler's Rest," in Berkeley County, where he remained till 1790, when he went to reside at New York. He died on the 10th of April, 1806, aged 77 years.

ALEXANDER WILSON.

Born in Paisly, Scotland, July 6th, 1766—emigrated to the United States, July 14th, 1794—settled in the County of Berkeley, now in West Virginia, shortly after his arrival, as a weaver. His residence here was marked by great poverty, and does not seem to have left very pleasant impressions on his mind, if we may judge by the following lines extracted from one of his poems—

> Farewell to Virginia—to Berkeley adieu,
> Where, like Jacob, our days have been evil and few.
> So few—they seemed really but one lengthened curse,
> And so bad that the Devil only could have sent worse.

He was a man of unconquerable resolution and energy, and of enthusiastic devotion to natural science. He had completed the seventh volume of his great work on ornitholigy before he died, and was engaged, when seized with his last illness, in collecting the materials for the eighth volume. Of the many active men whose biographies are before the public, there is not perhaps one whose life presents such heroic resolution in the pursuit of science. He died August 23, 1813, and was buried in Philadelphia.

DR. RICHARD McSHERRY

Was born in the County of Berkeley, upon the farm known as "Retirement," near Leetown, on the 28th of May, 1792, and was the eldest son of Richard and Anastatia McSherry, who both lived and died on the estate. He was educated at an academy at Fredericktown, Maryland, then at Hagerstown, and lastly at Georgetown College, D. C., where he went through a full course of instruction. He commenced the study of medicine under

Dr. Samuel J. Creamer, a graduate of Edinburg, and a very accomplished physician, residing at Charlestown. From thence he went to Philadelphia, and entered the office of Prof. Nathaniel Chapman, of the University of Pennsylvania, at which University he graduated in medicine in 1816. Meantime, while attending the lectures, the war of 1812 broke out, and he joined a company from his native county, and marched to encounter our British invaders; and upon the death of the medical officer attached to the command, he was commissioned in his place, and served as a surgeon in the army until the end of the war. In 1816, he commenced the practice of his profession in Martinsburg, and enjoyed an extensive and lucrative practice until 1871, when he withdrew from the practice. He was married in January, 1817, to Miss Ann C. King, daughter of Mr. George King, Georgetown, whose family were of the early Maryland colonists. He died in Baltimore, at the residence of his son, on the 20th of December, 1873, and his remains were interred in the Catholic cemetery of Martinsburg.

No man enjoyed a more enviable reputation than Dr. McSherry. As a physician he stood in the first rank of his profession and by constant study, kept progress with the advance of medical science. His mild and amiable temper, bland and courageous deportment to all, made him a general favorite. His reading extended beyond the scope of his professional studies, and his familiarity with history and general literature, made him at all times an agreeable companion. He was kind and charitable, and bore throughout life a reputation of unsullied integrity.

JOHN MYERS.

Born in the County of Berkeley, about the year 1765, and lived all his life in the mountainous districts of the county. He was a man of striding appearance, about six feet, four inches in height, with no superfluous flesh, and with a countenance indicating great natural intelligence and intrepid daring. His whole life was spent in hunting bears, deer and other game of the forest. He was universally known by the name of "Hunter John Myers." The chase was his pastime and his means of support. His rifle was unerring in its aim, and rarely did a wolf, bear or deer escape him. There was a savage wilderness in his features, which indicated very clearly how little he had mingled in the haunts of civilized life. If he was not the original from which the novelist Cooper painted his celebrated character of Natty Bumppo, or Leather-Stocking, he has by the force of imagination delineated with extraordinary accuracy the hunter of Berkeley. Myers, like Leather-Stocking, stands half way between savage and civilized life; a man with all the freshness of nature about him, and whose like is only to be seen at this day, amidst the wild and unbroken forests of the west. He died about the year 1835.

CHARLES D. STEWART.

For nearly half a century this gentleman held the office of deputy Sheriff of this county. Each successive senior magistrate as he attained the Sheriffalty, was pleased, as the law then stood, to farm out for a fixed compensation the discharge of its duties to one so distinguished for his honesty and humanity as Charles D. Stewart. Few men ever passed through so protracted an official service with so little complaint of his conduct. He was prompt in the execution of process, tender, yet firm and decided, and he administered his charities so quietly and silently that his left hand scarcely knew what his right had bestowed. He died of the cholera in 1854.

RAWLEIGH COLSTON

Was born in England; married Elizabeth Marshall, sister of Chief Justice John Marshall; purchased a large estate upon the Potomac River in the County of Berkeley, upon which he erected a handsome mansion. He, in conjunction with his brother-in-laws, John and James Marshall, purchased from the devisees of Thomas Lord

Fairfax, all their proprietary rights in the Northern Neck of Virginia. Lord Fairfax being an alien at the period of our revolution, and the State of Virginia treating him as such, and alien creditors and landlords having acquired rights under the treaty of peace of 1783, and Jay's treaty of 1764, much perplexity and difficulty existed in this and other counties embraced in the Northern Neck as to their land titles. These difficulties were adjuted by a compromise between those purchasers and the Commonwealth of Virginia, made on the 10th of December, 1796, by which the State confirmed the title of all persons claiming under Fairfax to the lands which had been specifically appropriated or reserved by Lord Fairfax or his ancestors for his or their use; the purchasers relinquishing their title to all the waste and unappropriated lands in the Northern Neck. Under this compromise, patents were issued without controversy for all lands not then covered by patents from Lord Fairfax.

Mr. Colston was a man of literary tastes, and of large commercial information, and took an active interest in the cause of religion. On the 13th of June, 1814, he was elected president of a Bible Society then organized in the County of Berkeley, and his address to the public in support of that cause, published in the Martinsburg *Gazette*, of that period, is a document marked by literary ability and deep Christian feeling. He died in 1823, and was buried at Honeywood, his county seat, in this county.

He left a large family of sons and daughters, among whom were Edward Colston, a representative in Congress from this district; Mary, a lady of extraordinary beauty and accomplishments, married to John Hanson Thomas, of Maryland, a lawyer of great genius and promise, who died in early life, and Susan, married to Benjamin Watkins Leigh, one of Virginia's distinguished sons.

LIEUTENANT DAVID HUNTER,

Son of Col. Moses Hunter, was born in Berkeley county.

When quite a young man he was appointed an officer in the United States army, and was assigned to duty on the northern frontier. He was killed on the 11th of November, 1813, near Williamsburg, on the shores of the St. Lawrence, Canada. He was advancing with great intrepidity upon a formidable column of one of the best appointed detachments of the British Army, under a shower of musketry and grape shot scarcely ever equaled, and was exhorting his men to behave in a cool and determined manner, when he was struck by a canister shot, which in a few minutes terminated his existence.

DANIEL BEDINGER

Was born in Berekley County. When in his sixteenth year he ran away from home and joined a company of volunteers and served throughout the revolutionary war. He was captured at the battle of Brandywine on the 11th of September, 1777, and was detained as a prisoner of war until the British army evacuated Philadelphia in the summer of 1778. After his exchange as a prisoner of war, although he had suffered incredible hardships during his captivity, he promptly returned to the army.— He bore the rank of ensign during the war, and was appointed Navy Agent at Gasport, Virginia, by President Jefferson, and remained in office during his administration. When the old frigate Constitution was dismantled he purchased the masts, which were used in the portico of the house which he built near Shepherdstown, and which house, then the property of Edmund I. Lee, who had married his daughter, was, by order of General Hunter, burned during the late civil war. He was a man of vigorous and original mind, with a decided talent for poetical satire, and lines from some of his poems are, after a lapse of nearly half a century, in the memory of many persons. He died at his residence near Shepherdstown in March, 1818, aged 54 years.

ABRAHAM SHEPHERD,

A captain in the revolutionary war. He volunteered as

a private in June, 1775, in the Berkeley County company, commanded by Hugh Stephenson. He was elected a lieutenant of that company in the place of Lieut. Thomas Hite, who declined the commission, and marched with the company to Boston in July, 1775. At the expiration of its term of service, which was one year, he was commissioned the senior captain in a rifle regiment commanded by Col. Hugh Stephenson. He was very energetic in filling his company, having enlisted out of the old company twenty men to serve for three years, and returning to Berkeley in a short time enlisted seventy-one and marched them to the field of operations in the north. On the 4th of October, 1776, he arrived with his company at Bergen Point, opposite New York, where he found Col. Rawlings in command of the regiment, Stephenson having in the meantime died. On the 12th of Novenber he was engaged for three successive days in severe skirmishing at King's bridge. On the 16th he was engaged in a severe action with the enemy, in which Col. Rawlings and Maj. Williams were severely wounded and taken from the field, and the command of the regiment devolved upon him. Finding himself overpowered by superior numbers he returned slowly to Fort Washington, about half a mile distant from the scene of action. The fort was captured and all in it made prisoners of war. Cap. Shepherd remained a prisoner until May, 1778. He then returned to Berkeley County and remained there until 1779. In the meantime the fifteen Virginia regiments were, by a resolve of Congress, reduced to eleven, and many of the officers became supernumerary. Capt. Shepherd called upon Gen. Washington and claimed his right to be in active service as a senior captain in the Virginia line. Gen. Washington regretted the necessity that compelled so many valuable officers to retire as supernumeraries, and added that if the country should hereafter want their services they would be notified to join the army. Capt. Shepherd consequently retired from active service as a supernumerary for the remainder of the war. He received a letter from Gen. Washington but two months before the General's death, speaking of him as a "valuable officer in the revolutionary war." He never filled any public civil employment, but was an active supporter and liberal contributor to local improvements. He died on the 7th of September, 1822, in the 69th year of his age.

PHILIP NADENBOUSCH,

Born in Bedford, Pa., on the 20th of October, 1773, emigrated to Berkeley County on the 4th day of July, 1799. He was commissioned a magistrate in 1807, and was twice commissioned sheriff of Berkeley County. He was the presiding justice of the county court for more than twenty years. He died on the 5th day of ——1863. He bore the reputation of an intelligent magistrate and of an upright man.

LEVI HENSHAW,

Born in Berkeley County on the 22d day of July, 1769. He was for many years an active magistrate and member of the County Court of Berkeley, and in 1821, 1822, 1830 and 1831, was elected a member of the House of Delegates of Virginia. He was highly respected and esteemed, and died at his residence on Mill Creek in the County of Berkeley on the 9th of September, 1743.

JOEL WARD

Was born in the County of Berkeley on the 4th of May, 1781. He was for many years one of the most influential citizens and magistrates in the county. The grasp and power of the intellect were admitted by all who come into contact with him. He was in 1819, 1820 and 1828 elected to the legislature from this county, and always discharged his public duties with singular fidelity and conscientiousness. He resided near Bunker Hill, on Mill Creek, where he died on the 17th of February, 1837.

REV. BERNARD C. WOLFF, D. D.

Was born in Martinsburg, Berkeley County about

the year 1795. He was the son of George Wolff, Esq., one of our most conscientious and respectable magistrates. When the writer of this sketch first became acquainted with the son in 1822, he was working at his trade of saddler in Martinsburg, then in the 28th year of his age. His intelligence, extensive reading and literary attainments, were the subject of general remark; while his frank and fascinating manners, social temperament public and unaffected piety, made him a universal favorite. Every enterprise looking to the educational moral and religious interests of this community found in him an ardent advocate and energetic supporter. It was therefore not a matter of surprise when it became known, that he, then in the 36th year of his age, decided to devote himself to the office of the holy ministry.— After several years of preparatory study in the theological seminary of the German Reformed Church at York, Pa., he received a call to the reformed Church at Easton, in that State. In this field he labored for nine years, and in the spring of 1845 was called to take charge of the Third Reformed Church in Baltimore. A vacancy occurring in the theological seminary at Mercersburg, he was elected to fill the vacant position, and in 1854 entered upon his duties as professor of dogmatic and pastoral theology. Owing to declining health, he resigned his professorship in 1864, and removed to Lancaster city.— Here he devoted much attention to the interests of Franklin and Marshall College. About two years before he died, he was attacked with paralysis and his active labor on earth ceased. Gradually failing in his physical strength, but with his mental powers still active, he calmly and peacefully departed this life on the 31st day of October, 1870, while the last rays of an autumn sun was illuminating the western sky with a flood of glory.

Bernard C. Wolff was no ordinary man. He was the model of a christian gentleman, always kind and courteous, yet firm and decided in his principles, and untiring in his work. His views of the ministry were of the most exalted character, and his conduct and conversations in the life fully corresponded with his conceptions of its divine mission on earth.

COL. DAVID HUNTER

Was born in York, Pennsylvania, on the 3rd of May, 1761. Sometime during his early boyhood his parents came to Virginia and settled near the site of Martinsburg, on what is still known as the "Red House Farm." The precise date of his coming is unknown, but there is reason for believing that the settlement was made during the Governorship of Lord Dunmore, and before the establishment of Berkeley County in 1772.

David, the youngest son of the family, acquired the rudiments of his education, in a log school house located near the present crossing of Queen and Burke streets, walking the whole way from his father's house (about two miles to the northward) through unbroken forests. Of his earlier life the traditions are few and vague and scarcely worth reading. He was for sometime employed as deputy assistant in the Clerk's office of Berkely County, held by his brother, Moses Hunter, between the years 1735 and 1748. About the year 1787 or '88 he went to England on some business connected with the interests of his family, and after his return about 1792, he married Elizabeth, eldest daughter of Philip Pendleton, and sister of the late Philip C. Pendleton. The county Clerkship becoming vacant by the death of his eldest brother, David Hunter, competed for the place with Major Henry Bedinger. Bedinger was elected by the vote of the magistrate, but it being apparant that some of the electors had been controlled by improper influences, the election was contested by Col. Hunter in the courts. After several years of litigation his case was sustained, and he was put in possession of the office in 1803, and held it until his death. About the year 1811 while walking out with some friends on the Walnut Flats, near Stephen's Dam, he attempted to leap a narrow gulley, fell and broke his leg, from the effects of which he was lame for life. Hence the cane and limp which are remembered by all who knew him in his latter days.

As the flower of his life passed during the interval between the Revolution and the War of 1812, Colonel Hunter was never in the military service and his title was probably derived from a commission in the militia, and while he was one of most generally esteemed and influential men in the district, the possession of the responsible and (then) lucrative Clerkship, effectually debarred him from seeking political distinction, then, as now, more honorable than profitable. He was nevertheless, like most of the gentlemen of his circle at that day, a strong Federalist, and when that party rejoiced in the downfall of Napoleon Bonaparte in 1813, he was chosen to preside at a barbecue dinner given in honor of the event by the Federalists of Berkeley and adjacent Counties of Virginia and Maryland. This celebration took place on the 16th of September, 1813, at Swearengen's Spring on the Potomac River above Shepherdstown, and was cleverly caricatured as "the Cossack Celebration" in some satirical verse written by a gentleman of the opposite party, and well remembered to this day. The motives and justification of the assembly are set forth however, in a document, still extant, bearing evidences of the sincerity and ability of its framers, and well worth perusal at this day.

Colonel Hunter died on the 22nd of March, leaving a large family of sons and daughters, only one of whom it is believed, is still living.

From the traditions of his earlier life, we learn that Colonel Hunter was a person handsome, athletic and graceful, courteous and dignified in manner ; in conversation full of humorous and entertaining anecdotes, the result of travel and observation, rather than reading and books. He was especially remarkable for his strong practical sense and keen insight into character, rarely erring in his judgment of men with whom he came in contact; yet kindly and generous withal—leaving the impression both in physique and character, of one of the finest types among our early settlers.

MAJOR GENERAL THOMAS SIDNEY JESSUP

Was born in the County of Berkeley, in 1788 and entered the army in 1808 as a second lieutenant of the seventh infantry. So rapid was his promotion, that in 1812 he was brigade major, and acting adjutant general to Brigadier General Hull. In 1813 he was major of the 19th infantry; transferred in 1814 to the 25th infantry as brevet lieutenant colonel, for distinguished and meritorious bravery in the battle of Chippewa, of the 5th of July, 1814. In November of the same year, he was breveted colonel for gallant conduct and distinguished skill in the battle of Niagara, of the 25th of July, 1814, in which he was severely wounded. On the reduction of the army in 1815, we was retained in the first infantry, and in 1817 was lieutenant colonel of the third infantry. In 1818 he was appointed adjutant general with the rank of colonel; and the same year, Quartermaster General, with the rank of Brigadier General; and was breveted Major General in May, 1828, for ten years meritorious service. He was assigned to the command of the army in the Creek nation, Alabama, in 1836, and succeeded Gen. Call in Florada on the 8th of December, 1836; was wounded in action with the Seminole Indians near Jupiter Inlet on the 24th of January, 1838; and was succeeded by Col. Z. Taylor on the 15th of May 1838; whereupon he returned to the duties of his department, which he managed with distinguished ability.

He continued at the head of the Quartermaster's department of the United States, until the period of his death, which occurred on the 10th day of June, 1860.—The writer of this sketch, who was himself at one time

Chairman of the committee on military affairs of the House of Representatives, knew Gen. Jessup well, and had an opportunity of estimating his valuable services to the country. To his fine military capacity in the field, he added great administrative ability. In the management of the vast concerns of the Quartermaster's department, he evinced great foresight, but the labor developed upon him by the Mexican war, in managing the details of the campaign in a far distant country, can only be properly appreciated by those who shared in its difficulties and responsibilities. A grateful country must ever bear in honorable remembrance the services of the veteran soldier and gentleman whose name and fame will go down to posterity as a portion of the brightest military records.

ROBERT COCKBURN, JR.,

The son of Robert Cockburn, of Cockburn Hill, east of Martinsburg, was born in 1775. When I first knew the father he was, at least 80 years of age. His long, flowing white hair, covering his shoulders and reaching far down his back, and his snowy beard sweeping to his waist, gave a striking and picturesque appearance to the old man. It was said, that he had been college-bred; that he had been educated in the best schools in Scotland and that he had amassed a rich fund of classical lore and historical knowledge.

"Cockburn Hill," as it was then called, with its extensive orchard of cherries was well known to every boy in Martinsburg; and often has many an idle and truant urchin roused the excitable temper of the old hermit by pillaging his fruit before it was quite ripe. When matured and proper to be eaten, no one could be more generous and liberal than he was in the license granted to gather it.

He had two sons, Adam and Robert. Adam was a dull and stupid boy; Robert the genius of the family, and upon him did the hopes of the old man repose. He was smart, loquacious, disputatious, and brimful of egotism, pertness and conceit. He had an extravagant idea of his scholarship and of his poetical talents. He selected the vocation of a schoolmaster. The birch and the ferule were no idle implements in his hands. He was self indulgent to his own vices, but inexorably severe on the peccadilloes of his pupils. He had all the learning at that period of our educational history, deemed necessary to an instructor of youth.

> 'Twas certain he could write and cypher, too,
>   Lands he could measure, terms and tides presage
> And e'en, the story ran, that he could guage.
>   In arguing, too, the parson owned his skill,
> For e'en tho' vanquished he could argue still.

But it was not in his character of a schoolmaster that he became entitled to be noticed in these humble sketches. His gay, frolicsome and social temper—his familiarity with all games and pastimes at rural entertaiments, his capacity for extemporaneous rhyming—made him the hero of all apple-butter boilings, quilting parties, cotillion assemblies and corn-husking festivities, for miles around. No party was deemed complete unless graced by the presence of "Bob Cockburn." He sang, played on the fiddle, told funny stories and extemporized verses for the relief of those who were amerced in poetical forfeits. But such a round of dissipation in those days of apple-jack and whisky—when no temperance lecturer had ever been heard of in the land—in the course of a few years began to tell on the habits of the frolicsome pedagogue—his nose began to blush—his eyes became weary and inflamed—and he soon fell under the dominion of that tyrant who has never been known to show mercy or compassion to his helpless victims.

Bob was a patriot as well as a poet; at least I am justified in thinking so from a poem of his which I have seen in an old number of the Martinsburg *Gazette* and what is the only specimen of his poetical genius which

Historical Pen Sketches. 101

has survived "the wreck of the matter and the crash of worlds." I can only take a short extract from it.

It was written in June, 1818, one of the gloomiest periods of our last war with Great Britian. Norfolk, Portsmouth and all the towns and cities on the Chesapeake Bay and James River were threatened by a powerful navy and military force of the enemy. Two of the finest companies from "old Berkeley" were then at the scene of battle, encountering the pestilential air of the swamps of Norfolk, and the fire of the enemy, in protecting the sacred soil of Virginia from invasion, pillage and murder.

The poem commences by representing a Berkeley youth deeply enamored of a charming girl dwelling on the crystal waters of the Tuscarora. He vows his love in most passionate terms; declares that for years her enchanting image has wholly absorbed his heart, and asks in a delirium of despair, *what he shall do* to assure him of the reward of his long and devoted affection for her. The Tuscarora maiden, in the spirit of Boadicea, thus replies to him:

> If you sincerely wish my favor
>   Then you possess a patriot mind;
> Your country droops, advance to save her,
>   Nor sighing, linger here behind.
> Hear the inspiring shouts of praise —
>   On to glory!—loud they call you!
> See youthful heroes crowned with bays
>   Their envied lot may yet befall you.

Robert Cockburn died on Cockburn Hill in 1824, in the 49th year of his age.

JOHN R. COOKE

Was born in 1788, in Bermuda, the son of Dr. Stephen Cooke and Catharine Esten. He came, with his parents, to Alexandria, thence to the vicinity of Leesburg, where his father had a place called the "Forest." He never went to college, as his eyes suddenly failed him whilst preparing for it. He settled in Martinsburg about 1810, where he commenced the practice of law. In 1814 he was elected to the House of Delegates from the county. He married in Martinsburg a daughter of Col. Philip Pendleton, and continued his residence there for a period of nearly twenty years. He subsequently removed from this county to Winchester, thence to Baltimore and thence to Richmond. Enjoying a high degree of popularity, political position might with him have been a matter of easy attainment, but, earnestly devoted to his profession, he resisted the appeals of that character which were frequently made to him. He was, with great unanimity, elected a member of the Constitutional Convention of Virginia of 1830, and there exhibited the nerve and ability to grapple with such intellectual giants as Leigh, Upshur, Randolph and Tazewell in the discussion of the great question of extended suffrage and equal representation before that body. His professional abilities were of the highest order and universally recognized. In the celebrated Randolph will case, argued in 1836, his great and peculiar powers of argumentation were strikingly exhibited. E. V. Sparhawk, the reporter of that trial, a very competent judge, and who heard all the arguments in the case, thus speaks of Mr. Cooke's effort: "It was a masterly production. He classifies and expounds his facts with great strength and clearness, and arranges his authorities and arguments in the most forcible manner. His method of arguing is superior to any man at the bar. Instead of dividing his strength upon the separate points, his whole speech was but one point, for the support of which all the other various facts and considerations of the case were brought together in pyramidal strength and harmony."

Mr. Cooke was a bold, trenchant and vigorous writer. His able and elaborate pamphlets published in 1825 entitled "The Constitution of 1776," followed by "The Convention Question," in 1827, and then again by "An

Earnest Appeal to the Friends of Reform" in 1828, attracted the attention of the whole State to him and largely contributed to the passage of the law organizing the Constitutional Convention of 1829 and 1830, of which he himself was an active and conspicuous member. Mr. Cooke opened the "great debate" in that body by an unsparing attack upon the then existing constitution of Virginia, and asserted for himself, beyond all question, the position of *leader of the friends of reform* in a body composed of the ablest men from Western Virginia.

In 1835 he yielded to the importunity of his friends and very reluctantly accepted the Whig nomination for Congress in this District. Once accepted, however, he entered into the canvass with his usual and characteristic energy and pluck. His address to the people in the several Court Houses of the district were models of lucid statement, pungent, invective and eloquent demonstration. The writer of this heard his address in Martinsburg. The court-room was crowded to excess. Not a man stirred or left the hall during the two hours that he was speaking. It was one of the most logical, perspicuous and powerful arguments that he ever hurled from the hustings.

No one was better qualified to judge of his intellectual merits than the late James Marshall, of Winchester. In 1866 he thus spoke of Mr. Cooke to a friend:

"The finest faculty of his mind was his power of reasoning—his clearness of judgment. His narrative in a case was the best I ever knew. It might be said of him as Webster said of Hoffman, that his case " once stated, was already argued." He was very rash in his charities, unbounded I may say in liberality. His power of labor was very uncommon. I never saw such great labor. He had the clearest mind I ever saw. If a witness or any one in a case was acting dishonestly, he attacked him without mercy. He was remarkable in philippic. He had a very keen appreciation of equity, morals and manners, and if they were wanting on such occasions he conceived a great contempt for the individual and denounced him bitterly and powerfully. He had a great practice."

David Holmes Conrad, in a letter, refers to him as "the model of lofty courtesy, chivalry and generosity." Another said that when he died "he did not leave an enemy on the bosom of the spacious earth."

This apparent hyperbole is undoubtedly near the truth. He was a man of extraordinary suavity and amenity—of unvarying sweetness of temper. In social life he rarely exhibited any feelings of anger, and was characterized by a remarkable patience and benevolence. His generosity knew no bounds. He seemed to place no value upon money. He gave it away to everybody and to every object.

He died in the city of Richmond in December, 1854, in the 67th year of his age.

MAGNUS TATE

Was born in Berkeley County in 1760. He was a man of superior intelligence and a farmer by occupation. He was twice elected from the county to the House of Delegates of Virginia, in 1797 and 1798. He was commissioned a magistrate in 1799, and twice commissioned Sheriff of the county in 1819 and 1820, and elected to the House of Delegates in 1803, 1809 and 1810. He had much of the old Virginia character about him in his tastes and habits. He was fond of dogs and horses, and in his younger days a keen fox hunter. His house was the abode of a generous hospitality, and the lovers of whist, music and the dance could always find an opportunity there to gratify their appetites for pleasures.

In January, 1815, he announced himself a candidate for Congress for the district composed of the counties of Berkeley, Jefferson, Hardy and Hampshire, and he was triumphantly elected. His address to the freeholders of the district prior to the election is all that now remains of this gentleman to show the temper of the man and the character of his intellect, and certainly his descendants have no reason to be ashamed of it, either upon the score of its sentiments or of its ability. We give it entire:

"*To the freeholders of the district composed of the counties of Berkeley, Hampshire, Hardy and Jefferson:*

FELLOW CITIZENS :—I offer myself to your consideration as a candidate to represent you in the next Congress of the United States. It is possible the curious may be disposed to inquire why I have become a candidate without the sanction of a committee. To this interrogatory I answer that the recent method of nominating candidates by committee, however highly I may incline to appreciate the practice, is, nevertheless, as it seems to me, no way preferable to the ancient custom which everyone understands. Again, I have been induced to declare myself at this time and in this way by the request of my friends, who think with me it is the wish of a majority of the freeholders of the district. If, however, we should be mistaken in this particular, whatever the result may be, I will cheerfully submit to when fairly ascertained on the day of election. All I desire is to give the people an opportunity of making a selection, and all I ask is an unbiased expression of public opinion. This manner of proceeding appears perfectly congenial with the first principles of our government, with all our political institutions, and consequently can be liable to no rational objection. Here, perhaps, it may not be improper to premise that I trust my deportment on this occasion will be found fair and manly, and that if I should meet with an opponent he shall receive from me all the politeness and decorum due from one gentleman to another.

To those gentlemen in the upper parts of the district with whom I have not the pleasure of a personal acquaintance, I am pursuaded I shall be exonerated from the charge of egotism and of complimenting myself when they are informed that I am a farmer, in the middle walks of life, and that if honored with their suffrages my circumstances are such that I will neither be driven from the path leading to the prosperity of our country by want or poverty, nor allured from it by avarice or ambition.

Citizens of the district, if an ardent attachment to my native soil ; if many friends and relatives whom I esteem and venerate ; if a numerous progeny intertwined with every moral perception of my heart ; if either or all these considerations firmly combined can rivet a man to his country and to liberty—these motives, these inducements, which, in my estimation, are the most powerful that can operate on the human mind, shall be left by me, as pledges."

He was associated in his legislative labors with such men as Henry Clay, Daniel Webster, John C. Calhoun, William Lowndes, John Randolph, William Gaston, Philip P. Barbour, Henry St. George Tucker and a host of others, all members of that House almost equally distinguished by their geniuses and reputations. In those days the committees of the House were few and small, and the active business of the body was left in the hands of its leading statesmen. Not as now, when every man in Congress, no matter how inferior, must have his hour, and grind out that hour in a written speech, whether listened to or not, or whether written by himself or by a clerk in the departments. The rule now is to put every member on some committee. The rule then was to put on committe duty only the most competent and distinguished.

Mr. Tate lived almost two and a half miles southwest from Martinsburg, on a farm since purchased by Wm. Walker. He left a large family of sons and daughters. He died on the 30th of March, 1823.

JOHN BOYD,

Father of Gen. Elisha Boyd and a native of England,

was one of the earliest settlers in the County of Berkeley. He acquired his land in this county by original grant from Lord Fairfax, the patents of which are still preserved by his descendants. He resided near the North Mountain, about five miles west of Martinsburg. He was a man of herculean frame of body, and some anecdotes are related of his hand to hand conflicts with the Indians, which demanded all his activity and strength, but in which he was generally victor.

He was married about the year 1754, to Sarah Gryfyth, a native of Wales, and died in the year 1800, leaving eight children, born in the following order, to wit: Charles, Margaret, Fulton, John, William, Rachel, Bayley, Elijah, Mary, Munford and Elisha; the first born on the 13th of April, 1756, and the last on the 6th of October, 1769.

His widow, Sarah Boyd, survived him some years, dying in 1806. With the exception of Elisha, the children were among the earliest emigrants to Kentucky. It is said that Hon. Lenn Boyd, of Kentucky, for several years Speaker of the House of Representatives, was one of that stock, and his striking resemblance to Gen. Boyd in stature, feature and general appearance would seem to confirm that remark.

WILLIAM SMITH,

most generally known as "Burgess Billy Smith," was born in Sleepy Creek about the year 1747, in that portion of the colony of Virginia which was subsequently embraced in the County of Berkeley. He had an insatiable ambition to become a member of the legislature. Shortly after the creation of the County of Berkeley in 1772 he became a candidate for the House Burgess, and continued his candidacy, without success, for several years, from which he acquired the soubriquet of "Burgess Billy." After the revolutionary war was ended and the State constitution of 1776 was adopted, dividing the legislative department into a Senate and House of Delegates, he pressed his claims for election to the House of Delegates from year to year, but still without success. When Morgan was formed into a separate county in 1820 he regularly entered the field every year for a seat in the legislature. At the April election in 1830 the aspirations and struggles of a long life were gratified by an election, but the adoption of the new constitution in the following August set aside the election and dashed and disappointed the hopes of his life. He never afterward had the heart to aspire to the place, and died a few years afterward, deeply impressed with the incapacity of the people to select competent and proper agents to serve them. He was a man of remarkable astuteness and cunning, and although unable to read or write, no one was ever found smart enough to take advantage of those deficiencies. He was said to have been the first child born in the Sleepy Creek Valley.

HENRY CLAY.

When this illustrious statesman was Secretary of State under the younger Adams, and when, like the antlered monarch of the forest, he was almost driven to bay by the fierce blood-hounds of party under the foul and loathsome cry of "bargain and corruption," he sought, in July, 1827, a temporary refuge from this pitiless storm of calumny in a visit to some of his cherished friends in Berkeley County. He spent some days in Martinsburg, and it is needless to say that he was received here with all the enthusiasm due to his exalted genius and patriotism. He decided to pay a brief visit to the Berkeley Springs, and a gentleman now residing in our county, accompanied him in a carriage. When, about 2 o'clock in the day, they reached what was called the Halfway House, a sort of tavern kept by Dick Sheckles, a man of enormous proportions, fat and unwieldy, and weighing near four hundred pounds, they found the old landlord sitting in the shade before his house, indulging in his usual habit in the hot days of summer, of keeping himself cool by burying his feet in the earth and piling it up around his legs nearly as high as his knees. The arrival of the carriage did not in the least disturb the placidity of the unwieldy landlord. When Mr. Clay approached the house his traveling companion presented him to Mr. Sheckles, saying: "Permit me to introduce to you the present Secretary of State, Henry Clay, of Kentucky." With that the old gentleman gazed for a moment at the tall, spare and erect figure before him, and rising to his feet said : "Did you say this was Henry Clay, of Kentucky? Why, I thought he was a great big man like a king!" "No, Mr. Sheckles," said Mr. Clay, "you are more kingly in your proportions than I am. You see in me nothing but a broken down public servant, worn almost to a skeleton by State and the calumnies of my enemies."

In May, 1844, Mr. Clay was invited by a public mass-meeting of his friends in this county to visit Martinsburg and to partake of the hospitalities of the county. We take an extract from the letter of invitation, as it contains some facts worthy of remembrance:

MARTINSBURG, VA., March 14th, 1844.

To the Hon. Henry Clay :

SIR—The County of Berkeley boasts of some historical recollections connected with your fame, which she is not disposed shall at the present period be lost sight of or forgotten. She looks with a becoming pride to that sagacity which prompted her sons some twenty years ago to seek to give in your person that direction to public sentiment which it is now receiving from the patriotism and sagacity of the whole Union. It was here, in this very county—by action of the people in primary assembly, on the 14th of June, 1824, that your name was first presented to the people of Virginia, as a candidate for that exalted station, for which you now stand nominated in the hearts of near two millions of your admiring countrymen. It was here—in this county—that the electoral ticket was framed and announced, which presents your claim to the suffrages of your native State. The short period which elapsed after the annunciation of that ticket, connected with the circumstance, that your claims were brought in competition with an elder of the Republican party, holding the same general principles of policy with yourself, and also a native of this State, prevented your receiving that support in this commonwealth, which none at that time denied to be due to your patriotism, exalted character and eminent public services. Still Berkeley by her recorded vote, preferred you then, as she has ever preferred you since and as she prefers you now, to all living statesmen, as the representative of her principles in the administration of the national government. She gave you her confidence without reserve in 1824, and she has continued that confidence without change or shadow to the present hour. She has with an abiding faith sustained you amidst all the fierce and bitter conflicts of party, confidently looking forward to the day now reaching its meridian splendor—when your name would kindle its just enthusiasm in every patriotic bosom, and all sections of this vast country hail you as the hope of this great Republic.

The invitation was declined for the reason set forth in his reply :

WASHINGTON, D. C., May 1st, 1844.

Gentlemen:

I feel greatly flattered, honored, and obliged by the invitation which you have transmitted to me to visit Berkeley County and partake of its hospitality, and by the friendly sentiments which accompany it. I feel, with gratitude, and acknowledge with pleasure, my great obligations to Berkeley, for its uniform and ardent attachment and confidence for me; and I should be most happy, under other circumstances, to meet and exchange friendly salutations with my fellow citizens of that county; but considerations, both of a public and private nature, in my judgment, require of me hereafter to avoid attendance upon large assemblages of my fellow citizens and I hope that the determination, to which I have come, on that subject, will command the approbation of you, gentlemen, and of those whom you represent. So numerous and constant are my occupations and so frequent have been the invitations which I have received, and am still receiving to public assemblages, that I am compelled to be much briefer, in my replies, than I would wish to be.

I pray you gentlemen to accept yourselves and tender to those whom you represent my respectful and grateful acknowledgments. I am with great respect,
    Your friend and obedient servant,
              H. CLAY.

Mr. Clay's second visit to the County of Berkeley was in January, 1848. He was then going to Washington to argue a case before the Supreme Court of the United States. Having some days to spare, he determined to spend a short time in this county, with a friend. The presidential question was then agitating the public mind, and it had not been determined whether the nominee of the Whig party would be General Taylor or himself. The private mansion at which he stopped was freely opened to all his friends and there are many now living amongst us who will remember with delight, the wonderful power and fascination of his conversation, when in unrestrained intercourse with his friends.

He spoke with his characteristic frankness and freedom of the pending Presidential canvass; made no secret either of his work or of his expectation of receiving the nomination of the approaching Whig convention; read a correspondence between himself and Gen. Z. Taylor, embracing several letters in which the old hero of Buena Vista whilst freely conceding the superior party claims of Mr. Clay to the nomination, and expressing his individual wishes that he might receive it, declares that he had no agency whatever in having his name presented in competition with Mr. Clay's, yet with modest firmness stated, that it was not his business to interfere with the progress of public sentiment, and the convention must be left free to make its selection in the best interests of the party and country.

The writer of this has never known Mr. Clay to be more joyous and cheerful than upon the occasion of this last visit to the County of Berkeley. He felt indeed that he was in the house of his friends. He seemed eager to promote universal enjoyment around him. He encouraged the dance, music—caressed the children, told amusing anecdotes to the ladies ; and when in his graver moments, he retired to the library, and there, surrounded by many of our citizens, portrayed the characters of our leading public men and expatiated upon what he deemed the true policy of the Government, all felt that they were in the presence of a patriot, orator and statesman, of whom the country might indeed be justly proud.

I have pondered over the inquiry, How was it that this bold and unequalled leader of a great party, this noblest type of American manhood, this most prominent orator, patriot and statesman of his day, could never reach the goal of his lofty and honorable ambition—the Presidency? Was he too bold, too independent, too little of the politician to suit the then cravings of party cupidity ? Is it a position only suited to men of inferior and moderate abilities? Are all of our really great men to be hereafter excluded from the enjoyment of its honors? Was it attributable to the secret influences of rival candidates, that Mr. Clay lost his nomination ? Was it to be ascribed to that natural jealousy which great, brilliant and commanding minds attract? Was it to the office seeking demagogues who fill our conventions, and who are ever on the alert to find out whom they think the most "available" candidate, without regard to merit? Or was it to that caprice and ingratitude which so often darkens the history of Republics, and which causes them to banish from their confidence, a citizen because they are tired of hearing everybody styling him "Aristides the Just?" These are questions which it may be well at some future day to consider, and to find their solution if possible.

MARTIN VAN BUREN,

Eighth President of the United States, made a visit to Martinsburg in 1830, whilst Secretary of State under General Andrew Jackson. He stopped at the Globe Hotel, then kept by William Kroesen. The writer of this sketch made a respectful call upon him, and spent a pleasant evening in his company. His trip was one simply of recreation. He spoke of the pleasure which he derived from his excursion, and was emphatic in his praise of the soil and scenery of this Valley. He was not at that time much of a favorite with our people, of either party, and but little enthusiasm was manifested at his presence.

FISHER AMES.

This distinguished orator and statesman, at the close of the session of Congress of 1796, being then in feeble health, paid a visit to the warm springs in the County of Berkeley, in the hopes of obtaining some relief from his increasing debility. He thought he derived much benefit from drinking the water; also from our pure and fresh mountain air, and relaxation from the unremitting cares of public life. In this visit he was the object of the most friendly and respectful attention, individual and public. Contrary to his expectations, he found many friends of the Washington administration during this visit, notwithstanding the lead taken by the Representatives of Virginia in opposition to that policy. In one of his letters from Berkeley he observes "Virginia has been misrepresented to us, as much as the measures of government have been to them; and many good men are here to be found friendly to the federal cause."

From his visit to Berkeley in 1796 his health continued to decline, with partial and flattering intermissions until death. He was a striking example of magnanimity and patience under suffering. Retaining always the vigor and serenity of his mind, he appeared to make those reflections which became his situation. When speaking of his illness, he observed, "I trust I realize the value of those habits of thinking which I have cherished for some time. Sickness is not wholly useless to me. It has increased the warmth of my affection for my friends. It has taught me to make haste in forming the plan of my life, if it should be spared, more for private duties and social enjoyments, and less for the splendid emptiness of public station, than yet I have done."

After an extreme debility of two years, the frame which had so long tottered was about to fall. With composure and dignity he met the approach of his dissolution.

Fisher Ames will ever rank among the great statesmen of this country. Excepting Daniel Webster, I know of no public man of the North whose fame rests upon a more indisputable basis of genius and merit. His speech in the House of Representatives on the British Treaty of 1790 has been regarded as one of the finest specimens of Congressional eloquence ever uttered in that body—and many passages of it of surpassing brilliancy are remembered and quoted to this day, although near a century has elapsed since they were delivered.

WM. H. CRAWFORD,

In his visit to the Berkeley Springs, spent several days in Martinsburg, going and returning in the summer of 1824. He was in the early part of that year, beyond all question, the most formidable candidate for the Presidency. He had withdrawn from the canvass in favor of

Mr. Monroe and was considered in some sense his destined successor. He was nominated as such by a Congressional caucus on the 14th of February, 1824—that being the mode which up to that day had been adopted by the Democratic party to indicate its choice for the Presidency. But the powerful opposition of four Democratic competitors—Calhoun, Jackson, Adams and Clay —followed by a severe attack of paralysis, blasted his prospect of election, he receiving but the solid votes of Virginia and Georgia and portions of the votes of New York, Maryland and Delaware.

It was to get relief from this crushing affliction that he visited the Berkeley Springs in the summer of 1824. But the healing waters of those celebrated springs were impoetnt to give the desired relief. During his passing visits to Martinsburg he received the warmest sympathies of its citizens, who vied with each other in showing him every attention and respect.

THOMAS DAVIS, M. D.,

Was born in Kentucky, and was a favorite protégé of the distinguised Dr. Lewis Marshall of that State. He became a resident and citizen of this county about the year 1820. He practiced his profession as a physician for about ten years in Martinsburg, but his excessive devotion to literature and history caused him to become indifferent to the practice of his profession, and after his marriage to the daughter of a very wealthy farmer of the county, he abandoned it altogether and retired to the country. He was a man of acute and powerful intellect, of extensive reading and a vigorous and forcible writer. In literary attainments and in profound historical research, he was almost without an equal. He left here for Natchez in 1843, with a view there of resuming the practice of his profession. Within a month after his arrival there, the yellow fever broke out with fearful mortality, and he fell a victim himself to the fearless discharge of his professional duties. The writer of this paid a visit to his grave in January, 1845, and dropped a tear to the momory of one of the noblest and truest of men. He founded the Martinsburg Library, which for so many years was supported and cherished in this place ; and in the important session of 1831 represented this county, with signal ability, in the House of Delegates of Virginia.

JOHN S. GALLAHER

Was born in Martinsburg, Berkeley County, Va., December 1st, 1796. His only school education was obtained between the ages of five and twelve, in the old stone school house in the north-eastern portion of the town, under the tuition of "an excellent Irish gentleman of the olden time," Capt. Jas. Maxwell, long the County Surveyor. On the fourth day of April, 1809, he entered the printing office of Mr. John Alburtis, editor of the Berkeley and Jefferson *Intelligencer*, afterwards the Martinsburg *Gazette*.

After an apprenticeship of five years, Mr. G. worked a few weeks in Baltimore, principally upon Nile's *Register*. In August, 1814, being in Charlestown, in charge of the *Farmer's Repository*, while its editor, Capt. Richard Williams, was in the military service at Norfolk, Mr. G. joined the volunteer rifle company of Capt. George W. Humphrey's, and served a month. In the course of this service the company had part in the sharp conflict at the White House Bluff, on the Potomac, in which Com. Porter undertook, with a few small field pieces and some riflemen, to stop the British vessels then descending the river, ladened with flour and other stores captured at Alexandria. On the conclusion of his military service, Mr. G. worked about a year in the office of the *National Intelligencer*, the model newspaper conducted by those well known gentlemen, Messrs. Gales and Seaton.

In May, 1821, Mr. Gallaher, with his younger brother, Robert, (who died in August following, after only four days' sickness, of a malignant fever then prevailing,) commenced the publication of the Harper's Ferry *Free Press*, now the *Virginia Free Press*—a paper which acquired great popularity. Mr. G. also published for four years, a literary paper called *The Ladies' Garland*.

In 1827 he purchased the *Farmer's Repository*, at Charlestown, and merged it with the *Free Press*, now published by his brother, H. N. Gallaher, and his nephew, W. W. B. Gallaher.

In the spring of 1830, Mr. Gallaher was elected a member of the Virginia House of Delegates, with the veteran Daniel Morgan as his colleague. The amended Constitution of 1829 being adopted, this election of delegates was set aside, and in October, 1830, John S. Gallaher and Edward Lucas were chosen. In this first session under the new Constitution, much of the legal talent of the Old Commonwealth was in requisition, and it was deemed no light honor to be a colleague of such men as Benjamin Watkins Leigh, Richard Morris, Thomas Marshall, Jas. M. Mason, James McDowell, etc.

Mr. Gallaher was re-elected for four successive terms, with slight opposition, except in 1833, when, having given a "State's Right's Vote" (in the nullification era), which displeased some of his ultra Whig supporters, a spirited canvass ensued, but he was re-elected by an increased majority. In the spring of 1835 he declined further legislative service, and removed to Richmond to take chief management of the *Richmond Compiler*, which he held for nineteen months.

At the close of his term, the elder Governor Floyd, in 1832, appointed Charles James Faulkner, of Berkeley, John S. Gallaher, of Jefferson, and John B. D. Smith, of Frederick, Commissioners to settle, in conjunction with a like number from Maryland, the boundary line between the two States, but Maryland did not appoint Commissioners, and nothing was done. Mr. Faulkner has since had the matter in charge under a new appointment, and has made much progress in the collection of interesting data.

In January, 1837, Mr. Gallaher purchased a third interest in the Richmond *Whig*, and for three years was associated with those eminent journalists, John Hampden Pleasants and Alexander Moseley. In 1840 he sold his interest in the *Whig* to his partners, and published for nine months a popular campaign paper—the *Yoeman*, in support of Harrison and Tyler. In the contest of that year the Whigs came within 1,400 votes of carrying the State.

In the autumn of 1841 Mr. Gallaher returned to Jefferson, in connection with his favorite *Free Press*, and in the spring of 1842 was again elected to the House of Delegates, and served two sessions. In 1844 he was nominated for the Senate by a Whig convention, and was elected in the then Democratic district of Jefferson, Frederick and Clarke, by a majority of 62 votes, in opposition to John Bruce, a gentleman of ability and scholarly attainments—his predecessor, Robert Y. Conrad, an eminent lawyer, having declined a re-election. This district, the same year, gave Mr. Polk a majority of one in the Presidential election.

In connection with Mr. Gallaher's career as a State Senator, it may not be out of place to mention, that near the close of President Tyler's term, in a conversation on the subject of the annexation of Texas, so confident was the President of the success of that measure, and of the consequent war with Mexico, that he offered Mr. G. a command in the army. This compliment was respectfully declined, for two reasons; first, that his term of civil service had not expired, and secondly, that his military aspirations had been satisfied with the command of a well-drilled company of riflemen at Harper's Ferry.

In 1848 Mr. Gallaher was again nominated for the Senate, and after an active canvass, was defeated by a majority of 22 votes, the principal opposition to him being on account of a school bill for the County of Jefferson, matured by him and carried through both Houses. Jefferson County having an area about 25 miles square, is particularly well adapted to an experiment with free schools; and the system, by the aid of the remakabie John Yates, a wealthy land holder, and the largest tax payer in the county, was successfully put into active operation, and resisted several attempts to repeal the act. Mr. Gallaher, in his retirement, had the proud satisfaction of seeing 27 schools, free for the poor, firmly established and successful until broken up by the disastrous four years' war, which also destroyed the labors of forty years of his life.

On the 22nd of October 1849, Mr. Gallaher was appointed by President Taylor to succeed that eminent accountant Peter Hagner, as Third Auditor of the Treasury, who had held the position from its creation in 1817, a period of 32 years. Declining health was the cause of Mr. Hagner's retirement.

Mr. Gallaher served as Auditor through President Taylor and Fillmore's terms, and was removed in April 1858, by President Pierce, to make room for Francis Burt, of South Carolina, a personal friend of Jefferson Davis, then Secretary of War. This change was made in opposition to the wishes of many prominent Democratic members of Congress, who were satisfied with the incumbent, and strongly protested against his removal.

Being prevented by the exigencies of the war from returning to Virginia, as he desired to do, Mr. Gallaher, accepted a position in the office of the Quartermaster General, at Washington, which position he continued to hold until a few months before his death, when age and disease rendered him unable to discharge its duties.

He died at his residence in the city of Washington on the 4th of February 1877, and his remains were conveyed to the Presbyterian church in Charlestown and interred in Edge Hill cemetery, in sight of his beloved hills, and beneath the soil of his native State.

No one took a livelier interest in the "Berkeley Centennial Celebration" than Mr. Gallaher. It seemed to touch the innermost chords of his heart, and to wake up, in vivid coloring, all the reminiscences of his early life. He anxiously desired to be present at the ceremonies of the day, but circumstances put it out of his power. For a few weeks preceeding the celebration scarcely a day passed that the Chairman of the Committee on Correspondence did not receive some communication from him—referring in that kind and genial spirit, so characteristic of the man—to those old citizens of the county, whom he had known, loved and respected in his younger days. It is due to him and cannot fail to interest our readers to make some extracts from this correspondence.

WASHINGTON, D. C., June 13, 1872.

Hon. C. J. Faulkner, Chairman, Martinsburg, W. Va.:

Dear Sir: I am proud of my native county and have had frequent occasions to refer to her honored history.

It would be egotistical in me to recount the ordinary events of my school-boy days during my attendance under twelve years of age in Capt. James Maxwell's old school house, in the northeastern portion of Martinsburg, over the site of which the locomotive now plies its busy wheels. The teacher being an adept in mathematics, and County Surveyor, had a number of grown up young men as students. I recollect Tillitson Fryatt, Robert V. Snodgrass, Jacob Myers, Dennis McSherry and Lawrence Wilmer among these. Three of them I met, after a lapse of twenty years, in the legislature of Virginia.

Among my earliest recollections of eminent public men I may cite a discussion at the old Court House in Martinsburg between Alfred H. Powell, Federalist, and Henry St. George Tucker, Republican, for the position of State Senator. It was a rich, intellectual treat to me, a discussion between two courteous and polished gentlemen, strongly impressed on my youthful memory as a model of forensic eloquence. Both these gentlemen were afterward eminent members of the national House of Representatives.

My memory naturally carries me back to the era in which prominent men of Berkeley were in the vigor of life and usefulness, such as Col. Elisha Boyd, Judge Philip C. Pendleton, Col. William Gregory, Maj. Andrew Waggoner, Maj. Jas. Faulkner, Capt. Rob't Wilson, Capt. James Mason and others, who were in military service in the war of 1812.

Among the regular army officers of 1812 who went to the northern frontier from Berkeley, I remember Capt. Lewis B. Willis, Capt. Hiram Henshaw, Lieuts. John Strother and David Hunter, the latter of whom was killed in Canada.

I cannot omit a reference to an early friend who kindly stimulated my ambition when struggling with adverse fortune—I mean the late John R. Cooke, eminent at the bar, and in the Constitutional Convention of Virginia—a gentleman in every sense of the term, "with a heart open to melting charity." Nor do I forget my apprentice days on the old Martinsburg *Gazette*, published by John Alburtis, one of the most even-tempered gentlemen I ever knew, and who, like my old teacher, Capt. Maxwell, seemed ever gratified at my success.

Well do I remember the venerable Edward Beeson—Beeson's mill, Beeson's orchard, (from which urchins like myself, of tender years, often were supplied with fruit) and Beeson's meadow, on Tuscarora Creek, upon which an Indian tribe of that name had frequent sanguinary battles with other tribes. The tradition on this subject is sustained by the frequent finding of arrow heads and various implements of Indian warfare. Other objects of interest abound. This recital may not be worth the time to read it, but the very suggestion of one's birth-place awakens memories of hills and valleys, teeming fields and gushing fountains, such as old Berkeley is blessed with most abundantly.

It would be interesting to ascertain how many now survive who trod those hills and valleys and laved in those waters,

Just one hundred years ago!

Yours truly,

JOHN S. GALLAHER.

In another letter of the following day he mentions:

"Ephraim Gaither, the dignified and gentlemanly proprietor of the Globe Hotel; Philip Nadenbousch, long a magistrate, whose sons worthily represent the name; Col. George Porterfield, also a popular magistrate and the Chesterfield of the County Court; Charles D. Stewart, for over fifty years the faithful deputy sheriff of the county; Rev. William Riddle, the preacher and teacher; Michael McKewan, Luke Pentiney, Alexander Cooper, Thomas C. Smith, Dr. Erasmus Stribling, Dr. J. S. Harrison, Jacob Hamme, Geo. Doll, Geo. Wolff, Adam Young, Wm. Somerville, the well remembered postmaster; Conrad Roush, Anthony S. Chambers, James P. Erskine, Jacob Poisal, John H. Blondell, W. Long, Ezekiel Showers, John Stewart, Conrad Hogmire, Daniel Burkhart, John Matthews—but my pen must stop; columns would not suffice to make up the record of my old friends and acquaintances."

John S. Gallaher was a man of strong and vigorous intellect, disciplined and improved to the highest point of which it was susceptible. His judgment was sound, practical and discriminating; his temper mild, just and generous; his habits those of constant and assiduous labor. Free from his business employments he delighted in history and Belles Letters, and his taste in literature was refined and chaste. He was patriotic and public spirited, and liberal in all his views of national and State policy. He was a careful and correct, but not dashing and flowing writer. He had none of the qualities of a public speaker, yet he always had at command such a fund of practical good sense, and was so familiar with the recognized maxims of human life that a few short, pithy sentences from him from the stump reached their mark more effectually than more accomplished oratory, and his sayings were remembered and treasured up by his audience. He was kind, grateful, charitable and whole-souled, and was universally esteemed for his integrity and for his merits and attainments as a self-made man.

FELIX GRUNDY

Was born on Back Creek, in the County of Berkeley, on the 11th of September, 1777. His father was a native of England, who settled in early life in the valley of Virginia. In 1780 he removed to Kentucky. The early childhood of Mr. Grundy was passed amid the perils and sufferings of Indian warfare. A striking picture is given in his own eloquent language in a speech delivered by him in the Senate of the United States in February, 1820, from which, however, we can only take a very short extract:

"Mr. President, I was too young to participate in these dangers and difficulties, but I can remember when death was in almost every bush, and every thicket concealed an ambuscade. If I am asked to trace my memory back and name the first indescribable impression it received it would be the sight of my eldest brother, bleeding and dying under the wounds inflicted by the tomahawk and scalping knife. Another and another went in the same way. I have seen a widowed mother plundered of her whole property in one single night, and from affluence and ease reduced to poverty in a moment, and thereby compelled to labor with her own hands to educate her last and favorite son, who now addresses you."

He was educated at Bardstown Academy, studied law,

and soon became distinguished at the bar. He commenced his public career at the age of twenty-two, as a member of the convention for the revising of the constitution of Kentucky; was afterward, for six or seven years, a member of the legislature of that State. In 1805 he was elected one of the judges of the Supreme Court of Kentucky, and was soon after made Chief Justice. In 1807 he removed to Nashville, Tenn., and became eminent as a lawyer. From 1811 to 1814 he was a representative in Congress from Tennessee, and during that period gave to the war measures of President Madison against Great Britain such ardent support that he was familiarly know as the "war hawk" of democracy. From 1829 to 1838 he was United States Senator, and in the latter year was appointed by President Van Buren Attorney General of the United States; in 1840 he resigned this position and was again elected Senator. He died at Nashville, Tenn , Dec. 19th, 1840. Whilst a member of the Senate he made a visit to Berkeley County to examine the spot where he had passed his early boyhood. But he found nothing but a dilapidated stone chimney to mark the place where had stood the cabin with its clapboard roof which had shielded his childhood from the storms of winter.

MICHAEL ROONEY

Was born in Ireland. His enemies contended that he had been a Corsair in early life, but this was believed to be an idle slander. Certain it is that he spent some years amidst the perils of the sea, in the British service, and he there acquired the reputation of an expert sailor and skilful navigator. He was familiar with the dead languages and thoroughly versed in some of the higher branches of mathematics. He emigrated to the County of Berkeley about forty years previous to his death, and purchased a large body of land on Cherry Run in that county, his dwelling-house having been built on the western side of that small stream. He was one of the most zealous and indefatigable magistrates of the county, and took special and peculiar pride in the discharge of all the duties of that position. When the County of Morgan was formed in 1820, and Cherry Run made the dividing line between it and Berkeley, thus throwing him into the County of Morgan, he promptly abandoned his substantial residence in that county and erected a new dwelling house on the Berkeley side of that run, a few yards distant from his former residence, that he might preserve his domicil in Berkeley and continue his magisterial functions. His strange and peculiar features and appearance, and his indomitable will and imperious temper; the ardor with which he entered into the examination of every case before him, and the sharpness and point with which he commented upon the law and facts as they arose in the progress of the trial, made his court at the old Robert Snodgrass tavern, on Back Creek, a place of great attraction and resort for the neigborhood for many miles around. He was elected high Sheriff of the county, and died in 18—, leaving a will emancipating his slaves, providing for their transportation to the colony of Liberia, and appointing Chas. James Faulkner his agent, with full power to carry his benovelent views into effect. But a testator often intends what he cannot accomplish. He could emancipate, but he could not transport without the consent of his freedmen. They received their emancipation papers with becoming gratitude, but they declined his generous offer to transport them across the ocean to that fiery continent from which their ancestors had been probably torn more than a century before. They concluded that this country was quite good enough for any white or black man to live in.

GEORGE PORTERFIELD

Was born in Berkeley County in the year 1740; in early life he was once or twice exposed to the imminent risk of losing his life from the Indians then inhabitating or making incursions into this county. His brother

Charles, then a youth about twenty years of age, was killed not far from his father's house by a body of Indians who had the previous day attacked Nealy's fort, near the Opequon, massacred the inmates and took off several prisoners on their retreat. Mr. Porterfield was among the most popular magistrates of the county, and when acting as senior justice of the county court, presided with unusual dignity. He was Sheriff of the county, and in 1808 and 1810 one of its representatives in the legislature. In 1814 he was elected chairman of the meeting for the organization of the Berkeley County Bible Society. He was remarkable for the equanimity of his temper and for his invariable courtesy, pleasant address and politeness. He died in 1824.

MARIA COOPER.

Born in Berkeley County; a lady of great intelligence, brilliant conversational powers, and of great religious fervor and piety. No person was ever more universally loved and esteemed in this community; and of the hundred and eleven estimable persons who fell victims to the cholera pestilence in the fall of 1754, there was not one whose death was so universally lamented. She left a will, bequeathing a large portion of her estate to charitable purposes. Among seven other bequests contained in her will was one for the founding of an academy in Martinsburg; but this, with all the other bequests in her will for charitable purposes, was declared by the Supreme Court of Appeals of West Virginia, to be invalid and thus, an institution which in anticipation of this fund, and to do honor to her memory, was incorporated as the Martinsburg Cooper Academy, perished under the illiberal policy and stern decree of the court. She published some time before her death a small work composed of original and selected matter, that gave evidence of high literary taste, and which proved that she was as graceful in composition as she was brilliant in conversation. She died in October, 1854, of an attack of the cholera.

JAMES STEPHENSON

Was born on March 20, 1764. He commanded a company in the disastrous defeat of General Arthur St. Clair in 1791, when thirty-eight officers and five hundred and ninety-three men were slaughtered by the Miami Indians, and twenty-one officers and two hundred and forty-three men were badly wounded. He was present at the quelling of the whiskey insurrection in Pennsylvania, and was promoted to the office of Brigade Inspector. He served in 1800, 1801 and 1802 as a delegate from Berkeley County to the Virginia Assembly, and was a representative in Congress from this district from 1803 to 1805, from 1809 to 1811, and again from 1822 to 1825. He raised a large and interesting family of children, boys and girls, and lived in the house now owned and occupied by D. H. Conrad. He died in August, 1833. An anecdote is told of an arranged duel between Major Stephenson and General Darke, both men of tried and approved courage. They were to fight with swords. Stepenson, who was a small man, came to the ground armed with a rapier. Darke, a man of gigantic proportions, brought with him a broad sword, as large as an ordinary mowing scythe. When the seconds were about to place them in position for the combat the disparity of size of both the men and of their weapons was so irresistably ludicrous that the seconds burst into an uncontrolable fit of laughter, which soon communicated its effect to the principals; the duel was averted, all points of honor settled and the two brave old soldiers shook hands and continued warm friends the rest of their lives.

JOHN MILLER

Was born on the Tuscorora Creek in Berkeley county. He was distinguished for his courage as an officer in the last war with Great Britain; soon after the struggle he was appointed Register of the Land Office, in Missouri;

subsequently elected Governor of the State, and was a Representative in Congress from 1837 to 1843. Died near Florissant, Missouri, March 13, 1846.

WILLIAM CREIGHTON,

Born in Berkeley county, Virginia, October 29, 1778; graduated at Dickenson College when quite young; studied law and was admitted to the bar at the age of twenty; in 1798 he settled in Chillicothe, Ohio, devoted himself to his profession, and holding many positions of public trust. He was the first Secretary of State, for Ohio; and was a Delegate in Congress from 1813 to 1817, and again from 1827 to 1833. Died at Chillicothe, October 8, 1851, having for many years previously declined all public office.

JOHN KERNEY

Was born in Berkeley county. The following extract is taken from an original certificate executed on the 17th of June, 1791, by William Darke, late Lieutenant Colonel commanding in Virginia Line, now in the possession of the writer of this sketch:

"I was, and am well acquainted with Captain John Kerney, of the county of Berkeley, Virginia; he engaged in the American service as first Sergeant to a company in July, 1775, in Col. Hugh Stevenson's regiment of infantry; he was taken prisoner at Fort Washington, suffered a long and painful imprisonment after which he continued in the American army and behaved as a brave and distinguished soldier, 'til he was appointed a lieutenant in a State Regiment, commanded by Col. Joseph Crockett, after which he succeeded to the command of a company in said regiment, and served until it was disbanded, which was not until the end of the war. During his whole service, he merited the esteem of his superior officers, and of his country."

Subsequent to the war, he returned to the county of Berkeley, held the position of a justice of the peace and member of the County Court, until about the year 1805 he emigrated to Kentucky, where he died.

NATHANIEL WILLIS

Was born in Boston, June 1780. When twenty-one years of age he established the first newspaper in Martinsburg, which was called the *Berkeley Intelligencer*. He continued to edit that paper until 1803, when he sold out to John Alburtis, left Martinsburg, removed to Portland, Maine, where he established the *Eastern Argus*. He was an active journalist for many years. He finally moved to Boston and died there May 26, 1870, nearly ninety years of age. It has been supposed by some that his distinguished son, N. P. Willis, the poet and journalist, was born whilst his father resided in Martinsburg, but this is an error. N. P. Willis was born in Portland, Maine, Jan. 20, 1806.

WILLIAM ALBURTIS

Was born in Martinsburg, and commissioned 2nd Lieutenant of infantry in the regular army of the United States on the 8th of March, 1827; promoted to the rank of first Lieutenant in July 1839; commanded in sortie from Fort Brooks, Orange Creek, March 2nd, 1841, against the Seminoles; was breveted as captain in August 1842, "for gallantry and good conduct in war against the Florida Indians;" was killed 11th of March, 1847, by a cannon shot at the siege of Vera Cruz.

JAMES R. STEPHENSON,

Son of Major James Stephenson, born in Martinsburg; entered the military academy at West Point in 1818; graduated with great distinction, and commissioned second Lieutenant of infantry in July 1822; promated to a first lieutenancy October 1825; commissioned a captain, December 1834. Died 26th of November, 1841, at Pilatlea, Florada.

MAJOR ANDREW WAGGONER, JR.,

Son of Major Andrew Waggoner, of Revolutionary

memory, was born near Bunker Hill, in the County of Berkeley, on the 24th of October, 1779. I have no information of his occupations and employments in early life. He was elected a member of the House of Delegates from this county, 1811. When war was declared in June 1812, by the United States against Great Britain, all the heroic qualities of his nature, and which he had so largely inherited from his gallant father, promptly developed themselves. He first volunteered as a private, soon was promoted to a captaincy, and then commissioned as a major of infantry. He was on Craney Island, in command of a battalion of the 4th Reg. of Va. Infantry, when the attack upon that Island was made by a combined military and naval British force, on the 22nd of June 1813, and although from the successful operations of the Artillery in repelling the attack, both by land and water, the infantry was not called into action, yet, all were impressed with the daring courage, and animated by the noble patriotism which he displayed on that occasion. He had to an extraordinary degree, the confidence of those under his command. Popular in his manners—frank and manly in his bearing—decisive in his movemens—with a face beaming with intrepidity and devotion to his country, he was the idol of the soldiery. No one doubted, had the enemy reached the Island, how gallantly he would have borne himself amidst the storm of battle.

After the war he removed from the County of Berkeley, to the vicinity of Point Pleasant, in Mason County, Virginia, to take possession of some valuable land on the Ohio River, in that county, which had been granted to his father in consideration of his Revolutionary service.

He was elected a member of the House of Delegates of Virginia, from the County of Mason in 1836. He soon became as great a favorite among the members of the Legislature, as he had been among the soldiers. All local measures for the benefit of his constituents were carried without opposition and almost by acclamation.

It being understood that he was on Craney Island, during that battle, a resolution was introduced into the body, without his knowledge, to vote him some signal honor for his assumed services in that conflict. But he promptly put a stop to the intended compliment by saying: "It is true I was on that Island during the attack ; but my command was not called into action. The artillery did the work, and I cannot be the instrument of robbing Major Faulkner who had supreme command of the artillery, of the honor and merit which belong to him." After this frank and manly declaration, all further proceedings in his honor, were dropped.

His estate was contiguous to Point Pleasant, the county seat of Mason, and he was almost a daily visitor of that interesting and old fashioned Virginia town. No man in the county was more generally loved and respected, and none whose sudden death was more universally lamented. He was killed on the 30th of March 1863, by a fire from a detachment of Federal soldiers, stationed in that neighborhood, as he was passing from the town to his farm. His son, Charles B. Waggoner, was a member of the recent Constitutional Convention of this State, and now holds an important office in the county.

CHARLES ROBERTS

Was chiefly remarkable for his longevity. He was a native of Oxfordshire, in England, but had resided in this county about eighty years. He died in Berkeley County, Feb. 17th, 1796, aged 116. During his life, he never knew sickness.

CAPT. NAPOLEON B. HARRISON, U. S. N.,

Youngest son of Dr. John S. Harrison and Holland Williams Stull, was born in Martinsburg, Va., February 19th, 1823. Entering the naval service of the United States as Midshipman February 28th, 1838, he acquired experience in his profession under various commanders in the West Indies, Brazil, the Coast of Africa and the Pacific Squadron. In 1844 he was promoted to the rank of Passed Midshipman, and under Commodore Stockton, during the Mexican war, he was distinguished among the younger officers for courage and ability. He here took part in the land expedition which rescued General Kearney's command from a desperate position and on another occasion, having volunteered to carry an important message to a distant command in an open boat, he was carried out to sea and unable to make land for five or six days. The violence and persistence of the storm was matched by the firmness and skill of the young sailor, who finally brought back his boat and crew unharmed.

In 1850 he was on duty at then Washington Observatory and in the year 1853 promoted to a lieutenancy and served as naval store keeper in the East Indies, Japan and on the coast of Africa.

In 1862 Lieut. Harrison was placed in command of the gun boat "Cayuga," attached to the Mississippi Squadron under Com. Farragut. In his dispositions for forcing the passage of the river, the Commodore arranged his fleet in three divisions, and in this programme, the Cayuga being a light armed vessel of only seven guns, stood last in the first division.

This undistinguished position was a source of great mortification to her gallant commander, who, nevertheless prepared to do his duty with patriotic resignation. In the meantime Capt. S. P. Lee, who had volunteered to lead the attack, objected to Capt. Bailey making the "Oneida" his flagship, fearing that the presence of the Division Commander would obscure his own position.

Baily promptly ordered the Oneida to the rear of his division, and proposed to Lieutenant Harrison, to make the "Cayuga" his flagship.

This unexpected transfer to the van of battle and post of danger was hailed with great delight. Just before daybreak on the 23d of April, 1862, Lieut. Harrison led the advance of the national fleet. Passing Forts Jackson and St. Philip, with their hundred blazing guns, the

Historical Pen Sketches. 133

"Cayuga" rushed into the midst of the enemy's fleet of iron-clads, rams and fire ships above the forts, and there sustained herself for half an hour unsupported.

During this brief and unequal fight, she repelled all attacks and destroyed three vessels of the adverse flotilla, and when relieved by the advance of the national vessels, she passed up the river with forty shot holes in her hull and rigging, and only six men wounded. She next covered the encampment of the Chalmette Regiment with her guns, and forced it surrender, with six thousand men. Next day, alone, she attacked the Chalmette Batteries, and persisted until the Hartford came up and the Batteries surrendered.

Captain Bailey, in his official report says: "From first to last, Lieutanant Commander Harrison showed a masterly ability in steering his vessel past the Forts under a hurricane of shot and shell, and, afterwards, in maneuvering and fighting her among the gun-boats, I cannot say too much of him."

The chivalric courage and intelligent coolness exhibited by Commander Harrison in this tremendous engagement, impressed all who were near him, and won for him the respect and admiration of the whole service. The following characteristic anecdote is currrent among his brother officers: During the hottest fire he found a gunner skulking; seizing the recreant by the collar, and dragging him before Captain Bailey, he said, "Captain, here's a fellow skulking; shall I shoot him or boot him?" The commander recommended the lighter punishment and the man was expedited back to his post with a vigorous kick. The remedy was efficacious and the man stuck to his gun afterward doing good service.

In recognition of his conduct in this engagement, Lieutenant Harrison was advanced to the rank of Commander, his commission bearing date July 15th, 1862.

He was soon after ordered to the "Mahaska," of the

James River fleet, and rendered efficient service during McClellan's operations at Harrison's Landing.

Late in the same year, in command of the flagship "Minnesota, he was with the North Atlantic Squadron, and took an active part in the naval operations on the coast of South Carolina, terminating in the evacuation of Charleston.

After the peace Commander Harrison had charge of the navy yard at Portsmouth, New Hampshire, where he remained until 1868. On the 28th of April, this year, he was commissioned Captain, and soon after ordered to duty at the Annapolis Navy School as Commandant of Midshipmen. From here, one year later, he was ordered to the command of the "Congress," flagship of the North Atlantic Squadron. While at Key West the "Congress" encountered a terrible norther, and in his solicitude for the safety of the vessel, Captain Harrison so exposed himself to the storm that he died two days after.

His remains are buried in Oak Hill Cemetery, Georgetown, D. C., and he leaves behind him the reputation of a gallant, able and faithful officer and an honorable, amiable and agreeable gentleman.

LEWIS P. W. BALCH,

The first Judge appointed for the Berkeley circuit after the close of our late civil war. He was far advanced in life when elevated to the bench, but preserved much of the vigor and eccentricity of his mind. He was eminently fitted to perform the duties expected of him at that sad period of our history. He was a slave to popular prejudice, intolerant in his opinions and overbearing in his conduct. He was inordinately vain of his judicial position, and brought his authority to bear on the unfortunate rebels, if not with the bloodthirstiness, certainly with all the buffoonery and vindictiveness of a Jeffrey. The character of his judicial administration may be inferred from the following extract from one of his opinions: "Common fame is *prima facie* ground for putting a person on trial for an offense. It is the duty of a magistrate to arrest on such evidence, and the *onus probandi* of innocence is on the accused." There was much freshness and originality in the character of his mind, while his heavy and grotesque figure, his bombastic and theatrical airs upon the bench, with the quaint and characteristic opinions to which he gave utterance, offorded a rich fund of entertainment to the usually crowded court room. A keen sense of the ludicrous was irresistably inspired by his appearance. He presided on this circuit from March 1865 to March 1866; but even his own party could tolerate him no longer. An accurate sketch of his personal appearance, has been preserved by one of our best native artists, and as we have rarely had such a specimen of judicial eccentricity, if not monstrosity, in this section of the country, he may be regarded as the natural outgrowth of the diseased and disjointed period in which he officially flourished; it is hoped, that the picture may be engraved and perpetuated, as a reminiscence of times never to be seen again.

He died at his residence near Leetown, in the County of Jefferson, in 1868.

REV. WM. HILL, D. D.

Was born in Virginia on the 3rd of March, 1769. In 1785, he entered Hampden Sidney College. He graduated at that college in 1788, and was licensed to preach the gospel by the Presbytery of Hanover, July 10th, 1790. Immediately after his license, he settled in Berkeley County. His stated field of labor was missionary ground, and though his labors here were prosecuted through many discouragements, they were marked by great vigor and boldness, and were followed by highly important results. He had already acquired a high reputation as a commanding and effective pulpit orator. In January 1800 he left his residence in Berkeley County, and took charge of the Presbyterian Church in Winchester. In

1816 the degree of Doctor of Divinity was conferred upon him by Dartmouth University. He died on the 10th of November 1852, in Winchester, in the 84th year of his age. His funeral sermon was preached by the Rev. A. H. H. Boyd, D. D.

His power as an extemporaneous preacher was very remarkable. He had not the learning and the close logical reasoning of Rice, nor the chaste and flowing style of Speece, nor the splendid imagination of Kirkpatrick; but there was a combination of excellencies in his preaching which made him a great favorite. His commanding person, his clear and powerful voice, the vividness of his conceptions, the distinctness and pungency of his appeals, and the deep earnestness visible in his countenance and manner of delivery, impressed his audience with the conviction that what he said was truth, and such truth as involved their most vital interest.

THOMAS WORTHINGTON

Was born in the County of Berkeley in 1796; emigrated to Ohio, and settled in Ross County in 1798. In 1803 he was a member of the State Constitutional Convention. He was a Senator in Congress, from Ohio, from 1803 to 1807, and again from 1810 to 1814, when he resigned; and from 1814 to 1817 he was Governor of Ohio. After his retirement from that office, he was appointed a member of the first Board of Canal Commissioners in which capacity he served until his death, which occurred 1827.

THOMAS VAN SWEARINGEN

Was born in Berkeley County, Virginia, and elected a representative in Congress from 1819 to 1821. He died in 1823 from a fatal bilious fever, which carried off the most prominent citizens of Shepherdstown.

WILLIAM MACKEY

Was born near Belfast in the north of Ireland in 1738. He emigrated to this country about 1762, landing at

Philadelphia, and thence removing to the Cumberland Valley, Pa He volunteered in the Revolutionary army in the beginning of the war, was promptly commissioned as captain, and continued in service until its close. At the battle of Brandywine, he fell, severely wounded, charging at the head of his company.

The battle of Brandywine (so called from the small creek near which it occurred) was fought on the 11th of September, 1777, and was one of the most interesting of the early conflicts of the Revolution. It grew out of the determination of General Washington to save, if possible, from capture, the city of Philadelphia, then the capital of the States, and the seat of the Continental Congress. If the magnitude of the prize at stake, the number of the troops engaged and the character of the military leaders on both sides, could give dignity to any battle, this possessed those elements in an eminent degree. General Sir Wm. Howe, aided by Lord Cornwallis and Gen. Knyphausen, had landed from the British fleet a well disciplined and admirably equipped army of 18,000 men—looking to the capture of Philadelphia. General Washington, assisted in his command by Gens. Green, Wayne, Muhlenburg, Sullivan. Stephens and Maxwell, with an inferior force of 13,000 poorly equipped men, was equally determined to save the city. The hostile armies met near the Brandywine Creek. The battle was fierce and bloody. On our side there was a loss of 1,000 killed and wounded. On the side of the British but 546 killed and wounded, this disparity of loss resulting from the superior arms and equipments of the enemy. Among the wounded was the Marquis de Lafayette. Our army was defeated, Philadelphia fell into the hands of the enemy. Washington made a masterly retreat and few prisoners were taken—none but those who were left severely wounded on the field of battle. Among those was Capt. Wm. Mackey. After several months imprisonment, he was exchanged, when he joined his regiment, still suffering from his wounds, and continued in service until hostilities ceased.

Shortly after the close of the war he removed to Martinsburg, where he continued to reside until his death. He had two children, William Mackey, and Sarah, married to James Faulkner. His residence was in the house directly opposite the Episcopal Church in Martinsburg.

After the termination of the Revolutionary war, being entitled by his service and position to be a member of the Society of the Cincinatti, composed exclusively of the officers of that army, who had served until the end of the war, he received his diploma as such, which bears the honored signatures of George Washington, as President and General Henry Knox, as Secretary and which may be seen gracing the walls of Chas. James Faulkner, his grandson, at Boydville.

As there may not be any future occasion to refer to this Society of the Cincinnatti, an institution which has excited so much attention and even hostile discussion in this country, a brief reference to it may not be uninteresting.

It was an association founded by the officers of the American Revolutionary Army, after the peace of 1783. Its object was to commemorate the success of the Revolution and to perpetuate sentiments of patriotism, benevolence and brotherly love, and the memory of hardships experienced in common. The original draft of the Constitution was made by General Knox and it is still extant. At the second general meeting of the Society in 1787, Washington was elected President General, and was re-elected trienially during his life. He was succeeded by Hamilton and the Pinckneys, and the Society was in all its vigor during the last visit of Gen. Lefayette to the United States, in 1824-5, who was then its only surviving Major General. It has branches in several of the States, but the general Society meets trienially in New York, of which Hamilton Fish is at this time the

President. It admits of honorary membership, among whom are to be found the names of Benj. Franklin, Andrew Jackson, Winfield Scott, Z. Taylor, U. S. Grant, etc. The oldest male decendant of any officer of the Revolution is entitled to regular membership.

William Mackey died in Martinsburg in 1812, and was buried with military honors. His wife preceded him to the grave a few years, she having died on the 23 of Oct. 1810. His will bears date the 28th of April, 1812, and is recorded in the Clerk's office of the County Court of Berkeley. By it, he devises his property generally to his grandson, J. H. Mackey, and his military lands in Ohio, to which he became entitled by virtue of his Revolutionary services, to his grandson, Charles James Faulkner.

The Martinsburg *Gazette*, of Friday, the 23rd of October, 1812, contains the following notice of his death:

"The deceased was born in Ireland, though no native son of America was ever more attached to the institutions of this country. He was one of the few surviving heroes of the Revolution that gave independence to the country. He entered the contest soon after the commencement of hostilities, and continued his useful services in the arduous struggle until our liberty was established. No one of equal grade rendered greater service to the country, and but few suffered as much. Blest with a strong constitution and filled with that ardor and enthusiasm, so natural to his countrymen, his zeal was unconquerable. At the memorable battle of Brandywine he had the command of a company, posted in one of the most important and dangerous situations; this post was supported by Capt. Mackey and his brave company, until every individual in it, except himself and one of his subordinates were killed. In this dreadful conflict Capt. Mackey was shot through the breast and made a prisoner. He was soon after exchanged, but a considerable time elapsed before the severity of his wound enabled him again to join the army. He was engaged in many other severe trials in which he was always distinguished for his determined courage and usefulness."

COL. WILLIAM CRAWFORD

Was born in Berkeley County. During the French war he distinguished himself by his bravery and good conduct, and was much noticed by Gen. Washington, who obtained for him an ensign's commission. He was a captain in Forbs' expedition in 1758. He was half brother to Col. Hugh Stephenson, of Berkeley county, who commanded a rifle regiment in 1776. At the commencement of the revolution, he raised a regiment by his own exertions, and held the commission of Colonel in the Continental Army. He was one of the bravest men on the frontier, and often took the lead in parties against the Indians, across the Ohio. In 1782, he accepted the command of an expedition to ravage the Wyandott and Moravian Indian towns on the Muskingum. On this expedition he was taken prisoner and put to death by the most excruciating tortures.

Dr. McKnight, a fellow prisoner, who subsequently made his escape, and who was an eye witness of the scene, thus describes the death of the brave Col. Crawford: "He was stripped naked, severely beaten with clubs and sticks, and made to sit down near a post which had been planted for the purpose, and around which a fire of poles was burning briskly. His hands were then pinnioned behind him, and a rope attached to the band around his wrist and fastened to the foot of a post about fifteen feet high, allowing him liberty only to sit down or walk once or twice around it, and return the same way. His ears were then cut off, and while the men would apply the burning ends of the poles to his flesh, the squaws threw coals and hot embers upon him. For three hours he endured these excruciating agonies with the utmost fortitude. When faint and exhausted, he commended his soul to God, and laid down on his face.

Historical Pen Sketches. 141

He was then scalped and burning coals being laid on his head and back by one of the squaws, he again rose and attempted to walk, but strength failed him, and he sank into the welcome arms of death. His body was thrown into the fire and consumed into ashes."

COL. HUGH STEPHENSON,

Of the Revolutionary Army, born in Berkeley county. In June 1775, under a resolution of Congress, he raised a company of volunteers in Berkeley county to serve one year in the Continental Army. William Henshaw, Geo. Scott and Thomas Hite were elected Lieutenants of this company. Among the privates were Robert White, afterwards Judge of the General Court of Virginia; Joseph Swearingen, Gen. Samuel Findlay, Maj. Henry Bedinger, Maj. Michael Bedinger, Abraham Shepherd and Nathaniel Pendleton, Esq., of New York. A few days previous to the departure of this company for Boston, Lieut. Hite resigned his commission and Abraham Shepherd was elected Lieutenant in his place, by the unanimous vote of the company. The company marched to Boston in July, 1775. Before the expiration of its term of service General Washington recommended to Congress the raising of a rifle regiment, which was accordingly organized by the appointment of Hugh Stephenson as colonel, Rawlings as lieutenant colonel. Otho H. Williams was the senior captain of the regiment. In August, 1776, Col. Stephenson died and was succeeded in the command of the regiment by Col. Rawlings. Stephenson's will, now on record in the County Court of Berkeley, bears date the 20th of July, 1775, to which there is a codicil annexed, bearing date the 3rd of March, 1776, and executed at "Roxbury Camp, New England." The will was presented for probate on the 20th of November, 1776. Among the executors appointed by the will is the name of his half brother, Col. Wm. Crawford—the bravest of Indian fighters, whose sad and excruciating death is mentioned in another part of these sketches.

REV. MOSES HOGE, D. D.

Born in Virginia, February 15, 1752; in 1787 moved to the county of Berkeley. He resided in this county for upwards of thirteen years, and acquired great popularity as a minister throughout this section of the State. In 1801, in consequence of the failing health of Mrs. Hoge, he left the county of Berkeley for a more southern climate. In 1807, he was appointed President of Hampden Sidney College. In 1810, as a testimonial of his great learning and eminence as a minister, the degree of Doctor of Divinity was conferred upon him by the college of New Jersey. He possessed a mind of uncommon vigor, capable at once of accurate discrimination and profound research, and richly stored with scientific knowledge. He died on the 5th of July, 1820, in the 69th year of his age.

JOHN MORE

Was born in Berkeley county in 1788. He was a Representative in Congress from the State of Louisiana from 1841 to 1843, and again from 1851 to 1853. Died in June, 1861.

JOHN FRYATT SNODGRASS.

Born in Berkeley county, Virginia, March 2, 1804; was a lawyer by profession, and practiced in Parkersburg, Virginia. He was a member of the Virginia Constitutional Convention, assembled at Richmond in 1850, and was a representative in Congress from 1853 until his death, which occurred while trying a case in Court in Parkersburg, June 5th, 1854. A sketch of his private, professional and political character may be seen in the Congressional *Globe* of the 9th of June, 1854, made by Hon. C. J. Faulkner, then a member of the House of Representatives in announcing his death to that body.

ALMON SORTWELL,

For many years principal of the Martinsburg Academy. He was a native of one of the New England States, but possessed but few of the characteristics of that steady and cool headed people. Striking and intellectual in his physiognomy, he labored under the same deformity in one of his feet that tortured the soul of Lord Byron during his life. In many respects the temper and character of the two men were not unlike. Fiery and intractable in his temper, constantly laboring under the suspicion that his club foot was an object of observation, his extreme sensitiveness especially in society, generated the most painful feelings in those around him. And yet, when he could forget his deformity, he was replete with wit, vivacity and good humor. He was a profound scholar, and did ample justice to the youths whose education was entrusted to him. He died in 1834.

JOHN STROTHER,

A son of Benjamin Strother, was born at Park Forest, in Berkeley county, November the 18th, 1792. At thirteen years of age he was placed in the county clerk's office at Martinsburg, and became an inmate of the family of David Hunter, then clerk of Berkeley county. When war was declared against Great Britain, in 1812, he volunteered for the defence of Norfolk, as second lieutenant in Capt. Faulkner's artillery company, but having in the meantime applied for a commission in the regular army, he received a notification of his appointment to a lieutenancy in the 12th infantry, in camp near Fredericksburg. He thereupon resigned his commission in the State company, was succeeded by Edward Colston, joined his regiment on the Canada frontier, was engaged under Wilkinson in the unsuccessful enterprise against Montreal; participated in the famous passage of the Long saut of the St. Lawrence, and was in the command of his company at the battle of Crisler's Field, where out of twenty-four men present for duty, the company lost eight killed and wounded. For good conduct in the battle, he was promoted, and afterwards appointed adjutant of the regiment. After the war, he returned to Martinsburg, and on the 8th of September, 1815, was married to Elizabeth Pendleton, eldest daughter of David Pendleton. In 1829 he was elected clerk of the County Court of Berkeley made vacant by the death of David Hunter, and held that office until 1833, when a change in the constitution of Virginia making a new election necessary, he was superseded by Harrison Waite, Esq. In 1832 he was appointed by Judge Richard Parker to the Clerkship of the Supreme Court of law and chancery for the county of Berkeley, and continued in that office until by another change in the Constitution it became elective by the people, when he declined competing for the office, and retired from its duties after having been connected with the Berkeley clerkship for forty-five years. Constrained by the limited income of his office, and by ill-health, brought on by the close confinement to his clerical duties, he had some years previously, in 1833, opened a boarding house at Berkeley Springs, and latterly, between 1845 and 1848, erected a large hotel at that place. The remainder of his business life was devoted to that enterprise. In the recent troubles which agitated the country, he was a firm and intrepid champion of the rights of the Union, and asserted his opinion with a courage that commanded the respect of both friends and enemies. He died at the Berkeley Springs on the 16th of January, 1862, in the midst of his family, his last words expressing solicitude for his beloved country, and his absent son, then serving in the Federal army. His remains were carried to Martinsburg, where they were interred with masonic and military honors.

JOHN S. HARRISON

Was one of the most highly educated and accomplished physicians that up to that day had sought a home in Berkeley county. Descended from one of the most respected of the old families of Maryland, he was born on West river, Anne Arundel county in 1790. At the age of thirteen, he was sent to St. John's College, in Annapolis, and there spent six years in completing his elementary, classical and scientific studies. At the age of twenty he was sent to Europe, where he spent four years in the medical and surgical instructions of France and England, preparing himself for the practice of his profession. In 1805 he was married to Holland Williams Stull, the niece of that distinguished patriot and hero of the Revolution, General Otho Holland Williams, after whom she was named. In 1806 he removed with his young bride to Martinsburg, which he sought as a permanent home, purchasing as a residence the property at the northwest corner of King and German streets, which he occupied during his life.

His pleasant and social manners, frank and manly deportment, with the general recognition of his high attainments in his profession soon introduced him to a profitable practice; and as there were no physicians at that time in the county, beyond the limits of Martinsburg, his practice was soon co-extensive with the county. His patients had unbounded confidence in his skill and judgment and his opinion upon all medical questions soon came to be regarded as oracular.

He was a man of ardent temperament and gave expression to his views on all subjects with frankness and decision. He was a Jeffersonian Democrat, and regarded as one of the acknowledged leaders and representatives of that minority party in this county.

At that day what were called the "Federalists" had complete control of the county. Most of its then leading and influential families adhered zealously to the principles of that party, such as the Pendletons, Hunters, Colstons, Waggoners, Porterfields, Orricks, Newkirks, Shearers, Snodgrasses, Campbells, Vanmetres, Gorrells, Burns, Boyds, Tabbs, Stephensons, Wevers, Tates, &c. There was much exclusiveness in the distribution of patronage, and it rarely happened that one of the opposite party was honored by any official or political preferment.

The Federalists wrecked their party by violent opposition to the war of 1812-13 with Great Britain. The military and naval victories of that war and its glorious and triumphant results utterly annihilated all opposition to the conquering Democracy. From that time a more conciliatory spirit was manifested by the ruling party, and among the first evidences of that change of policy was the recommendation in 1818, of Dr. Harrison for a seat as a justice of the peace, upon the bench of the County Court of Berkeley. He accepted the position and for near ten years discharged its duties with intelligence and promptness.

Upon the death of Maj. Faulkner in 1817, he qualified under his will, as one of his executors, and by his kind, generous and parental attention to the writer of this sketch, justified the confidence reposed in him.

For some years before his death he was confined to the house by a severe attack of gout, under which he suffered until he expired in October, 1838.

He left a large and interesting family of children, some of whom and the descendants of others are still in this community.

REV. ANDREW H. H. BOYD, D. D.,

Second son of Gen. Elisha Boyd, was born at Martinsburg, in the year 1814. He received his academic education at Martinsburg and Middleburg; when fourteen years old, he entered the junior class of Jefferson College, and graduated with distinction in 1830. Shortly after entering college he joined the Presbyterian Church and resolved to preach the gospel. After graduation in Jefferson College, he spent two years at New Haven, to perfect himself in particular studies; completed a regular course of theological education thereafter at Princeton; and subsequently visited Europe and attended lectures delivered by the celebrated Dr. Chalmers and Sir William Hamilton in Edinburg, Scotland. He was licensed to preach the gospel by the Presbytery of Winchester in 1837; entered upon his first charge over the churches of Leesburg and Middleburg in 1838; accepted a call to Harrisonburg in 1840; and to Winchester in 1842. He was called, during all parts of his ministry to a number of distinguished churches in the great cities, but being wholly independent in his pecuniary circumstances, preferred to remain in Winchester, to the people of which city, and the County of Frederick, he exhibited a strong attachment. His prominence as a citizen during the late civil war, residing within the Confederate limits, caused him to be seized as a hostage, and held in retalliation for the arrest of other citizens attached to the cause of the Union. He bore the illegal and unjustifiable imprisonment consequent upon this seizure with all the patience and fortitude of a Christian minister, but a fatal blow was given to his health by the rigors of his long imprisonment. He never enjoyed a day of perfect health after his restoration to liberty. His valuable ministry of three and twenty years at Winchester was terminated after a mournful and protracted illness on the 16th of December, 1865. A funeral address was pronounced over his remains by Rev. Joseph C. Stiles, of Georgia, which was published in pamphlet form and is worthy of extensive perusal.

Dr. Boyd was a man of fine intellect. He was endowed with quick and clear perception, a sound, discriminating and comprehensive judgment, and especially with strong and active reasoning faculties. He loved study and ever felt both its necessity and obligation. He was a man of extensive and useful information. On almost every topic of literature and science he discoursed like one who had given exclusive attention to those subjects, while in his proper department of didactic and polemic theology, ecclesiastical history and biblical criticism, few men in the country had made such eminent attainments.

During his illness the presbytery met in Winchester

and appointed a committee to convey to Dr. Boyd their christian salutations and to assure him of their sincere condolence in the painful and protracted trial which he was then enduring. He received the distinguished attention with such humble and touching gratitude to his brethren, and in such calm and assured submission to the will of God, that on the return of the committee the chairman reported to presbytery that "he had seen Bunyan's Pilgrim on the banks of the river, joyfully awaiting his transportation to the opposite shore."

THOMAS MASLIN,

Son of Wm. and Ann M. Maslin, was born in Gerardstown, Berkeley County, on the 28th day of October, 1808. At the early age of fifteen years and with but a very limited education, he was placed in a store at Harper's Ferry and continued there and in similar situations until in 1830, when he removed to Moorfield. In 1831 he commenced the mercantile business in that place without capital and relying exclusively upon his own energy, integrity and capacity for business. In this pursuit he continued actively and successfully for a period of thirty years. In 1837 he was commissioned a magistrate of Hardy County, and continued to hold that office until the magistry became elective under the constitution of 1850. Under that new system he was elected to the same office, and was made presiding justice of the County Court until the County of Hardy was embraced in the newly created State of West Virginia. When the Bank of the Valley established a branch at Moorefield, in 1853, he was elected a director and made President, and re-elected every year until the bank was closed by the war. In 1861 he was elected by an almost unanimous vote of the people to represent the County of Hardy in the Virginia State Convention, called together by the exigencies of the opening civil war. In 1871 he was elected by a large majority to represent the counties of Hardy and Grant in the Constitutional Convention of West Virginia. He also filled various other offices in that county—was treasurer of one turnpike company and President of another.

He died at Moorfield on the 21st of September, 1878, after a protracted illness of more than a year.

JOHNSTON MAGOWN,

For many years one of the most efficient and active magistrates in the County of Berkeley. He resided in Martinsburg, and kept his office in the frame building attached to the Stewart Hotel. He was a man of strong mind, with clever common sense views of the law. Few, if any, appeals were ever taken from his decision, for all had abounded confidence in his integrity and sense of justice. He possessed much quaint and original humor. His memory was stored with anecdotes, and being a bachelor, with none of the cares of a family about him, his office, in which he also slept, was the regular resort of a coterie of visitors during the long evenings in winter. He died after a short illness, in 1836, to the regret of all who knew him.

MAJOR GEN, ADAM STEPHEN.

There is now upon the lands of Charles J. Faulkner and within the recently enlarged limits of Martinsburg, the remains of a monument, under which repose the ashes of this distinguished soldier and patriot. By whom this structure was erected—whether by the executors and legatees of the deceased, or by the grateful contributions of his countrymen, is not known. There is nothing in the will nor in the detailed account of the executors to throw any light on the subject. The design of the monument is obviously a rectangular pyramid, with a base of twenty feet square. Its supposed altitude from the vertex to the plane of the base may have been from six to nine feet. It has now an elevation of a little more than four feet. The large stones used in its construction— some of them twelve feet in length, are hard silicious mountain stones, and must have been transported, at great expense, from a distance, as they are not natives of this valley. I think a careful examination of the remains will lead to the conclusion (contrary to the present popular belief) that the monument was once finished according to its original design, but being much exposed and unprotected—a play spot for the boys—the apex was first thrown off, and stone after stone injured and removed, leaving only what remains of the original structure. It is at present within the limits of our city, and since it has been in the possession of its present proprietor since 1339, (now thirty-three years ago) has been protected from further injury.

General Stephen's life and fortunes are intimately identified with the County of Berkeley. He was one of the earliest immigrants to this locality—he became the owner of large tracts of land in this neighborhood; he was one of the most active agents in having the County of Berkeley established, and one of the most prominent actors in its early civil and judicial history. It was upon his land that the city of Martinsburg was located; here he lived a long and prosperous life, and in her soil have his remains been interred. The people of Berkeley, therefore, should feel an interest in learning something of his history, and a pleasure in seeing his memory vindicated from any unjust and unmerited reproach cast upon it.

General Stephen was born about the year 1718, and is believed to have been a native of Pennsylvania. He emigrated to this portion of Virginia about 1738, a few years after the first settlements were made in this valley. He must have derived the most of his land by direct grant from Lord Fairfax.

Military History.

The earliest notice we have of the military movements of Adam Stephen, is in immediate connection with Washington. Information reached the colonial authorities at Williamsburg, that the French and Indians had taken possession of the northwestern portion of Virginia, on the Monongahela, murdering and driving away the settlers of that section. The General Assembly authorized the raising of six companies for the recovery of that territory. The command of this force was tendered to Washington, but because of his youth he declined it in favor of Col. Joshua Fry, an experienced English officer, and Washington became Lieutenant Colonel. Stephen had raised a company from the settlers hereabouts, and by Washington's order, met him with his company at Winchester on the 20th of March, 1754. This assembled force started for the frontiers, but Col. Fry having died, the command necessarily devolved upon Washington, and Stephen, in June, 1854, was appointed Major. On August the 14th, same year, the regiment was re-organized with Washington as Colonel, Stephens as Lieut. Colonel and Andrew Lewis as Major. They pursued their difficult and wearisome march through the wilderness until they reached the Great Meadows, and there unexpectedly encountered a hostile force, greatly superior to their own, and were defeated in battle. They took shelter in Fort Necessity, but they were, after a gallant resistance, compelled to surrender, but upon terms which allowed them to march out with flying colors and with all the honors of war. Col. Stephen was then placed in command of Fort Cumberland, the frontier out post of that period. In 1755 he was in the memorable battle of the Monongahela, usually called Braddock's defeat, and was wounded, though not seriously. In 1756 he resumed his command of Fort Cumberland. In 1757 he accompanied Washington in his expedition to Fort Du Quesne, where they recovered possession of that territory, and captured Fort DuQuesne, which they subsequently named Fort Pitt, the site of the present city of Pittsburg. In the same year he proceeded, by order of Congress, to the South, to quell the hostilities of the Creek Indians in that section. In August, 1763, the colonial government ordered out a force of 1,000 men—500 of whom were to be raised from this section of the colony and were placed under the command of Stephen, for service on the North-western frontier; and 500 to be raised in Greenbrier and the adjoining counties, and placed under the command of Col. Andrew Lewis, to protect the South-western portion of our territory. The object of these expeditions was to repel an attack upon our people, by a formidable alliance of Shawnees, Delawares, Wynadotts and other Indian tribes, acting in alliance with Pontiac.

Sir Jeffery Amherst, then in command of all the British forces in America, thus notices these expeditions in a letter of the 27th of August, 1763, addressed to Sir William Johnson, Superintendent of Indian affairs:

"An effectual stop will be put to these outrages; particularly as Col. Stephen with a body of 500 men of the Virginia militia, is advanced as far as Fort Cumberland and Bedford, with a view not only of covering the frontiers, but of acting offensively against the savages. That public-spirited colony has also sent a large body of the like number of men under the command of Col. Lewis for the defence and protection of the South-west frontiers. What a contrast this makes between the Pennsylvanians and Virginians, highly to the honor of the latter; but places the former in the most despicable light imaginable."

Again, in a letter of September the 14th, 1763, to the same person, he says:

"The attempts against the Shawnees are certainly very necessary, and I heartily wish Col. Stephen success in his expedition. His chief danger will be his retreat up the river."

Mr. Bancroft thus describes the sad condition of our frontier in June, 1763, which it was the object of the expedition under General Stephen to avenge and redress:

"Nor was its garrisoned stockades only that encoun- the fury of the savages. They roamed the wilderness, massacring all whom they met. They struck down more than a hundred traders in the woods, scalping every one of them; quaffing their gushing life blood, mutilating their bodies. They prowled around the cabins of the husbandman on the frontier, and their tomahawks struck alike the laborer in the field or the child in the cradle. They passed the mountains and spread death even to Bedford. The unhappy emigrant knew not if to brave danger or to leave his home and his planted fields for wretchedness and poverty. Nearly five hundred families from the frontiers of Virginia fled to Winchester, unable to find so much as a hovel to shelter them from the weather, bare of every comfort, and forced to lie scattered in the woods." (*vol. 5th, page* 124.)

After aiding to quell these hostile Indian movements, Col. Stephen returned to the east and was placed in command of Fort Loudon at Winchester, charged with the protection of our entire Northwestern frontier.

All further dangers being removed from the frontiers, our troops were disbanded and Col. Stephen, now a Brigadier General in the State Militia, returned in 1768 to his home in Berkeley County—after fourteen years of almost continuous service in defense of the people and territory of Virginia.

That General Stephen at that period enjoyed in a high degree the confidence of Washington is not only obvious from the preceding narrative, but is further shown by the fact that when, in 1756, he was required to visit Boston on important public business, he left Col. Stephen in command of all the troops in the service of Virginia.

In continuation of the history of his military service we pass for the present over the intervening period of time.

At the commencement of the revolutionary war he was, in December, 1775, commissioned by Virginia Colonel of one of the regiments raised by that State. Isaac Reed was at the same time chosen Lieut. Colonel, and Robt·

Lawson Major of this regiment. On the 13th of February, 1776, he was transferred, with his regiment, to the Continental line. On the 4th of September, 1776, he was appointed by Congress a Brigadier General of the Continental troops, and on the 9th of February, 1777, promoted to the rank of Major General. Gen. Stephen was with Washington in 1776, at the battles of Trenton and Princeton—in his celebrated retreat of ninety miles through the Jerseys—the most critical and disastrous campaign of the war, but which was marked by brilliant stratagems and daring exploits. He continued with him in 1777, and at the battle of Brandywine was in command of a division as Major General, giving entire satisfaction by his bravery and good conduct.

We now approach the most painful period of the military history of General Stephen. On November the 4th, 1777, was fought the battle of Germantown. Washington was defeated. The enemy triumphed. Gen. Stephen was charged with "unofficer-like conduct," and the specification was that he was "intoxicated" on that day. He was found guilty and dismissed from the army.

The friends of General Stephen, whilst not questioning a fact ascertained by a court of competent jurisdiction, have nevertheless complained of the harshness and unkindness of the sentence of dismissal. They thought in view of his long and valuable military services and in view of the further fact, that his intoxication in no wise contributed to the disasterous befeat of that day, it should have been overlooked, or a milder penalty inflicted. They say, further, that as strict a deciplinarian as Washington was, he was more than usually severe and exacting in this case, with a view of creating a vacancy in that high grade of the army, for his friend and favorite, the Marquis de Lafayette. On the 26th of November, 1777, he wrote to the President of Congress, urging for military and political considerations, the appointment of Gen. Lafayette to a division of the army. This authority was given to him by Congress on the 1st of December, and in three days afterwards it was proclaimed in general orders that he was to take command of the division recently under General Stephen, who had been dismissed from the army.

I have read with great interest, the account of the battle of Germantown, as given by our best historians to see if our defeat was in any way attributable to the misconduct of General Stephen, or of the division of which he had commanded, and I cannot find a single imputation upon his conduct, personally, during the battle— none upon his division except what is satisfactorily explained.

Washington Irving in his "Life of Washington," referring to the delay of General Knox, in this battle, says:

"This half hour's delay of nearly one half of the army, disconcerted the action. The divisions and brigades thus separated from each other, by the skirmishing upon Chew's house, could not be reunited. The fog and smoke rendered all objects indistinct at thirty yards distance; the different parts of the army knew nothing of the position or movements of each other, and the commander-in-chief could take no view nor gain any information of the situation of the whole.

"Green and Stephen, with their divisions, having had to make a circuit, were late in coming into action, and became separated from each other, part of Stephen's division being arrested by a heavy fire from Chew's house and pausing to return it.

"At this moment a singular panic seized our army. Wayne's division, which had pushed the enemy nearly three miles, was alarmed by the approach of a large body of American troops on its left flank, which it mistook for foes, and fell back in defiance of every effort of its officers to rally it. In its retreat it came upon Stephen's division, and threw it into a panic, being in its turn mistaken for the enemy ; thus all fell into confusion and our army fled from its own victory."

Mr. Bancroft, who may be regarded as one of the most impartial and perhaps one of the most censorious of our historical critics, in describing that battle, utters not a word in disparagement of Gen. Stephen.

"His (Washington's) plan was to direct the chief attack on the enemy's right, to which the approach was easy ; and for that purpose, to Greene, in whom of all his generals he most confided, he gave the command of his left wing, composed of Greene and of Stephen, and flanked by Macdougall's brigade."

Again, "Greene should by this time have engaged the British right, but nothing was heard from any part of his wing." Again, "and where was Greene? From some cause, which he never explained, he reached the British outpost three quarters of an hour later than the troops of Washington ; then at a very great distance from the force, which he was to have attacked, he formed his whole wing, and thus in line of battle, attempted to advance two miles or more through marshes, thickets and strong and numerous post and rail fences. Irretrievable disorder was the consequence ; the divisions became mixed and the line was broken."

Again, "Greene on that day, 'fell under the frown' of the Commander-in-Chief. Had the forces entrusted to him acted as efficiently as the troops with Washington, the day might have been fatal to Howe's army."

Thus Greene and Woodford are censured by the historian, for their conduct in this battle ; not a word of censure is cast upon Gen. Stephen. From all which I infer, that whilst he may have been proved to have been intoxicated on the day of battle, there is nothing in these accounts to show that his intoxication disqualified him for command, or that the country sustained any injury from his improper indulgence in the use of liquor.

Thus ended the military career of this distinguished

soldier, after a service of 14 years in fighting the French and Indians, and two in fighting the enemies of our liberty and independence. I have seen no evidence in his previous career, and none in his subsequent life, that he was habitually addicted to the use in excess of ardent spirits. For this one violation of military discipline he seems to have been treated with unusual harshness.

Civil History.

After the return of Gen. Stephen from military services, in 1768, he gave his attention to his private affairs, and was chiefly instrumental in having the county of Berkeley created, by an act of the General Assembly. Its limits were so arranged as to make the present site of Martinsburg about the centre of the county. So perfectly was this understood that the justices appointed by Lord Dunmore assembled at that point on the 19th of May, 1772, and formed the first court of the county. General Stephen was one of the justices so appointed and also at the same time commissioned first High Sheriff of the county. Prompt arrangements were made for the erection of all the necessary county buildings, and there being no town then established, it was only known as the Berkeley Court House. Gen. Stephen being withdrawn from the county, by his services in the Revolutionary army, no steps were taken for the establishment of a town, until his return in 1777. In 1778 Martinsburg was by an act of General Assembly laid out on 130 acres of land, granted for that purpose by Gen. Stephen.

Mr. Bancroft, incorporated into his great historical work, a letter of Gen. Stephen, written in advance of the war, vindicating the position then being taken by the colonies, that would have done honor to the patriotism and public spirit of a Henry or a Jefferson.

In 1788 Gen. Stephen and Gen. Darke were elected by the voters of Berkeley county to the convention which assembled in Richmond on the 2nd of June of that year to determine whether Virginia would give her consent to the adoption of our present Federal Constitution. It is difficult to imagine a higher and more important trust that could have been confided to two of her citizens. The convention was nearly equally divided on the question of the ratification or rejection of that Constitution. In favor of its adoption were such men as Jas. Madison, John Marshall, Edmund Pendleton and Geo. Wythe; for its rejection were such men as James Monroe, Patrick Henry, George Mason and Theodore Bland. The vote stood 89 for adoption, 79 against it. It is almost unnecessary to say that the delegation from Berkeley stood by the Constitution in all their votes from the beginning to the end of the session. For this alone, if for nothing else, we owe them a debt of gratitude.

The speech delivered by Gen. Stephen in favor of the adoption of the Constitution may be seen on pages 642, 643 and 644 of Elliot's debates of that convention, and does great credit to his ability, eloquence and patroitism. The speech is so honorable to him that it should be incorporated into this sketch but it is too long for present publication.

Gen. Stephen, died in Martinsburg in 1791, possessed of a large real and personal estate. His will, bearing date the 5th of June, 1791, was admitted to record in the Winchester District Court, at the September term, 1791. He has left many descendants in the States of Virginia and West Virginia, and many collateral relatives, the grand children of his brother Robert.

Gen. Stephen, at his death, must have left many valuable papers in the hands of his executors, and especially his military correspondence. But after inquiry I learn that not a single paper has been preserved to throw light upon his long and eventful career. A sketch of his life can only be gleaned from the general histories and public records of the country.

MOSES T. HUNTER,

Born in 1790, was the son of Moses Hunter, one of the

early clerks of Berkeley, County, and one of the Presidential electors who cast the vote of Virginia for George Washington. He was educated at Princeton, New Jersey, and after completing his collegiate course commenced the study of law in Winchester, under Henry St. George Tucker, his brother-in-law, at that time one of the most eminent and successful practitioners in Virginia. When admitted to the bar he took up his residence for a brief period in Martinsburg, but his tastes at that time being more to literary than to legal pursuits, he removed to his fine estate called the "Red House" farm, inherited from his father, about one mile north of the town.

The "Red House" was a well-known spot in the annals of Berkeley County. It was, as stated, the property of his father, Moses Hunter, and it was here that the court held its session from May 19, 1772, until by virtue of a writ obtained by Gen. Stephen from the Secretary's office its sessions were removed to Morgan's Spring, near the present site of Martinsburg.

The jail, a temporary wooden structure, was located in the public square, where the old market house subsequently stood, near the property of Admiral Boarman. The Clerk's office was at the corner of Queen and John streets. Where the stocks or whipping post and pillory, (an essential inheritance from our English ancestors) were placed, I have no means of ascertaining. I can well remember its dark and menancing outline when I was a boy. It stood directly opposite the Court House door— about thirty feet from the present curbstone, and more than once have I witnessed the writhings and contortions of human flesh, both of whites and blacks, under the lash of the jailor, as I passed to and from old James Anderson's school house. The pillory as a punishment, was established in England as early as the reign of Henry III, and only abolished during the reign of the present

Queen, Victoria, in June, 1837, a few years subsequent to its abolition in this State.

The residence of Mr. Hunter in the country was in no wise profitable to him. He had no taste for agriculture; he lived extravagantly, spent his money wastefully; and his house and furniture having been consumed by fire, he determined to return to Martinsburg and enter earnestly upon the practice of his profession. His circuit embraced the counties of Berkeley, Jefferson, Morgan and Frederick; especially the District Court of Chancery, held at Winchester, which had jurisdiction over some fifteen or twenty counties. It was in Jefferson that he seemed to make his deepest impression upon the popular mind, and there, that he attained his largest and most lucrative practice.

When I first recollect Mr. Hunter, which was in 1825, he was of medium height and strongly tending to corpulency, but for a person of his bulk, active and alert on his feet. His countenance, when in one of his gay and pleasant humors, beamed with a benevolent expression; his eye sparkled with wit and intelligence, and his demeanor was marked by courtesy and affability, but in his crabbed and disagreeable moods—and they were by no means uncommon—his face became as dark as a thunder cloud, his tongue was tipped with venom and sarcasm, and his manners were repellant, morose and offensive. He had some of the finest qualities of an orator—a rich and poetic fancy, a brilliant imagination, wit, humor—a taste enriched by classical reading and high powers of logical analysis. His voice was the most agreeable that I have ever heard at the bar—musical from its lowest to its highest tones—and was admirably adopted to give effect and emphasis to whatever he said, whether in the department of wit, humor, sarcasm, pathos or denunciation. His powers of vocal mimicry were extraordinary, and if there was anything peculiar, quaint or ludicrous in the voice or deportment of the witnesses, he could reproduce them at the bar in a manner to covulse the court room with laughter. He was the only lawyer I ever saw who could literally "laugh a case" out of court. His keen sense of the ridiculous was such that he would seize upon every incident in the prgress of a trial that was capable of being perverted into a source of humor and fun, and drive the poor plaintiff or defendant out of court amidst the laughter of bench, bar, jury and bystanders. His style of writing was rich, classical, perspicuous and condensed, the best specimens of which that I have seen were his 4th of July oration delivered in 1825 and printed in the Martinsburg *Gazette* of that period, and his Masonic oration, delivered in 1826 in the old Presbyterian church on King street, now a ruin. I heard them both, and was delighted with their delivery, and have often since read them with much pleasure.

When a youth, just from college, the writer of this sketch would often saunter to the Court House to hear the able lawyers then practising at this bar. The cases which now dwell most especially in his memory were those of James Parsons vs. James Gibson, and William Vance vs. James Parsons, all leading and influential men. They were both celebrated causes and removed from Hampshire to this county, and both cowhiding assaults and batteries, growing out of the same ugly feud. Among the counsel engaged were Alfred H. Powell, John R. Cooke, Moses Hunter, Wm. Nayler and Elisha Boyd. They gave rise to much eloquent speaking, but were finally compromised to the satisfaction of all parties.

The case of Alexander Stephens and Isaac S. Lauck vs. Matthew Ransone, was also among the causes *celebres* in its day. Both plaintiffs and defendants were owners of large merchant mills near Martinsburg, and all were men of large influence and great wealth. Ransone was charged with deliberately diverting the Tuscarora stream so as to deprive the lower rival mill of its proper supply of water. The case was fought with determined zeal and obstinacy on both sides. Cooke's opening was in his finest style of perspicuous narrative. Powell and Boyd put forth their strongest powers in the defense. Hunter commenced his closing argument with the quotation :

> "When Greek meets Greek,
> Then comes the tug of war,"

alluding to the wealth, energy and influence of the contestants, and followed it with one of the most striking and masterly arguments that I ever heard at our bar. The jury brought in a small verdict for the plaintiffs—but it was accepted without costs—a sort of drawn battle.

The first civil case in which I ever appeared at the bar was an action of ejectment, brought by my client, Jonas Hedges, vs. the well known Hunter John Myers, to recover a tract of land on the Meadow Branch, west of the North Mountain. Both had patents for the same land, but Hedges held the elder patent. The case was in the county court. Hunter was my opponent. He vehemently assailed the validity of the Hedges' patent for vagueness in its entry and irregularity in its issue. He dwelt with power and effect upon the ungenerous conduct of Hedges in securing his patent in the manner he did, and upon the noble and primitive virtues of the great Natty Bumppo, of Berkeley. It was in vain that I presented the clear and indisputable law bearing on the subject—he carried court and jury by storm. The law was submerged under the flood of his eloquence. My client was turned out of court. But his triumph was only short lived. I removed the case by writ of supersedeas to the Superior Court, where the ruling of the county court, admitting improper evidence and giving wrong instructions, were reversed, the verdict set aside and the case sent back with such instructions as precluded all further controversy. Hedges recovered his land, with costs in both courts.

Some idea may be formed of the high powers of Mr. Hunter, as an advocate and jurist, when we find the following notice of his first effort at the bar, in a written opinion, delivered by Chancellor Carr in the District Court of Chancery, held at Winchester:

"These points were maintained with great ability, and I must be permitted to say that I have seldom heard so powerful an argument as that delivered by the opening counsel. It gives me pleasure, in passing, to pay this just tribute to the first essay in our court of a young practitioner."

A high compliment to be embraced in a judicial opinion from the pen of Dabney Carr.

Mr. Hunter was a Democrat, and as such, had given his ardent support to Mr. Clay in 1824. His speech in support of the Kentucky statesman, in the Berkeley Court House, was much admired at the time, and presented some of the most captivating views of Mr. Clay's noble and lofty character. But he had an unextinguishable hatred to the Adams family, and when Mr. Clay by his vote and influence made John Quincy Adams President in 1825, Mr. Hunter gave him up and joined the cry of that opposition, which in the language of Richard M. Johnson, had combined to crush the administration for the "original sin of its election, even tho' its acts should prove it as pure as the angels of heaven."

Although the storm of political excitement was raging wildly in the Spring of 1827, in Tennessee, Kentucky and some of the Northern States, its influence was not felt in the county of Berkeley. We had then no railroads, telegraphs, or telephones—few newspapers were taken beyond the county, and outside intelligence reached us slowly through the weekly or semi-weekly lumbering stage coach. An evidence of the total absence of party feeling is found in the fact that in April, 1827, Edward Colston, Federalist, and a Clay man, and Moses T. Hunter, Democrat, and a Jackson man, were both elected to the House of Delegates without opposition, and with the concurrence of all the voters of the county.

Mr. Hunter's career in the Legislature opened brilliantly, but terminated painfully. He made some speeches which gave him high reputation—whilst his attic wit, his captivating conversational powers, his wealth of anecdote and his pungent satire, made him a great favorite in the social circle. But Richmond was not at that time a safe place for one having the tastes and propensities of Mr. Hunter. He relapsed into habits of dissipation, under which his system became disordered, and he was attacked with a serious, and which proved fatal malady.

He returned to Martinsburg in bad health and died, after a long and painful illness, on the 4th of June, 1829, at the residence of his brother-in law, Chancellor Tucker, in Winchester, in the 39th year of his age.

There are some now living in this county, who can recall with pleasure the many occasions when they have hung with rapture upon the glowing eloquence, powerful argument, brilliant and irresistable flashes of wit and humor that marked his professional efforts.

EDWARD COLSTON

Was born at Honeywood in the County of Berkeley, in 1788. He graduated with distinction at Princeton College, New Jersey, in 1806. He passed through a regular course of legal studies, municipal and international, with no view to the practice of the profession, but to qualify himself for the intelligent discharge of any public duty which in a Republic like this, the people might devolve upon him. He was an ardent Federalist, in perfect accord with the predominant sentiment of this county, and as a young man of talent and high promise, was cordially welcomed as an important accession to the party. At twenty-five years of age he was elected a member of the House of Delegates; and when but twenty nine years old, elected a member of the United States Congress from the district composed of the counties of Berkeley, Jefferson, Hampshire and Hardy.

In June, 1814, he was married to Jane Marshall, daughter of Charles Marshall, of Fauquier County. She died on the 5th of March, 1815, in giving birth to a child, ten months after marriage, and in the 21st year of her age. The papers of that day are full of tributes to her many virtues and entrancing loveliness. The child was buried in the same grave with the mother.

When Mr. Colston took his seat in the 15th Congress (1st Monday of December, 1817), he found himself associated in his legislative labors with many distinguished men, among whom were Henry Clay, General Harrison, subsequently President; Henry Baldwin, John Sergeant, Philip P. Barbour, John Floyd, R. M. Johnson, subsequently Vice-President; Henry St. George Tucker, Charles Fenton Mercer, etc. Although but a young man and a young member, he took an active and prominent part in the proceedings of that body. His speeches on the "Commutation of soldiers' pay," for relief to the "Surviving Revolutionary soldiers," in favor of "the Internal Improvement powers of Congress," upon "the Migration of Slaves," upon "the Reduction of the Staff of the Army," and especially his elaborate speech on the resolution of the Military Committee condemning the conduct of General Jackson, for the execution of Arbutnot and Ambrester in the Seminole war, show not only his ability and self reliance, but the extent of his information, and his capacity to take a leading part in any deliberative assembly. He seems to have participated in all the discussions of that body; to have grappled in debate with the foremost intellects, and to have maintained his opinions with firmness and ability.

After the close of his most creditable service in Congress, Mr. Colston found it necessary, in consequence of the increasing age and infirmities of his father, to give his attention to the Honeywood estate in this county and also to the extensive landed possessions of his father, in Virginia and Kentucky.

Mr. Colston was elected to the House of Delegates from

this county in 1823 and 1824, and was again a candidate for Congress in 1825. In this contest he was defeated by Wm. Armstrong of Hampshire. The Martinsburg *Gazette* of the 28th of April, 1825, in referring to the defeat of Mr. Colston :

"We were present on Monday last and heard Mr. Colston address the voters. He exposed in a concise, eloquent and convincing manner the glaring calumnies that had been industriously circulated against him, and left a deep impression on the minds of the people of the gross injustice which had been done him by those slanders and which had resulted in his defeat."

No doubt Mr. Colston was grossly caluminated in that canvass, but the real cause of his defeat was the disorganization and disruption of the party of which he had been so conspicuous a member. The Federalists ceased to exist as a National party after the close of the war with Great Britain, and whilst that may not have been the direct issue involved, yet he had been too distinguished in its history, not to be made to share the consequences of its fall. Some amend, however, was made to his disappointed ambition by his unanimous election to the House of Delegates, in 1826, by the voters of Berkeley. He was again re-elected in 1827, 1833 and 1834.

Whilst in Richmond he formed the acquaintance of Miss Sarah Jane Brockenbrough, the intelligent and accomplished daughter of Judge William Brockenbrough, to whom he was married—from which marriage has resulted a highly educated and interesting family of sons and daughters.

Mr. Colston was commissioned a magistrate of the County Court in 1818, and no one could have taken a more lively interest in the performance of its important and responsible duties than he did. His intelligence, his knowledge of law, his integrity, his high sense of justice, gave to all his decisions, whether on the Bench or *in pais*, a weight and authority accorded to but few of his brethren. He was also commissioned High Sheriff of Berkeley County and acted as such in 1844 and 1845.

Although a Federalist and concurring with his party in opposition to the declaration of war against Great Britain, yet when war was declared by the constituted authorities, he volunteered as a member of Captain Faulkner's Artillery Company, soon reached the rank of Lieutenant and was present, near Norfolk, when the combined military and naval attack was made by the British upon the defences of that important city. He bore the reputation of a brave and conscientious soldier.

Mr. Colston was a member of the Episcopal church—a sincere and practical Christian and an ardent promoter of all institutions and enterprises looking to the advancement of religion, and to the spread of the life saving doctrines of the Redeemer of the world.

Mr. Colston died suddenly — unexpectedly, in the twinkling of an eye—from some affection of the heart, on the 23d of April, 1851. He left a will, devising his whole property, subject to the payment of his debts, to his estimable widow, Sarah Jane Colston, and appointing her, Chas. J. Faulkner and his brother-in-law, Willoughby Newton, of Westmoreland County, Va., executors of his will.

An intelligent gentleman from Eastern Virginia, who had just come from spending two weeks at Honeywood, thus speaks to the writer of this sketch, of Mr. Colston, in 1838:

"I consider Edward Colston, the finest specimen of a country gentleman whom I have yet met in Virginia. His manners are courteous, polite and dignified; his conversation highly instructive and interesting, and his hospitality free and cordial, without being oppressive. He is fond of agriculture, history and general literature. He has a noble inheritance and a magnificent library. He is loved by all his neighbors, for his kindness and charities and they look up to him as a friend, adviser and counsellor. He has a charming family and a delightful residence. What more need any man want to ensure his happiness in this world?"

It is deeply to be regretted that Mr. Colston did not himself cherish the views expressed by this intelligent visitor. He was unhappily not content with the rich blessings which then surrounded him. The activity of his mind led him to engage in milling enterprises and speculations. He became, in the honesty and unsuspecting integrity of his heart, the sport of fortune, and the victim of accomplished villains, and that " noble inheritance" has thus passed from his widow and children, to discharge forged obligations and unfortunate speculations in trade.

JAMES FAULKNER,

Son of George and Rebecca Faulkner, was born on the 2nd of April, 1776, in the county of Armagh, Ireland, a few miles from Newry. The family, as the name itself sufficiently indicates, was of English origin, their ancestor having emigrated to Ireland in the reign of William and Mary. Having been left an orphan by the death of both his parents, at the early age of ten years, he accepted the kind offer of Richard McSherry, a friend of the family, to accompany him upon his return to America. They arrived in the port of Baltimore in the latter part of 1786.

Richard McSherry had some years before emigrated from that part of Ireland, and had gone to the Island of Jamaica to improve his fortunes. He was a man of energy and enterprise, and soon got occupation as the manager of a large sugar plantation. He remained there for several years, until he succeeded in accumulating quite a respectable fortune. He then visited the United States, and purchased a fine farm in the then County of Berkeley, near to the present village of Leetown. Not being able to get immediate possession of his purchase, he availed himself of the interval to pay a visit to his old home in

Ireland. It was upon his return from this visit, that the boy Faulkner accompanied him to America. It is said that Richard McSherry was the first person who introduced from Jamaica into this country, the tomato and okra, as esculents for the table.

Young Faulkner was brought to Martinsburg and placed under the charge of Michael McKewan, an Irishman, who then kept a retail store in that town. He remained in his service until he was of age, in 1797, when he purchased the property at the southeastern corner of Burke and Queen streets, and commenced business on his own account.

On the 15th of December, 1803, he was married to Sarah Mackey, only daughter of William Mackey, of Martinsburg.

He was not particularly fond of the mercantile business, and from 1804 until 1808, he spent much of his time in correspondence with Hon. James Stephens, and Hon. John Morrow, the representatives in Congress from this district; with Henry Dearborn, the Secretary of War, and President Jefferson, in endeavoring to gratify his military tastes by procuring a commission in the regular army of the United States. But our army was then small—there were few vacancies or promotions. and his efforts in that direction were unsuccessful.

Towards the close of Mr. Jefferson's administration in 1809, the relations between this country and Great Britain had become very critical. The affair of the Chesapeake had occurred ; the sensibilities of the nation were deeply aroused by the habitual impressment of our seaman ; by the contemptuous deportment of England to our representatives, and by the destruction of our commerce, and an intense war spirit prevaded the land, which was alone held in check by the extraordinary influence of Mr. Jefferson, and by his determined peace policy. It nevertheless became apparent to all men, that unless Great Britain altered her conduct to this county, which was hardly anticipated, war would be inevitable in a year or two. It was under these circumstances that Mr. Faulkner, unable to procure a position in the regular army, determined to organize a volunteer artillery company in Berkeley County, to meet any of the probable demands of war. This was promptly accomplished. James Faulkner was elected Captain, Robert Wilson 1st Lieutenant and William Long 2nd Lieutenant. Among the names familiar to our people who thus volunteered as privates, were John R. Cooke, Edward Colston, John Alburtis, Alexander Stephen, William Campbell, James Newkirk, Tillotson Fryatt, Adam Young, Jacob Snyder, John Mathews, Jacob Poisal, Chas. Pendleton, James Shearer, Nicholas Orrick, and some fifty others. It will be conceded that no other vounteer company in the State was better drilled ; was composed of more reliable material, or could boast of men more determined to stand by their country in any hour of difficulty or trial.

On the 18th of June 1812, war was declared by the United States against Great Britain. During that year and the earlier part of 1813, the fighting was mainly confined to the Canada frontier, where notwitstanding some brilliant victories upon our part, the British, aided by the Northwestern Indians under Tecumseh, inflicted some severe defeats upon our armies.

In the Martinsburg *Gazette* of the 7th of February, 1812, is found the following extract from an address to the artillery company :

"You have upon two former occasions, volunteered your services to the government, the commander hopes your patriotic and military pride will not be damped by the circumstance that you have not been ordered into actual service. He flatters himself that as there is now every probability of a war that you will authorize him to offer your services to march wherever you may be required. He returns his thanks to those patriotic young men not belonging to the company, who enrolled themselves to march with him on a former occasion, and flatters himself that they, and others who feel a desire to serve their country in the ranks of its defenders, will come forward and join the parade on Saturday, the 22nd inst., the anniversary of the birth of the immortal Washington.

JAMES FAULKNER,
Feb. 7th, 1812   *Captain 1st M. Artillery.*

As early as March, 1812, there were satisfactory reasons to believe that a formidable military and naval demonstration of the enemy would, in the course of the summer, if not earlier, be made upon Norfolk and Portsmouth, in Virginia. Accordingly general orders were issued on the 24th of March, for the assembling of a considerable portion of the State militia at those points. Among the companies so ordered into service was Captain Wilson's Berkeley Artillery, for such it then was. Captain Faulkner had been, early in March, promoted to the rank of Major of Artillery, was thus separated from his company; and was ordered by Governor Barbour to report to him at Richmond, and to take command of all the artillery companies then assembled at the capital. He reported to the Governor on the 10th of April, and taking command of these companies he proceeded with them to the seat of war.

Early in June Admiral Warren with a large naval and military force arrived in the Chesapeake Bay; the land force being under the command of Gen. Sir Sidney Beckwith. The appearance of this formidable force in the Chesapeake Bay created much uneasiness in the more considerable cities situated upon its waters. Baltimore, Annapolis and Norfolk were threatened. But the fleet directed its course toward Hampton Roads, and it was evident that the cities of Virginia were to receive the blow.

About four miles west of Norfolk and commanding the approach to that city, lay Craney Island. This was the exposed outpost of our military line — the nearest in contact with the enemy—a position of great importance as the key to the harbor, and which it was indispensable that the enemy should possess before they could reach the cities of Norfolk and Portsmouth.

Among the general orders issued by Major General Taylor, Commander-in-Chief, on the 13th of June, are the following:

"Major Faulkner of the regiment of Artillery will to-morrow take the command of all the artillery and fortifications of Craney Island.

The commander of artillery will direct Capt. Wilson's company of artillery to some place near the entrenchments in the rear of Fort Norfolk."

On the 22nd of June occurred the battle of Craney Island. I am not disposed to repeat the details of that battle. They can be seen in the various histories of the late war with Great Britain, and in the recently illustrated history of that war by Benson J. Lossing, which contains a portrait and autograph signature of Major Faulkner.

It can also be seen in the elaborate report of a Committee of the House of Delegates of Virginia, who were appointed to take testimoney, and to make a thorough examination into the details of that battle, and which report, with the resolutions and evidences accompanying it, unanimously concurred in by the House, is the proudest monument that could be erected to the memory of Major Faulkner.

It is sufficient to say the battle of Craney Island was won; that it was won exclusively by the *artillery* engaged in its defence; that a force of near 3,000 British soldiers were signally repulsed; that the cities of Norfolk and Portsmouth were saved and that the results of that battle were hailed throughout the country as a National balm for our defeats on the northwestern frontier.

On the 5th of July Major Faulkner was placed in command of Forts Barbour and Tar and a mile of breastwork extending between the two forts, with his headquarters at Norfolk.

Major Faulkner was not a man of robust constitution, but rather of delicate physical organization, and the effect of that low-land summer climate, with the fatigues and exposures of the service, gave a shock to his system from which he never recovered. He was an invalid from the close of the war until his death, which occurred on the 11th of April, 1817, in the 41st year of his age. He was buried with military and masonic honors in the Norborne cemetery, where a granite monument now stands erected to his memory.

Postcript.—When the facts connected with the battle of Craney Island were under examination by the Legislature of Virginia, Major Faulkner's official report of that battle was not before the committee. Indeed, it was not known that any copy of it had been preserved or was in existence, as the substance of it had been incorporated into the account of the battle as given by Major General Robt. B. Taylor, then Commander-in-Chief. Since that that time a copy of it has been found, in the hand-writing of the author, inclosed in a letter to Col. Elisha Boyd under date of the 6th of July, 1813. It is deemed unnecessary to publish it in full, as in all its prominent facts it is in harmony with the received histories of that battle and in accord with the conclusions of the legislature. Had it been before the committee it would have removed all doubt upon one point upon which the committee expressly refrained from announcing any opinion; that was to whom the credit was due for the successful shot which sunk Admiral Warren's barge.

The committee say:

"Scarcely had the enemy been driven, by our well directed fire, from their assailing position on the land, when fifty of their largest barges, filled with men from the ships supposed to contain about 1,500 sailors and marines, begun to approach within the range of our artillery. They were advancing towards the island, in column order, in two distinct divisions, one following the channel between the island and the main land, led on by Admiral Warren's barge, the Centipede, a boat upwards of fifty feet in length, rowing twenty-four oars, with a brass three pounder in her bow, under the command of Capt. Hanchett, of his Majesty's ship Diadem ; the other directing its course to some point on the north of the island. Whilst the barges were approaching, Captain Emerson observed to Major Faulkner 'Are they near enough to fire?' 'No, sir,' replied the commander of artillery, 'let them approach a little nearer.' In a few moments afterwards the word 'fire' was given, when our whole battery, except the disabled pieces, opened upon the nearest division of boats a brisk and heavy discharge of grape and canister. The barges, however, continued to advance in the face of this destructive fire until they could no longer maintain themselves under it, when the Centipede and the boats immediately following her were observed to change their direction toward the division of barges aiming at the north of the island, at which moment the Centipede was sunk by a shot from one of the guns passing through the boat, in the wake of the afterthwart, wounding several, and among them Capt. Hanchett, the commanding officer of the division, severely in the thigh. At this time, so quick and galling was our fire, that the enemy were thrown into the greatest confusion, and the order was soon after given for a hasty retreat to the ships."

Again the committee say :

"Much of the eclat which attached to the guns under the immediate command of Lieut. Neale, resulted from the general impression and belief that it was a shot from the 18-pounder which passed through and sunk the Centipede. Whether that result was produced by a shot from the eighteen, or one of the six-pounders, this committee will not undertake to determine. There are strong and confident statements and opinions sustaining either view, which will be found in the appendix accompanying this report."

Had this report been before that body there could have been no doubt announced on this point, for Major Faulkner expressly states in his report: "Captain Emerson and Lieutenant Neale informed me that their guns were pointed and in readiness to bear upon the leading boat, which proved to be the Admiral's barge. I immediately ordered them to fire, when the second fire of Lieut. Neale had the desired effect and sunk the barge."

He concludes his report as follows:

"The officers principally enged in the action were Captain Rook, of the ship Manhattan; Lieut. Neale, of the frigate Constitution; Capt. Emerson, Lieuts. Howle and Godwin and Sergeants Young and Butt, of the Portsmouth Artillery, who, for their skill and bravery in repelling so large a force of the enemy, deserve the thanks of the country. Lieuts. Shubrick, Saunders and Breckenridge, of the Constellation, with their crews, as brave and determined a set of men as I ever saw, gave substantial aid and assistance in the defense."

MAJOR HENRY BEDINGER,

Was born at Little York, Pennsylvania, October 16th, 1753. His father emigrated to Berkeley County in 1758. In June, 1775, he volunteered in a company raised in the County of Berkeley, under the command of Capt. Hugh Stephenson, which marched in July of that year to the siege of Boston. At the expiration of one year, their term of service having expired, this company was disbanded. Immediately thereafter a rifle regiment was organized, of which Hugh Stephenson was appointed Colonel and Abraham Shepherd commissioned as senior Captain of one of the companies. Young Bedinger was commissioned as Third Lieutenant in this company, and his original commission as such signed by John Hancock,

President of Congress, may be seen, framed and hanging in the house of his grandson, H. B. Davenport, Esq., near Charlestown. After three days' severe fighting at King's Bridge, this regiment, then commanded by Colonel Rawlings, was forced to capitulate, and surrendered themselves as prisoners of war in the capture of Fort Washington. This occurred on the 16th of November, 1777, and Lieut. Bedinger was confined as a prisoner on Long Island until the summer of 1781. After having thus endured the rigor of imprisonment for four years, he was exchanged, and, returning to the army, he was commissioned a Captain in the 4th Virginia Regiment and ordered to Yorktown, but before he reached that point the surrender of Lord Cornwallis and his army had taken place. At the close of the revolutionary war he returned to Shepherdstown, then in the County of Berkeley, and there entered into the mercantile business. Upon the death of Moses Hunter he was, in August, 1798, elected Clerk of the County Court of Berkeley, when he removed to Martinsburg, its county seat. Prior to this time he had been elected and served one year as a member of the House Delegates of Virginia. The validity of his election as Clerk of the County Court was vigorously contested by Col. David Hunter, his competitor for that office. This led to protracted litigation, in which the ablest counsel in the United States were employed—John Marshall, Luther Martin and Walter Jones being of the number, and party spirit then running very high, Bedinger being a Jeffersonian Republican, and Hunter an ardent and prominent Federalist, the contest excited deep interest throughout the country. The venue of the trial of the case was changed by the General Court of Virginia at its November term, 1799, from the Winchester District Court to Staunton, but subsequently sent back to Winchester. The suit resulted in a judgment, rendered December, 1803, setting aside the election of Major Bedinger and the transfer of the office to his opponent, Col.

Hunter. Some of the remains of that litigation are to be seen upon the records of our courts as late as 1830. He was a member of the Society of the Cincinnatti, and his diploma as such, handsomely framed, still adorns the parlor of one of his decendants. After his amotion from the office of Clerk, he removed to his fine estate "Protumna," five miles south of Martinsburg. He was a careful farmer and an enthusiastic cultivator of fine fruits. He possessed an extraordinary memory and delighted in his hospitable mansion to dwell upon the incidents of our revolutionary war. He could remember, with great distinctness, even in very advanced life, the company, regiment, rank and service of almost any officer in the Virginia line, and it was through his retentive' memory that many received that justice from their country which otherwise, from lost and mutilated records, they could never have obtained. He bore the reputation of a patriot and good citizen up to the period of his death, which occurred on the 14th of May, 1843, then nearly ninety years of age.

ALEXANDER WHITE

Was among the earliest of those who presented their licenses and qualified as practitioners of law in this county. This was on the first day that the first court was held in Berkeley county, May 19th, 1772. The proper oath of an attorney-at-law was duly administered to him, Philip Pendleton and four others. On the same day, as the record reads.

"Alexander White having produced a commission from the Attorney General of this county, appointing him deputy attorney for this county, the same being read, he having taken the usual oath, and sworn Deputy King's attorney for this county."

Mr. White was elected the first member of Congress from this District, under the present Constitution of the United States. He was a man of marked punctuality and system, and a slight evidence of this may be seen in the fact, that he was the only member of Congress from Virginia who was present on the first day of its session. The *Annals of Congress* are meager in the debates of that period, although accurate so far as they give the substance of the remarks made—a practice that should never have been departed from. Mr. White took a prominent part in all the debates of that term of Congress, and as our enlightened statesmen were then laying the foundation of our legislative system, the subjects before them were necessarily numerous, important and interesting. He bore the reputation of a man of learning, of great ability and of ardent patriotism.

Mr. White was re-elected to the 2nd Congress in 1791, over his two competitors, Generals William Darke and James Wood.

In 1798 he was commissioned as magistrate of Berkeley county.

Mr. White was dragged from his retirement to represent the county of Berkeley in the House of Delegates of Virginia, during the important sessions of 1799 and 1800, when the celebrated report and resolutions of Mr. Madison were the subject of such earnest debate, and which gave such an impulse to the Revolution which brought Mr. Jefferson into power.

As has been already stated Alexander White was the first representative in Congress from this District under the present Constitution of the United States. That election occurred on the 2nd of February, 1789. At that time no census had been taken of the population of the States, and the Constitution provided "until such enumeration was made," Virginia should be entitled to ten members in the House of Representatives. The General Assembly therefore laid off the State into ten districts, making the counties of Berkeley, Hampshire, Shenandoah, Hardy, Monongalia, Ohio, Randolph and Frederick the first district. It was from this district that Mr. White was elected in 1789, and re-elected in February,

Historical Pen Sketches. 179

1791. After the census of 1790 was completed and Congress had fixed the ratio of reprsentation, Virginia became entitled to 19 representatives and the legislature then divided the State into 19 districts making "Berkeley and Frederick" the first District, which so continued until after the census of 1800. The first election under this apportionment was on the third Monday in March, 1793, when Robert Rutherford was returned. He was re-elected in 1795, General Daniel Morgan in 1797; and David Holmes, subsequently Governor of Mississippi and U. S. Senator from that State, was then elected and continued in Congress until the District was changed under the apportionment of the census of 1800.

HON. ROBERT RUTHERFORD,

Of Berkeley was elected to the 3rd Congress in 1793, from the District composed of the counties of Berkeley and Frederick. He was re-elected to the 4th Congress in 1795, thus serving four years as a representative in Congress from this District. He was a candidate for re-election to the 5th Congress but was defeated by General Daniel Morgan. He contested Morgan's election before the House, but the decision was in favor of the right of Morgan to the seat.

Mr. Rutherford does not seem to have participated very actively in the general debates of the House, and yet, in January, 1794, he delivered quite an elaborate speech on "The Commerce of the United States," and in March, 1776, participated in the great debate of that period upon the "Constitutional Powers of Congress," in reference to treaties and in April, 1696, gave his views at large in opposition to the provision for carrying the British treaty into effect. All his views would seem to class him with the Democratic rather than the Federal side of the House.

It might afford some interest to take a few extracts from these speeches (especially as the reporter declares them to be authentic, they "having passed the revision of the Speaker") as illustrative of Mr. R's. views and opinions, but they must be passed by for the present.

Feeling that he was, in his public course, acting in opposition to the recommendations of Washington, he thus refers to their personal relations:

"Much stress has been laid on the patriotism of the President, which makes it necessary for me to reply, lest I may be taken for one uninformed. I have had the honor of the President's acquaintance well nigh, or quite, forty years, and he has supported every character with merit, dignity and unswerving attention. I have acted with him on trying occasions, sometimes equal, oftentimes in a subordinate sphere, and tho' senior in point of years, yet, I uniformly looked up to him as a parent—my head and my guide; yet I am independent of the President—an unchangeable friendship excepted."

Judging of Mr. Rutherford by the impression made upon me by his speeches in Congress I would say that he was a man of strong and original mind—honest and sincere in all his convictions—upright and independent in his bearing, but not of much mental cultivation, nor deeply imbued with the facts of history, nor the lessons of statesmanship.

I have heard traditionally and seen in print many anecdotes of Mr. Rutherford illustrative of his homely manners, the simplicity of his dress, the frugality of his mode of living, and of his awkwardness in society, but these stories may or may not be true—and as they touch none of the substantial merits of a man—are not worthy of being remembered or repeated.

GENERAL DANIEL MORGAN

Represented this county and district in the 5th Congress of the United States—that is from 1797 to 1799. The military history of this distinguished soldier, has been so frequently written and is so familiar to the public mind, that it need only here be briefly glanced at.

He is mentioned in these sketches only because of his connection with the County of Berkeley.

He was born in New Jersey in the year 1737. At the age of eighteen, he emigrated to Virginia and obtained employment from farmer Roberts, of Berkeley County. He delighted in the management and use of his team, and acquired throughout life, the subriquet of the "old wagoner." He shared in the perils of Braddock's defeat, probably as a wagoner, and was wounded by a bullet through his neck and cheek. The profit of his business as a wagoner enabled him to purchase a tract of land in Frederick County, where he lived at the commencement of the Revolutionary War. In June, 1775, he was appointed a captain by Congress. He was in the expedition against Quebec, and contributed to the capture of Burgoyne. He defeated Tarlton in January, 1781, in the battle of Cowpens, taking upwards of 500 prisoners. For this action Congress voted him a gold medal. Soon afterwards he retired from the army and returned to his farm.

The excise, or as it is most usually called "The whiskey Insurrection," is an interesting episode in our early history. It was the first open, defiant and formidable opposition of the Federal government, after the adoption of our present constitution. It grew out of an act of Congress imposing an internal revenue duty on distilled spirits. Much dissatisfaction existed throughout the United States at the imposition of this excise duty. But it was in Western Pennsylvania, and especially in the four counties of Alleghany, Washington, Green and Westmoreland, that this dissatisfaction broke out in open rebellion. The revenue officers were seized, tarred and feathered. The houses and barns of those supposed to be friendly to the Government were burnt. Many acts of extreme violence were perpetrated. No civil process could be executed. Lawlessness universally prevailed. Armed bands of forty and fifty, and even as high as five hundred, were organized to resist the government. It was boldly asserted that the insurgents could bring into the field seven thousand well armed troops. It could not be supposed that such men as President Washington and Secretary Hamilton would tamely submit to see the new Government thus paralyzed and defied in the performance of one of its most important and vital functions. A proclamation was issued by President Washington, calling upon the insurgents to disperse. This not being obeyed, a requisition was made upon the States of Pennsylvania, New Jersey and Virginia for 15,000 troops to crush the insurrection. The requisition was promptly complied with. General Henry Lee, of Virginia, was placed in command of the army. Gen. Morgan was assigned to the command of the Virginia troops. Hamilton left the Treasury Department and remained during the expedition at the headquarters of the commanding general. Washington proceeded toward the scene of strife as far as York, and designed taking command in person, but public business (Congress then being in session) called him to Philadelphia. The appearance of this formidable army in the disaffected district under such able, popular and experienced commanders soon brought the insurgents to their senses. They rapidly disbanded and dispersed. Some of the leaders were indicted for treason, but no convictions followed, and Gen. Morgan, with a body of Virginia militia, was left for some time in the disaffected district to see that no further violence was attempted.

In 1797 Gen. Morgan was elected from the district composed of the counties of Berkeley and Frederick, as a member of the 5th Congress. His opponent was Robt. Rutherford, whom he defeated. The election was contested before the House, but the committee reported in favor of Morgan, and as Rutherford did not appear to contest the conclusions of the report, it was unanimously concurred in by the House.

General Morgan submitted no motion and made no

speech during his term of service. He was a rough, uneducated man, and while he felt perfectly at home on the field of battle, he, with sensible modesty, knew his deficiencies in civil life, and felt like a child in the presence of the enlightened statesmen then around him. But if he did not know how to speak, he knew how to vote with his party, and if the records of Congress be searched there will be found no name that adhered so loyally to its allegiance to the Federal organization as Daniel Morgan. He had able and accomplished leaders in the persons of Harrison, Gray, Otis and Robert Goodloe Harper, to point out to him the path of party duty, and he followed them with the same unfaltering fidelity with which he had followed Washington in the field of battle. He voted for the bill to punish "usurpation of Executive authority," and against the repeal of the alien and sedition laws, and at the close of his term published an address to his constituents vindicating the administration of the elder Adams. No one doubts that he was an honest and conscientious politician, however much they may differ in opinion from him.

When, in view of a war with France, a provisional army was organized in 1798, President Adams favored the appointment of General Morgan to its command, subject, of course, to the supreme command conferred upon Washington. But General Washington insisted upon that position being given to Hamilton, which was acceded to with a bad grace by Adams, as he hated Hamilton most cordially.

Morgan died in Winchester on the 6th of July, 1802, aged 65 years.

DAVID HOLMES,

Born in Winchester, was the son of Col. Joseph Holmes, of Frederick County, Va., and a brother of Major Andrew Hunter Holmes, so distinguished during the recent war with Great Britain for his talents and high military qualities. He was killed in the battle of

Mackinaw, on the northern frontiers, on the 4th of August, 1814, and a sword voted to his heirs by the General Assembly of Virginia, in consideration of his gallantry and good conduct. Also brother to Judge Holmes, who occasionally presided in this judicial circuit, and brother to Ann Holmes, married to Gen. Elisha Boyd, of this county. He was a member of the 5th, 6th, 7th, 8th, 9th and 10th Congresses.

At the close of his service in Congress he was, in 1809, appointed by President Madison Governor of the territory of Mississippi, and when admitted into the Union as a State he was elected Governor by the people. He was subsequently, in 1820, elected a Senator in Congress for six years, from the same State, but resigned before the end of his term of service. He died in Winchester on the 20th of August, 1832.

Although twelve consecutive years a member of the House of Representatives, and six in the Senate, the records of Congress show nothing but his votes. It does not appear that he ever submitted a motion or made a remark in either body. And yet there must have been something very remarkable in the intellect and bearing of a man who could, with a different constituency, thus pass so triumphantly through all the stages of political life, without any of the adventitious aids of public speaking. When elected to the 5th Congress he was a resident of Shenandoah. Gen. Morgan then represented Berkeley and Frederick in that Congress. In 1799 (6th Congress) Holmes having removed back to Winchester, was elected from the district of Berkeley and Frederick; so in the 7th Congress he represented this district. When the district was re-arranged after the census of 1803, he represented Frederick and Shenandoah from 1803 to 1809, thus consecutively representing three distinct districts of the State within the twelve years of his service in the House.

Gov. Holmes was a man of modest and retiring habits,

but of captivating manners, and bore the reputation of marked ability and of great integrity of character. He was the uncle of David Holmes Conrad, now residing in this county, after whom he was named.

GENERAL ELISHA BOYD

Was born in the County of Berkeley, at the eastern base of the North Mountain, on the 6th of October, 1769. Up to the age of 14 he enjoyed only the limited means of education which the common country schools of that period afforded. During that time he attended a small school not far from the present site of Martinsburg. Our thriving town was then a forest, and whilst its eligible locality, its gushing springs and valuable water power invited to such a destiny, few, if any at that time, contemplated it as a seat of population, manufactures and trade.

In 1785 he was entered as a student of Liberty Hall Academy, (so baptised amidst the revolutionary fires of 1776,) in Rockbridge County, Va., a most excellent and patriotic institution then under the rectorate of the Rev. William Graham, largely patronized throughout the south, and yielding a rich harvest of patriots and statesmen. Although bearing the modest title of an academy, it had all the attributes of a college, with power to hold land, confer degrees, etc. Like the great Virginia State University, springing from the germ of "Albemarle Academy," it grew into "Central College," and then reached its present grand proportions; so did this spirited academy, expanding in dignity, reputation and importance, first develop into "Washington College," and recently—in 1871—into "Washington and Lee University." Amongst those well known in our State who were associated with young Boyd as schoolmates, were Dr. Archibald Alexander, of Princeton, Hon. John Baker, of Jefferson County; Chancellor John Brown, Judge John Coalter, Col. James McDowell and many others distinguished for their worth, learning and ability.

He studied law in the office of Col. Philip Pendleton, one of the earliest as well as one of the ablest lawyers that ever qualified for practice in our courts. Mr. Boyd was elected to the House of Delegates in 1797, with Richard Baylor as his colleague, and also in 1796, with William Lamon as his colleague. In 1798 he was chosen by the County Court of Berkeley as its attorney for the State, which office he continued to fill for forty years. He was married in 1795 to Mary, the daughter of Major Andrew Waggoner of revolutionary memory, by whom he had one child, a daughter, Sarah Ann Boyd, who was married to Philip C. Pendleton on the 25th of November, 1813. For forty years he gave his almost undivided time to the practice of his profession and to attention to his several farms in this county, varied at occasional intervals by military service, a seat in the House of Delegates and Senate of the State, and in the Constitutional Convention. During all this time he had probably the largest and most lucrative practice of any lawyer in this section of Virginia.

Some years after the death of his first wife he was, in 1806, married to Ann Holmes, daughter of Col. Joseph Holmes and sister of Gov. Holmes and Major Andrew Hunter Holmes. By her he had four children—Ann Rebecca Holmes, married to Humphrey B. Powell, of Loudon County; John E. Boyd, Rev. Andrew H. H. Boyd and Mary, married to Charles J. Faulkner.

Mrs. Ann Boyd died on the 20th of July, 1819. An eloquent and impressive funeral sermon was preached over her remains by the Rev. J. B. Hoge, which was printed in pamphlet form, and copies of it are carefully preserved by the family.

He had command of the 4th Regiment of Virginia militia in 1814 during the war with Great Britain, when the cities of Norfolk and Portsmouth were threatened by a second attack of the British land and naval forces. The Norfolk *Herald*, 1814, contains an interesting correspondence between the officers of that regiment and Col. Boyd when the term of service of that regiment was about to expire. It bears date the 1st of August, at Camp Peach Orchard. The officers say that they cannot permit the occasion to pass by "without paying to Col. Boyd the tribute of their highest respect and esteem." "They have at all times felt confident that when the hour of danger arrived that on his patriotism and courage they could, with the utmost confidence, rely to lead them on in defense of the country." They also take pride in declaring that whatever military knowledge they have acquired is due to that strictness of military discipline which has uniformly characterized the 4th Regiment since he had the command of it. "And if they ever should again be called into the service of their country, it is their wish that they should be placed under his command." To this complimentary letter Col. Boyd replied, which is also published in the same paper. He was subsequently elected a brigadier general by the General Assembly of Virginia. He was a member of the convention of 1829-30, which framed the first amended Constitution of Virginia, serving in that body with Madison, Monroe, Marshall, Giles, Tazwell, Leigh, Barbour, Johnson and many other of the most distinguished men of Virginia.

In the election which occurred after the adoption of the "Amended Constitution" in 1830, he was chosen without opposition, and by the unanimous vote of the counties of Berkeley, Morgan and Hampshire, to a seat in the Senate of Virginia.

He was commissioned a magistrate of the County of Berkeley, in 1838, upon the resignation of his office of State's attorney.

He was an earnest and sincere advocate for a reform of the "Old Constitution" of Virginia, and for placing its government upon a more liberal and republican basis. He was generally selected as Chairman of the county meeting held here, and a delegate to the State Reform Convention.

He took an active interest in the educational institutions of the county; and had the principal agency in establishing the Martinsburg Academy, not far from his residence.

He was a third time married and then to Elizabeth Byrd, of the Westover family, who died on the 16th of November, 1839, leaving no issue.

Gen. Boyd departed this life on the 21st day of October, 1841, and was buried in the family graveyard adjoining Norborne Cemetery.

He was a man of vigorous mind, and of indomitable energy and perserverance. His power at the bar consisted in his unflaging attention to business, his thorough capacity to master details, and in his earnest, direct and manly appeals to the common sense and intelligence of courts and juries. He was a man of perfect system and of extraordinary capacity for labor; and he commanded universal confidence by his stern and unbending integrity of character.

HON. JOHN BAKER

Was born in Berkeley County, Virginia, about the year 1769. He was entered as a student of Liberty Hall Academy, Rockbridge County, Va., between the years 1783 and 1789, and among his fellow students of that period, were Dr. Alexander, of Princeton, and General Boyd of this county. He took up his residence in Shepherdstown, on the Potomac River, then the most flourishing town in the lower valley, and soon rose to the distinction of an able and accomplished lawyer.

He was nominated by the Federal party, and elected to the 12th Congress from the District of Berkeley, Jefferson and Hampshire, embracing the term from 1811 to 1813.

The *Annals of Congress* give no report of any speech

made by him, yet the Martinsburg *Gazette*, of January the 24th, 1812, publishes some very forcible and eloquent remarks made by him in Committee of the Whole, on the 26th of December, 1811, in favor of pensioning the surviving officers and soldiers of the Revolutionary War. The omission of this speech from the "Annals" is to be explained by the fact, that it was delivered in the Committee of the Whole, and no report, it seems, was usually made at that time of speeches made in the Committee.

On the 4th of February, 1812, he presented a petition from Jefferson County, asking Congress to make certain improvements near Georgetown, that would give to the farmers of the upper county a choice of markets for their flour between Alexandria and Georgetown. It was stated that 300,000 barrels of flour were then annually conveyed to market by the river, in boats, and the trade was increasing.

Mr. Baker was an ardent and uncompromising Federalist, and voted steadily with his party against a declaration of war against Great Britain, and all other measures in aid of that belligerent movement. He was one of the 34 members of Congress who published, after the rising of Congress, an able and elaborate defence of their opposition to the war. The Federalists of Berkeley were much pleased with his votes and on the 12th of August 1812, gave him a public dinner to express their approval to his course in Congress. Among the toasts of that occasion was the following:

"The war rashly and unnecessarily begun. May it be speedily terminated by an honorable peace."

The sentiment announced in honor of Mr. Baker was "A disciple of Washington and true to his principles."

In the summer of 1813 Shepherdstown was visited by a violent bilious epidemic, scarcely less fatal than the yellow fever. Many of her most prominent citizens fell under the terrible visitation. Among the number was Hon. John Baker, who died on the 18th of August, 1823, leaving an estimable widow and an interesting family of children. One of his daughters was married to T. W. Gilmer, Governor of Virginia, and Secretary of the Navy.

Mr. Baker was universally respected for his high attainments as a lawyer—for his many virtues as a private citizen—for his courage, firmness and consistency as a politician.

COL. EDMUND P. HUNTER

Was born in Martinsburg on the 24th of March, 1809, and after enjoying the advantages of a collegiate education at Jefferson College, was admitted to the Berkeley bar, in 1831. Shortly afterwads he became the proprietor and editor of the Martinsburg *Gazette*, and continued as such until March 1845, when he was succeeded in the control and management of the paper by James E. Stewart, Esq.

On the 2nd of August, 1832, he was married to Martha Crawford, daughter of Captain John Abell, an intelligent and highly esteemed farmer of Jefferson county. The author of this sketch participated in the ceremony, as first groomsman, and for some days enjoyed the kind hospitality of that charming and interesting family.

This may be an appropriate occasion to notice very briefly the history of that venerable journal. It was establised in 1801 by Nathaniel Willis, the father of the distinguished poet, N. P. Willis and then called the Berkeley *Intelligencer*. In 1803, he disposed of his interest in the paper to John Alburtis, who at first styled it the Berkeley and Jefferson *Intelligencer*, but a newspaper soon making its appearance in the recently formed County of Jefferson, its name was changed to the Martinsburg *Gazette*, which name it retained until the opening of our civil war, when its publication altogether ceased. It was under the control of John Alburtis from 1803 until 1823, of Washington Evans from 1823 until 1833, of Col. Edward P. Hunter, from 1833 to March, 1845 ; of

James E. Stewart and subsequently of Stewart & Gregg, from March 1845 to March 1847. It then passed into the hands of Charles H. Lewis, and lastly under the control of A. T. Haupin, boasting, a continuous and prosperous existence of sixty years.

In May 1832, he attended as a member the memorable "Young Men's Convention," in Washington city, upon which occasion Mr. Clay appeared before that body and electrified it with one of his most eloquent and stirring speeches.

General Boyd having held the office of county attorney for forty years, resigned it at the March court, 1838, when an animated contest took place for the succession, between Edmund P. Hunter and David Holmes Conrad. The power of appointment was then vested in the county court, and the justices having been all summoned for the purpose, a full court was present. The contest excited unusual interest and for a time its result was deemed doubtful. But Hunter obtained a majority of the votes and was declared elected. It is unneceseary to say that he filled the office for many years, not only with ability, but with justice to the State and with judicious clemency to the accused.

He enjoyed a high degree of popularity in the county, and was elected a member of the House of Delegates of Virginia, in 1834, 1835, 1839 and 1841. His course as a member of that body gave great satisfaction to his constituents, as it was uniformly marked by dilligent attention to their local interests, and by a faithful expression in their sentiments on all the questions of State and national policy.

He was Colonel of the 67th Regiment of Virginia militia and took a deep interest in all the details of its organization. When dressed in full military costume it would be difficult to find a more striking realization of imposing manhood than he presented.

He was an ardent and enthusiastic member of the

Masonic order, and worthily rose to the highest honors of the craft in Virginia.

He was in the latter portion of his life a sincere and exemplary member of the Episcopal Church, and exhibited in his conduct, a thorough conviction of the truths of revealed religion.

In September, 1854, the Asiatic cholera—that terrible pestilence "which walketh in darkness, and wasteth in noonday"—struck the affrighted population of Martinsburg. There are those amongst us yet, who can well remember the alarm and terror which its unwelcome appearance excited here. Hundreds fled from the place with precipitation. Many families whose wealth and means ought to have caused them to stand by their friends in their sad affliction, abandoned their homes for the mountains and cities. The carnage was that of a battle field. One hundred and eleven of our citizens fell victims to its fury. Among the first of those who perished was the lamented Colonel Edmund P. Hunter, who died on the 7th of September, 1854, in the 45th year of his age.

Edmund P. Hunter was not endowed with any very high or extraordinary quality of intellect, but he possessed such a rare combination of excellent qualities, both moral and intellectual, as more than compensated for the want of any particular brilliancy of parts. He was a man of sense and of good judgment; lucid in his mental perceptions, and capable of expressing his convictions with clearness and force. Superior to all artifice himself, he was proof against the arts of sophistry and deception in others. He was a fair speaker and a sound and manly reasoner, and these, with his open-heartedness and honesty of character, made him always formidable at the bar. He had something of his father's fondness for broad humor and a joke, which occasionally flashed out in the trial of a case, but was more particularly observable in the social circle. All his impulses were kind and generous. His hospitality was proverbial. He was a stranger to envy, hatred, malice, and all uncharitableness. He was firm and steadfast in his friendship, and ever outspoken and candid in the expression of his opinions. I dare not penetrate the domestic sanctuary and speculate, to what extent, his loss must have agonized that sacred circle; but I can truly say, that his friends and brethren of the bar have never ceased to lament the day that deprived them of his joyous presence and attractive companionship.

> The sweet remembrance of the just
> Shall flourish when he sleeps in dust.

GENERAL WILLIAM DARKE, A DISTINGUISHED WEST VIRGINIA PIONEER.

[*By Virgil A. Lewis, of Mason City, W. Va., in W. Va. School Journal.*]

In the settlement of the western wilderness, what is now West Virginia can boast of pioneers whose names are as honored and should occupy as high a place upon the temple of fame as any that appear in the pages of pioneer history. But alas! many of them have been lost in oblivion, while those known to us, some who merit enduring monuments, scarce found a tomb. The great Roman lyric poet informs us that, "The names of the heroes who flourished before the days of Agamemnon were lost for want of a recording pen." This is true, too, of many of those who first planted the standard of civilization within the present confines of West Virginia. What a valuable contribution to the literature of the State would the record of their lives be? But much is irretrievably lost. Then let that which has survived the lapse of a century, be carefully preserved and cherished by a generation now enjoying the fruits of the toils and privations of the men and women who reared the first cabin homes within the confines of the "Little Mountain State."

On the bank of Middle Creek, a tributary of Opequon River, in the southern part of Berkeley County, stands the little village of Darkesville, which was made a town by an act of the Virginia Legislature December 7, 1791, when Washington had served two years of his first term as President of the United States. Who that now visits the little town or sees dimly marked on the map of the State, "Darkesville P. O." stops to enquire why it was so called? And who, that does, will not be surprised to learn that it commemorates one of the most distinguished names which appear in frontier annals—that of General William Darke.

He was born near Lancaster, Pennsylvania, in 1736, and in 1741, when but five years of age, accompanied his parents south of the Potomac, where they reared their cabin home within a few miles of the present site of Shepherdstown, now in Jefferson County, W. Va. Here they were on the outmost boundary of civilization, while to the west of them lay the vast, untrodden American wilderness. Their nearest neighbors appear to have been Thomas Shepherd, the founder of Shepherdstown, and Robert Harper, whose name is preserved in that of Harper's Ferry. Here, among wild solicitudes, young Darke grew to manhood. Nature made him a nobleman; he was endowed with a herculean frame; his manners rough; his mind was strong but uncultivated, and his disposition was frank and fearless. From infancy he was familiar with "war's dread alarm," for throughout his youthful years he had listened to the recital of the bloody drama then being enacted on the frontiers of Virginia and Pennsylvania. This familiarity with the story of savage warfare aroused within him a spirit of adventure and daring, and he longed to engage in "struggles fierce and wild." The opportunity soon came. In the spring of 1755, General Edward Braddock arrived in Alexandria, Virginia, with an army of two thousand men, consisting of the 44th and 48th Royal Infantry

Regiments. This force proceeded up the Potomac, and at Fort Cumberland—now Cumberland City, Maryland—was joined by a regiment of Virginia Provincials, in the ranks of which were many Valley men, one of them being William Darke, then but nineteen years of age.

The march into the wilderness began. Slowly the splendid pageant moved on; the long line of scarlet uniforms contrasting strangely with the verdure of the forest, while strains of martial music filled the air—sounds so strange beneath the dark shades of the American forest. It was the evening of the 8th of July, 1775, when the English columns for the second time reached the Monongahela, at a point ten miles from Fort Duquesne. On the next day a crossing was effected, and once across the stream the order to march was given, but scarcely was the column in motion when Gordon, one of the engineers, saw the French and Indians bounding through the forest. At once a deadly fire was poured in upon the English, who returned it with but little effect. Braddock formed the regulars into squares, as though he had been maneuvering in the fields of Europe, and thus they were shot down in heaps. Of the twelve hundred men who crossed the Monongahela, sixty-seven officers and seven hundred privates were either killed or wounded. Braddock was among the fallen, and of all his aides, Washington alone was left. Many Virginians were among the dead, but a sufficient number were left—among whom was William Darke—to form a line and cover the retreat of the shattered army back to Fort Cumberland, whence Colonel Dunbar marched the regulars back to Philadelphia, and the Virginians returned to their frontier homes, there to withstand a storm of warfare then raging fiercer than ever before.

During the next fifteen years, Captain Darke was engaged in defending the Virginia frontier against the incursions of the savages, and associated with him in the same daring and noble work, were many destined to leave a name behind them, and some to leave an impress upon the age in which they lived. Among them were George Washington, George Rogers Clark, William Clark and Andrew Lewis.

When the storm of revolution came, Captain Darke hastened to join the patriotic army in which, because of meritorious service, he was soon promoted to the rank of lieutenant colonel. He, together with the greater part of his regiment, was taken prisoner at Germantown and detained on board a prisonship until November 1, 1780, when he was exchanged and returned to his post in the army. During the next spring he recruited his regiment (known as the "Hampshire and Berkeley regiment") at the head of which he marched to Tidewater, Virginia, and was actively engaged during the siege of Yorktown, at which place, on the 19th of October, 1781, he witnessed the surrender of Cornwallis' army to the combined forces of America and France. At the close of the Revolution, Colonel Darke, like his illustrious chieftain, returned to his home and engaged in agricultural pursuits until called upon to serve his State in another capacity than that of a soldier.

Soon it was seen that while the Articles of Confederation had bound the country together in the time of war, they were not adapted to the new order of things; and for the purpose of forming "a more perfect union," the Federal Constitution was framed. Its firmest supporters were the great men who had led the armies of the Republic and achieved its independence.

The convention which assembled in Richmond in June, 1788, to ratify that instrument, was composed of some of the most illustrious men of Virginia. The names of Marshall, Madison, Monroe, Mason, Nicholas, Henry, Randolph, Pendleton, Lee, Washington, Wythe, Harrison, Bland, Grayson and a host of others, shed a lustre on the deliberations of that august body, which has never been surpassed in the annals of the Old Dominion. The debates display a degree of eloquence and talent, certainly, at that time unequalled by any gathering of public men in this country. There sat General Adam Stephen, the founder of Martinsburg, and General William Darke, as the delegates from Berkeley county. Both were ardent Federalists, and both voted for the ratification of the Federal Constitution, despite the powerful opposition at the head of which was the immortal Henry.

From the halls of the convention General Darke retired to his Berkeley county home, where he continued his agricultural pursuits until the renewal of the Indian war in 1791. With it came the call to arms and once more General Darke, aroused by the military spirit within him, entered the army as colonel commanding the Second Virginia Regiment. Descending the Ohio his force reached Fort Washington—now Cincinnati—where the army was collecting for invasion of the Indian county. General Arthur St. Clair was placed in command, and in October of the above named year the march into the wilderness began.

On the 3rd of November the army encamped near the present boundary line between Indiana and Ohio, on the bank of the St. Mary's river, a tributary of the Wabash, but which St. Clair believed to be a branch of the Miami of the Lake. Here, at day break the next morning, it was attacked on all sides by the combined strength of the western tribes, at the head of which was the distinguished chieftan Little Turtle, and for five dreadful hours was continued a slaughter unparalleled in the annals of forest warfare.

At the time of the attack Col. Darke's regiment, together with two battalions, occupied the second line, and when the first gave way his regiment received almost the entire shock of battle, the men executing every order of command. During the dreadful hours which followed, he was the coolest man on that bloody and chaotic field, and his escape seems to have been almost miraculous. Possessed of a tall, striking figure, in full uniform and mounted on horseback, he headed three desperate charges against the enemy, in each of which he was a conspicuous mark. His clothes were cut in many places, but he escaped with only a slight flesh wound. In the last charge the ensign of his regiment, a youth of seventeen, was shot through the heart and fell in the rear of the regiment, which was then returning to its original position. An Indian, attracted by his rich uniform, sprang up from the grass and rushed forward to scalp him. Col. Darke, who was then at the rear of the regiment, suddenly wheeling his horse, dashed at the savage and cleft his skull with his broadsword. By this act he drew upon himself the rapid discharge of more than a dozen rifles, but escaped and joined his regiment, though forced to leave the body of the ensign to the enemy. Among the killed in this charge was Captain Joseph Darke, the youngest son of the Colonel. At length the troops yet alive began a rapid retreat which was covered by Darke's regiment to Fort Jefferson, a distance of thirty miles, which they reached the same night. Here a council of war was held and Colonel Darke urged the expediency of an immediate attack, believing that the savages flushed with victory were unprepared for a second contest, but he was overruled.

Stowed away among the archives in the office of the Secretary of War at Washington, deposited there during the administration of that office by General Henry Knox. "The Artillerist of Revolution," is a production in which is told a melancholy tale of sadness and woe. It is the official report of General St. Clair, written after the return of the shattered army to Fort Washington, and bearing date November 9, 1791. In it he speaks at length of the heroic bravery exhibited by his men when hundreds of them were being shot down on the banks of the St. Mary—falling under the fierce fire of an unseen enemy—and then says:

"Colonel Darke was ordered to make a charge with a part of the second line and to turn to the left flank of the enemy. This was executed with great spirit, and at first promised much success. The Indians instantly gave way and were driven back three or four hundred yards; but for want of a sufficient number of riflemen to pursue this advantage, they soon returned, and the troops were obliged to give back in their turn. At this moment they had entered our camp by the left flank, having pursued back the toops that were stationed there."

From the same sad recital we are, told farther on, that Col. Darke's Virginians made a second charge, in which every commissioned officer of the regiment was killed except three, and of them—Captain Greaton—was dangerously wounded. Of the Virginians who yielded up their lives on that fatal field, *eighty* are said to have been from Berkeley county, now in West Virginia. Long years after the mournful story of their fall was rehearsed around the hearthstones in the mountain homes of West Virginia, old soldiers chanted "St. Clair's Defeat," which told in plaintive accents how

"We lost nine hundred men on the banks of the St. Mary."

From Fort Washington Col. Darke returned to Berkeley county, which he almost continuously represented in the General Assembly until his death which occurred November 20, 1801, when he found a grave near the spot where early in life he had found a home.

Thus passed to rest a representative of the Pioneer Age, which was to West Virginia what the Heroic Age was to Greece. The men with whom he lived and acted were as fearless and hardy a race as ever braved the perils of the wilderness. Time has waged a merciless warfare upon the memorials of the age in which they lived, and that which has survived should be placed beyond the possibility of destruction.

CHAPTER IX.
SLAVERY—MODE AND MANNER OF PUNISHMENT—FREEDOM.

HISTORY records no data for the introduction of Negroes, or slaves, that were held in bondage in this county, earlier than the time of Lord Fairfax, about the year 1738. It will be noticed that in several of Fairfax's grants, a number of slaves were included, at which period he kept over a hundred at one time. They were then sold and purchased at that day, in the same manner as we would handle dumb brutes at the present day. The earliest Court record concerning slavery, dates back to April 17, 1772, when a commission was received by the first justices who were appointed to transact the business of the county, by the Governor of the Colony. The following is taken from the original copy, now on file in the County Clerk's office:

"*Virginia, sct.*: John, Earl of Dunmore, his majesty's lieutenant and governor general of the colony and dominion of Virginia, and vice-admiral of the same. To Ralph Wormley, Jacob Hite, Van Swearingen, Thomas Rutherford, Adam Stephen, John Neville, Thomas Swearingen, Samuel Washington, James Hourse, William Little, Robert Stephen, John Briscoe, Hugh Lyle, James Strode, William Morgan, Robert Stogdon, James Seaton, Robert Willis and Thomas Robinson, gentlemen of the County of Berkeley; greeting: Whereas, pursuant to an Act of Assembly, made at a General Assembly, begun and holden at the capitol, in the city of Williamsburg, in the fifth year of his present Majesty's reign, entitled an act for 'amending the act entitled an act directing the trial of slaves committing capital crimes, and for the more effectual punishing of conspiracies and insurrections of them, and for the better government of Negroes, Mulattoes and Indians, bond or free,' the governor, or commander-in-chief of this colony, for the time being, is desired and empowered to issue commissions of Oyer and Terminer, directed to the justices of each county, respectively, empowering them, from time to time, to try, condemn and execute, or otherwise punish or acquit all slaves committing capital crimes within their county: Know ye, therefore, that I, the said John, Earl of Dunmore, by virtue of the powers and authorities to me given by the said act, as commander-in-chief of this dominion, do assign and empower you, the said [the above named parties] or any four or more of you, whereof any of you, the said [the above named parties] shall be one, justices, in such manner, and by such ways and methods, as in the said acts of the General Assembly, are directed, prescribed and set down, to enquire of and to hear and determine, all treasons, petit treasons, or misprisons thereof, felonies, murders or other offences, or capital crimes whatsoever, committed or perpetrated within the said county, by any slave or slaves whatsoever; for the better performance whereof, you, or any four or more of you, as aforesaid, are hereby required and commanded to meet at the court house of the said county, when thereunto required by the sheriff of the said county, for the trial of any slave or slaves, committing any of the offences above mentioned, and any such slave or slaves, being found guilty, in such manner, and upon such evidence, as the said acts of the General Assembly do direct, to pass judgment as the law directs for the like crimes, and on such judgment to award execution, or otherwise to acquit, as of right ought to be done, or to carry into execution any judgment by you given on such trial. Given under my hand, and the seal of the colony, at Williamsburg, the 17th day of April, 1772, in the twelfth year of the reign of our Sovereign Lord, GEORGE the Third. DUNMORE."

The first offence committed and recorded is as follows: "Phil, Sambo, Joe, Will, Jack, Sam, Anthony, Ede, Hannah, Peggy, Betty and Peg, negroes, belonging to Mathew Whiting, being bound to appear at this court for stealing hogs, the property of John Cranes, appeared according to their master's recognizance; on hearing the same it is the opinion of the Court that the said Jack, Joe, Phil and Will, are guilty of the said offence, and it is ordered that the sheriff give them thirty-nine lashes on their bare backs, at the public whipping-post, well laid on, and that the others are not guilty; ordered that they be discharged."

To give the reader an idea of the treatment toward slaves, in this section of country, it may prove of interest to publish the following extract as told by Samuel Kercheval: "My residence was in a neighborhood where slaves and convicts were numerous, and where tortures inflicted upon them had become the occurrences of almost every day, so that they were viewed with indifference by the whole population of the neighborhood as a matter of course. I had not been long in my new habitation, before I witnessed a scene which I shall never forget. A convict servant, accused of some trivial offense, was doomed to the whip, tied with his arms axtended upwards to the limb of a tree, and a bundle of hickories thrown down before him, which he was ordered to look at, and told that they should all be worn out on him, and a great many more, if he did not make confession of the crime alleged against him. The operation then began by tucking up the shirt over his head, so as to leave his back and shoulders naked. The master then took two of the hickories in his hand, and by forward and backhanded strokes, each of which sounded like a wagon whip, and applied with the utmost rapidity and with his whole muscular strength, in a few seconds lacerated the shoulders of the poor miserable sufferer with not less than fifty scourges, so that in a little time the whole of his shoulders had the appearance of a mass of blood, streams of which soon began to flow down his back and sides. He then made a confession of his fault, one not worth naming; but this did not save him from further torture. He put his master "to the trouble of whipping him and he must have a little more." His trousers were then unbuttoned and suffered to fall down about his feet; two new hickories were selected from the bundle, and so applied, that in a short time his posteriors, like his shoulders, exhibited nothing but laceration and blood. A consultation was then held between the master and the bystanders, who had been coolly looking on, in which it was humanely concluded "that he had got enough." A basin of brine and a cloth were ordered to be brought, with which his stripes were wased, or salted as they called it. During this operation the suffering wretch writhed and groaned as if in the agonies of death. He was then untied and told to go home, and mistress would tell him what to do."

"It frequently happened that torture was inflicted upon slaves and convicts in a more protracted manner than that above described. When the victim of cruelty was doomed by his master to receive the lash, several of his neighbors were called on for their assistance. They attended at the time and place appointed. A jug of rum and water were provided for the occasion. After the trembling wretch was brought forth and tied up, the number of lashes which he was to receive was determined on. Who should begin the operation was decided by lot or otherwise, and the torture commenced. At the conclusion of the first course the operator, pretending great weariness, called for a drink of rum and water, in which he was joined by the company. A certain time was allowed for the subject of their cruelty "to cool," as they called it. When the allotted time had expired the next hand took his turn, and in like manner ended with a drink, and so on until the appointed number of lashes were all imposed. This operation lasted several hours, and sometimes half a day, at the conclusion of which the sufferer, with his hands swollen with the cords, was unbound and suffered to put on his shirt. His executioners, to whom the operation was rather a frolic than otherwise, returned home from the scene of their labor half drunk. Another method of punishment still more protracted than this was that of dooming a slave to receive so many lashes during several days in succession, each whipping, except the first, being called "tickling up the old scabs." Wagoners in the neighborhood have been known to fasten the slaves, and, with a jug of rum, amuse themselves by making the deepest scores on their back for wages."

It has been stated by several in their writings that through the Shenandoah Valley slaves were treated with the utmost cruelty, and the further South it penetrated the worse the barbarity.

The following is taken from an old court docket of 1792: "At a court held in Berkeley County the 4th day of November, 1792, for the examination of Nell, a Mulatto woman slave, on suspicion of feloniously stealing from Amos Davis one muslin sheet, one white linen sheet, one girl's slipp, one flannel petticoat, a large shawl, one white linen handkerchief ruffled, and one black lace tippett. PRESENT: John Cook, David Hunter, James Maxwell, John Kerney and Nicholas Orrick, Gentlemen Justices. THE PRISONER being led to the bar, and it being demanded of her whether she was guilty of the facts wherewith she stood charged or not guilty, said that she was in nowise thereof guilty. Whereof sundry witnesses were examined, on consideration of whose testimony, and the circumstances attending the same, it is the opinion of the Court that she is guilty of petit larceny only. Therefore it is ordered that the sheriff do take her to the public whipping post and there give her thirty-nine lashes on her bare back, well laid on, and then discharge her."

The old dockets show a number of similar cases, in which both male and female were treated with the utmost and most cruel barbarity.

I might here relate many other methods of torture, such as the thumb screw, sweating, the birch, etc.; but it is enough—the heart sickens at the writing of such cruelties. There are several incidents that occurred in our present town, worthy of note, of which Capt. Wm. Hoke, now living, is my informant:

For a long while a whipping post and pillory stood in front of the Court House, (the present site) and was considerably used. It was afterwards removed to the East side of the present jail, and stood between it and the building adjoining, then used as the Clerk's office. Capt. Hoke says he saw three negroes whipped here, Hannah Henson, Taylor Piper and George Casion; and Jim Piper placed in the pillory. The pillory was built above the whipping post, about ten feet from the ground and had a small platform. It was composed of an upright piece, and a top piece laid crosswise, in the shape of a cross. In the top piece was a hole large enough to admit the neck, while a smaller one on each side was made for the two arms. Casion had committed a petit larceny of some kind, and was doomed to the pillory for three or four hours. The day was very rainy, and a number of small boys formed a brigade, under the command of Adam Cockburn, somewhat larger. They then proceeded to rob the hen-nests that were expected to hatch in a short while, and carried off the contents. With their hats nearly filled with eggs, they marched to the pillory and formed in a line in front. Here quite a lively time was had by firing at Casion's head, and occasionally, when a rotten egg would strike, a loud yell went up. In those days this was considered big sport, and participated in by nearly all the boys of the neighborhood.

I asked the Captain whether the authorities made any objection, to which he replied, "No, and I wouldn't doubt but what the authorities put the boys up to it."

Many wars, bastiles, prisons, crosses, gibbets, tortures, scourges and fires, in the hands of despots, have been the instruments of spreading desolation and misery over the earth. Those means of destruction, and their extensive use in all ages, are regarded as indices of the depravity and ferocity of man. From the bloodstained pages of history, one now turns with disgust and horror, and pronounces an involuntary anathema on the whole of his race. The time came, however, in which the master and slave changed situations. The American Revolution was the commencement of a new era in the history of the world. The issue of that eventful contest snatched the scepter from the hands of the monarch, and placed it, where it ought to be, in the hands of the people.

After the foreign war conducted by the United States (which ended February 2, 1848,) the slavery question was considerably agitated, and as years went by the discussion of its merits increased in bitterness. As the country grew rapidly in wealth and population, many began to hope for some compromise that might preserve the national peace, and deemed the abolition of slavery expedient. As each presidential election went by the issue became more clearly—that of slavery or freedom. In 1860 Abraham Lincoln was elected President by the Republican Party on a platform which, while leaving to each State the right to order and control its own domestic institutions, insisted that freedom was the normal condition of all the territory of the United States. On the other hand, the Southern States had made the declaration that the election of a President pledged to oppose the extension of slavery would be a violation of their constitutional rights and a moral invasion of the slave States. In adherence to this declaration, in December, 1860, South Carolina seceded from the Union, and her example was followed by Mississippi, Georgia, Alabama, Florida, Louisiana, Texas, Virginia, Arkansas, Tennessee and North Carolina. Shortly after, (April following,) hostilities were opened by the Confederates and a severe conflict ensued. On the 1st of January, 1863, President Lincoln issued the Emancipation Proclamation. The war continued until April, 1865, in the conduct of which nearly 1,800,000 Union soldiers had been enlisted and a debt of $2,000,000,000 was incurred. During this conflict the negro, (with all due respect to his race) took his stand, and no sooner had the order "to arms" been given than he had taken up in defense of the Union. Numbers have fallen and shed their blood upon the battle plain with a courage that far surpassed many of the white soldiers.

A few weeks after his inauguration for the second term, in April, 1865, President Lincoln was assassinated at Washington, D. C., by J. Wilkes Booth, who was hunted down and killed a few days later. Vice-President Johnson became President, and the work of political reconstruction was begun. The Thirteenth Amendment to the Constitution, abolishing slavery within the United States and places subject to their jurisdiction was duly ratified and proclaimed. In April, 1866, the Civil Rights Bill was passed by Congress over the President's veto, thus insuring protection to the freed slaves and giving to the federal courts enlarged jurisdiction in the matter. In the following June the Fourteenth Amendment was passed, whereby equal civil rights were guaranteed to all, irrespective of race or color.

At the present day this race of people is represented in almost every trade and profession throughout the country. Our county is largely inhabited by them, among whom are to be found energy and enterprise. Some own considerable property and are well to do. They have built and ably support churches and schools of their own, and deserve much credit for the manner in which they have prospered under such marked disadvantages.

CHAPTER X.
LATE WAR OF THE REBELLION—BERKELEY COUNTY'S SITUATION.

INTRODUCTORY REMARKS.

HISTORY indicates that the old County of Berkeley was well represented in the different wars, for nearly one hundred and thirty years past, which form so important a part of the country's history. First, in the year 1755, the French and Indian war broke out, before this county was formed, and the citizens of this section shared in the disastrous defeat of General Braddock. They afterwards served under George Washington, the illustrious Colonel who built Fourt Loudon in the fall of that year, and established himself at Winchester, Frederick County. A terrible conflict with the Indians followed, and these intrepid men took a gallant part, continuing to serve their country against the frequent attacks of the cruel savages, while their depredations lasted. In 1774, two years after the county was formed, a full representation of Berkeley's gallant sons shared in the dearly bought victory over the Indian allies of the British Government, at Point Pleasant. It occurred in the Summer of that year, and was virtually the first battle of the Revolutionary War. About eighty of the volunteer soldiers from Berkeley, under Colonel Drake, were killed in St. Clair's defeat by the Indians. The pages of the country's history, during the Revolutionary War, have been embellished and brightened by the heroic deeds of many of Berkeley's patriotic sons, who aided materially in the cause. The names of many of her gallant sons, who enlisted and served during the long, dark days of that struggle, are not mentioned in history, but its pages record their deeds. A number of them arose to the highest distinction in the army. They were again called upon in the War of 1812, and the county was represented by about 200 men, in the troops which gained one of the most brilliant victories of this war—at the battle of Craney Island, June 22, 1813. In 1844-45, in the war with Mexico, the valorous deeds of Berkeley and Jefferson County men are an important matter of history.

On the 17th day of April, 1861, Virginia passed the ordinance of secession at Richmond, and the people of the State were called upon to take a decided stand upon one side or other in this important issue. Credit must be given those who, after a calm deliberation, and from principles which their best judgment declared to be righteous, took up arms, or exercised their best talents in advocating the cause of the State. Too much credit cannot be given to those who sundered the tender ties that bound them to the homes of their nativity or adoption, sacrificed or endangered all their property interests, and devoted their lives to the defense of the Union— from a high sense of loyalty to the General Government. "Greek met Greek," brother encountered brother, friend stood opposed to friend upon many a hard-fought and bloody battle-field on the soils of Berkeley and Jefferson Counties, and southward in the valley. The adoption of a neutrality was attempted by some, who, perhaps, were the ones to suffer most in the sacrifice of property during the war. They were looked upon with suspicion, and little leniency was shown them by either party. The character of the questions at issue were deemed to be too grave and important to be regarded with indifference by any citizen.

The minds of the grandsons of Berkeley were pervaded in 1861, by the same spirit which animated the heroes of 1776 and 1812, and emulating their noble example, a full representation volunteered who were willing to take up arms, and, if need be, sacrifice their lives in defense of the principles which they had adopted. These heroic men enlisted on both sides. Men equal in intelligence and courage, honesty of purpose and stubborn determination, whose forefathers had fought side by side for the independence of their country during the Revolutionary War; only differing, perhaps, in the circumstances and influences which had educated them into a decided opinion upon the great questions then at issue. This state of affairs was not by any means confined to Berkeley and Jefferson Counties, as it was very general along the border, and notably so here. These men, as heroes, met each other in battle, and did not pause to consider whether the quondam friend, in deadly array against him, came there "through error, perversity, conscience, weakness or chance," but duty of the hour which governed them was to do or die for the cause which they had espoused.

GOING TO WAR.

Berkeley and Jefferson Counties saw much of the war, being located at the northern portal of the Shenandoah Valley—that bloody arena where so many tremendous conflicts occurred. Details of the marching and counter marching of armies, and their frequent engagements, which are incident to this locality, can be read in many a well-written work, and no attempt will be made to record them here in full, but an account of some of the interesting occurrences will be given.

The following reflections of "A Virginian," as he leaves the home of his boyhood, to take up arms in defense of his country, against his native State, but echo the sad thoughts entertained by thousands of others, who, through a lofty devotion to principle, abandoned their homes and cut asunder the closest ties of kindred and friendship, to follow where their duty called them. From the front porch of a house at Fairview, (on the turnpike,) can be had a beautiful and comprehensive view of the Shenandoah Valley, extending as far up as the Massanutten Mountain, above Front Royal and Strasburg. The towns of Williamsport, Martinsburg, and Shepherdstown are distinctly visible, while the sites of Harper's Ferry, Charlestown and Winchester can be distinguished. Upon this azure map the whole circuit of the late campaign could be satisfactorily traced. An old resident living near by stated to the author that he often visited this spot, and that "each field, each house, each clump of trees, recalled some friendly face, some youthful sport, some genial hour of past delight. There, from childhood to maturity, I had lived, opulent in friendships and social sympathy. That fair valley was now the land of mine and my country's enemies; among them I could see whole squadrons of my kindred and former friends—the kindly and generous companions of the olden times. It mattered little to me now how they came to be there—through error, perversity, conscience, weakness or chance. The Potomac that flowed between us now, rolled a fathomless gulf of blood and fire. On this side I was alone. There was neither friend nor kinsman, nor neighbor to whom I might turn for countenance or counsel in those hours of soul-weariness, which oppress one whose individuality is too heavily taxed. On this side I found none nearer to me than the acquaintances of yesterday, marching together as champions of a common cause, but strangers to the heart. I felt the weight of my position. I was an exile indeed—poor, weary and dispirited. Yet I had taken my course after calm and full deliberation. I had asked no man's counsel, and confided my conclusions to one alone."

FIRST APPEARANCE OF "GRIM VISAGED WAR" IN MARTINSBURG.

On the 13th of June, 1861, General Johnston, who in command of the Confederate Army of the Shenandoah, had occupied Harper's Ferry, after burning the railroad bridge and other property at that place, retreated to

Winchester. At this time, General Patterson was advancing, with his army, from Pennsylvania, *en route* through Maryland, for Virginia; General McClellan was also on his way, through Western Virginia, toward the valley. General (afterward "Stonewall") Jackson (in anticipation of the arrival of the Federal troops) was sent, with his brigade, to the neighborhood of Martinsburg, to aid Stewart's cavalry in destroying what they could of the Baltimore and Ohio Railroad stock, and thus check the advance of these opposing armies.

What was known as the "Colonnade Bridge," a beautiful structure, erected in Martinsburg by the company as an especial compliment to the city, was at that time destroyed. The citizens who witnessed it will never forget this, the first appearance in the city of the terrible reality of the war which followed. The bridge was fired one calm and beautiful evening, about eight o'clock, and the saddening effect upon the minds of the large concourse of people who witnessed the destruction was a lasting one. After the burning of the bridge, the troops, by fire, partially destroyed thirty-five large locomotives that stood in the yards west of the bridge. This was a sad error on the part of the Confederates, for there was nothing to prevent their running these engines to Winchester, via Harper's Ferry and the Winchester and Potomac Railroad. Some time afterward, these same engines had their wheels furnished with broad iron tires, by the Confederates, and were hauled a distance of twenty-two miles, over the Martinsburg and Winchester turnpike to the latter place, where they were put in repair and used. Thirty-two horses were required to each engine, to accomplish this feat, and the task of getting them up the hills, through the streets of the city, and on to the straight road to Winchester was accompanied with great difficulty. At the same time the machinery of the railroad shops was taken, and used in the arsenals at the South during the war. It is a remarkable fact that this machinery and all the locomotives but one were regained by the company after the close of the war.

ARRIVAL OF PATTERSON'S TROOPS IN THE CITY.

On the 2nd of July, 1861, Patterson and his troops forded the Potomac at Williamsport, and advanced, by the main pike, towards Martinsburg, and Jackson, at the same time, fell back toward Falling Waters, over the main road leading from Martinsburg to that village. On the morning of the 3rd of July, a company of Patterson's infantry encountered a small force of cavalry near a school house, a few miles north of Martinsburg, where a skirmish ensued, and one of the Confederates was killed, the balance retreating. In the afternoon, the whole column marched into Martinsburg, amid demonstrations of joy and welcome on the part of the great majority of her citizens. A detachment of troops was sent forward to reconnoitre, and Jackson was encountered in a position where he had formed his men in line of battle, with four guns directly across the turnpike, along which the former were advancing. A sharp encounter here ensued, which lasted about an hour, when Jackson continued his retreat, joining the main army under Johnston, at Winchester.

An order which had been issued to Patterson to advance to Winchester and give battle to the Confederates under Johnston, was countermanded, and on the 9th of July, the former renewed a previous application to transfer his army to Leesburg, making that his base of operations, which was granted, but an order from General Scott directed him to continue demonstrations in front of Winchester, until after the battle of Manassas, which was expected to occur on the 16th. On the 15th, Patterson's army proceeded to Bunker Hill, where it remained two days; thence to Charlestown, where they remained in position until the 23rd, when they marched to Harper's Ferry, and, the time of the three months men having expired, they returned home, many of them to reenlist for the war. It was on the 23rd, that the news, so disheartening to the Union Cause, of the defeat at Bull Run was received.

AFTER THE BATTLE OF MANASSAS.

One of the saddest nights of the war, to many of the citizens, was soon after the first battle of Manassas. Two brothers and a cousin fell in that fight, at almost the same moment, and side by side. The brothers (Holmes and Tucker Conrad) were the sons of an old and esteemed citizen—a lawyer of rare ability—Holmes Conrad, Esq. Previous to Virginia's act of secession, Mr. Conrad had taken an active part in favor of adherence to the Union, and made a most eloquent and stirring speech in the Court House, which had great influence, and was afterward published in the National *Intelligencer*. His two sons, both quite young, left their home without the knowledge of their father, and nearly the first news which reached him concerning them was the intelligence of their death. One of the participants in the last sad rite says: "We buried them, with their cousin, Captain Peyton R. Harrison, together in one tomb

> "By the struggling moonbeam's misty light;
> Our lanterns dimly burning!"

"This circumstance is worthy of mention, as the name was a beloved one in our country, and, although we lost many noble ones, on both sides, none more fair, bright and promising than these."

A great awe seemed to have quelled the spirits of the people at this time.

Those who had deceived themselves, or had been deluded by others into the belief that the dismemberment of the nation would be accomplished without bloodshed, now began to realize the true character of the contest that was opening. In the first ebullition of their zeal, the elite of the Virginia youth had rushed to the field, many serving as privates in the ranks. The slaughter at Manassas fell heavier, proportionately, upon this class than any other. In many an aristrocratic mansion, horror and mourning veiled the joy of victory for a season.

GENERAL BANKS' RETREAT.

On the 25th of May, 1862, occurred Banks' disastrous defeat by Jackson, at Winchester, and his retreat, via the Martinsburg and Winchester turnpike, to the Potomac. Those who witnessed the rush of the panic-stricken troops through Berkeley and Jefferson counties will never forget it. Hundreds of wagons, loaded with commsisary, quartermaster, medical, ordnance, and other military stores and supplies, were scattered all along the route, greatly to the delight of many, who, on account of the difficulty of obtaining them, had been living on short rations, and with a scant supply of blankets and clothing. Notwithstanding the efforts of the retreating troops to destroy them by burning the wagons, many of these supplies fell into the hands of those who no doubt badly needed them. For some time afterward, the skill of the dyer was called into requisition, to obliterate the tell-tale material blue, and hardtack became a popular article of diet. This celebrated retreat occurred on Sunday—a day that seemed destined as a season of excitement in this section, Early in the morning, cavalrymen made their appearance in squads of two or three, and about 11 o'clock a. m., four-horse wagons, carrying pontoons, filled with absconding negroes, swept through the streets at a full gallop. It was one of the most disgraceful scenes of the war. In due time, the General and his staff arrived, and dismounting at the principal hotel in town, went into the parlor. Looking into a mirror (the first glimpse, no doubt, which he had caught of himself for several days) Banks remarked: "Well, General, you *do* look worsted."

THE MARTINSBURG HOME GUARDS.

D. H. Strother, (Porte Crayon), in his "Personal Recollections of the war," contributed to *Harper's Monthly*, has the following to say, regarding this quasi-military band, that was organized in the spring of '61: "Not to fall behind the times, the citizens had formed a volunteer Home Guard, for the purpose of police duty and watching over the general welfare of the community. They kept their headquarters at the Court House, sat up of nights, arrested each other, and everybody they found prowling about. It was shrewdly suggested that the peace of the lonely village might have been better preserved if everybody went quietly to bed and minded their own business. But, in times of revolutionary excitement, people cannot keep quiet, even in view of their own safety, and along the border every man seemed to suppose he had the right to constitute himself a special constable, to arrest and cross-question every other man he met, with whose business he was unacquainted. One night, Dick Ganoe, a harmless and well-meaning citizen of the Home Guard, arrested a stranger who was riding into town from the direction of Winchester. Dismounting his prisoner, Ganoe led the way to the Court House, lounging along with his musket under his arm, and his hands in his pockets, as was his wont. The stranger, who followed in apparent acquiescence, quietly drew a pistol and blew the citizen's brains out, then mounted, and continued his journey northward. This shot also terminated the volunteer labors of the Home Guards. It abdicated, and was heard of no more."

EFFECT OF THE WAR ON THE CITY.

Business was almost entirely suspended in Martinsburg during the first years of the war, and at times a great deal of distress prevailed, for lack of the necessaries of life, which were hard to obtain. Considerable damage was done to buildings, but not as much as would naturally be supposed, considering the fighting that was done here, and the length of time the town was occupied by soldiers. From the commencement of the war to the close, there were camps of either Union or Confederate soldiers in the town. Every church and public building was used as barracks, hospital or stable. The court house was continually occupied by troops, during which time valuable papers and records were ruthlessly destroyed. This unwarranted act has caused endless trouble, and it is doubtful if the effects of it can ever be remedied. Fourteen volumes of records of court proceedings and deeds, and many valuable papers are missing from the office of the Clerk of the County Court, and numerous others are badly mutilated.

A great many self-appointed detectives, or spies, existed at this time, who found excellent opportunities to gratify some petty spite against a neighbor, and at the same time cover themselves with glory and obtain great credit for patriotism either in the Union or Confederate cause, as the case might be. A short experience with these enthusiastic reformers, however, and the investigation of cases reported to them, led the officers in authority, upon both sides, to treat them with deserved contempt.

It frequently occurred that a change of occupants would occur in the city several times in one day. At one time, "Hampton's Brigade" (then under command of General "Jeb" Stuart,) numbering about 3,000 cavalry, came into town, and at noon they were driven out by the cavalry under General Kilpatrick; the latter was in turn dislodged in the evening, and forced to retreat across the Potomac at Shepherdstown, fighting all the way—a distance of ten miles. Quite a remarkable occurrence happened upon this occasion. The only piece of artillery that Kilpatrick had with him was commanded by the grandson of the late Philip C. Pendleton, then one of the oldest and most respected citizens of the town. It was planted on the eminence which is now occupied by Green Hill Cemetery, and the first shot that was aimed by the young man at the Confederates, as they retreated southward, penetrated the cone of the roof of his grandfather's house, without, however, doing any material damage. The citizens had many shells left with them as mementos, during the frequent skirmishes that happened about the town. One of them penetrated the walls of the Catholic Church, without exploding, where it remained until several years after the war, before it was removed.

CARE OF THE SICK, WOUNDED AND DEAD.

After the battles of Antietam and Gettysburg, Martinsburg became one grand hospital. Many of the churches were occupied in this way; in many instances, their interiors were completely destroyed. The citizens were as loyal as any situated near the border, and Union soldiers were as kindly treated, and as faithfully nursed, when wounded, sick and suffering, as many of them could have been in their own homes, and the same kindness, was shown to those of the Confederate army. There are many of them living to-day, who bless the good citizens of Martinsburg for their unselfish acts of kindness at this time. The honored dead of the contending armies lie buried in the city cemeteries, and large numbers were committed to their last resting place with the beautiful, sublime service of the Episcopal church. At one time, the rector of Trinity church was the only minister in town, and officiated for all parties for whom his services were required. The German Evangelical Church was composed of Germans, or those of that descent, many of whom were in the United States service. On the evening of February 13th, 1863, Captain G. W. Hicks, of the Ninth Virginia Infantry, arrived in the city, as escort of a government train from Winchester, and quartered in the church building owned by this society valued at $3,500. Through the carelessness of the occupants, it caught fire and was burned to the ground.

THE BLACK HORSE CAVALRY.

The renowned Black Horse Cavalry figured frequently

during the war in Berkeley and Jefferson counties. Their organization was commenced in Fauquier County, Virginia, June 18th, 1859. The first service which the command was ordered to perform was to report to Governor Henry A. Wise, at Charlestown, West Virginia, at which point were being collected the volunteer companies of the State, to insure the execution of John Brown and his associates. A detachment of this company escorted the prisoners to the place of execution, while the rest of the command was employed in keeping the streets clear, for it was feared, even to the last moment, that an attempt would be made to rescue Brown. The day before the ordinance of secession was passed by Virginia (April 16th, 1861,) orders were received by Lieutenant Robert Randolph, commanding the Black Horse Cavalry, and by Captain Turner Ashby, of the "Mountain Rangers," to assemble their respective commands and proceed at once to Harper's Ferry for the purpose of capturing the stores and munitions of war stored there. After remaining there for several days on picket duty they were ordered on similar service to Berlin Bridge. They took a prominent part in the battle of Manassas, and soon afterward were selected as the body-guard of General Joseph E. Johnston. Jackson was accompanied by this cavalry in his expedition to Williamsport, Martinsburg and Harper's Ferry. They continued in the service during the entire war, and became renowned for their exploits.

Considerable time and labor has been given to deep researches concerning our military organizations during the late war. The above mentioned cavalry was organized in Fauquier County, but figured prominently in Berkeley. The different companies organized in this county, with the names of the participants, happenings, etc., are given below. Among the names included are mostly those who enlisted at the time of organization. A number of our men enlisted in other companies, but in nowise pertaining to a Berkeley organization.

COMPANY C, THIRD REGIMENT, WEST VIRGINIA CAVALRY —BERKELEY COUNTY.

[*United States Army.*]

The members of this company were enlisted in the United States service, mainly from Martinsburg and Berkeley County. This regiment was organized by the consolidating of a number of companies that had already seen much service, at Charlestown, West Virginia, in December, 1863. From there they marched to Parkersburg, and thence were transported to Martinsburg. Here it began its summer campaign under Sheridan, through all of which it followed him, participating in all its battles and skirmishes. The history of the regiment is written upon every page that records the conflicts and victories of the Middle Military Division. Its story cannot be more eloquently told than in the simple list of battles it has fought. Among the names upon its banners are: Carter's farm, Newton, Winchester, Bunker Hill, Martinsburg, Hagerstown, Hancock, Moorefield, Martinsburg (second,) Bunker Hill (second,) Bucklestown, Bunker Hill (third,) Stevenson Depot, Winchester (second,) Fisher's Hill, Mount Jackson, Brown's Gap (two fights,) Milford (two fights,) Front Royal and Mount Jackson (second.) The enlistments were as follows:

Captain, Peter Tabler.
First Lieutenant, John E. Bowers.
Second Lieutenant, Albert Teets.
First Sergeant, Jas. W. Kneedler.
Second Sergeant, John Falkenstein.
Third Sergeant, Michael Ferrel.
Fourth Sergeant, Sylvester Ridgway.
Fifth Sergeant, Edmond Wagely.
Sixth Sergeant, Wm. Clendening.
Seventh Sergeant, Levi J. Welshaus.
Eighth Sergeant, Edward N. Loy.
First Corporal, Levi F. Miller.
Second Corporal, Adam Wolf.

Third Corporal, James O. Ross.
Fourth Corporal, Alex. Horner.
Fifth Corporal, Ulysses Davis.
Sixth Corporal, William Deets.
Seventh Corporal, Benj. F. Statter.
Eighth Corporal, Franklin Spencer.
Bugler, David Kiser.
Bugler, Alfred Porter.

PRIVATES.

Anderson, Eri.
Anderson, Jas. W.
Allison, John.
Butt, David.
Burch, George.
Barthlow, William.
Bricker, Levi.
Butt, William.
Colbert, Jesse.
Colbert, Clarkson.
Cross, John A.
Cockran, Hiram.
Cockran, Charles C.
Crowe, James B.
Deets, James.
Fravell, John.
Fizer, John T.
Frushour, Wm. A.
Fleming, Wm.
Gardener, John W.
Hart, Jacob H.
Hays, Jos. H.
Hower, Edmund.
Homer, Robert.
Jenkins, George.
Kline, John W.
Kiser, Isaiah.
Kiser, John.

Lamaster, Theodore.
Lamaster, John H.
Lazzel, Wm. G.
Long, George.
Miller, Isaac.
Myers, Wm. C.
Myer, William.
Murphy, John W.
Murphy, James W.
Murray, Samuel E.
Morgan, Edmund.
Morgan, Elijah.
Morgan, Robert.
Myers, Samuel.
Myers, Jacob.
Novington, John W.
Piles, Edgar C.
Price, George L.
Ridenour, James.
Ridenour, Charles.
Racey, William.
Ramsburg, Elijah.
Reynolds, Elijah.
Stansburry, H. R.
Stafford, John.
Shrout, Andrew J.
Smith, John.
Stoneking, Lewis S.

Stoker, Thomas.
Strawson, H. W.
Street, William J.
Teets, Elisha.
Tichnal, Samuel.
Taylor, James.
Taylor, Samuel H.

Taylor, Ephriam.
Vanansdal, Jerry.
Woodward, Chas. W.
Wise, Thomas.
Wister, Benj. K.
Welsh, Patrick P.
Welsh, Thomas S.

RESIGNED.

Benson, Joseph A.
Shaw, William B.

Stahl, Jonathan.
Wade, Alexander.

PROMOTED.

Conger, Seymour B., to Major, July 29, 1863.

Perry, James S., to First Lieutenant.

DISCHARGED.

Barnes, Lemuel.
Barthlow, Joshua.
Curry, Alonzo H.
Deen, George W.
Green, David S.
Hart, Jacob.
Kines, W. E.
Mercer, Marshall.
McKinney, Alex.
Myers, Enos.

Morgan, Enoch.
Perry, James S.
Pullin, William.
Prossman, William.
Roby, Middleton,
Rude, George. W.
St. Clair, James P.
Shaffer, Balser.
Statler, Andrew J.

TRANSFERRED.

Awman, Benjamin.
Hickman, Gilaspie.

Shaffer, David.

DESERTED.

Butler, Thomas J.
Fitzpatrick, David.

Smith, Mathias B.
Volgarmott, Moses.

CASUALTIES.

Dilly, John R., killed in action May 10, 1864.
Hoffman, John E., killed in action Nov. 24, 1863.
Johnson, Moses, died Oct. 9, 1862.
Light, Isaac J. killed in action April 24, 1862.
Mock, James M., "   "   Aug. 7, 1864.

Pitcher, John W., killed in action Aug. 7, 1864.
Piles, Osborne H., died October 9, 1862.
Pitcher, Chas. W., died Nov. 19, 1864.
Siler, Philip, killed in action Aug. 7, 1864.
Slater, Henry M., killed in action May 10, 1864.
Teets, John,   "   "   "   Oct. 11, 1863.
Yoho, Ezra,   "   "   "   Aug. 7, 1864.

COMPANY B, FIRST REGIMENT, VIRGINIA VOLUNTEERS— BERKELEY COUNTY.

[United States Army.]

This organization was mustered in under Col. Ward Lemon, and organized at Williamsport, Md., May 17th, 1861. At the time of its organization it was composed entirely of Berkeley County citizens. The company was uniformed at Williamsport, where it first entered service to guard a wagon train to Martinsburg. They next returned to the former place, from whence they were ordered to Hancock, Md. Upon crossing the river they were attacked by Ashby's Cavalry, when Lieutenant Hancock was wounded.

The next order received was to proceed to Dam No. 4, and upon their arrival they learned that the Confederates were robbing the store of A. McQuilken, at Hard Scrabble. A number of the company were detailed and crossed the river, wounding two men and capturing a horse. From here they again returned to Hancock, where they had several skirmishes. From Hancock they were ordered to Orleans Road, thence back to Williamsport, thence to Shaffer's Mill on the river, thence to Falling Waters, and from here to Baltimore, where they arrived on the 5th day of February. Three days afterward they were transferred to the 3d Maryland Regiment, under command of Col. David D. Witt. From Baltimore they were transferred to Harper's Ferry, on the 23d of May, 1862, and after a skirmish on Bolivar Heights, they fell back to Maryland Heights. From here they proceeded to Kernstown, thence to Cedar Creek, thence back to

Warrington, Va. At the latter place Captain Joseph Kerns and Lieutenant James Fayman tendered their resignation. The company was them ordered to Little Warrington, Va. Among the principal battles fought upon its banners are: Cedar Mountain, Antietam, Winchester, Fredericksburg, Chancellorsville, Three Days Fight at Gettysburg, Raccoon Ford, and others. Shortly after these battles the company was divided—one half serving under Grant, and the other half under Sherman, until the surrender at Appomattox. The entire company had bravely participated in all the important fights throughout the war, and history records many valorous deeds of this company, though their names are not mentioned.

Berkeley County was most ably represented, and many of her noble and heroic sons have died upon the field in the defense of their country. Like those of the centending enemy, they believed their principles to be just, and took up arms against friend or foe. As far as the roll can be ascertained from surviving members, it is given as follows:

Captain, Joseph Kerns.
First Lieutenant, James Fayman.
Second Lieutenant, John Lowman.
First Sergeant, D. J. Weaver.
Second Sergeant, Wm. Smith.
Third Sergeant, Robert Lowery.
Fourth Sergeant, Jerome E. Pompell.
First Corporal, M. H. Harman.
Second Corporal, Robt. Thompson.
Third Corporal, Harry Strausbaugh.
Fourth Corporal, J. Lewis Cleary.
Fifth Corporal, Benj. Lowery.

PRIVATES.

Ashkettle, J.
Adams, Frisky.
Batch, C.
Bender, Jno.
Bishop, Jno.
Burriss, E.

Ball, Jno.
Bateman, C.
Brown, Wm.
Clevinger, R.
Coyle, James.
Colbert, Geo.
Cann, P.
Claspey, James.
Dickerhoff, Isaac, killed.
Dailey, Arthur.
Denan, A.
Ditman, Jno.
Davis, Joseph.
Davis, Samuel, killed.
Ebaugh, C.
Espenhine, G.
Fahey, Thomas.
Finigan, Patrick.
Gagle, John.
Giser, Christopher.
Goodman, John.
Grace, Israel.
Grindes, R.
Harker, C.
Hipper, A., killed.
Henry, R.
Harman, Hewitt.

Henlane, Henry.
Ingless, Joseph.
Ingram, John.
Israel, Edward.
Johnson, John.
Jones, James.
Johnson, Wm., hung.
Killgore, C.
Korcross, John.
Lincoln, C.
Lupman, Daniel, killed.
Lowery, Benj., killed.
Lowery, Robert.
Murphy, Denis.
Mathews, Frank.
Martin, John.
Prescit, B. F.
Perkins, C.
Potter, R.
Shirk, John.
Sadler, John.
Smith, David.
Sisco, John, killed.
Sisco, Joseph.
Thompson, Samuel.
Unger, John.
Vanmetre, Isaac.

COMPANY "D," SECOND REGIMENT VIRGINIA INFANTRY—"BERKELEY BORDER GUARDS."

[*Confederate States Army.*]

Under the supervision of J. Q. A. Nadenboush, Esq., this company was organized October 31st, 1859. It was composed almost entirely of Berkeley men, who volunteered their services in defence of what they deemed a just cause. This company acted on duty during the Brown raid, and stood guard at Charlestown during the hanging of Brown's men, on the 16th of March, 1860, It was first ordered into service by the Governor of Virginia, to report at Harper's Ferry on the night of April, 1861. It participated in all the important battles fought by the famous "Stonewall Brigade," and ably represented its county. Among its ranks were Berkeley's most gallant and heroic sons. Like all the different companies, the author has been unable to obtain the roll accurately, and with the assistance of surviving members, gives it at the time of organization, as follows:

Captain, J. Q. A. Nadenbousch, wounded at second battle Manassas, August, 1862,—promoted Colonel Sept. 17th, 1862.

First Lieutenant, P. S. Cunningham.

Second Lieutenant, Robt. W. Hunter, promoted Adjutant-General.

Third Lieutenant, Peyton R. Harrison, killed at first battle Manassas, July 21st, 1861.

First Sergeant, Maj. Israel Robinson, resigned to take his command in 67th Virginia Militia Regiment.

First Sergeant, Jno. A. Dugan, wounded at first battle Manassas, July 21st, 1861.

Second Sergeant, C. W. Welsh.

Third Sergeant, E. L. Hoffman, wounded at battle of Kernstown, March 23rd, 1862,—promoted Captain.

Fourth Sergeant, S. H. Fowler.

Fifth Sergeant, Holmes E. Conrad, killed at first battle of Manassas, July 21st, 1861.

First Corporal, E. Ryneal.

Second Corporal, Wm. Kline, promoted Sergeant, Aug. 4th, 1861.

Third Corporal, T. Bentz.

PRIVATES.

Armstrong, Jno. S., wounded at first battle Manassas, July 21st, 1861.

Albin, Wm. B.

Austin, Thos.

Albin, James, killed at second battle Manassas, Aug. 27th, 1862.
Blake, V. B.
Brady, Peter.
Bell, Alfred.
Bales, Adam S.
Boyd, B. R.
Brocies, Wm.
Buchannon, Thos., wounded at first battle Manassas, July 21st, 1861.
Barnett, A. J., killed at battle Mine Run, November 27th, 1863.
Carlysle, Jas. A.
Cline, David A., promoted Corporal August 4th, 1861.
Conrad, H. Tucker, killed at first battle Manassas, July 21st, 1861.
Cage, James.
Custer, Ephraim G., promoted Sergeant Aug. 4th, 1861.
Copenhaver, T.
Chambers, R. D.
Chambers, Jno. M.
Caskey, Wm.
Chevalley, ———.
Day, Jas. W.
Drebbing, C. L.
Doll, R. M.
Dieffenderfer, Wm.
Dugan, Jas. A., wounded by accident in camp, June 28th, 1861.
Dandrigde, E. P., wounded at first battle Manassas, July 21st, 1861.
Dalgarn, S. S., slightly wounded.
Englebright, Jno.
Earson, Joseph.
Fisher, James.
Fisher, John L., killed at battle Chancellorsville, May 3rd, 1862.

Fravel, Geo.
Fryatt, John T., killed at Manassas, July 21st, 1861.
Griffin, Michael, wounded at battle Cold Harbour, June 27th, 1861.
Gardner, Jarvus.
Glass, G.
Hollis, T. W.
Hodges, N.
Homrich, Jas. M.
Hollis, J.
Hollis, T. P.
Halem, M.
Hill, Joseph.
Harrison, ———
Hedges, Owen T., killed at battle of Gettysburg, July 23d, 1863.
Hunter, John C., promoted Sergeant, August 4th, 1861, —wounded at first battle Manassas, July 21st, 1861.
Helferstay, ———
Harman, Wm., wounded at battle of Kernstown, March 23d, 1862.
Harrison, John S.
Hambleton, Wm., promoted Corporal, August 4th, 1861.
Huff, Benj., killed.
Harley, Patrick, wounded at battle Cold Harbour, June 27th, 1862.
Joy, J. F.
Kilmer, George H.
Kearfott, William P.
Kearfott, James L.
Koiner, L. K., wounded at battles of Payne's Farm, Wilderness, and Seven Days' Fight around Richmond.
Kearns, Joseph, deserted.
Lewis, Walter, wounded at second battle Manassas, August 27th, 1862.
Larkins, Thomas.

Leshorn, James W., wounded at first battle Manassas, July 21st, 1861.

Light, William H., wounded at first battle Manassas, July 21st, 1861.

Lewis, Lewis, killed at second battle Manassas, August 27th, 1862.

Leathers, John H.

Meachem, Richard, killed at battle Chancellorsville, May 3d, 1862.

Maupin, T. A., deserted, June 30th, 1861.

Moody, John P.

Miller, Jonathan.

Matthews, Henry C.

McMullen, Charles.

McIntire, John F., wounded at first battle Manassas, July 21st, 1861.

McCleary, Trip, wounded at first battle Manassas, July 21st, 1861.

McGeary, William, wounded at first battle Manassas, July 21st, 1861.

Muhlenburg, Charles.

Marikle, John B., wounded at second battle Manassas, August 27th, 1862.

Marikle, Thomas T.

McWhorter, James W.

Marikle, Joseph S., killed at second battle Manassas, August 27th, 1862.

Nicholson, Thomas.

Oden, Archibald.

Painter, Joseph.

Phillips, William.

Piper, John R.

Parker, Richard.

Rust, William.

Simmons, W., wounded at first battle Manassas, July 21st, 1861; discharged Dec. 5th, 1861.

Scheig, George.

Staub, R. P. H.
Sailes, ———, died of disease.
Suddith, Joseph.
Smith, John, deserted July 5th, 1861.
Smith, William.
Sherrer, George.
Suiter, Charles.
Siler, John.
Steward, T. W.
Staub, John F.
Smeltzer, C. W.
Saville, Albert, killed at second battle Manassas, August 27th, 1862.
Thrush, John M.
Titlow, R.
Vorhees, George F., wounded.
Weaver, Charles, wounded by accident in camp, June 28th, 1861.
Weaver, George.
Webster, R. A.
Wolff, C. A.
Weaver, John, killed at second battle Manassas, August 27th, 1862.
Whitson, Geo. D., wounded at first battle Manassas, July 21st, 1861.

MUSICIANS.

E. B. Hooper, Drum Major.
Wm. Hayden, Assistant Drum Major
E. G. Tabler.
Samuel Hutchinson.
Charles Shober.

While Jackson was retreating from Winchester, by direction of Capt. Hoffman, Lewis Lewis fired the first shot at a Federal scout on the famous Fisher's Hill, where one of the most important battles was fought.

COMPANY "B," WISE ARTILLERY—BERKELEY COUNTY.
[*Confederate States Army.*]

This company was organized in November of 1859, immediately after John Brown's raid upon Harper's Ferry, and was named in honor of Governor Henry A. Wise, of Virginia. The first section of this battery was stationed at Charlestown during the execution of John Brown. On the evening of the 18th of April, 1861, Capt. E. G. Alburtis received orders from Governor John Letcher, of Virginia, to prepare his battery for the march and proceed early the next morning, via. Baltimore and Ohio Railroad, to Harper's Ferry, and there report for duty. History records many heroic and valorous deeds of this company, which participated in the most severe strugles during the war. Its simple list of battles fought, as placed among the names upon its banners are : battle of Manassas, Williamsburg, Seven Pines, seven days' fight around Richmond, Cold Harbor, Savage Station, Frazier Farm, Malvern Hill, Second Battle Mannassas, Boonsboro' Gap, Sharpsburg, Fredericksburg, Chancellorsville, Gettysburg, Chattanooga, Seige of Knoxville, Tenn., Wilderness, Spottsylvania Court House, second battle Cold Harbor, Drewey's Bluff, Five Forks, Siege of Petersburg, Va. The company surrendered with the Army of Northern Virginia at Appomattox Court House, April 9th, 1865. The enlisments were as follows :

Captain, E. G. Alburtis, resigned 1861.

First Lieutenant, James S. Brown ; promoted Captain, January, 1862 ;—wounded at battle of Sharpsburg, June, 1862.

Second Lieutenant, Geo. H. Murphy, transferred to cavalry, 1861.

Third Lieutenant, —— Witherow, resigned in 1861.

Lieutenant, J. C. Pelham, instructor; promoted Captain and chief Stewart's Horse Artillery, 1861.

Surgeon, Dr. J. D. Newman.

Bugler, Jos. Sherrer.

Ensign, John R. O'Neal.
First Sergeant, Frank Smith, transferred.
Second Sergeant, Oliver King,   "
Third Sergeant, Robert Lowery,   "
Fourth Sergeant, John Maxwell, promoted Second Lieutenant, January, 1862;—transferred to cavalry.
Fifth Sergeant, J. R. Couchman, promoted Quartermaster Sergeant, January, 1862.
First Corporal, Henry Wentz, promoted First Sergeant, 1862.
Second Corporal, Barney Stewart, promoted First Sergeant, May, 1861.
Third Corporal, John Hines, transferred.
Fourth Corporal, John S. Robinson, promoted Third Sergeant, June, 1861.
Fifth Corporal, John H. Weddell, promoted Second Sergeant, November, 1861; promoted Second Lieutenant, June, 1862; promoted First Lieutenant for gallantry upon the field of battle, May 1st, 1863; wounded at United States Ford, May 3d, 1863; wounded April 5th, 1365.
Sixth Corporal, Joseph Lantz, promoted First Corporal, June, 1861,—killed at battle of Gettysburg, July 3d, 1863.

PRIVATES.

Alburtis, Samuel, transferred.
Auld, Charles.
Armpriest, Wm.
Boyer, John A.
Blakeney, Edward.
Blakeney, Harry, wounded at battle of Antietam, June, 1862.
Blanchfield, John.
Beard, Geo., wounded at Seven Days' Fight Around Richmond, June 27th, 1862,—wounded in front of Bermuda Hundred, February, 1865.
Bell, Harry, promoted Sergeant, 1862.

Britton, Edward, transferred to Cavalry.
Bowers, John, transferred.
Chambers, G. W., wounded at battle of Spottsylvania Court House, and died, June, 1864.
Clarke, Wm., wounded Seven Days' Fight Around Richmond, June 27th, 1862.
Conway, James, discharged.
Commiskey, Thos.
Cox, Samuel.
Cunningham, David.
Causemenia, ———, wounded and died, June, 1864.
Faulkner, E. Boyd, wounded at first battle of Manassas, July, 1861,—promoted Captain, 1861,—transferred.
Feaman, James, discharged.
Frazier, James.
Fiske, James, discharged.
Fultz, Thornton, discharged.
Gruber, J., discharged.
Hedges, B. S.
Herndon, Thomas.
Harley, James, killed, April 29th, 1863, at Chancellorsville.
Helan, Patrick, discharged.
Hazard, Charles, killed at Cold Harbor, 1864.
Helferstay, Wm.
Hess, Aaron T.
Hill, Christopher.
Iradella, ———, discharged.
Israel, Gilbert.
Johnson, Wm., discharged.
Kisner, Wm., discharged.
Kisner, Wash., discharged.
Kearns, Cyrus, promoted 3d Lieutenant, April, 1862,—killed at Seven Days' Fight Around Richmond, June 28th, 1862.
Kearns, Robert, discharged.
Keyes, John.

War of the Rebellion.

Lucas, Charles, killed, at Seven Days' Fight Around Richmond, June 27th, 1862.
Lucas, Benj., promoted 1st Sergeant.
Lucas, O. M., promoted Corporal, January, 1862.
Lowery, Benj., discharged.
Lantz, Christian.
Lowman, James, discharged.
Lowery, Wm., discharged.
Landers, Michael, discharged.
Mahoney, Patrick, promoted Commissary Sergeant, January, 1862.
McLaughlin, Franklin.
Mulligan, Patrick.
Murray, Patrick.
Moore, J.
Moore, Andrew M.
Markel, Samuel, promoted Corporal, 1862.
Mooney, J. B.
Myers, Wm.
Noland, Wm.
Palmer, Kearney.
Prior, Thomas.
Pendleton, P. C.
Rose, A. P.
Ryneal, P.
Ridenour, Martin.
Reardon, John.
Robinson, Edgar.
Reed, John.
Reed, J. F.
Strayer, A. P.
Sullivan, Edward.
Schultz, Wm.
Sisco, John.
Sisco, Peter.
Shea, John.
Seibert, Joseph.

Suter, T. C.
Scheig, Adolphus.
Strainey, Edward.
Titlow, Robt.
Tate, Robt.
Thomas, B.
Tabler, Martin.
Vogel, John.
Walker, E. M., promoted 1st Lieutenant, January, 1862,—transferred to cavalry.
Walker, G. W., promoted Corporal, 1862.
Wert, H. T.
Wollett, P., discharged.
Wann, John.
Westphall, Chas., discharged.
Whitehurst, James, killed at Knoxville, Tenn., 1863.
Young, John.

COMPANY "B," FIRST REGIMENT, VIRGINIA CAVALRY—
BERKELEY COUNTY,
[*Confederate States Army.*]

About the year 1860 this company was organized, with John Blair Hoge as Captain, and took an important part in the battles of the late civil strife. Composed of loyal and intelligent men, its part was well played. Upon its banner are to be found the names of the largest and most importaant battles fought. The first conflict for which they were ordered out, was the battle of Manassas, which occurred July 21st, 1861. After this they were engaged with the Confederate troops in the various long and bloody battles fought. Among the number are: Battle of Seven Pines, (or seven days fight around Richmond), Wilderness; Fredericksburg; Second Battle of Manassas; Antietam; Gettysburg; Spotsylvania Court House; Petersburg, Five Forks, and others. Berkeley was ably represented by this command, of whose number, many have strewn the battle-Field with blood and life in defense of their just principles. With the army of Northern Virginia, they surrendered at Appomattox, April 9th, 1865. The enlistments at the time of organization are as follows:

Captain, G. N. Hammond, killed at Yellow Tavern, May 12th, 1864.

First Lieutenant, Wm. K. Light.

Second Lieutenant, Wm. T. Noll, promoted as first Lieutenant,—wounded at Gettysburg, July 4, 1863.

First Sergeant, John B. Seibert, discharged.

Second Sergeant, Charles Weller, discharged.

Third Sergeant, Robert .H. Stewart, promoted as 2d Lieutenant,—wounded at Mt. Olivet, October 10, 1864.

First Corporal, James N. Cunningham, promoted as Captain,—wounded at Front Royal, August 21, and at Rood's Hill, November 23, 1864.

Second Corporal, Aquila Janney, detailed in Quartermaster's Department.

Third Corporal, James W. Cushwa, promoted as 2d Sergeant.

PRIVATES.

Armstrong, Archibald, wounded at Spottsylvania, May 8, 1864,—killed at Martinsburg, July 1, 1864.

Auld. Thos. E.

Boley, Benj. F., wounded at Rood's Hill, November 23, 1864.

Bowers, Richard H.

Boyd, John E., promoted as Fourth Sergeant.

Breathed, James W., transferred,—promoted as Captain and Major of the Stuart Horse Artillery.

Bryarly, Robert P., promoted as Third Corporal,—wounded at Tom's Brook, October 9, 1864.

Buchannon, J. C.

Burkhart, R. C.

Carper, Geo. W.

Catrow, John W., wounded at Slatersville, May 9, 1862.

Chapman, Jacob A., transferred.

Combs, J. L. E., bugler; discharged.
Couchman, David, wounded at Slatersville, May 9, 1862.
Cunningham, Charles, killed at Winchester, September 19, 1864.
Cunningham, W. L., wounded at Gettysburg, July 4, 1863.
Cushen, R. D.
Cushwa, Daniel.
Cushwa, David, promoted as 1st Corporal,—wounded at Rood's Hill, November 23, 1864.
Cushwa, Seibert
Frieze, A. J., wounded at Spottsylvania, May 9, 1864.
Frieze, George.
Gageby, John N., promoted as 1st Sergeant.
Gladden, George.
House, Thomas.
Janney, W. H. H.
Jefferson, William M.
Kearfott, James, killed at Rood's Hill, November 23, 1864.
Kearfott, John P., wounded at Kennon's Landing, June 5, 1864.
Kilmer, B. S., wounded at Mount Olivet, October 10, 1864.
Kilmer, Daniel.
Kilmer, David, wounded at Yellow Tavern, May 11, 1864.
Kilmer, H. D., transferred.
Lemen, W. M., Medical Sergeant.
Lyle, R. G., discharged.
Manning, Dennis, wounded at Raccoon Ford, October 13, 1863.
Marshall, Geo. W., promoted as 3d Sergeant,—wounded at Spottsylvania, May 9, 1864.
Marshall, Joseph, died from disease.
Mason, James A.

McClary, Geo. W.
McKee, Mayberry.
Miller, Daniel.
Mong, Wendel, promoted as 4th Corporal.
Murphy, James B., killed at Rood's Hill, Sept. 19, 1864.
Murphy, Richard.
Myers, W. H.
Payne, J. Trip.
Payne, Martin L., wounded at Anandale, Sept. 1861, at Spottsylvania, May, 1864, and at Cedar Creek, February, 1865.
Payne, O. F., wounded at Mount Olivet, Oct. 10, 1864.
Rainer, George.
Roberts, E. S.
Roberts, Geo. D.
Roberts, William, wounded at Cedar Creek, October 19, 1864.
Roush, Charles, wounded at Winchester, Aug. 28, 1864.
Seibert, Abraham, wounded at Manasses, July 21, 1861, —discharged.
Seibert, Eli.
Seibert, John B., discharged.
Seibert, Wendel, promoted as Second Corporal,—wounded at Spottsylvania, May 9, 1864.
Shepherd, James, transferred.
Showers, George E.
Silver, Frank, wounded at Rood's Hill, Nov. 23, 1864.
Silver, Henry.
Small, David.
Small, William
Strayer, D. J. R., wounded at Manassas, July 21, 1861.
Strode, P. H.
Stump, John H., wounded at Yellow Tavern, May 11, 1864.
Tabb, E. W. discharged.
Thatcher, David, killed at Buckland Mills, Oct. 19, 1863.
Thomas, Jacob.

Weaver, Charles.
Weaver, George, killed at Slatersville, Va., May 9, 1862.

COMPANY "E," SECOND REGIMENT, VIRGINIA INFANTRY—
BERKELEY COUNTY.

[*Confederate States Army.*]

This company was organized in the fall of 1859, in the town of Hedgesville and vicinity, immediately after the John Brown raid, when the Southern people became impressed with the idea that their institutions were menaced by northern fanatics. M. C. Nadenbousch, Esq., was its first Captain, and R. T. Colston, a graduate of the Virginia Military Institute, was First Lieutenant. Capt. Nadenbousch having had no military training, very shortly resigned, and Lieutenant Colston succeeded to the captaincy and brought the company to a high degree of proficiency. When the war cloud burst, Captain Colston was ordered to report, with his company, at Harper's Ferry. Company "E" was assigned to the 2nd Virginia Regiment, which formed a part of the famous "Stonewall Brigade," and participated in all the battles in which that gallant corps was engaged. It contained within its ranks some of Berkeley's bravest sons, always bearing itself bravely in every fight. The following is a roll of the company, as near as can be gotten at this late day, obtained from surviving members thereof:

Captain, Raleigh T. Colston, promoted to Lieut. Col. in 1862,—to Col. in 1863, and killed at the battle of Mine Run, Nov. 23d, 1863.

First Lieutenant, David Manor, killed at the first battle of Manassas, July 21st, 1861.

First Sergeant, Wm. B. Colston, wounded at Kernstown, March 23rd, 1862,—promoted to First Lieutenant, April, 1862,—wounded at Fredericksburg, Dec., 15th, 1862,—promoted Captain, May, 1863.

Second Sergeant, John T. Hull, promoted Second Lieutenant, April, 1862,—wounded at Chancellorsville.

Third Sergeant, Chas. W. Manor, wounded at first battle of Manassas, July 21st, 1861,—promoted Orderly Sergeant, April, 1862.

Fourth Sergeant, W. H. Lingamfelter.

PRIVATES.

Bane, Newton.
Basore, Emanuel.
Blamer, James.
Brown, Charles.
Criswell, John L.
Couchman, Geo. W., wounded at second battle of Manassas.
Dugan, James L., lost arm at Seven Pines.
Eversole, John W.
Eversole, Jacob H., wounded at Chancellorsville.
Eversole, Isaac, killed.
Fiery, James, killed at Chancellorsville.
Guinn, James V.
Haines, John J., promoted First Lieutenant, April, 1862,—wounded at Fredericksburg, Dec. 15th, 1862.
Hill, Abraham.
Hull, Geo. W., wounded.
Hull, Dallas, wounded at Port Republic.
Hunter, David, killed at Fisher's Hill, 1864.
Hunter, John A., detailed on signal service.
Jenkins, Asa.
Johnson, William.
Keisecker, Newton, killed at Chancellorsville.
Keyser, John, killed at Fredericksburg.
Lanham, Jeremiah.
Light, Wm. E.
Merchant, Isaac N., wounded at Chancellorsville.
Miller, Geo. W., killed at first battle of Manassas, July 21st, 1861.
Myers, Cromwell L., wounded at Kernstown.
Miller, Harvey A.
Merchant, W. S., wounded at Cedar Mountain.

O'Connor, Michael.
Pike, Frank, Jr., killed at Kernstown, March 23d, 1862.
Pryor, John, wounded on several occasions.
Porterfield, Milton, wounded at battle of Wilderness.
Porterfield, Alexander, killed.
Perregory, William.
Riddle, John, killed.
Rockwell, George W., promoted 3d Lieutenant, 1863.
Sperow, Jacob, killed at Kernstown, March 23d, 1862.
Sperow, George.
Snodgrass, Porterfield.
Sharff, Nicholas.
Stuckey, Samuel A.
Stuckey, John W., killed at second Manassas, 1862.
Small, Reuben.
Small, John M.
Turner, William, killed.
Triggs, Harrison.
Wilson, Valerius.
Weddell, Geo. W., wounded at Kernstown, March 23d, 1862,—at Monocacy in 1864.

COMPANY "A," SEVENTEENTH BATALLION, VIRGINIA CAVALRY—BERKELEY COUNTY.

This company was organized in October, 1861, at Martinsburg, principally of Berkeley County men, with a number from the surrounding counties. It was first stationed at Martinsburg, and acted on picket duty along the border, where it remained until about February 24th, 1862. From here they proceeded to and around Winchester, and afterward fell back up the valley. They next went to Strausburg and Woodstock, afterwards serving on picket duty several days at Millwood and White Post. They were then ordered to Middletown, Harrisonburg and Two Bridges, and from the latter place a detachment of fourteen men were sent to Fort Republic to guard the bridge and prepare it for burning. Here they engaged in two very severe fights, which occurred on the 11th and 12th of May, at Cross Keys and Lewis' Bottoms. From here they went down the valley in rear of Jackson's army and fought at Winchester on the 24th of May of that year, with a part of the company acting on picket duty at Front Royal. They again returned to the border and remained about three days, from whence they fell back with Jackson, who then crossed the Blue Ridge and went into Virginia. This company participated in all the important battles fought during the late civil strife, and many of Berekeley's brave and heroic sons have fell within its ranks in defense of what they deemed a just and worthy cause. It was known during those days as the "Wild Cat Company."

It has been an impossibility to obtain its roll of members full and correct, as the author has been unable to gain any other information than that given by several survivors of the company. The following is a list of Berkeley County men, with officers, etc., as can best be ascertained:

Captain, G. W. Myers, of Baltimore, Md.
First Lieutenant, George Wells.
Second Lieutenant, —— Murray, of Baltimore.

PRIVATES.

Albain, ——
Brittner, Thad, killed.
Blondel, Charles.
Bets, James.
Butler, John.
Carney, J. V., wounded at Darkesville, Sept. 17th, 1862.
Chapman, ——.
Gore, ——, killed at Buckner's Station, May 23d, 1862.
Hedges, Anthony, killed.
Kensel, John J.
Leech, Sid.

Miller, Harvey A.
Mingle, John.
McNemar, Michael, wounded.
Patterson, Frank.
Ronk, Benj., killed at Mt. Jackson, 1863.
Seibert, J. B., promoted Lieutenant.
Strode, Joseph.
Saderfield, ———.
Sayles, William.
Seckman, T.
Turner, John A., promoted Captain.
Teack, S.
Wilson, J. L., killed at Warrington Springs.

This Company left Martinsburg with about 50 members, and was composed of men from Berkeley, Morgan, Frederick and Jefferson Counties, with several from Maryland.

THE BLUE AND THE GRAY.

I.

"By the flow of the inland river,
  Whence the fleets of iron have fled,
Where the blades of the grave-grass quiver,
  Asleep are the ranks of the dead;—
    Under the sod and the dew,
      Waiting the judgment day;
    Under the one, the BLUE;
      Under the other, the GRAY.

II.

"There, in the robings of glory,
  Those in the gloom of defeat,
All, with the battle-blood gory,
  In the dusk of eternity meet;—
    Under the sod and the dew,
      Waiting the judgment day;
    Under the laurel, the BLUE;
      Under the willow, the GRAY.

III.

"From the silence of sorrowful hours,
  The desolate mourners go,
Lovingly laden with flowers,

War of the Rebellion.

Alike for the friend and the foe;—
Under the sod and the dew,
Waiting the judgment day;
Under the roses, the BLUE;
Under the lilies, the GRAY.

IV.

"So, with an equal splendor,
The morning sun-rays fall,
With a touch, impartially tender,
On the blossoms blooming for all;—
Under the sod and the dew,
Waiting the judgment day;
Broidered with gold, the BLUE;
Mellowed with gold, the GRAY.

V.

"So, when the summer calleth,
On forest and field of grain,
With an equal murmur falleth
The cooling drip of the rain;—
Under the sod and the dew,
Waiting the judgment day;
Wet with the rain, the BLUE;
Wet with the rain, the GRAY.

VI.

"Sadly, but not with upbraiding,
The generous deed was done;
In the storm of the years that are fading,
No braver battle was won;—
Under the sod and the dew,
Waiting the judgment day;
Under the blossoms, the BLUE;
Under the garlands, the GRAY.

VII.

"No more shall the war-cry sever,
Or the winding rivers be red;
They banish our anger forever,
When they laurel the graves of our dead;
Under the sod and the dew,
Waiting the judgment day;
Love and tears, for the BLUE;
Tears and love, for the GRAY.

REMINISCENCE.

People's National Bank
— OF —
⇒*MARTINSBURG, WEST VIRGINIA,*⇐
COR. QUEEN AND BURKE STREETS.

DESIGNATED DEPOSITORY OF THE UNITED STATES.

A. J. THOMAS, Pres.   J. B. WILSON, Cashier.

Capital, $50,000.   Surplus and Undivided Profits, $20,000.

A GENERAL BANKING BUSINESS TRANSACTED.

ACCOUNTS OF BANKS AND BANKERS, CORPORATIONS, MANUFACTURING FIRMS, MERCHANTS AND INDIVIDUALS SOLICITED.

COLLECTIONS

RECEIVED UPON ALL ACCESSIBLE POINTS, AND RETURNS PROMPTLY MADE AS DIRECTED. CAREFUL ATTENTION GIVEN TO THE BUSINESS OF CORRESPONDENTS.

Domestic and Foreign Exchange Bought and Sold.

PRINCIPAL CORRESPONDENTS:

FIRST NATIONAL BANK, New York City,
COM. EXCHANGE NATIONAL BANK, Philadelphia,
WESTERN NATIONAL BANK, Baltimore,
SECOND NATIONAL BANK, Washington.

CHAPTER XI.
HISTORICAL REMINISCENCE OF MARTINSBURG, FROM THE YEAR 1832 TO THE YEAR 1861, WITH STATEMENTS COVERING MANY EVENTS OCCURRING SINCE THE CLOSE OF THE LATE CIVIL WAR.

BY JOHN W. CURTIS.

[*Written especially for the author of this work, and copyrighted according to law. All rights reserved.*]

DURING my early childhood days there were still many Revolutionary heroes, old, and in many cases, decrepid, who would often entertain company at the hotel, by relating personal experience of the times through which they had passed; also, many yet who had been engaged in the Indian wars. Among them was one Peter Cook, who had been in St. Clair's defeat in Ohio Territory. He would exhibit the effect of a terrible struggle which left him maimed for life, and was one of only 123 that reached the white settlement from the defeat. His right foot was cut off diagonally up to the instep of the foot, leaving only the little toe. He shot an Indian who feigned death, and went to get his arms, when the Indian arose with tomahawk and cleft his foot off at one blow. He had a severe struggle, and finally getting the tomahawk, he buried it in the top of the Indian's head.

Many thrilling instances of escape, as well as personal struggle in border warfare, would be related in which the parties were personally engaged. There seldom passed a week that more or less Indians, in their native dress and natural ferociousness of character, came through town. They would be fully equipped with bow and arrows, and tomahawk, with knife hanging to a band of undressed deer hide around their waist. They would often shoot at coin placed in a split stick—if hitting, it was theirs; upon missing, they would throw on the ground the same coin. Our silver coin at that time was the Picayune, or 6¼ cent piece. The bit of 12½ cent piece, and the Hispanola of Pillar, 25 cent piece, were all Spanish coin. The Mexican Pillar or Spanish, and the American silver dollar, copper half and one cent pieces, were used as American coin. I have no early recollection of seeing the American five, ten, twenty-five and fifty cent pieces until after passing up to full youth.

The Indians generally passing through our valley were from Kentucky and Tennessee, and were enormous eaters. On one occasion four arrived and stopped at the hotel. Three at once commenced shooting at coin, and the other came in and asked for food. A full large loaf of bread, with an ordinary size ham, was placed before him, and he was left to help himself. Upon returning nothing was left except the bone of the ham.

When a child the whipping post occupied ground directly in front of your present, and also old Court House door. One Christmas morning it was found blown to pieces. Parties had bored holes in the stock and charged them heavily with powder, destroying it for all future use. A new one was afterward erected in the space between the jail and next house east, which was then the Clerk's office.

The first event to make a lasting impression and fix itself upon my mind was of a political character, and will show the devices resorted to at that period to claim and hold party fealty. It was in my fourth year, and had my home at a large hotel, the headquarters of the Democratic and Republican parties. During the congressional canvass of 1832 General Jackson was President, and a procession and barebcue was held late in the evening, and the Democracy addressed from a stand in front of the hotel. On the street was a wagon drawn by six horses, beautifully caparisoned, and fixed upon it was a good-sized hickory tree in full leaf and foliage. Upon each twig, branch, limb, in fact all over it, was hung the American silver dollar, tied by blue ribbons, and at every vibration of the tree the delightful tingling money sound would strike upon the ear. This device was to show the Democrats' hostility to the then Federalists' financial system and United States Bank, which had absorbed and held in its vaults nearly, if not all, coin in the country, ruinous to all commercial pursuits and crippling the Government very seriously in its Treasury Department. My entire boyhood days were spent at this hotel, and up to almost middle life it was the headquarters of the Democracy, and every meeting of the county was held there. Old Tammany or Billmire's Hotel was situated on the southwest corner of King and your present German streets. It was not for many years that any other streets had names, except King and Queen, they being then as now, the principle business streets.

The other hotels were the Globe, Wm. Kraesen, proprietor, occupying the site on King street opposite your St. Clair Hotel, as far up as Grantham Hall east, and adjoining property now owned by E. Herring, Esq.; a hotel with different proprietors, called the Claycomb House, where the present Lambert saloon is, on Queen street; the Gardner House, owned by Peter Gardner, an eccentric good old German, which is now the Eagle Hotel, on Queen street; also the Kelley House, (proprietor unknown) located on your present Martin street, directly opposite the home of Dr. Myers. The old town up to the year 1837 was what might be called a good-sized village, with possibly 800 and could not have exceeded 1,000 inhabitants. Each day four stages arrived and departed— one to Hagerstown, one to Shepherdstown, one to Winchester, and one to the Warm Springs, now known as

Berkeley Springs. All traffic and trade was carred on by wagons and teams. Every hotel tried to secure the custom, and it was very evenly divided. No such things as a railroad was thought of in our every-day life, although occasionally I could hear among the drivers of teams about the horse railway from Baltimore to Ellicott's Mills. The manufacture of wools was carried on largely at a factory belonging to the Gibbs family. It occupied the present locality of or about your pump-house for water works; also a large foundry on same locality, of which the Gibbs were proprietors, and superintended by John Keys, who raised a large family, one of whom, Philip, is now living at Keyser. Distillers for whisky and fruit were scattered around, the principle one being Flaggs', east of town. Flour was largely manufactured and shipped. The Stevens mill, now owned by Geo. M. Bowers; the Ransom mill, now Hannis'; the Tabb and Hibbard mills on Tuscarora, west of town, now Kilmer and Bender's mills, were all large grinders. Each farmer had his own grain ground for toll, and sold the flour as needed at home, or else hauled it to Baltimore markets, bringing back for the merchants dry goods, groceries, etc. At the site of the present Fitz mill was an oil mill, where flax-seed was ground and oil extracted for sale. Blacksmithing, wagon-making, furniture manufacturing, cooperage, saddle and harness making, tailoring, shoe-making, watch repairing, house carpentry, tinning, white-smithing or lock making, brass foundry and copper kettle making were carried on extensively, and many manufactories had wagons on the road selling their articles of trade.

Our fathers and mothers were an active, busy people. The mode of preparation of food by cooking was of an entire different character than at present. We had no stoves and knew nothing about them, except the old ten-plate All our cooking was done in stew pans with long handles, Dutch ovens, spitts, frying pans, etc., on an open hearth, using live coals from the chimney where full cord wood had been burnt down. Our bread was baked in ovens specially built for such purposes. In preparation for baking, batch was set in large dough-trays over night and worked out in the morning into loaves, each of which was placed in a bread-basket made of straw, closely knit together by hickory withs. In these baskets the bread was again raised for baking, and afterwards turned upon a large paddle used in placing it in the oven, where it rested upon the heated floor, and generally came out with a crisp, nice crust, and was fit for the stomach of an epicure.

The sports of the day were of similar character to the present. Boys played town, ring and corner ball, ran the fox, and at certain seasons played marbles in various games, shooting in holes being much in vogue; in winter enjoying skating. A large pond of water was near town, known as the Waite lot, where many days of sport in skating were enjoyed. Hop, skid and jump, mumbly meg, hide and seek, and many other games were indulged in. The older boys took much delight in flying large kites, sending up hot air paper balloons, throwing fire balls, etc. The men would get up bull baits, where they would have a large, fierce bull tied by the horns with a cable rope, and fastened securely to a stake planted deeply in the ground. They would try the metal and ferocity of a class of fierce bull dogs. One to three at a time turned on the animal, and which ever dog took a nose hold and threw the bull, received the reward of champion, and possibly its owner some compensation. Much betting was engaged in as to the merits of the different dogs. There was also a weekly chicken or cock main fought somewhere in town. They also passed much time in pitching quaits, wrestling and jumping, and on everything betting was prevalent. Much drinking was done,—persons usually buying liquor by the pint or half pint, and drinking it at a table from little tin cups called jiggers. This was the general custom up to 1837, when drinking at the bar by glasses became customary. No liquor was sold except at regular licensed hotels, and no license granted except upon condition, that stable room for not less than three horses and beds for nine men, were on the premises; and they were then licensed as *ordinary's*, not as hotels or inns.

The school accommodations of the times were limited, in the extreme. Old Capt. Maxwell taught for years in a house on your present Burke Street. In the basement of the Lutheran Church different persons taught. My first day at school was under the present church site, the teacher being a Mr. Young, who by his filthy habit of profuse tobacco spitting on the floor, was disrespectfully called by the scholars "Old Peal Garlic." He was better known by that than his own name. He was succeeded by a Mr. John Byers, from Shepherdstown, who continued a long time as tutor, and many of my age then going to him, owe him a deep and mighty debt for his loving care over us, both as to morals as well as the secular knowledge he gave us. I think your good citizens, J. E. Hill, Joseph Painter, Jacob Swartz, and possibly others will join me in his praise. On the hill near the Catholic and Episcopal cemeteries was a stone building called the accademy, then taught by a Mr. Bascom, succeeded by a Mr. Caney and others whose names have passed from memory. In the building now occupied by the priest, in charge of the Catholic Church, a Mrs. Little taught exclusively, a female school. This embraced all the schools of the town, until after the year 1840, which I will enumerate when I reach that year.

The Presidential campaign of 1836, with Martin Van Buren for President, and R. M. Johnson* for Vice-President, as Democratic candidates, with Henry Clay as the

---

*Johnson was called old Tecumseh, having the reputation of killing this great Indian Chief in the Indian war of 1834, in the then territory of Indiana.

Whig candidate, passed without much excitement, although the great questions of the day being as is now. The Whig measure was Tariff for Protection, or Tariff for Revenue, with incidental protection a Democratic policy. The Democratic measure was the recharter of the old U. S. Bank, advocated by Henry Clay, as against the Sub-Treasury system. The Democrats being successful in the election of Van Buren and Johnson, with a large majority in the lower House and Senate, everything remained quiet politically.

In 1837 the old town was moved wonderfully. A large camp, having 37 canvas tents, suddenly appeared on level ground beyond the present Green Hill Cemetery. They proved to be the Surveying corps, locating the route of the Baltimore and Ohio Railroad, among whom were a Mr. Latrobe as principal, and his immediate officer in charge, a Mr. Shipley, and many others with whose names I was once familiar, but have now passed from memory. It gave new life and impetus to everything. The house, known afterward as Everett House, was improved and converted into a hotel, of which my uncles, John and Mike Billmire, became proprietors for the years 1838 and 1839. This house became headquarters in town for Civil Engineers when from camp. They removed their camp to the ground now occupied by Mr. J. W. Bishop, above the Fitz mills, and remained there for several years. On the 22d of February, 1839, the citizens of the town tendered an honor to the Civil Engineers, which they accepted, and a grand ball was held at the old Tammany House, to which my uncles were caterers. The military spirit of the people of Martinsburg was always good, and at that time the Lafayette Guards, under command of Capt. John S. Harrison, was a crack company. Under superior drill and beautifully uniformed, was present also many soldiers from Cumberland, Md., belonging to a company called the Continentals. Their dress consisted of navy blue cloth, with buff facing on the breast; buff vest, many of yellow tanned deer skin; short knee breeches with white hose attached by large buckles, and low slippers, something like an Indian moccasin. They made a beautiful appearance, and taking all in all, the ball was a grand occasion.

The churches of the town from 1832 to 1840 remained unchanged. There was on the corner of John street and the graveyard an old log building, which had been occupied in common by the Lutheran and German Reformed denominations, services being conducted in the Dutch language. It was abandoned when I first knew it. Inside it was weatherboarded to the apex of the roof, with the entrance on the corner. The quaintest high back pews were placed diagonally across the church, in order to face a pulpit nearly, if not fully, fifteen feet high, as it was reached by 17 steps, ascending spirally from the corner of the chancel. It was capped by a box that came above the waist of an ordinary sized man, and just big enough for him to stand in without a seat, from which he delivered his sermon. Above the entrance was a gallery in which was a large pipe organ, and above was a small belfry. The bell used here is said to be the one now in use on the German Reformed church, at least when that church was erected it was so stated. The M. E. Church had a stone building on East John street, and is now occupied as a residence. The Presbyterians had a church on King street, which was destroyed by soldiers during an early period of our late civil strife, the lot being still unoccupied. The German Reformed worshipped in this church for a number of years. The Catholics had a stone church located near the centre of their present cemetery. Protestant Episcopal church had an abandoned church structure of stone, and its location was at the entrance to their present cemetery. I cannot recall where they worshiped until the present church was erected, which was near 1850—although I knew the pastors in charge of Parish, a Mr. Johnson and Tallifaro, after which came Rev. Mr. Chisholm, who volunteered and nobly entered in company with the then Catholic Priest, Rev. Mr. Plunkett, as nurses for afflicted yellow fever patients in Norfolk and Portsmouth, both of whom died in discharge of christian duty and charity. The Lutheran Church has always occupied the present site on corner of Queen and Martin Streets, much improved from its original structure, which was very plain and unobtrusive.

During the years 1838, '39 and '40, business began to expand and stretch away from the centre of the town. All the stores, dry goods, groceries, druggists, etc., had been on the now Grantham corner, also Wilson and Boreman property, up to the business house now occupied by Frank Doll & Co., and were confined within that limit. Railroad contractors began to come in, and established stores in order to supply their employees, selling and trading with the public just as the regular established merchants. In 1832 we had but one drug store, located in Commodore Boreman's house, with Israel Young as proprietor. Grantham Hall corner was occupied by Thos. C. Smith; Wilson corner, by John K. Wilson and William Anderson; Continental corner, by Isaac Locke; opposite corner, now Sheriff's office, by Alex. Robinson; Frank Evans tobacco store, by Daniel Burkhart and Geo. Doll; store house of C. Thumel, by Wm. Long & Sons; Frank Doll & Co's stand, by a Mr. Hogmire. The corner of the then Faulkner property, now occupied by the People's National Bank, was used by Robt. Rush, a son-in-law of Daniel Burkhart. Jacob Hamme and James Stevens did business in the old Baker building. Their trade was general merchandise, groceries, hardware, queensware, and whatever people wanted. No one branch was confined to itself as is now often the case. It is a noted fact, often spoken of in my presence as true, that every merchant doing business under the old regime and system failed.

In the fall of 1838 Wm. Lucas, father of Hon. D. B. Lucas, was the Democratic candidate for Congress. His opponent was a Col. Barton, of Frederick County, the Whig candidate. Mr. Lucas was elected, the district being overwhelmingly Democratic, embracing, if my memory is not at fault, the counties of Jefferson, Clarke, Page, Warren, Frederick, Berkeley, Morgan, Hampshire and Hardy. The system of voting was *viva voce*, or open spoken ballot. The right of suffrage was only given to land owners and other property qualification. A land owner could vote in each county where his name was entered in the Land Book if he could reach a voting place within three days, for which time the polls were kept open. This system continued up to the year 1851 and 1852, at which time the new Constitution was adopted, that extended the right of suffrage to every white man 21 years of age and over, not disqualified by pauperism or mental incapacity. The elections were confined exclusively to Presidential, Congressional, State Senate and Legislature. All county officers were appointed by the Governor of State. Berkeley County was one of the reliable old Federalist and Whig counties of the State, and Democracy was frowned upon with apparent contempt. Under the old regime of restricted suffrage all the wealthy and leading citizens seemed to belong to that party. General Boyd, whom I just remember, Col. Ed. Colston, Moses Hunter, Col. E. P. Hunter, Judge Philip Pendleton, Capt. Van Doren, Col. R. V. Snodgrass, Col. Jacob Myers, Benjamin Comeqy, Wm. T. Snodgrass, Samuel Henshaw, William Cunningham, Andrew McCleary, Dr. Allen Hammond, Hon. C. J. Faulkner, Tillitson Fryatt, Barton Campbell, Jacob Weaver and many others were leading, wealthy citizens, and each one an ardent Federalist and Whig. On the other side ardent Jackson Democrats were such men as Col. Robinson,

James W. Gray, Wm Barney, George, Jacob and David Seibert, Moses S. and Lewis Grantham, lame Mike Seibert, Dr. John Hedges, Dr. John S. Harrison, Dr. Thos. S. Page, Dr. Chas. Magill, John and Jacob Painter, Alex. and Geo. Newcomer, Abraham Williamson, Geo. and William Sperow, Rev. John Light, Jacob, John and Daniel Lefever, Samuel and Hezekiah Hedges, Peter Gardner, John and Michael Billmire, and many others.

The Democrats never failed having a candidate in the field, but invariably met with defeat in county elections for Legislature. For the State Senate the District was always reliably Democratic, as was also the case for Congress. The Presidential election of 1840,—M. Van Buren, Democratic candidate, with W. H. Harrison and John Tyler as candidates of the Whig party, was the most exciting and strongest contest and furor that this county has possibly ever passed through. General Harrison was a noted successful Indian warrior, and very popular as the Governor of Northwest Territory. He lived in a plain log cabin on the prairies of Indiana, and gave full, free entertainment to whomever called. His customary drink was hard cider, handed in a common gourd cup. His cabin was covered with coon skins. This gave the Whig party the opportunity to build log cabins on a wagon—the interior holding in large casks his favorite drink, with live coons confined by chains on the roof or wherever they could get a foothold. The Democrats tried to bring the canvass within the province of principles and discussion of political questions, but were overthrown by the public furor and excitement of honoring a good old soldier who had spent the flower of his life in dangerous public service on the frontier. They could not be drawn from giving him the deserved honor. He was a Whig President without policy or chart, and only lived one month. When dying he was succeeded by John Tyler, the elected Vice-President, who had, all his previous life, been recognized as a Democrat, and it was no surprise when in forming his cabinet, with the exception of Daniel Webster, Secretary of State, that his selection should be of the conservative Democratic element. He was cursed by the Whigs, but ardently supported by Democrats.

The year 1841 was uneventful, except the fact that process of grade and bridge building on the railroad was in progress, with a large number of employés, most generally of a foreign element. From about Vanclevesville, on the East, to North Mountain, west of town, the employés were all from Ireland. Beyond that to near Sleepy Creek, they were German—growing out of the fact that contractors were Irish at one place and German at the other. A Mr. Wm. O'Neal had the contract East of town, from Green Hill Cemetery to about one mile East of Opequon Creek. Immediately through the town a Mr. Eads was contractor, and beyond Dry Run, West, a German by name of Rotterman, was contractor. I knew them all personally, as they were boarders at my home.

On St. Patrick's day of this year, an old gentleman by name of Gallaher, was honored by the jokers of the town in having a "paddy" hung upon a tree in front of his residence. He took it in as a good joke, and carefully taking it down, gave it to us school boys that were present, provided we would carry it upon a board as a bier and he would walk as chief mourner on the street to the Everett House, which we did. The "paddy" was left there in the care of a colored man for future use. On the night of the 31st, "paddy" was removed to Tuscarora Creek, at foot of John street,—carefully placed in the water with one foot showing boot sole near the top, and the balance of the body seen under water, which to every appearance was a drowned man. Wm. Reed, on his way to the factory, made the discovery. He immediately reported the fact to the Coroner, Mr. Anthony Chambers, who summoned a jury of inquest, and to the disturbance of many a breakfast. Citizens of the town hastened to this ghastly sight. The jury was placed solemnly on each side of the bridge, and parties detailed to bring the body out for view before them. One seized hold of the floating leg, when off came the boot, exposing the straw filling of the "paddy." At this moment arose the cry loud and long, "April fool." It would be impossible to describe the angry, vengeful excitement of the coroner, jury and citizens, who had been so fearfully fooled.

In the month of December of this year, 1841, the trial of a colored man name John, charged with the murder of a white man named Colbert, who lived near the mouth of Opequon Creek, occurred before the County Court. Jacob Weaver was Chief Magistrate, with four Associate Justices, and the full bench were present. He was convicted and sentenced to be hung—time fixed in February, of 1842. It was the only public execution that had taken place since about 1830, of which event I only have a traditionary knowledge. Three colored men were charged and convicted of highway robbery, and were executed by hanging on the Winchester road near town. They claimed innocence, and predicted that it would be attested by a fearful storm before the people dispersed from the ground. It seemed to be a well established fact that such storm did occur - of wind, rain and hail, which was very destructive to growing corn, and also grain crops, just harvested. The sympathy of the public was much excited in behalf of this poor colored man John, and great efforts were made for his reprieve, but without avail. Time arrived for execution, and an immense crowd assembled to witness it. He was placed upon his coffin in an open barred ladder wagon at the jail door, and was guarded by the Lafayette Guards, squad walking in close double file on either side. Immediately following were the sheriff and Deputies—C. D. Stewart, D. C. Burns and Cornelius Comeqy, with Rev. Charles Martin, of the Lutheran Church, his spiritual adviser. The column commenced moving, John, singing in a quiet, plaintive-touching tone the hymn "When I can read my title clear to mansions in the skies, I'll bid farewell to every fear and wipe my weeping eyes," which he kept up until the gallows was reached. The place was just beyond Norborne Hall, or Cumberland Valley Depot, in a deep ravine surrounded by rising rocky ground. I witnessed his ascent to the platform—and farewell with the minister, and immediately hastened away. The rope broke and a fearful cry arose from the lookers on. John was helped up and again ascended to the platform, from which he was soon suspended. He was buried beneath the gallows, from where his remains were removed and dissected by the physicians of the town, in an old abandoned brew house on Spring alley, near Liberty Spring. He was skinned and his hide tanned by a colored man named Wm. Piper, who gave to a friend of mine a strip of the hide that I have often seen used in sharpening a razor. Nothing unusual, that I can recall, occurred this year, 1842.

As usual and according to law, in the month of May each year, the militia met for field evolution and marching, and to answer to the call of their name from the record of the regiment, as a member of the militia of the State. It was preceded by four days drill of officers, Captain and Lieutenants, with Major, Adjutant, Colonel and other officers. Sometimes the General of Division would be present. General Carson, of Winchester, is the only live militia general that I had ever seen. Our Colonels of Regiment 69, during my early days, were E. P. Hunter, R. V. Snodgrass, and last, Jacob Sencindiver, who was in command on last general muster in May 1861. During the years 1842 and '43, rail-laying began and passed beyond the town. One of the most wild and excited times, occurred on general muster day, in one of these two years. The regiment had just been formed in marching order, when suddenly, and for the first time, the piercing whistle of a steam engine broke upon the ear. Regiment, officers and men broke ranks, and running pell-mell, were soon on the hill beyond the mill now owned by Geo. M. Bowers, waiting with anxiety the arrival of this monster. There was no more mustering, and the day was given up to general drinking, carousing, rioting and fighting.

In 1843 I became fully identified with the business of the town, entering the store of R. P. Bryarly & Co. The other merchants were G. and C. W. Doll, John H. Likens, Mevorel Locke, D. S. White, Hamme & Stevens, John W. Boyd, John Jamison, Washington Kroesen and possibly others; drug stores, Wm. Dorsey, W. H. Hezeltine, and Adam Young. We had no clothing stores. Cloths and cassimeres were manufactured into clothing by regular tailors, who were Hiram Bowen, Hugh McKee, Pat. Cunningham, Ezekiel Showers, Wm. Billmire and John and Wm. Hoke, each of whom employed journeymen with many apprentices. One confectionery and cake stand was kept by George Raenhal. During this year one freight train with a passenger car arrived in the early morning, and returning East in the afternoon. The depot was a small shed roof building, occupying site of stone wall on your present platform, and Mr. John Jamison was the agent. At or about this time Archibald Oden opened his house as a hotel, where the present St. Clair stands, and it became the leading hotel of the town. Wm. L. Boak occupied the Everett House as an hotel. The market house for the town occupied a space in front of King Street Hall, which was then the M. E. church. It was a rough stone structure, with roof reaching very near the ground, and open lattice wood-work for the front—standing square on Queen street on a line with Commodore Boreman's residence. There was space all round for market wagons. A good joke was played off by the bad boys of the town upon two eccentric characters named Gano, father and son. Jim and Dad were the only names I ever heard for them. They attended market often, and would drive their wagon behind the market house, and there leave it for the morning. On this occasion they were loaded with buckwheat flour. The boys unloaded the wagon, detached the wheels, taking it by pieces upon the roof and there replacing it in perfect running order, carried up the buckwheat, reloaded it and left. The opening of market was from 2 to 3 o'clock A. M. On this particular morning it was dark, rainy and a heavy fog prevailing. The wagon being missed an alarm was raised, and officers of the town employed to find the stolen property, without avail. When daylight came, lo, and behold! on the roof of the building was found the stolen property intact with nothing missed. Ever after, however, Dad and Jim took good care to drive their wagon into the hotel yard. Another good and surprising joke was perpetrated sometime previous to this. A Mr. Wm. Thompson had running at large, and very tame, a small jackass. The boys got hold of him one Saturday night, took him up in the Court House, and from the floor of the gallery raised him by block and tackle into the steeple, and placing his head out of a window just below the hall, secured him and left. He was a great animal for braying and gave always a very hideous sound. On Sabbath morning, the people on their way to church, were greeted by him looking out of the steeple window. Mr. Thompson and the town authorities offered large rewards to discover who committed this offence, however, without success. Nothing that I can recall of moment occurred during this year.

In 1844 came on the Presidential election. The Democrats presented James K. Polk for President and George M. Dallas for Vice-President. The Whig party Henry Clay and Theodore Frelinghuysen. The contest was carried on fairly and honorably, with each advocating clear and distint principles much animated, but no furor and excitement. The question of admission of Texas as a State being advocated by the Democrats and bitterly

Reminiscence. 265

opposed by the Whigs, seemed to be the leading question, and gave success to the Democracy. It is my impression that before Polk took his seat, on March 4th, 1845, Texas was admitted by action of the Senate and lower House, and approved by President John Tyler.

Early in 1845 John C. Fremont raised a company of volunteers for the purpose of exploring the Rocky Mountains. Among the number was a native of our county, Henry Vincenheller, a millwright by trade, which identified us with the grand undertaking and claimed our interest with its success or failure. No one ever appeared to know what became of him. Many of the volunteers perished before Freemont was heard from, as the conqueror of California in part. There was great activity in raising recruits for the army, and many of our young men enlisted, only two of whose names I can recall— Samuel Caskey and John Myers. During the fall months the question of war with Mexico was constantly before us, finally reaching a climax by the call of the Government for volunteers. In the month of December daily the fife and drum passed through the streets, morning and evening each day, a new face appearing in the company. Capt. E. G. Alburtis, Daniel Poisal, Otho Harrison, a Mr. Gray, William Sherrard, Samuel K. Stucky, John and Jim Bear, John Gallaher, John Ott, a young Blondell and John Jamison were among the first. After several weeks a company of 46 men was formed, of which Dr. John H. Hunter and Wm. Keefe were part. Col. Hamptrammeck, of Shepherdstown, Hon. C. J. Faulkner and others spoke at a public meeting, and it was not a great while until a company was fully formed and left for Fortress Monroe, the place of rendezvous for Virginia volunteers. One came back, not passing examination from loss of one eye. One, the young Blondel mentioned, died at the fort. All the others, I believe, returned after peace was declared without injury in any way, except Lieutenant Gray, of whom no information was ever given as to his fate. The war closing, the country was prosperous and largely extended in territory.

The year 1849 arrived, at which time came wonderful reports of gold discoveries in California. Nearly every one seemed disposed to strike out for the wealth said to lay on the surface of the ground, only waiting to be picked up and brought into use, Many of our young men joined companies and left, very few of whom have ever returned, and many have perished from disease, want, and neglect to provide and equip themselves for such a trip through the wilds of the Rocky Mountains, which previous to Fremonts's exploration was termed the Great American Desert. From the year 1844 up to the year 1849, I occupied the position of Deputy Postmaster under John H. Likens, and the position gave me wonderful opportunity to know the people of both town and county. In the Presidential year of election, 1848, the Democrats presented Lewis Cass for President—name for Vice-President not remembered. The whig party presented the grand old warrier, General Taylor, with Millard Fillmore for Vice-President. Owing to dissension in New York, M. Van Buren was run on a local state question to some extent, and brought up for the first time the question of Free Soil on Free Territory, as against the Extension of Slavery. James Birney also ran as an avowed slavery Abolition candidate—the result being the defeat of Cass and success of Taylor; the slavery question entering largely into the contest nationally for the first time in my knowledge. Taylor lived but a short time and was succeeded by Millard Fillmore, Vice-President, who was a good man—conservative and national in his recommendations and acts, but not popular with the extremists of the south. There was wonderful agitation and excitement, and almost war, which was averted only by a compromise measure offered by Henry Clay, but which opened up a question called the Missouri Compromise, and again in a few years opened up the full agitation of the slavery question. The South was kept in a continuous condition of excitement, by the strong and vicious talk of war for the protection of slavery. The rights of the South and their violation by the North, was a constant theme of discussion, both public and private. There was no peace or quietness to be found in any community south of the Potomac River.

In the year 1851, a convention for constitutional change was called for and held. The delegates from our district elected, were Dr. Dennis Murphey, Hon. Andrew Hunter, Hon. C. J. Faulkner and one other, whose name I forget. The constitution was presented before the people and approved by popular vote, which extended the right of suffrage to every white man not disqualified by mental incapacity or pauperism. This gave Berkeley County a large Democratic majority for the first time in its history, except on two occasions by dissension among the Whigs, during the years 1846, '47 and '48; growing out of arbitrary action by the County Court against the protest of many Justices, who resided outside of town. The bridge crossing on South Queen street was washed out by a great flood. The County Court, without summoning a full bench, appointed a committee to rebuild, also to place under contract, which was greatly opposed. However, the contract was given to Wm. Lester, and a large debt created against the county. At a full bench of Justices, the bonds of the county were issued upon a very small majority vote. This gave rise to the cry "Court House Clique," and many positive Whigs determined to defeat them in any nominations they might present for Legislature. James E. Stewart, now Judge in Page County, ran as an independent candidate as against Whig nominees, and was elected, I believe. At the next Legislative election, Dr. A. C. Hammond was an independent Whig, who joined with Lewis Grantham, Democratic nominee, and they were elected, defeating Col. E. P. Hunter and Col. Edward Colston, Whig nominees.

The election for county officers, under the new constitution, came off in May, 1852. Jacob Van Doren, Jr., Whig, was elected Sheriff; E. G. Alburtis, County Clerk, and Israel Robinson, Circuit Court Clerk, Democrats, which party was generally successful for all officers in the county and for State Legislature, all through my early boyhood days. The County Clerks office and records were kept in a small stone house, east of the present jail. About the year 1848, the county erected the brick house on public square, now owned and occupied by Dr. W. D. Burkhart as a residence and store, which was used for County and Circuit Clerks' office until after the new Court House was erected. The clerks, Circuit Court, Col. John Strother, under appointment for years; and Harrison Waite, County Clerk, after whose death Capt. Jacob Van Doren became successor, held offices until newly elected officers' terms commenced.

The Baltimore & Ohio Railroad, about the year 1849, commenced the foundation for an engine house and machine shops, and made Martinsburg a first-class station. Washington Kroesen erected a log store house directly opposite the present depot, facing the railroad with switch coming up to platform of house. He did a large grocery business, and commenced the erection of the stone building, formerly the Railroad Co's. depot and freight house, which was occupied first by W. H. Cronise & Co. They did a rushing business, but soon failed, and John H. Likens, my employer, was engaged in business therein, I being his chief clerk and salesman. At this time the Martinsburg and Potomac turnpike was put under contract—M. C. Kyne and P. J. Mussetter, contractors for first 5 miles; Henry Haines, 2 miles; Charles Downs, 4 miles; and Jeremiah Sullivan, remainder to the river. Daniel Burkhart was President, and John H. Likens, Secretary, the records and books being kept by myself as his clerk. Messrs. Kyne and Mussetter threw up the contract, which Burkhart and Likens took up and finished. Then I became time keeper and paymaster to the employés. The State subscription was three-fifths, and personal subscription two-fifths. Collections from the State were secured by approval of report by members of the State Board of Improvement, and upon their requisition the money was drawn from the old Valley Bank in Winchester. The members of the Board were a Mr. Pendleton, of Clarke Co., and Gen'l Carson, of Frederick Co., and it invariably devolved upon me, in person, to visit and secure their names and order for payment of money from the bank—thus becoming closely identified with this, the first turnpike road in the county. The Winchester pike was commenced a few years later.

The town then began to expand. J. W. Boyd purchased the vacant land on the south side of East Burke street, and subdividing in lots, they were soon owned and improved by buildings. The first, just beyond the bridge, was purchased by Jeremiah Smith, an old railroad employé. On the opposite side J. W. Hooper purchased, and immediately erected a building and ten-pin alley, which was the first drinking saloon that I can recall. He also erected a brick dwelling beyond. A Mr. Chevally purchased a large body of land, and commenced a vegetable and fruit garden. A Mr. Lohr erected a large brick house, which stood alone for several years on the present High street. Benj. R. Boyd erected the stone building east of the railroad, on Queen street, and C. M. Shaffer the stone store house, now occupied by C. M. Shaffer & Son. Daniel Burkhart erected the small brick houses on the south side of the street. The only house between the railroad and Daniel Burkhart's old residence was a small wooden structure, owned and occupied by Mrs. Kane and family, mother of Bishop Kane. A Mr. Strine came, and purchasing from Mr. Burkhart, improvement by building immediately commenced. This I think was after 1850 or 1851. The old mill, then a grist or corn mill, consisted of about one-story, 16x20 feet, and occupied the present Fitz mill site with a saw-mill opposite. The water way from each ran on either side of a tongue of land, on which was a fine large spring of clear, cold water. The streams joined a short distance below, and formed a wide, shallow water, through which the street ran. The hill from town was very rough and rocky, and the means of crossing was a narrow log on either side of this tongue of land, on which was the spring. Where the railroad crosses Tuscarora was a spring, and when the bridge was built, an arch was left open in the side of it so as to give access to the spring, which I suppose is still to be found there. John H. Likens erected the large stone building on the south side of the railroad. About this period my direct business relations with the town ceased. I moved to Bedington, (Sulphur Springs,) yet was in town every week, more or less.

Circuit Court being in session in the spring of 1852, and contest for nominations of congressional candidates, Henry Bedinger, having been our representative for several previous terms, was bitterly opposed, and Wm. Lucas sought the nomination in his stead. Democrats were greatly divided in sentiment, and Bedinger succeeded in securing the nomination. At the dinner table of old Tammany were all, or nearly all, leading Democrats of the county. The subject came up, and many, if not all, expressed their determination not to vote for Bedinger. Some one suggested that Mr. Faulkner be urged to run as an independent candidate, and in that conference it was determined if he would give to them certain pledges regarding his vote for speaker they would vote for him. A committee was informally appointed, and before the hour of the next morning a circular was posted announcing Mr. F. as an independent union candidate for Congress. He was elected, and again re-elected as a full-fledged Democrat for the next term. About this period Hon. John Blair Hoge, in his young manhood, took unequivocal positions as a Democrat. The Presidential election approaching, there arose in Philadelphia a party naming themselves the "American Party," who announced themselves as hostile to the vote of foreigners—naturalized citizens coupling with that hostility to the Catholic Church, denying them the right to vote or hold office. The national conventions having met, the Democrats presented for President Franklin Pierce, and for Vice-President Wm. R. King. The Whigs nominated General Winfield Scott for President; Vice-President not remembered. Previous to this election in the fall, Hon. Henry A. Wise was nominated for Governor by the Democrats, and Hon. W. L. Goggin by the Whigs—election occurring in May.

During the month of February, as one would pass on the street, he would notice a large number of small three-cornered pieces of paper with the word *Sam* written thereon. During the evening, towards dark, citizens would be asked to take a walk, and would find themselves generally introduced into a long, one story stone building, used as a school-house by a Mr. Webster, and located on Raleigh street, near C. V. Depot. There, if disposed, they would join the Darklantern Knownothing Organization, known publicly as the American Party. Personally, I was solicited time and again to take the walk. When the exposure came by a withdrawal of a number of Democrats, I then became familiar with their mode of securing adherents. Wise was elected Governor with the entire Democratic ticket. In the fall Pierce and King were elected with almost unanimity, Scott carrying only three or four States. The administration proved very popular with both North and South.

About the year 1853 the cholera visited Harper's Ferry, and an epidemic violent in form. Many citizens left for safety. A family by the name of Crowl, owning a farm in the vicinity of Gerardstown, moved part of the family—the old gentleman, wife and three daughters.

They brought the disease with them, and all died, besides many in the neighborhood. A son coming from the Ferry hired a horse and buggy from George Swimley, proprietor of the Everett House. It was a very popular hotel and filled with permanent boarders. On one Sunday evening the son returning, drove up in front of the hotel, but remained sitting in the buggy. Some one, upon going to him, found him in what is termed a collapsed state of cholera. The alarm was raised, and Mr. Swimley coming forward, took the man in his arms and, carrying him in, proceeded to his own bed-room, where he placed him in bed and sent for physicians. Immediately the guests began to leave, when Mr. Swimley came to the head of the steps and announced that all might leave—that he would care for the sick man, let the consequences be what they might. His house was closed for three days by the town authorities, except at one door on Burke street, at the end of which it was announced the young man was getting well. The alarm ceased, and he was deservedly more popular than before. He exhibited the true charity of the good Samaritan, and although his manners were unrefined and his habits possibly would not meet the approval of many, yet, thank God for such unselfish Christian characters as he.

Coming into Martinsburg in the early morning for market, in the latter part of June or early in July, 1854, I heard proceeding from the house on corner of Race and Queen streets, the most piercing screams. Proceeding up Queen the same sounds of agony came from a house opposite the present Valley House. Turning the corner of Martin Street, the same greeting met me from the house in the rear of the Lutheran Church. Being at my old home, I learned that Mrs. Geo. Raenhal had died from cholera, and upon going down town, by nine o'clock, I found that nine persons were dead from cholera. On the Monday previous, Miss Kate Homrich and Thos. Turner died. From this time forward the town was in a fearful condition, more or less deaths occurring every day, until toward the latter part of August when it abated. It again broke out in violence about the middle of September, and continued with less fatal effects until some time in November. The first body buried in Green Hill Cemetery was that of Mrs. Geo. Raenhal or Horace Woodward, an engineer in the railroad service, who also died from this fatal disease. A lawyer of the town, David H. Conrad, organized a relief or nurse body of volunteers, who would agree to give two nights a week, if necesrary, in waiting upon the sick and seeing the dead properly prepared for the grave. It proved an important aid to physicians. In the month of November, B. L. Jacobs, Railroad agent, being very ill, solicited me to take charge of the Railroad ticket and freight office for him temporarily, which I did; the freight depot being on North Queen street, about where present house stands, and the passenger and ticket station being at foot of Martin street, as at present. Washington Kroesen built a brick hotel, which became a passenger eating house, and was conducted by Henry Staub for several years, during which time the railroad company built a fine brick hotel on North Queen street opposite Bishop's store. They removed and located the passenger and freight business at that point, where it remained until the property was burnt in early part of civil war.

The years 1855, '56 and '57 were uneventful, except for rapid progress in business and population. During the years 1853, '54 and '55, Mr. Sam'l Fitz purchased from Daniel Burkhart the old oil mill, and began improvement by sinking Tuscarora and building the present grand mill in part, and his foundry and machine shops; the creek being spanned by the bridge, and the street filled to its present level. In 1858, my connection with town and county business by being elected teller of the Bank of Berkeley, gave me an opportunity for gathering much knowledge of the business affairs of the county and surrounding country. During and preceding this period, from possibly 1848, flour was manufactured and shipped to Eastern markets in very large quantities. Alfred Ropp, D. D. Rees, James McWhorter, and some one from the J. E. Boyd mill, at Bunker Hill, were large shippers; as also the Newcomer mill, on the Opequon; the Hibbard and Tabb mills, west of town; the Geo. H. McClure, now Hannis mill; and the Bower's mill, in town, and Thos. G. Flagg, east of town. Daniel Burkhart had a small distillery on Dry Run, where the present large Hannis distillery now stands, and F. G. Flagg distilled liquor at his place east of town.

On the morning of the 9th of October, 1859, a citizen, W. N. Riddle, Esq., was seen to hastily enter the Court House, and soon the bell was pealing forth a rapid and excited sound, which only occurred in case fire was prevailing. Citizens began hastily to collect, and as they assembled it was announced that Harper's Ferry Armory had been captured, and citizens of the town were being shot down upon the streets, and were calling for aid to capture and discover what it meant. It was announced that a train of cars would be ready to proceed there, carrying volunteers, who would arm themselves with such weapons as they could. In a short time Capt. E. G. Alburtis, an old Mexican war veteran, was selected to command, and other officers appointed. By 11 o'clock they were ready, and going to the depot, took the train, which proceeded to the Ferry, accompanied by a large number of unarmed citizens. Our men were stopped this side of the Ferry, and ordered to enter the Armory yard at west end, and there remain for further orders. Instead of which, in impetuosity, they pressed forward until they came under fire from Brown's men, who had been driven into the small engine house, from which the Marines under General Lee captured them. George Murphy, our Prosecuting Attorney, was wounded through the calf of his leg; J. N. Hammond, our Deputy Sheriff, had the point of his hip shot off; a young man in the railway service was shot through the stomach; George Wollett, assistant in the service, was shot through the hand; and George Richardson, a railroad watchman, had his right eye shot out. It was always claimed, that if they had been properly supported, they would have succeeded in capturing the invaders before the marines arrived. No one could describe the excitement prevailing.

At about 6 o'clock in the evening, our wounded boys came back. They and the citizens could only say that it was a negro insurrection commenced, which only increased the excitement and alarm. During the night it was announced that the marines had captured them, and that old John Brown, known as a Kansas Free State Fighter, was the leader, with negro and white men as abettors. It was remembered with alarm that for months a deaf and dumb strange negro man had appeared in peculiar dress upon the streets of the town, marching as if under military orders, always near sundown. His plug silk hat was adorned with a feather from a turkey's tail, and a band of red flannel round the body of the hat. He was generally supposed to be insane, and no attention was ever paid him. It is certain, however, from this day forward he was never seen again. Hence he has always been coupled, in my mind, as an aider of the Brown gang. From this day forward, until the final close of the civil strife by surrender of General Lee, in April, 1865, we were under military surveilance and control. The business of the town, although disturbed, still continued unobstructed. Personally, I removed from town to the residence of my mother-in-law, on the Potomac River, going to and from town each day and familiar with what was occurring. Scouts and military organizations were going to and returning from different points along the Potomac every day, on the lookout for further forays by such wicked fanatics as John Brown and his gang. Daily reports of a startling character being stated of a large organization of rescuers of Brown, who was in Jefferson County jail, were coming in on us at any hour. It was a period of unrest and disquietude, indeed.

The Presidential election of 1860 coming on, Democratic dissension placed John C. Breckenridge and Stephen A. Douglass before the people. The then lately organized party, under the name of Republican having absorbed the Whig party North, selected Abraham Lincoln as their candidate—the Union Party, as called, presenting John Bell, which largely absorbed the Whig element South. The election came off, resulting as known in the selection of Lincoln. The already inflamed and excited people of all parties flew almost at once into an attitude of war in the South. In the early months of the year 1861, we were startled with news of the burning of Government property at Harper's Ferry, by the officers and soldeirs, who had been stationed there as guards, and their rapid movement to Washington. In a few days it developed, why it had been done by the concentration of military forces, representing as stated, state authority. It had been distroyed by orders from the war department, in order to defeat its capture of arms and ordinance stored in the Armory, by the Southern men. From this time forward, Harper's Ferry was the scene of many exciting circumstances. Shortly after this the Armory proper was dismantled,—all the machinery for arms and manufacture were removed; some said to Richmond, others to North Carolina.

Our yearly General Regimental parade coming on in month of May, 1861, occasioned wonderful excitement. The officers determined to march under the State Flag, discarding the stars and stripes of the country. Personally, being an ardent supporter of the Government as against secession, I joined with others in securing a large part of the Regiment, who carried and marched under the grand old Stars and Stripes, in defiance of orders from the officers. It almost brought on personal rioting and fighting, and if arms had been at command, it is probable much blood would have been shed. This gave occasion for officers in command at Harper's Ferry to send a military company here to keep down the Union sentiment. It was the Rockbridge Guards, under command of Capt. Letcher; and they proved good fellows, largely in sympathy with the Union sentiment. Capt. Letcher was ordered to burn the Railroad bride crossing Opequon Creek. He refused to obey orders, was put under arrest and removed, his company also returning to Harper's Ferry. In their stead the Clarke County Greys were sent up, and under orders they burnt the bridge. This incensed Union men very much, and members of the company would, individually, receive an unexpected lick or knock-down whenever opportunity occurred in the hotels of the town. They had headquarters in Grantham Hall building, and every afternoon would drill in the square. One Saturday afternoon it was noticed that many persons, citizens, and employés of the Railroad Company, collected on the Court House pavement. The military formed as usual in time, in front of the Col. Hoge, now J. B. Wilson residence, facing the crowd. On the Court House pavement commenced loud and vociferous comments upon their appearance and drill, and finally some one threw a stone, striking a gun in the hands of a member of the company. Many in the company brought their guns to shoulder, ready to shoot. The crowd made a break toward them, but before reaching them, they had dispersed and were mounting steps to their headquarters. The crowd hooted and howled for some time, but the soldiers kept within their quarters, and finally the crowd dispersed. This was the only assault on the military I ever witnessed in town.

A Regiment of cavalry, under the command of J. E. B. Stewart, came next, and camped in the county, scouting along the Potomac River. They were seldom in a body in the town—hence, no collision ever came up.

Still continuing my trips daily, to and from town, attending my bank duties, I passed through cavalry camp morning and evening; they being in the orchard of John C. Small, on Martinsburg and Williamsport pike. Holding a pass from Col. Stewart, I was surprised one evening upon arrival at picket post by arrest, being conducted to Col. Stewart's tent. I was met with the charge of being dangerous in conveying news to the enemy, then in force on the Maryland side of the river; my residence being in sight of the river and my sentiments being hostile to the South. I offered simply innocence of having conveyed information, or of having such disposition. Hoge being present, appealed in my behalf, and I was released with a more far reaching pass than I had before. On the 2nd day of July, 1861, the Bank closed up its business, all its funds, books, bonds, etc., being placed in the hands of a committee for safe keeping. From this time forward to 1872, I was only a casual visitor to the town. In 1863, I became identified with the railroad service, located at Cumberland, Md. In January 1864, I was in charge of Harper's Ferry agency, and was every week a visitor to your town in transaction of business for the company with the military authorities—hence, I know but little of the history of the town after 1861.

The fight between General Jackson and Patterson's forces, near Falling Waters, was under my view. Shortly after it opened, in company with John Marshall and Henry Myers, who lived at Bedington, we passed out to see what was on fire, a dense smoke appearing, and found Wm. Porterfield's barn burning. The Confederate's were in battle array on the hill between Mr. Hill's residence, just where the road turns off to the Falling Waters church. Unexpectedly we found ourselves captured by the 4th Wisconsin Regiment, who were flanking to the south side of the burning barn. When we recovered our surprise the Confederates had retired, and we supposed, continued their retreat to and beyond Martinsburg. On our way to have a hearing one dead man with a ball through his head was seen lying on the pike, and was a member of the 4th Wisconsin regiment. At Mr. Porterfield's residence was found five severely wounded Federals, and under an apple tree was a dead man, supposed to be a Confederate by his dress. At the house of John Gonter three wounded Federals were found, one of whom had the most singular appearance I have ever seen. His head lay perfectly level on the right shoulder, and on his neck, under the left ear, appeared a large blood blister. His body was paralyzed. The surgeon said it was caused by abrasion—a small sized six-pound canon ball having passed between the ear and shoulder, not striking, but just rubbing against the skin. The wounded Federals were placed in ambulances and went back to Maryland. The dead Confederate was buried in the field back of Porterfield's barn.

The seasons, winter and summer, in our latitude, are generally uniform, but there have been exceptions. I cannot recall the year, but it was from 1836 on to 1840—one summer it was uniformly cold, with frost occurring more or less in each summer month—during which, about the middle of July, an old revolutionary veteran was buried. His remains were taken to a graveyard in the country, possibly at the old Baptist Church, near the Newcomer mill ; anyhow it was out that way. Being buried with military honors, the boys of the town naturally would be present. I distinctly recollect the fact that whilst the salute over the grave was being fired, it commenced snowing and continued until the ground was covered fully three inches, becoming fiercely cold. The past year, 1887, being a noted year for fierce blizzards and wonderful snow storms in various parts of our country, calls my attention to a wonderful snow storm which we had in 1842, in the early part of February. It commenced snowing on Friday, about noon, falling rapidly and continuing all day Saturday, Sunday and Monday; and in the afternoon of Monday, still snowing, a fierce driving wind came on. On Tuesday morning the entire country was blocked up, and in front of my home, on the southeast corner of Shaffer's property, a large drift was standing which reached the roof of the house. A gentleman by the name of Vincenheller, seizing me, caught me by the clothing and threw me into this drift headforemost. Unfortunately, I fell too far near the edge, sustaining a wounded right shoulder by striking on the ground. I could not rise, and he becoming alarmed, had to take a snow bath through the drift in order to relieve me. This accident gave me the pleasure of a daily sleigh ride all over the county, as he was fond of the sport and had a fine team to make amends for his act, and would take me with him. No fences could be seen in any direction, and in many places in the woods the lower limbs of the trees were hid under the snow. This was the most severe snow storm we may have ever had in the valley. In 1856 there were great snow falls, and the railroads, also country roads, were blocked up, but no such continuous storm as that of 1842.

The resident ministers of the town from 1828 to 1861, as far as I can recall, were: Lutheran—C. P. Krauth, Sr., Medtart Schaffer, Weizer Martin, Sprecher Seip, Winter Krauth, Jr., Schonucker Fenk Kopp; 1861, C. Martin. German Reformed—Revs. Robt. Douglas, Daniel Bragonier; both these churches were united usually with Shepherdstown. Presbyterian—Revs. Peyton Harrison, John Boggs, a Mr. Berry and A. C. Hopkins. Protestant Episcopal—Revs. Johnson, Talifaria, Chisholm, Davis, Sprigg and others. Methodist Episcopal—Revs. Riley, Watts, Hodges, Goheen, Coffin, Dulin, Mercer, March, Moorehead and many others. Baptist—Revs. Wm. Herndon, W. S. Penick and others. Catholic— Rev. Wheelan, afterward Bishop of Diocese of W. Va.; Revs. Plunkett, O'Brien and Talty.

Among the professional men were: Physicians—Drs. Richard McSherry, Kownsler, Hollingsworth, John S. Harrison, Sr. and Jr., Charles Magill, Dennis Murphy, F. D. Dellinger, Wm. Snodgrass, Thos. S. Page and E. B. Pendleton. Dentists—John Little and W. P. Withrow. Judges of Circuit Court—J. R. Douglass, of Jefferson County, and Richard Parker, of Frederick County. Lawyers—D. H. Conrad, E. P. Hunter, C. J. Faulkner, Edmond Pendleton, J. Blair Hoge, Frank Thomas, Norman Miller and Andrew Kennedy. Editors—Washington Evans, Col. E. P. Hunter, James E. Stewart and Norman Miller, of *Gazette;* E. G. and Samuel Alburtis and Major Israel Robinson, of the *Virginia Republican.*

From my earliest days the parish, (now called the poorhouse,) occupied the present building known as Norborne Hall. A Mr. James Moon was the keeper, and supplies were furnished by J. W. Boyd. At one time there was quite a political scandal in regard to the improper use of inmates, and the enormous profits made in supplying the house, which finally resulted in the Court buying the present farm and buildings on Tuscarora. I think this was about the year 1850. The old Court House occupied in part the locality of the present one. It did not come to the corner of Queen street, but left a space fully thirty feet. The corner was occupied by a frame building with brick back dwelling house, and was the best store stand in town. It occupied the space now about where Sheriff's office stands.

The first telegraph office that we had in town was in a frame building, occupying the corner of Grantham Hall, the line coming direct up King street and diverging from the railroad at the Bower's mill. I was boarding at the corner of Spring and King streets, and opposite on the jail steps, upon one occasion, sat two of our aged men, Jesse Hayden and Adam Schoppert.

Adam says: "Jesse, how does this thing work, anyhow? I have been watching it for the last hour and nothing has gone over it yet."

Jesse replied: "Why, Adam, it is a liquid and flows inside the wire, and you can't see it. When it gets to the end it comes out."

"How's that," says Adam, "I seen Joe, my son, get a telegraph from Harper's Ferry, and it was just like any other letter."

"Well," replied Jesse, "it is a d—d puzzler, anyhow, and I believe a fraud."

Without solving the problem of the telegraph they closed their conversation, and I expect they were not the only ones who were puzzled over the same matter.

We had many eccentric characters about town, and amongst others was one Adam Cockburn. He owned and lived on the property now owned by E. Herring, directly opposite Green Hill Cemetery. Every day Adam was in town, usually visiting the various bar-rooms until full, and he would then perambulate the streets, making fun for everybody. Personally, I only have a vague knowledge of him and his habits. His place was long used as a resort for the boys of the town, as a play ground. Many a pleasant hour have I passed with my boy friends in playing ball on the familiar Cockburn Hill. The community yet has in it a representative of the long ago, Alexander Grimes. He has always been a peculiar character. His home for a long time was with my relatives at old Tammany. Much of the filling, grading and macadamizing of King and Queen streets was done with his assistance. His habits for a long time were very dissipated. However, he made up his mind to quit drinking, and purchasing a pint of liquor he took it to his sister Polly, telling her he would only drink from that bottle, and that she should refuse to give it to him. The plan worked splendidly, and from that day to the present I have never known him to be under the influence of liquor. (If seen he will verify this statement.) He has always been noted for sharp repartee, and quick to take advantage in a bargain. I recall an occurrence between himself and one of our prominent lawyers. He was occupying a house, the owner of which wished to dispossess him, and he applied to this lawyer for advice, receiving and acting upon it. He retained the property, and the lawyer told him his fee was five dollars—all right. Some weeks after, in passing the garden of the lawyer, he found the wife assisting in measuring off beds, by holding the tape line for her husband. He was invited to come in, and the lawyer taking him around, showed him what he wished to do, and would every now and then say, as an old gardener, do you think that would suit? Aleck, (as he is called,) would give his opinion, and the lawyer would thank him. After passing some time Aleck says, "I believe I owe you five dollars for your advice about the house." The lawyer said "yes," and looked expectantly at the prospective coming fee, but was surprised to hear Aleck say, "Well, my fee for garden advice is ten dollars, so you are in debt to me five." The lawyer honoring it as a good joke, immediately paid him the difference. Another good and sharp practice occurred between Aleck and a Jew, by the name of Pfeiffer. They occupied the same house on Queen street, where Lambert's saloon now is. The Jew had a cord of wood to be cut for stove use, and he applied to Aleck, who did that kind of work, but would not agree on the price demanded. Finally Aleck agreed to cut the wood for the chips, which Pfeiffer agreed to. They used in common the cellar, and Aleck had his children picking up the chips and throwing them down. Commencing, he would cut two-thirds of the stick into chips and the remainder into stove wood. When Pfeiffer discovered the fraud practiced, he sued Aleck, but his bargain was such that Aleck gained it.

We had a very good but eccentric character, James Hutchinson, engaged in watch and clock repairing at the present Hyde stand. He never walked on the street, but was invariably in a run. A noted character, Smith, the razor strap man, visited our town, and his cry was always "only a few more left—who takes the next?" He sold at auction on the street, and Mr. H. desiring one of the wonderful straps, started in his usual running gait. Catching the words "only a few more left," he called out, "Save me one." Smith seeing him and hearing what he said yelled out, "Only one more left." Mr. H. quickened his run, and reaching the crowd took the "one more." Looking down he noticed seven baskets full, and left at once, muttering as he passed, "Oh, what a liar!" The first railroading that I ever saw occurred with himself and family. The track was laid as far as the bridge at the foot of Green Hill Cemetery, and a truck was standing on the track chucked. The old gentleman, on his way to church on Opequon, placed his wife and younger children upon it, and himself and eldest son pushed it. After passing a short distance a down grade commenced. The old gentleman or son could neither stop the car, or yet keep up with it. It got away from them, and mother children soon passed out of sight. Brown Calvin and myself being near Flagg's Mill, followed the car and found that it had come to a halt near Opequon, having struck a rising grade. After some time the old gentleman came in sight in his usual run, and was very grateful, apparently to Calvin and myself, for saving his family.

Peter Gardner, the old hotel keeper whom I mentioned before, was a grand caterer to his guests, and no one ever set a better prepared or more plentiful supply upon a table. On a court occasion his country guests were detained on account of a German boarder whom he would not delay. He placed upon the table a good-sized roast pig, and the single boarder took his seat and helped himself. After awhile Mr. G., upon going to the room, was surprised to see none of the pig left, and the boarder, in

Reminiscence. 285

a deep German accent, said, "Have you any more little hogs? I likes 'em." Mr. G. at once dismissed the boarder as unprofitable.

Very few of the old landmarks of my boyhood days are left around or in the town. The Burkhart property, Hannis mill, Bowers mill, Boyd's store, in Young's, now Herring's property; Lamberts saloon, formerly Claycomb Hotel; Eagle Hotel, formerly Lutheran Church; Blondel dwelling, Dunn property, opposite Market House; Long property, now owned by C. Thumel; brick store-house adjoining Continental Hotel; Boreman property, Conrad, McSherry, Cunningham, Stewart, Reed, Campbell, Pendleton and Harrison Waite, on Queen street, are all improved considerably, but some are recognizable as they were in the thirties. On King street the Diffenderfer, Rousch, Shaffer, Wolff, Swartz, Snodgrass, old Harrison, Shaffer, Poisal, Somerville, now Shaffer; Locke, now Young; Alburtis, jail, old stone house corner opposite jail, Seaman, Gerard and Bowers' mill and dwelling, all improved but still recognized as of old. On Water street, where the Riddle and Showers properties are now situated, was a long one-story building used as a bark shed for Divinney's Tannery, and long owned by James Brown. On the opposite side was a general stone quarry for the town. Tuscarora was noted as a fine fishing stream. Many a fine sucker and eel have I seen and caught therefrom. Above the Hannis mill was called Ransom's Bottom, and the evidence of a great Indian battle having been fought there was very clear. Many a skull and bone of a dead Indian have I seen ploughed up, and the only tomahawk I ever recollect of handling was one found by a young boy named Alex. Gregory. We were fishing and playing, when in tumbling he struck the handle and drew it out. Your Dr. John H. Hunter may recall this, as I think he was one of the company.

It was a very great pleasure during my young days to visit in the surrounding country, near town, on the Winchester road, the families of Martin Rousch, Snodgrass, old Jimmy Beard and John Jamison. On Tuscarora road the Kearneys, old Jacob and George Seibert, the Mong family, Barley Tabb, Hugh Campbell, the Cushwas, Kilmers, Hibbards, Janneys, Wellers and Walters families, all of whom would welcome you cordially and entertain you royally. Hospitality and good fellowship was the order of the times. There has always been an idea that there was more real honesty and integrity at that period of our history than since. It is a noted fact that farmers would loan each other money without passing anything more than their word on such a day it should be returned, and very seldom a failure of promise would occur.

Many of our people of the present day do not recollect the beautiful stone-pillowed bridge that occupied the ground now filled with solid stone structure, from Burke street to beyond the Bowers mill. The rebels destroyed it in their frenzy of insanity and destruction of railroad property during the civil war. Quite a number of engines were fixed up and permitted to run off into the street below, which was obstructed for a long time. One of the most unusual sights was witnessed in our town during the war. The Rebels wishing to get some engines to Winchester, hauled them by horse-power over the road. They had hitched to one engine from twenty to twenty-four horses, a driver being provided for each four. They succeeded in getting them through, but it must have been a difficult job. The destruction of railroad property was immense around and in Martinsburg. As a matter to satisfy my curiosity, I rode from Tabb's crossing to road crossing just above town, and in that space counted over four hundred cars destroyed by fire, the rails removed and ties burnt. At one point I found a rail wound around a tree four times. They had heated the centre, and then taking hold of ends, wound it round and round. The station and hotel buildings at head of Queen street, and the engine and machine shops, were destroyed and dismantled. It was my misfortune to be absent from town when this was done, but the wrecked and ruined condition was seen by me often. It afterwards became my duty as an employé at Cumberland of the Company, to see that material for rebuilding the track and bridges was sent forward, so that I became very familiar with the whole subject.

The subject of fires is one that, from your present efficient organization and water supply, gives your people very little uneasiness. When I was a boy we had a hand engine, and our water supply was from cisterns on public streets—one at Court House, one at Lutheran Church corner, one at Presbyterian Church on King street, now vacant lot. Each family was furnished with two leather buckets, one of which hung out at the door, and was to be filled with water every night, the other kept conveniently inside, also filled up. This was the instruction from the town authorities. We had no Mayor and Council then, that I can recall. The first fire that I recall was the burning of a large stable belonging to the Globe Hotel, and occupying site of your present public school in third ward. It was about noon that alarm was given, and quite a number of horses, belonging to country people, were burned. After this the factory at lower end of town, where water works now stands, was burnt, and occurred late at night. It was never thought possible to save a house, and all effort was directed toward saving the surrounding property. Next came the destruction of the Globe Hotel, after which the corner house, then occupied as a telegraph station and located on site of Grantham Hall, was burned completely up. The most alarming fire that I can recall was the burning of four houses on King street, opposite the late J. M. Wolff residence, which commenced between 12 and 1 o'clock, P. M., in the cabinet-maker's shop of Andrew Bowman.

The wind was blowing almost a hurricane from the West, and it was but a few moments until the entire row of houses was in a blaze. Shingles were on fire and sparks innumerable were settling everywhere, and in a short time, on South side of street, fully twenty house-roofs were on fire. It became necessary for from ten to fifteen persons to be upon each house, in order to save them. I doubt if your old town has ever experienced a more exciting time from fire. The buildings burnt were very old and dilapidated. The Kelley Hotel on Martin street, a very large weatherboard building, was also burnt, belonging to Capt. Gardner. He was vexed about the loss, and coming to the church corner, tried to throw supply hose out of the cistern. In doing so he slipped and passed into the cistern feet foremost, but being a large man he was caught about the hips and there held, until he was relieved after great efforts. Col. Strother's house, on site now occupied by H. C. Berry, was burnt one night in the month of February, when it was so cold the water froze in the hose and disabled the engine.

The water supply of our old town was from public wells on the streets. One was in front of Lambert's saloon, one at the Schoppert corner, one on the corner of Burke and German streets, one in front of the Janney property on King street, which belonged to Conrad Rousch, and one at John Shaffer's residence. Many persons had wells upon their own premises, and large supplies were hauled daily from the various springs around town. It was between 1848 and 1860 that the system of cisterns was introduced. Messrs. S. B. and N. Mead brought into use the cement and concrete cistern, which is still much in use by builders. The condition of country around the town has changed wonderfully. At the road leaving the pike at lime kiln, north end of town, there was a nice grove of woodland, frequently patronized by Sunday School pic-nics. Just above the Hannis Mill, where the Cumberland Valley bridge crosses the B.

& O. R. R., woods commenced, and you could keep in woodland without break until you reached Hedgesville. On Tuscarora road, just beyond toll-gate, a heavy piece of woodland occupied the ground. Immediately in rear of Gen'l Boyd's residence, coming up to his yard, woodland commenced and continued without break above the Big Spring, except one field. Then a good deal of cleared land, belonging to the Tate and Snodgrass families. Then came in a body of woodland on the west side of the Winchester road, which extended almost without a creak until Apple Pie Ridge was reached, where the Lyle's, Henshaw's, and other large farmers lived with much land cleared and cultivated. Just back of the Jamison, late Bentz farm, a body of woodland commenced and continued to the mountain with very few, if any breaks.

Out near the present residence of A. J. Thomas was a grand grove, where almost every celebration of the 4th of July was held, in barbecue style. But few, if any of the new generation are familiar with the system of a barbecue, and I will therefore try to describe the manner of preparation of the food. The entire carcass of a number of sheep and hogs, and sometimes the full carcass of a steer, would be prepared for the feast. A deep pit was dug and filled with such fuel as would burn down to a bed of live coals. This was spanned with bars of iron, on which was laid the carcass for broiling, and along side would be a large pot filled with liquid butter, lard, etc., which would be applied by a mop to the cooking meat. As one side became partially done, the other would be turned to the fire by heavy pieces of wood, used as a crowbar. When fully roasted or broiled, no one ever tasted sweeter food. It generally came, however, after fatigued marching and late in the afternoon, hence was always appreciated. The meat was always accompanied with good bread, and generally new potatoes and beans—"Oh, for one more old-fashioned fourth of July celebration."

I have given a few names of farmers in the immediate vicinity of Martinsburg. It was my good fortune to become well and familiarly acquainted with persons who lived at a distance, and whose representatives are still in your county. No more clever class of people could be found than many in and around Arden, among whom were the Chenowiths, Millers, Gladdens, Lyles, Henshaws, Sencindivers, Sanakers, Thomas, McDonalds, Daniels, Throckmortons, Irelands, Meyers, Bayarlys, Tablers, Campbells, Walkers, Pitzers, "of the old stock";—and again on Tuscarora and Dry Run, Thatcher's, Small's, Noll's, Lame Mike Seibert, Chisty's, Emmerts, Dubles, Cushwas, Walters, Gross, Groves, Tabbs, Porterfields and a host of others, whom it gives me pleasure to recall. On Williamsport road lived J. C. and Henry Small, Ben. Comeqy, Geo. Reynolds, Sam'l and Ben. Harrison, James Turner, Henry Haines, Andy McIntire, Wm. Hill, Daniel Lamaster, Dr. John Hedges, Henry River, Andrew McCleary, Wm. Porterfield, Jacob Lafevre, Rev. John Light, Jacob Light, Peter Crowl, Dan'l B. Morrison, Hamilton Light, Christ. Tabler, Jas. L. and S. O. Cunningham, Joseph Unger and others of a pleasing disposition, many of whom have passed on to eternity—only one or two now living. They were true and honorable in life, and are still respected in death.

Along the mountain range were A. and Jas. Robinson, H. J. Seibert, Mike Seibert, Josiah and Hiram Hedges, Rev. L. F. Wilson, Casper Weaver, Josiah Harlan, and Bro. James Criswell, Jacob and Aaron Myers, Conrad Robbins, Jacob Lingamfelter, Willonbey Lemon, W. O. Cunningham, Christ. Tabler, Elliott Tabb, William and Benj. Couchman, Henry Myers, Mike Couchman and other noble men of the olden time. In enumerating the old farmer citizens of the county, on the lower or Jefferson line, I was not so well acquainted, yet I take pleasure in naming some whom I did know, viz: the Billmire family, Conrad, John, Solomon, David and Martin, all of whom were good, true men, and successful in life; Maj. Lewis B. Willis, a retired army officer; James Mason, George and John Holliday, Jacob and Wm. Rush, I. Van Doren, Drs. Vorhees and Magruders, S. B. and Thos. Vanmetre, A. R. McQuilken, who is yet one of your townsmen, Janifer Hudgel, E. B. Southworth and others whom I cannot just now recall. In the Northern end of the county were Jacob and Daniel Ropp, Poland and Amos Williamson, Col. Ed. Colston, Jacob Price, William Wilson, G. W. Robinson, Adam Small, W. H. Harley, Wm. Leigh, Robt. Lemon, Peter Light, Wm. Jack, Wm. Hitzer, Wm. Sperow, Joseph Criswell, John Horner, Warner Emerson, Jacob Basore, Dr. A. C. Hammond and Jacob French. I knew them all personally, and at some period of my life transacted business with the larger number. They have left representatives in almost every case, and their descendants can claim the respect which is always due an honorable and true life.

The second election for county officers, under the new Constitution, came off in May, 1854. The Democrats nominated Barnet Cushwa for Sheriff, and Alex. Newcomer, a professed Democrat, ran independent. It was a very animated canvass, and the result very close, Mr. C. having only seven majority. A contest was held before the County Court, and they decided that no one was elected, calling for another election in July, which was held. In the meantime, *Sam*, or the Know-Nothing party, became very active in behalf of Newcomer, and for the first time in our county's history, steeped men with whiskey and cooped them up in out-of-the-way places, so as to control their votes on election day. It was discovered, and every active Democrat was on the alert to expose and thwart their villiany. I was present at the break-up of one crop, near Whiting's Neck, where nine unfortunates were held. They were taken out, and by the next morning were over the mountain near Shanghai, where they were comfortably cared for in a farmer's house, and voted there the Democratic ticket as they all wished to do, except one who wished to vote for Cushwa and the other portion of the ticket opposite. After a hard fight Cushwa was elected by 67 majority. This election was also contested, and it is supposed would have been annulled, but cholera intervened and court adjourned without action. Before it convened again the law gave Mr. Cushwa the office. He proved to be one of the most efficient officers we ever had before, and his efficiency secured Democratic rule in the county up to the beginning of the civil war.

After 1852 it became apparent that Martinsburg was a town of importance and prosperity. Business began to expand largely—G. Baker and Bro. opened a wholesale grocery in the Shaffer room, east of B. & O. R. R.; D. E. Shipley, Conrad & Son, M. and N. Stine, R. S. Pendleton, D. E. White, Hughes & Baker, Vanarsdale & Gosnell, Wm. T. and Ezra Herring, W. H. Wilkens, J. F. Harrison, Robert. and Thos. Turner, Jno. F. Staub, Mason & Smith, Jas. W. Grantham and hosts of others were engaged in business. The town also improved in school facilities—John Sellars, J. F. Gardner, W. S. Saffell, J. W. Page, Mrs. Phelps, Mrs. Armstrong and Miss Chisholm taught schools. Rev. Wm. Love completed an old blacksmith shop, located where Hon. W. H. H. Flick's house now stands, and taught therein. It was only one story in height. About this time the town became wonderfully excited by a ghost, which walked the street all night rattling a chain. Many of us young men determined to find out the mystery. Preparing ourselves with pistols, loaded alone with powder, and being nine in company, we stationed ourselves on the corner of Burke and German streets, dividing each in companies of three. We soon heard the chain approaching, as it turned the corner toward King street. Some placed themselves directly in its rear, while others on either side of the street kept pace quietly in his rear. When about half way to King, the three in the centre of the street, fired their pistols. The ghost commenced running, and one of those in the street fell, leaving only two of the crowd to continue the chase. We all followed and soon found our two chums looking carefully among a lot of wagons, plows, etc., in front of the shop located where Flick's residence now stands, but failed to find his ghostship. It was, however, his last appearance in that character, yet it afterward came out fully, and the party came near being our representative in the pen at Richmond.

It was my good fortune to know many of the older citizens West of the Mountain, and among the number I recall that noble old gentleman, Wm. Barney, who has two sons, John and William, yet in your midst; also Lewis and Moses Grantham; Robert K., George W. and Israel Robinson; Jacob, Samuel and Michael Stuckey; Peter Keys and his brother Philip, Mrs. Jones and Miss McKeever, B. M. and Henry G. Kitchen, at each of whose residences I have been hospitably entertained in the regular old Virginia style. There was a noted hunter who was given the name of Wolff Myers. He lived at Meadow Branch, and almost every week during the winter he would be in town with venison, bear and other wild meat, also wild turkeys by the dozen. He also had a secret which I have no doubt died with him. Time and again have I seen him sell to the stores native lead, which he would smelt and bring in in square blocks. No one could ever get his secret from him, and it is a strong evidence that the native ore exists somewhere in the vicinity of his residence. A representative of his family still lives at Meadow Branch; at least he was there a few years ago, and is a grandson of Thomas Myers. About fifteen years ago I personally gave attention to the mineral interests of our county. There is, on the property of the late J. W. Chenowith, near Arden, a wonderfully rich deposit of ore, also on the property of the late Hon. C. J. Faulkner, at south end of town. The latter was developed and worked for a short period, and found to contain not only a rich deposit of iron ore, but with it a fair per cent. of zinc. This is an interest that your people should endeavor to develop, and in concluding my reminiscence I could do no better than to encourage greater honorable efforts for full development of the grand old county—rich in good lands, well cultivated farms, and laying undeveloped almost every source of wealth which man may demand.

In the past years Martinsburg boys would have their sport in swimming during the summer season. The places of resort near town were at the old oil mill dam, now Fitz's mill; the Bowers dam, directly opposite the railroad shops, and to the small boys a place called the "slip," just above the residence of Mr. Frazier and back of your present planing mill. These places at that time were very private and retired. No residences were around the entire space from John Fitz's residence to Ransom's, now Hannis' mill, it being an open common. The larger boys and young men frequently went to the Opequon, at a place called the "turn hole," possibly a mile or more above the county bridge, crossing at Vanmetre's, on the Shepherdstown road. It was a very dangerous place for bathers, and I have witnessed some terribly exciting scenes there in efforts to rescue those in danger, often proving successful, but in several instances the reverse. I recall the drowning of a young man by the name of Hugh McGackey. The family resided in the property on Queen street adjoining Commodore Boreman's residence. The father was a contractor, who, with a partner by the name of Scott, erected the stone bridge crossing the Tuscarora, on B. &. O. R. R., below the cemetery. Hugh went off on Sunday morning with other boys of the town, and the father and family went to the old Presbyterian Church, on King street. About noon, as the congregation was dispersing, a horseman arrived and informed the father that Hugh was drowned.

I have never seen such agony as the father, mother and sister exhibited. They fainted and were carried apparently dead to their home, all the congregation following. In a short time his body was brought in, which was certainly a solemn occasion. He was a bright young man, just turning into full manhood, and very popular in the community.

This being a period of much excitement on the temperance question, I purpose giving my knowledge of the first temperance organization which existed. In 1842, an announcement was made that a reformed drunkard from Baltimore would address the public in the Presbyterian Church, and especially inviting those who drank to excess. It being a new thing under the sun, everybody went Wm. Dorsey was made chairman of the meeting, and I then learned for the first time that there was a society pledged to refrain from drinking whiskey, brandy, gin and rum, but allowed to drink every kind of wine. My knowledge of the business was such that, boy as I was, I laughed at the idea, as I could see the effects of wine—not quite so quick but equally potent, and when once under wine influence, more difficult to sober up than even with heavier drinks. However, the reformed drunkard in a plain, square, unvarnished manner, told his life experience, and stated that in Baltimore, in a bar-room, twelve men just like himself had pledged each other to quit drinking and go out through the entire land, exhorting their fellow men to do the same. He also said they called themselves Washingtonians. He called upon any one present, who knew they were drunkards, to rise, and if any one wished to give their experience, they should raise the right hand. Several did so, and a very large number rose up, showing their honesty. At the present time, if you would ask in a large assembly for any one to rise and acknowledge they were drunkards, not one would do so; and yet there are more to-day, especially among young men, than there were then. A very large number signed the pledge, and I am proud to say, that nearly all proved faithful. I recollect one particular case. He was terribly given up to the habit, and for three days he remained in his shop, his meals being carried to him by members of his family. On the fourth day he came out and made for the back yard of my uncle's house. He came in with a frightened look upon his face, and at once began to beg for a drink. My uncle, although engaged in the trade and continuing in it for years, says: "No, Mike, you want to quit, and I know it is for your good. Now pledge me right here again, that you will not drink liquor of any kind, and then come with me." After a little hesitation, Mike took the pledge. My uncle took him to the kitchen and gave him a good meal, with plenty of good, strong coffee, and for years after this man was true to his obligation. The Washingtonians were succeeded by the "Sons of Temperance," and the "Boys' Cadets of Temperance." They did a great deal of good in reforming and keeping men from intemperance. The subject of prohibition had frequently been advocated under the old State before the war, and at one time it was thought would be embodied in the Constitution of 1851 and '52.

In my young childhood, John H. Blondel, generally called "Tebeaus," was a young man and associated with the circle of females and males, young men and women who were familiar with my relatives. He was a splendid performer on almost any character of musical instrument, and although of a very quiet manner, I expect had more real fun and sport in him than any one I ever knew about our town. For many years he was the leader and trainer of our bands, and had the reputation of being the finest performer on the bugle that could be found. Often at night has the old town been enlivened from some of the surrounding hills by his delightful music, sometimes from the bugle, accompanied by the claironet, flute, etc. He usually had a number of companions with him.

Many of your older citizens will recall with pleasure the amusing and laughable stories he would relate, among which were "Old Mrs. Schoppert and her song or hymn," accompanied by the violin; "Snuff-taking, sneezing and pipeing voice of conversation;" "Capt. Foley's visit and dinner at the residence of Gen'l E. Boyd;" "The coon hunt, with black dogs of old man Stuckey;" and many others that I cannot recall. It was a pleasure to meet him in a company, and wherever found he was sure to be a source of much amusement. He was a good and worthy citizen, filling his position of life with honor and credit to himself and family. I have frequently heard him relate that his mother and father were in San Domingo when the terrible Negro Insurrection arose, and that his mother, in order to save herself and him from death, walked out into the sea until the water touched her chin, and for several hours held him aloft out of the water in her raised arms until she was rescued by a vessel. Husband and wife were separated, neither knowing the other was living. The vessel that rescued Mrs. Blondel sailed for Philadelphia, and she, knowing her husband had relatives there, called to see them and found her husband safe. It was a joyful meeting to both. They moved to Martinsburg; and during my younger days, I had occasion to see them frequently. The shop occupied by him, in the tin and brass foundry business, was a small wooden structure, occupying the same corner now having upon it the fine brick building, in which the son of John H. still carries on the tin business.

In enumeration of worthy and good citizens I entirely forgot a section of the county, that possessed some grand men,—the upper Opequon region. Among the residents were Samuel Miller, John Burns, Benj. Boley, Joseph Gorrell, Joseph and John Burns, Isaac Franklin; Joshua, Daniel and John Burns, all of whom moved to Missouri years ago. There was also Jacob Vanmetre, called Easy Jake; Joseph Hoffman; the Roberts family, William,

Edward F. and Josiah; Abram Williamson, John P. Kearfott, Abram Deck, Morgan Vancleve and others,—all worthy gentlemen, and whose posterity in many cases are still citizens of your county.

The system of lights at night were entirely different from the present. Every family used the candle on a candlestick, and in many families nothing but the small grease lamp was used. A piece of cotton cloth would be cut about two inches wide, doubled together, and lard put in a small cup made of iron with a sharp prong, which would be put in a crack, usually of the chimney jam. In the stores and hotels the walls would be hung with sconces, made of tin, in which a candle was burnt. In some of the wealthier families they burned sperm oil in lamps. The churches were often lighted by side wall lights of candles, in sconces. It was a singular thing if any of the younger generation could define and give the meaning of the word *sconce*. Between 1840 and 1850 etherial oil was introduced, which gave a bright and beautiful light, but a very dangerous one as it was more liable to explode than the present kerosene so much in use. We knew nothing about gas, and in fact coal was not much in use, except by blacksmiths. Most generally charcoal was used.

The trade in charcoal and tar was carried on extensively in our pine regions. It is very doubtful whether one charcoal kiln is now burnt in the county in a year. At one time hundreds of them could be found in what was termed the Pine Hills. The mode of making charcoal is not fully understood, hence I can only give the fact that logs of medium size would be placed in a pit in the ground and covered over with earth, with only one vent hole to give draft to fire. It would be closed up after the kiln was fully fired, and kept constantly covered with earth until the smoke ceased to rise. It generally made a mound from six to eight feet high, which gradually sank almost to a level. When it was opened and occasionally sprinkled with water, the wood looked to be solid, but when stirred it broke up into lumps possibly three or four inches. A kiln generally yielded from 500 to 800 bushels of coal.

CHAPTER XII.
THE B. & O. R. R. STRIKES AT MARTINSBURG.

THE incidents bearing upon the beginning of trouble with the Baltimore & Ohio Railway began about the 16th of April, 1877. All along the line tramps, communists and turbulent organizations had given rise to much dissension among the railroad employés. John W. Garrett, a business man of acquired reputation, was made president of the company in 1856. He found its stock quoted low, its dividends small, and the road in a very poor condition. Mr. Garrett proved to be the right man in the right place, and displayed splendid executive ability during the civil war, which came on shortly afterward. He surrounded himself with capable assistants, and having considerable influence with the Secretary of War, secured the most profitable contract that, in a short while, fully restored the credit of the corporation and extended the road until it became one of the largest and most prominent lines in the country. However, about the month of July clouds began to hover about the president's head. A storm was impending which, before it could be controlled, would involve the nation from the Atlantic to the Pacific and from Pennsylvania to Texas, in untold loss and misfortune. At a meeting convened on the 11th of July, '77, by means of an official circular, the president informed the employés that a preamble and resolutions had been adopted to the effect that all officers and operatives of the road receiving sums in excess of one dollar *per diem* would be reduced ten per cent., and after the 16th of the same month the change would take effect. Every man engaged upon the main line and branches east of the Ohio River was embraced in this rule, including the trans-Ohio division and the roads leased by the company. It was stated in the notice that action in this direction would be postponed until after their competitors had made similar retrenchments, hoping that business would revive in a short while and a decrease of expenses be avoided. They were disappointed in this, and the principal reason brought about the action taken, which was on account of general depression of business interests over the country. The earnings of all railways were unavoidably and seriously affected. A change had to be made—in fact the call for it was imperative.

Persons superior to those of the ordinary observer, by means of information, supposed that the low wages movement was undoubtedly canvassed along the great trunk lines and decided upon by representatives of various roads directly after the close of Vanderbilt's freight war in the spring. During the month of May the Pennsylvania road put it in force, and the reduction of ten per cent. was accepted by the employés. This was followed by the Erie and New York Central roads, to take effect July 1st, and in both cases they were duly informed beforehand of the changes to be made. As asserted in its circular, the Baltimore and Ohio road was nearly the last to take action in this matter, and several days before the rule was to be enforced a number of the firemen at once decided to strike. They declared their intention that they *could not* and *would not* stand any reduction from their wages. The Trainmen's Union was in full blast all along the line, which had been effectively instituted previously by a traveling delegation from the Pennsylvania road, and taking advantage of affairs, a real strike began.

The workingmen claimed that their grievances were unbearable—that the treatment received at the hands of merchants and boarding-house keepers along the route, for such necessities as trainmen were compelled to have, was inordinately rash. Their belief was that whatever turn made in affairs could not make them much worse off. Their earnings were low, rents high, and for their heavy demands at the scanty stores at the stations, extravagant prices were charged. Extortion pressed them on every side, and coupled with compulsory credit purchase from month to month, they began to nurse a hatred and antagonism against the company and general public. At this time the road carried a moderate amount eastward, but owing to competition were unable to get sufficient to the westward to load its cars. This caused a large reduction of the hands employed, and created much discontent.

President Garrett, Vice-President King, and second Vice-President Keyser, upon learning of the strike, and the movements of the Brotherhood of Engineers and the Trainmen's Union, pronounced it untimely, ill-advised, and fated to meet no great success. The road, like all others, was now passing through the darkest days of its experience. A financial stringency was staring it in the face, and business falling off where an accession had been calculated upon—the results of competition and unproductive extensions of line. The officials stated that a reduction had to be made for the curtailment of expenses, and when the demands of the strikers were made known, they promptly refused them. Knowing that a stoppage would lead to heavy losses, yet they preferred to let the road stand idle, rather than be dictated to and cause a reinstatement of the former rates of wages. On account of this, the strike was simply suicidal on the part of those engaged in it. Meetings were held by the Brotherhood of Locomotive Engineers—advice given and received, and many were led to believe that they would take no part in the strike. With the consent of this organization, the Trainmen's Union assisted in starting the important movement all along the line. On the 16th of July, 1877, the day that the reduction of wages on the B. & O. R. R. was ordered to take effect, the strike was commenced in our city and the first actual violence committed. Here occurred the first important incidents of the great strikes of '77, on the night of July 16th. Notice had been given the crews of all trains, by the strikers, that after a certain hour no person should move an engine under penalty of death. Engineers on the road were paralyzed,—while the managers hastened to make good their usual trips and secure men to take the places of the strikers. However, they met with only partial success.

It was in our happy neighborhood, which had rested in peace and quietude since the war, that the combination of railroad men imbued their hands in blood and met their first loss of life, in attempting to carry out their communistic ideas. On Monday morning, the 16th of July, a large number of train hands left Baltimore, and with those coming in from the West, began to concentrate at Martinsburg. Near the dispatcher's office could always be found a number of locomotives on the tracks, and it was no unusual occurrence for employés to congregate there. But at this time it was noticed that something more than ordinary was transpiring, or about to transpire, when the men collected in groups at the depot, the machine-shops, the switch-stands, along the tracks and other localities. An explanation of these mysterious gatherings was, in a short while, made very plain, when a fireman notified the dispatcher that a cattle-train was compelled to stop there, as the entire crew had struck and no one could be found to take the vacant places. The fireman also stated that he thought no more trains would be allowed to move from this point in either direction. The news soon spread, and in a short while people began to collect from all directions to see what was going on. The policemen put in their appearances, and sauntered leisurely around, waiting to see if their services would be called for. In a short while the engines were detached from the trains, and run into the round-house. When questioned by the officials concerning their action, the strikers replied that no more trains would be run over that road, in any direction, until the company withdrew the ten per cent. reduction of trainmen's wages. They intended to refrain from work, and would not allow their places to be filled by a new set of men. The freight trains were kept on a stand-still, while the mail trains were allowed to pass, but eventually they were stopped. The increased crowd of spectators, by this time, was stirred with interest, and the news spread until it reached every citizen. It was taken up by the press and soon scattered broad-cast over the country.

The Mayor, Captain A. P. Shutt, and the policemen were sent for, who promptly put in their appearance, and backed by a trio of municipal guardians, held a conference with the railroad officials. Mayor Shutt, willing to do all in his power, proceeded to speak to the strikers, using mild and temperate language, and advised them to return to their work and trust to the fairness of the company in the settlement of their grievances. But the mob, following the general rule, had reached that point where reason ceased to be a virtue, and their madness and violence had only been increased. The Mayor was hooted at, derided, and his good counsel turned to ridicule. He failed to impress the strikers with any of his mild-mannered notions, and could not make them understand that it would be best to run their locomotives to their destinations. In fact, his speech only served to add fuel to the fires already fiercely burning, and, giving it up as a hopeless task, he ordered his policemen to arrest the ringleaders. Frantic efforts to obey were made by the powerless policemen, while the strikers laughed in their faces. The Mayor's appeals were equally fruitless—the men refused to work—and the engineers found an excuse for refusal by saying they dare not enter their cabs. The firemen and trackmen would not allow others to take their places, holding back with all their strength. Finally the Mayor and policemen withdrew from the scene, leaving the situation at the undisputed command of the strikers. The machine shops, depot and round-houses were all deserted by midnight, except by a number of Union men who were left to guard the tracks and see that no trains were allowed to pass that point. The strangers from Baltimore were provided for by their fellow-strikers, and a number lodged at the hotels. The telegraph manager communicated the information of the strike to President Garrett and Vice-President King, of Baltimore, and after midnight Capt. Thos. B. Sharp, General Master of Transportation, was brought to the spot. After carefully surveying the condition of affairs, which was in no wise difficult of comprehension, a full report of his investigation was telegraphed to the principal office. The matter was duly considered by the Baltimore officials, who prepared a telegram and at once dispatched to Governor Mathews, stating the facts as here given, and asking him to provide some method to abandon violent measures and allow trains to move in safety. Through the promptness of the Governor, a telegram was sent to Col. C. J. Faulkner, at Martinsburg, dated at Wheeling, about midnight, ordering him if necessary, to call out his command, the Berkeley Light Infantry, to aid and protect the civil authorities, and to make due report to the executive office of the existing state of affairs and his operations.

Col. Faulkner was informed of the Governor's wishes July 17th, about 12:30 A. M., and returned answer by telegraph, stating that the strikers would not allow trains to move either east or west from Martinsburg, and asked if his instructions extended any further than merely protecting the peace—if so, he desired an answer in full. Meanwhile the Colonel issued orders for an immediate assemblage of the militia command, prepared for active duty, at their armory. The call was promptly responded to by the militia, among whom were many railroaders, and possibly connected with the Trainmen's Union. A number of the militia, as well as numerous citizens, felt a deep and hearty sympathy with the men engaged in the strike. In a short while Col. Faulkner received another message from Governor Mathews, advising him if possible, to avoid using force, and at the same time give all necessary aid to the civil authorities, and see that the laws were duly executed. At the conclusion of the message the Governor stated: "I rely upon you to act discreetly and firmly."

Mr. Sharp, Master of Transportation, fixed upon 5 o'clock as the hour for moving trains on Tuesday morning, and secured an engineer and fireman, who agreed to take the stock-train through to its destination, if properly protected. A request was then made of Col. Faulkner, his command of militia, Mayor Shutt and police, County Sheriff and posse, to be present and see that the strikers did not interfere. Col. Faulkner, before retiring from the scene, asked Governor Mathews by telegraph: "Must I protect men who are willing to run their trains, and see that they are permitted to go east and west?" In a short while the Governor answered: "I am informed that the rioters constitute a combination so strong that the civil authorities are powerless to enforce the law. If this is so, prevent any interference by rioters with the men at work, and also prevent the obstruction of the trains."

Upon receiving this communication, Col. Faulkner at once repaired to the armory to take charge of his command, knowing plainly what his duty was. The known orders for the gathering of militia, the marching of uniformed men on the streets bearing arms, accompanied by the excitement of the strike, caused such a restlessness that there was but little sleep visited the eyelids of the citizens on that eventful night. Groups of persons, white and colored, could be seen gathered on the corners in knots, discussing the unusual state of affairs, and wondering what the morrow would bring forth. The city has never experienced such a sensation since the close of the war.

At about five o'clock the next morning, W. H. Harrison, Master Mechanic of the company, with Mr. French, arrived here from Cumberland. A consultation was held with Capt. Sharp and the remaining local force of the road, after which a locomotive was fired up and attached to a cattle train, and with an engineer and fireman they were ready to start matters anew. At about sunrise the attempt was made to set the driving wheels once more in motion, but was prevented by the strikers guard from the round-house, who swept down upon them and ordered the non-striking men to hold hard or they would be killed. The throttle was promptly shut and the engine brought to a stand-still, which probably saved their lives. However, the men remained with the train for a short time, expecting to rush it through, but finally left. Up to this time the militia and town officials had not made their appearance. The president and officers of the company were informed of the circumstances, and at once instructed Capt. Sharp to make the attempt until his efforts were crowned with success. The consequent sounding of the shrill steam whistle, in the early dawn of the day, startled the excited inhabitants of the city, and in a short while the streets were flocked, all anxious to learn what was going on. Among the citizens were the strikers belonging to the city, and reinforced by those from Baltimore and the West. They congregated about the basement doors of the present depot, and gathered in small squads over the surrounding ground.

It seemed as though the railroad men, by agreement, separated from the others, and concentrated a formidable force near the company's buildings. Mr. Harrison, the Master Mechanic, conversed with them and endeavored by every means in his power to influence their minds peaceably, and bring about an amicable adjustment of the prevailing troubles. A number of employés were well disposed towards Harrison, but exhibited no change of heart. Harrison finally returned to Sharp, after exhausting his arguments, and reported that the rioters would not change their decision in regard to stopping all freight trains, and if anything, their resolution had become more firm than ever. Mr. Sharp was a cool, determined man, of iron will, and upon receiving this information, concluded that no favorable or peaceful solution of the surrounding difficulties would be reached. The strikers had accused Sharp of being at the bottom of the rough treatment to which they were subjected, and believed him to be the cause of the reduction in wages. In truth, he was bitterly opposed to the cutting-down system, and in favor of restoring the pay to its original amount. The enemies were ignorant of this, and when they saw him walk up to a locomotive and order the engineer forward to his destination at all hazards, they cast scowling glances upon him and were greatly enraged.

The engine had not moved a single length of rail, before the mob swarmed upon the foot-board, over the coal in the tender and thence into the cab, driving the newly-engaged men from their positions. The locomotive was uncoupled from the train and run into the round-house, leaving the cars on the track no nearer their destination than before. By this time their numbers had increased several hundred, and no further damage was done. The crowd then gathered nigh, in almost a solid mass, to watch the proceedings. The engineer and fireman had escaped, and again Sharp was defeated, of which he informed the company as before. Meantime the crowd of spectators and array of strikers continued to increase. At about 9 o'cjock, four hours later than the appointed time, the sound of fife and drum was heard, and presently the gleaming arms and accoutrements of the Berkeley Light Infantry were seen advancing towards the depot, headed by Col. Faulkner. Loud hurrahs and shouts of welcome went up as the militia filed down the steep steps and marched to the round-house unopposed. The engineer and firemen had again been discovered and brought to the spot, and another cheer went up. They were closely followed by their wives and children, who threw their arms around their husbands necks, frantically embracing and urging them to refrain from the perilous attempt. But they tore themselves from the grasp of their families, and started on a swift pace to the round-house, where they mounted the engine, which had already been fired up. The engine was then moved out, with soldiers on either side, bayonets fixed and guns loaded, and proceeded in the direction of the distillery. Squads of the militia had been arranged and several placed on the engine. Their progress was slow and snail-like, owing to the pressure of the close forward ranks of the strikers. At this moment the rioters rose to white heat, when the third experiment was made for starting with the trainmen guarded. At the suggestion of Mayor Shutt, Col. Faulkner then proceeded to address the mob, and if possible stay further violence. In a courteous, firm and impressive manner, he warned them of the result if they interfered any further, and if they touched the engine it would be at their own peril. They only laughed at him, as though they would accept none other than brute force to obtain their rights.

The engine was moved in the direction of the distillery, where it was attached to a cattle train on the siding. A switch led this track upon the main road, which, it seems had been tampered with by the strikers. The train was made up about 10 o'clock, and squads of militia were placed on the engine, and on either side of the train. John Poisal, a militiaman was sitting on the cow-catcher, and as the train steadily and slowly drew near the switch, his attention was attracted by the position of the switch ball. Unless some change was made, Poisal knew the train would be thrown off the right track. With musket in hand, he immediately jumped to the ground, and ran to the switch. Just as he was in the act of reversing it, William Vandergriff, a striking fireman, who had tampered it and was standing near to see the result, yelled out:

"Don't you touch that switch!"

"I'm not going to see the train run on a siding if I can prevent it," replied Poisal, as he firmly grasped the iron. Before Poisal could change the switch, Vandergriff had drawn a small pocket-pistol from his belt, and fired two shots in rapid succession upon him. One of the bullets plowed a jagged furrow on the side of Poisal's forehead, just above the ear, while the other flew wide of its mark. Upon receiving the shot, Poisal quickly raised his gun, and with a steady aim fired on Vandergriff. Another soldier near by fired at the same time, and both balls lodged in Vandergriff's body, one in the arm and the other penetrating the thigh. He fell, mortally wounded, which was followed by the explosion of several small arms, but no injury done. At this onslaught the mob pressed closer on the soldiers, while a lively scattering was made among the woman, children, and more peaceably disposed citizens. Poisal and Vandergriff were taken to their homes, and medical aid procured. In a short while the strikers again had things all their own way, completely overpowering the militia. The sound of fire-arms drew larger crowds from the city, and the excitement was more intense than ever. By this time the fireman and engineer had escaped from the train, and left the locality.

Col. Faulkner fully appreciated in a minute, that his militia, however brave and trustworthy, under these circumstances would not attempt to kill their relatives and friends. He at once reported to Capt. Sharp, stating that his men were powerless and many in sympathy with the strikers, and that he would have to march them back to the armory. They were then ordered home, and the road left blocked up with trains of loaded cars, subject to the caprices of the infuriated and angry mob.

For several days afterward Vandergriff lay upon his bed, suffering terrible agony. The best nurses and physicians the country afforded attended him, and everything possible was done for his recovery. However, on the 28th of July he breathed his last, and on the Sunday following was buried in Green Hill Cemetery. Poisal, whose injury was slight, made his appearance on the street in a few days, appearing as well and hearty as usual. The story of this incident was spread abroad by the press, and if credit was given them, one would suppose that civil war surely reigned in Martinsburg. The actual number of strikers was estimated to be upwards of seventy-five or eighty, but were backed by many citizens and other working classes. The press greatly exaggerated this strike, and in a few days the torch of communism was burning brightly throughout the whole country.

After the militia had left the scene, the confusion ceased, and the railroaders retired to their former position at the shops. The locomotive, as before, was uncoupled and returned to the round-house. Col. Faulkner became disgusted with the part he had been forced to take in the riots. He had given his men no orders to fire, and therefore run no risk of his commands being disobeyed. His desire was to perform his duty and enforce the law without shedding blood, but met with no success. Information was at once furnished Governor Mathews of the proceedings and results. Later on Col. Faulkner telegraphed the Governor that it was impossible for him to do anything further, and that a number of his command, being railroad men, would not respond. The Governor, in response, dispatched that law-abiding citizens must be protected, and the peace preserved, by whatever means was necessary to accomplish it. He also stated that he could furnish a company from Wheeling, who would be used in the suppression of riot and execution of the law, and also spoke very highly of Col. Faulkner's appeal to the rioters.

The mob had full possession of all the railroad property from Monday night until the succeeding Wednesday morning, July 18th. At about 7:30 o'clock, the Mathews Light Guard arrived from Wheeling, under command of Col. Delaplaine, and a conference was held between Attorney-General White, Wm. Keyser, Second Vice-President, Col. Sharp, and others.. During this time the rioters made no further demonstration, but remained quiet and apparently content with the work they had done. The Trainmen's Union at Baltimore, Grafton, Cumberland, Pittsburgh, and other points were kept posted by the strickers concerning their doings.

The strikers visited the railroad shops on the evening of the 18th of July, and ordered the laborers then at work to stop, which they refused to do. In the meantime the mail trains were allowed to pass unmolested either way. Finally the cars loaded with cattle were arranged for by Mr. Mantz and shipped over the Cumberland Valley and Western Maryland roads. The Wheeling Light Infantry had charge of the town for several days, encamped at the Court House and railroad, and no action was taken by them with the strikers, as it was deemed best to await reinforcements. On the 18th of July Governor Mathews, at the urgent request of Mr. Garret, telegraphed President Hayes, and after explaining the situation, asked for United States troops. No freight operations were started until Brevet Major-General W. H. French, Colonel of the Fourth U. S. Artillery, arrived with two hundred men armed as infantry, and no sooner had they reached the town than quiet and order reigned supreme.

President Hays issued, previous to this, his proclamation, and directed it to the citizens of West Virginia. He admonished all good citizens in the United States and within its territory of jurisdiction, against aiding, countenancing, abetting or taking part in such unlawful proceedings. A warning was given those engaged in or connected with said domestic violence and obstruction of the laws, and orders given them to disperse and retire peaceably to their respective abodes on or before 12 o'clock meridian, of the 19th day of July. ᶠIt bore the signatures of President Hayes and F. A. Steward, Acting Secretary of State, accompanied by the great seal of the United States. This permanently settled affairs at Martinsburg, and the rioters had to retire, as they could not fight the Government of the United States.

CHAPTER XIII.

LIFE OF THE LATE HON. C. J. FAULKNER—THE STORY OF A LIFE FULL OF BUSTLING ACTIVITIES—LEFT AN ORPHAN—A FIGHT FOR AN EDUCATION — DEBATE WITH TOM MARSHALL—ENTERS PUBLIC LIFE IN 1832—GOES TO CONGRESS IN 1852—A DIPLOMAT AND A PRISONER OF STATE—THE REWARD OF INDUSTRY.

WRITTEN BY COL. FRANK A. BURR IN 1884.

I.

*" Time, hath, my Lord.
A wallet at his back, wherein he puts alms.
For Oblivion's sake.
These scraps, are good deeds past.
Forgot, as soon as done."*

HAD Shakespeare his normal inspiration when he penned these lines? And is it true that good deeds live to spur succeeding generations to emulation and success? It is the general judgment of the world that notable acts survive forever, and burnished by the lapse of time, are brighter when picked up from the dust of years. Of such a one I write. One whose life has been full of strange vicissitudes and bustling activities. It is now sloping to a close, as calmly as the sun goes down after a stormy day. He began life in an humble way. When eight years of age he was left an orphan, with no kith nor kin on this broad continent. He grew to manhood, and to old age, in the little town in which he was born, and in which he now lives. His home to-day is almost within the shadow of the grave of a grandfather, shot down in the Revolution, and of a father, who perished from service in the war of 1812. His mother died before he could hardly understand the value of a mother's care, and his father was buried before he could comprehend the meaning of the word "orphan." He was reared by strangers, and whatever he has been or is, he chiefly gained for himself, by as hard a struggle with the world as a man ever made. Perhaps it was best for him that his lot was cast in rough places, and that he had to make the journey of life alone. His father's advice and influence might have given his character a different bent, and a less fortunate one. He was a soldier, a major of artillery, and was filled with a soldier's ambition, and a soldier's *bonhomie*. Therefore, he died poor, and left his son, when a child, to make his own way, with no other capital than the sturdy qualities inherited from good Scotch-Irish stock on both sides of the family tree.

The village doctor gave him a home, but he himself learned the valuable lessons of industry and self-reliance that have stood him so well in hand through all his busy years. Like many of the youth of the country, when impelled by vague, yet strong ambitions, he early began the study of law, at the famous law school of Chancellor Tucker, in Winchester, and in much less than the usual time of probation and reading, he was admitted to the bar. He was never accounted a brilliant boy, nor has he ever been noted for that quality as a man. He got his start in life by untiring industry and close application; he early trained his mind to methodical effort. While others slept he worked, and it has been a tireless energy, more than any single quality of his nature, that has made him a name and fame as a successful man.

He had little more than attained his majority when he took a leading position at the bar, and in the politics of his native county.

The decade beginning in 1830 was filled with important history, and with its opening year Mr Faulkner practically began his public life.

The Constitutional Convention of that year had completed its work and the people of Virginia were to decide whether the Constitution of 1830, largely the work of Watkins Leigh, was to be the fundamental law of the State. There was a strong feeling for and against it. The famous Tom Marshall, of Kentucky, was one of its most bitter opponents. He had been living a year or more in Berkeley County, on a visit to his relations, the Colstons, and had gone to Richmond during the sessions of the Constitutional Convention. There he had engendered an intense dislike for Watkins Leigh. When he returned to Martinsburg he took open ground against the instrument and assailed it as "Watkins Leigh's Constitution." By the time the canvass came on, when the people were to decide for or against it, he had aroused a good deal of feeling in relation to its provisions, and it was thought best by those who favored it that a great public public meeting should be called, at which its provisions should be discussed before the people. Mr. Faulkner had taken a position in its favor, believing it an improvement on the old, and it was arranged that he and Tom Marshall should present its merits or demerits to the people at a meeting in Martinsburg, the county town. A great crowd gathered to hear the debate. It was the first public discussion of Mr. Marshall, as well as the first of Mr. Faulkner. Each young man appeared at his best, but Mr. Marshall, at that early day, gave ample evidence of those great powers of mind and tongue that afterwards made him so famous. The discussion lasted for several hours, and Mr. Marshall carried the crowd by his wit and eloquence; but Mr. Faulkner, by his industry, secured for the Constitution a large majority at the polls of Berkeley County.

II.
ENTERING PUBLIC LIFE.

An important decade in our national history began with the adoption of the new Constitution of Virginia. The nullification schemes of Calhoun were being hatched in its first year, and in 1832, when Mr. Faulkner was called to his first public position, President Jackson had just issued his famous "proclamation of force," which boldly asserted the supremacy of the Government of the United States over the government of any State. And there was then such imminent danger of armed resistance to the Federal authority that Congress placed in the hands of the President the power of military coercion. Clay was then engaging the public attention with his scheme of protection ; then, too, Andrew Jackson was pushing tricky Martin Van Buren for the Presidency, and sitting upon the aspirations of Calhoun with the whole power of his administration. It was amidst these striking events and upon the threshold of the Presidential election of 1832 that Mr. Faulkner took his place in the Virginia House of Delegates. He was then only a boy in age and appearance, but a man in mind. The Virginia Legislature of that period was composed of men, who in their day and in the great era following, left their imprint on the annals of their time. With those men Mr. Faulkner took a leading position, and at once gave evidence of his power to originate ideas, coupled with the courage to proclaim them. Taking heed of the differences between Jackson and Calhoun, looking at the then condition of Virginia and seeing in the temper of the political factions the seeds of a contest upon the slavery question, he submitted to the Legislature and advocated a proposition for the abolition of slavery upon the *post nati* principle. The north had liberated its bondsmen upon the same principle, and by the provisions of his proposition all children of slave parents were to be born free after July 1st, 1840. He supported this proposition in a speech of great power, which was widely circulated and was severely condemned by the radical slave-holding element. It did not, however, greatly shock public opinion in Virginia at the time, and in many sections of the State the idea was received with decided favor. The slave-holding element undertook, however, to make it an issue the following year, when he was a candidate for re-election, but he was returned upon that issue by what was practically a unanimous vote.

Comment upon this speech and action of Mr. Faulkner was not confined to the South alone. It was extensively read throughout the country. Once a year for many years after it was delivered, William Lloyd Garrison printed that speech in full in the *Liberator*, amused himself by sending Mr. Faulkner a copy, and circulated it widely as evidence of the growing sentiment in the South against slavery.

The opening of the year 1833 witnessed the beginning of the abolition crusade, and it seemed to destroy all the sentiment there ever was in the South in favor of emancipation, gradual or otherwise. It had the effect to combine all elements together in resistance, forcible and positive, to the attempted legislative encroachment upon the established institution of the South. I have often heard Mr. Faulkner say, "but for this impertinent and illegal intermeddling of Northern fanatics, emancipation would have become the predominant sentiment of Virginia, and would have worked out its results without ruin and bloodshed."

Mr. Faulkner finished his first legislative experience in 1833, and after declining a third election was appointed a commissioner on behalf of Virginia, to examine and report on the disputed question of the boundary line between Maryland and Virginia ; the controversy embraced all of that rich section of country lying between the north and south branches of the Potomac River. Mr. Faulkner's report was extensive and conclusive ; it settled the controversy between Maryland and Virginia, giving to the old mother of States a clear title to large proportions of the present counties of Hampshire, Mineral, Hardy, Grant Pendleton and Randolph, for which Maryland was contending.*

Mr. Faulkner first met Andrew Jackson while engaged upon this famous report. The interview was characteristic and interesting. It was in that nullification era when Congress had delegated to the President the power of coercion, and he had used it to crush South Carolina's secession proclivities. John Floyd, then Governor of Virginia, and Mr. Tazewell, then in the Senate, were, although still members of the party, bitterly denouncing Jackson's nullification proclamation, and pressing their theory of State Rights. Governor Floyd had asked Mr. Faulkner to go to Europe to obtain data from the original records in relation to the boundary line, but having no funds to pay the expenses of the voyage, he requested him to call upon the President. explain his proposed visit to England, and request that he be given passage as Virginia's representative, in a government ship. Mr. Faulkner visited the President, for this purpose, and as soon as he stated the object of his visit. "Old Hickory" replied:

"Certainly, sir, I will grant you passage in the ship Delaware, now lying in the Potomac, about to sail for England," but, he continued, "doesn't it strike you as a little strange that Governor Floyd, with his peculiar notions of States Rights, and ideas of the limited powers of the National government, should ask a service of this kind from it, in a purely State matter? I will grant the request with pleasure, but I cannot help thinking that it is an apt illustration of the absurdity of the doctrine of State Rights, as Governor and Senator Tazewell declare them." Mr. Faulkner at once transmitted an official announcement of the success of his application to the President, and at the same time wrote a letter to governor Floyd, which he marked "private and confidential," giving his conversation with the President. Floyd sent

---

*The report here mentioned will be found on page 67.

to Tazewell, and together they became greatly incensed. Floyd returned the letter to Mr. Faulkner, with the request that he strike out the words "private and confidential," that Tazewell might make it the basis of an attack for both of them, upon Jackson and his administration, upon the floor of the United States Senate. Mr. Faulkner refused, and years after Governor Floyd thanked him, as did Tazewell, for saving them from the premature open quarrel with "Old Hickory" which they had resolved upon having. The circumstances, however kept Mr. Faulkner from going to Europe on the vessel, and his report on the boundary question was made without consulting the archives of the mother country.

III.
QUITS POLITICS FOR THE LAW,

In 1833, after the completion of the report on the boundary, Mr. Faulkner was married to the daughter of Gen. Boyd, an old and distinguished Virginian, who for many years had taken an active part in her public affairs. For the next fifteen years politics commanded little part of his time and attention. He devoted himself with great zeal to the practice of his profession, and in a short time took a leading place at the bar of Virginia, which was in those days one of the strongest in the Union. His cases were many and his fees large, and before he again appeared in public life he had acquired a fortune which has enabled him to live independently ever since. Having acquired this independence, he again turned to politics, partially for relief from the exactions of legal work, and partly because he was ambitious to leave something behind him besides money ; because he believed that an ambition for public service was a laudable one after a man had acquired a competency. This ambition for a place in history was in perfect keeping with his character, and he devoted himself to it with the same earnest, untiring energy that he had brought to bear upon every task he had undertaken, from his childhood up. This very quality, which people applaud in most of the relations of life, has been belittled and derided by many not broad enough in mental grasp to comprehend the fact that in politics, as in business, a man wins success by the efforts which he makes to deserve it.

In 1841, he responded a second time to the call of his fellow citizens, and was elected to the State Senate of Virginia. Finding, however, that the office made too great demand upon his time, he resigned, in the spring of 1842; he did not, however, cease to take an active interest in public affairs. In 1843 he was an earnest advocate of the annexation of Texas, and in 1846, was one of the earliest and warmest supporters of the Mexican war. In the raising of troops from Virginia, for service in Mexico, Mr. Faulkner was prominent and successful, but all these, and many other public acts, were merely incidents in a life which, during this period, was chiefly devoted to the practice of the law. In 1348, however, Mr. Faulkner was again elected to the House of Delegates of Virginia. During that session he introduced into the Legislature a bill which was passed, and by the Legislature transmitted to the Senators and Representatives and became the famous Fugitive Slave Law passed by Congress, in 1850. Indeed, it was his avowed purpose, in being elected to the Legislature, to do all in his power to bring the whole moral force of the State of Virginia to demand from Congress, a law for the protection of slave property. During this session he was chairman of the special committee of the Virginia Legislature charged with the investigation of the whole fugitive slave question, and it would have been unnatural if he had not, from the beginning of that session, been a central figure in a Legislature of strong men. But it was not only in the discussion and consideration of this grave question, that Mr. Faulkner was prominent. In the revision of the code of State laws, which was the chief work of that Legislature, he took a leading part. His service in this

Legislature, and his work in a previous term was memorable for himself and fruitful to the State. During all the years after his entrance into public life it had been apparent to him, as to every thinking man, that the Virginia Constitution, of 1830, was not sufficient to meet the demands of a rapidly advancing civilization, and when the reform Constitutional Convention of 1850 assembled, it found Mr. Faulkner one of its members. This was the first occasion during his public life that an opportunity had been afforded him to combat the persistent discriminations of the government of Virginia against that portion of the state which lay west of the Blue Ridge. Eastern Virginia had always borne heavily upon the western portion of the State in taxation, in the distribution of public improvements, and had defrauded her out of her proper representation by establishing a mixed basis of population and property, which alone could give the Eastern slave-holding section of the State the power to control the policy of the entire State.

IV.
IN THE REFORMED CONVENTION OF 1850.

Mr. Faulkner's contest against these unjust discriminations began when he first entered the Legislature, and never ceased while he had a voice in that body. It 1841 his opposition to the unjust attitude of the majority towards the section of which he was a native was such that he presented a proposition to remove the capital from Richmond to some point in the Shenandoah Valley. But while these contests vexed the public mind in the East, because they served to call attention to the hardships endured by Western Virginia, there were no practical means presented of striking at the root of the evil until the reform convention of 1850 was called.

The proceedings of this convention were very important, and Mr. Faulkner was prominent in its sessions. He paid little attention, however, to the abstract or theoretical questions which arose, no matter what might be their seeming importance, but reserved all his influence and energy for a bold advocacy of the rights and interests of Western Virginia. To this, his native section, taxation and the basis of representation were far more important matters than any other questions before that body. The importance of these issues had been recognized by all sections of the State, and strong men from the East, as well as the West, had been sent to deal with the important issues to be decided by that assemblage. Governor Henry A. Wise, John Y. Mason, John Minor Botts and George W. Summers were a few of the great men in that convention. Mr. Faulkner's most significant battle in that body was upon the basis of representation, and in the debate upon that question he ran counter to all the leading men representing the eastern section of the State. This was especially the fact in his course upon the question of representation; it was to his great honor that at that early day he was the steadfast and eloquent champion of basing representation upon voters and not upon chattels; that he demanded representation should be wholly upon the free whites and not in part upon property, whether slave or otherwise.

In his advocacy of this measure his speech was able and exhaustive; he commanded the close attention of the convention during the two days which were occupied by its delivery. It made a profound impression, and deciding the question under consideration in consonance with Mr. Faulkner's views, gave to Western Virginia that position in the Councils of States to which she was entitled. The debate in relation to taxation was equally interesting and important. Mr. Faulkner bore the brunt of that task, as well as the debate upon representation. Henry A. Wise was the champion of Eastern Virginia ideas and interests on the subject of taxation, while Mr. Faulkner stood in the same relation to Western Virginia. The debate between these two leaders of diverse interests has been preserved and was regarded as a leading incident of the convention, and his position was sustained. With this eminent service to his State, and especially to his native section of the Old Dominion, Mr. Faulkner broadened into the domain of national politics.

The compromise measures of Mr. Clay of 1850 changed the political affiliation of many men, especially in the South. Mr. Faulkner was one of those who drifted to the side of the Union in the ensuing division. The South, equally with the North, was dissatisfied with the terms of the compromise; the North with relation to the Fugitive Slave Law clause, and the South because of the feeling that too much had been conceded to the anti-slave power. The planting States, with South Carolina in the lead, were ready then to secede, but they could not depend upon the help of the other Southern States, and hence there was no open revolt. This may be said to have been the opening of the division in the South upon the question of union or disunion.

In 1851 Henry Beddinger, of Jefferson County, was a candidate for Congress in the district in which Mr. Faulkner lived. He took the position of South Carolina on the compromise measure of 1850 as his platform. Mr. Faulkner was brought out as an indepedent candidate against him, in behalf of the Union cause and against further sectional agitation. Ben Hill, of Georgia, was a candidate the same year in his State on the same platform. The first contest of Mr. Faulkner for a seat in the national legislature was a memorable one. Mr. Beddinger was the regular Democratic candidate, with a majority in the district of several hundred in his favor, and he made war to the knife against his opponent. Extracts from Mr. Faulkner's speech in favor of the abolition of slavery in 1832 were printed in red letters and posted everywhere in the district, and every possible effort was made to array public opinion against him on account of the first conspicuous act of his political life. With that unwearying industry and zeal which have always been characteristic of Mr. Faulkner, he entered into this fight and made an active canvass, holding a public discussion with his opponent at least once in every county of the district. He was elected to Congress by a good majority in a district which was largely Democratic, but where the Union sentiment was at that time roused into fervid action.

V.
IN CONGRESS.

When he took his seat in Congress the old parties were undergoing rapid disintegration, and in July, 1852, Mr. Faulkner, in an address to the people of the country, joined Alexander H. Stephens and Robert Toombs, of Georgia, and several other Whig Representatives in Congress from the South, in declaring that as General Scott was the candidate of the Free Soil wing of the Whig Party, opposed to the compromises of 1850, they could not support him for the Presidency. Thus Mr. Faulkner, with those other great Southern leaders, left the Whig Party and joined his political fortunes with Democracy. In the heated discussion of the hour the Whig party charged the Democracy with opposition to the compromise measures of 1850. To refute this charge Mr. Faulkner prepared and delivered a speech in Congress, August 2, 1852, which, in the printed edition, was entitled "The Compromise—The Presidency—Political Parties." It was a great effort, an exhaustive review of the issues which had disrupted the Whig party, and a complete refutation, from a Democratic standpoint, of the charge that the Democracy, as an organization, was opposed to the compromise measures. It was also a splendid effort in behalf of Mr. Pierce for the Presidency. This speech at once attracted public attention, and was made a campaign document by the Democratic party.

Mr. John C. Rives, the noted Congressional printer, in a letter written in December, 1852, says: "I printed for the National Democratic Committee 93,000 copies of Mr.

Faulkner's speech, made in Congress before the close of its last session. I would have printed more if I could have procured paper in time. Although I have been engaged in the printing business here twenty odd years, I do not recollect to have printed so many copies of any other speech. The speech was printed at other offices, but I do not know how large the editions were."

The fact is that more than 125,000 copies of the speech were printed and distributed, and it was the text for every stump orator for the Democracy during the memorable campaign of that year. This change of Mr. Faulkner of his political affiliations naturally created him new adversaries at home, and he returned there to combat them. He took the stump, and in a series of speeches justified his course, carrying his district for Pierce by a handsome majority. This fixed his position definitely in the Democratic party. For four successive terms he was elected to Congress over popular candidates, and as early in the service he had attained, so to the end he maintained a leading position in the national legislature. He was made chairman of the Military Committee of the House at the beginning of his second term, and had a leading place on other important committees. His eulogy upon Henry Clay attracted great attention, as did his speech in favor of opening the way to promotion in the army to merit, without reference to the place of education, which was intended to be, and was, a blow at the military oligarchy which has its origin at West Point. Naturally there are many others in Congress and upon the stump worthy of equal commendation, as it was known of him that he was the most ceaseless of workers, and his only recreations during his public life were at intervals to take part in those social reunions where he could enjoy contact with the best minds of the nation. It was also true of him that at home, as well as when engrossed in the cares of public life, he gave close application to his private affairs and the interests of his clients.

His law office was near, but apart from his house, and that office had been his workshop for more than half a century. It was a trite saying in the little town in which he lived that the light was never out in that office until after each new day was born.

When the Know-Nothing craze was at its height Mr. Faulkner made a memorable canvass in Virginia in conjunction with Henry A. Wise, the key-note of which was the declaration, in the language of Mr. Faulkner in Congress, "I am not, never have been and never expect to be, a member of any oath-bound, secret political association. I claim communion with but one political organization—and that is the great National Democratic Party of this country—a party that has shown itself, after the most ample experience, broad enough to embrace all the vast interests of liberty and humanity, and strong enough to uphold in its firm and conservative grasp the Constitution of my country and the Union of these States."

Mr. Faulkner followed this struggle against the intolerance of Know-Nothingism by attending the National Democratic Convention in Cincinnati, in 1856. He was with a majority of the Virginia delegation in his preference for Mr. Buchanan as the nominee of that body. For the conspicuous services he had rendered the party he was chosen Chairman of the Democratic Congressional Committee for the conduct of the Presidential campaign. But for the action of the Electoral College of Virginia, in recommending John B. Floyd as the preference of the State for a Cabinet position, Mr. Faulkner would have been made Secretary of War upon the accession of Mr. Buchanan to the Presidency. The new President, however, tendered the distinguished Virginian the hardly less inferior position of Minister to France. But Mr. Faulkner was in Congress, and Hon. John Y. Mason, of Virginia, who was a personal friend, was the Minister of the United States in France. Mr. Faulkner therefore declined the mission, rather than disturb an old friend in his place. Mr. Mason having died during the pendency of the canvass of 1859, Mr. Faulkner was nominated and confirmed as our new Minister to France, and repaired at once to his new post of duty.

VI.
MINISTER TO FRANCE.

His services as a diplomat were useful to his country and honorable to himself; it was through his efforts that the right of expatriation was first admitted by the government of France, and naturalized citizens of the United States given the right to visit the land of their birth without molestation, or fear of military espionage The great bulk of Mr. Faulkner's dispatches while a foreign minister have never been given to the public by the State Department, but when, in 1866, the Senate called for the correspondence of that Department upon the great question of the claims of European governments to exact military service from naturalized citizens of the United States, those of Mr. Faulkner were presented, and in this way the general public was for the first time made aware that in less than a month after his presentation at the Court of Napoleon III., he pressed the issue upon that sovereign to a conclusion in harmony with the wishes and demands of the United States, despite the strenuous opposition of M. Thouvenal, the French Minister for Foreign Affairs. For this he received the thanks of the President in his annual message to Congress. During his term of service at the French Court, there were no great overshadowing questions, except the one to which allusion has been made, between the two countries, until the armed conflict between the North and South in this country became imminent. The sympathies of Napoleon, it is well known, were early enlisted upon the side of the South, and this fact naturally made the position of Mr. Faulkner at the French Court exceedingly delicate. As a citizen of the South, whatever he might do, or omit to do, was sure to meet with misrepresentation at Washington. But he was so circumspect in his conduct that he was not only held blameless, but received the thanks of the government for his services.

It was not to be expected, however, that in a period so stormy, his services, however meritorious and conspicuous, would protect him from detraction; malignant aspersions upon his loyalty to his country and fidelity to his official trust, were carried from Paris to Washington, and these became so frequent and persistent that soon after the inauguration of President Lincoln, Mr. Faulkner took notice of them in a letter to Mr. Seward, Secretary of State, in which he took occasion to deny in strong terms that either in his official or private capacity, he had been disloyal to the United States. It is unnecessary to present in detail the leading acts in Mr. Faulkner's service as a diplomat; but it was always creditable, for in all his mental characteristics he was eminently fitted for such a career. A man of great self-poise, equable temperament, and while of strong convictions, knowing how to hold them in check, it is not singular that he was able to walk in the paths of diplomacy without danger or difficulty, either to himself personally or the country he represented. Besides the power of presenting his points strongly, he could put them adroitly, and had the rare quality of making words persuasive. He showed this attribute early in life. In his many contests in a district that might oftentimes be called turbulent, Mr. Faulkner not infrequently softened the asperities of political warfare and won enemies to his support. A good story is told of him in his native village, which illustrates this point. Old Daniel Burkhardt, a conspicuous personage in the business circles of Martinsburg, was a quiet and eccentric man. He was exceedingly critical, and was at times in favor of Mr. Faulkner, while at other periods he opposed him. In one closely contested election he severely criticised some of Mr. Faulkner's political acts, when one of that gentleman's friends said to him:

"Mr. Burkhardt, you ought not to be against Mr. Faulkner. Why don't you see him, and he will explain to your satisfaction the matter of which you complain."

"Of course he will," was the prompt reply. "He never did anything in his life he could not explain to the satisfaction of anybody. That is the reason I keep out of his way."

Mr. Faulkner, however, did not permit Mr. Burkhardt to escape him, but made the explanation of which the latter was in fear, and thus gained his support. This incident not only illustrated the persuasive power of Mr. Faulkner, but it also allowed his extraordinary gift in gaining and ever afterwards retaining, the friendship of those who had been personally or politically inimical to him.

Mr. Faulkner was relieved of his diplomatic duties early in 1861, by Hon. Wm. L. Dayton, of New Jersey, who had been appointed as his successor by President Lincoln. He left France with the respect of the government to which he had been accredited, and the good wishes of the many American citizens with whom he had been brought into personal or official relations. He had so conducted himself in his delicate relations to the French government, growing out of the anomolous condition of affairs in his own country, that there was not even a pretence that he had been unfaithful in his conduct. He, from the first, refused to discuss these matters with M. Thouvenal, and never but once expressed an unofficial opinion as to the action of the government toward the seceding States. Just before his departure M. Thouvenal asked him if he believed his government would use coercion to preserve the autonomy of the Union. To this Mr. Faulkner said that he did not, but added that he felt compelled to decline to discuss the policy of his government, as Mr. Dayton was then on his way to France, with definite instructions from Washington upon that and cognate matters.

VII.
A PRISONER OF STATE.

After Mr. Faulkner returned to the United States, some American newspapers contained long accounts of Mr. Yancey and other Confederate diplomatic commissioners having been received by Mr. Faulkner, presented to the French Minister of Foreign Affairs, and even to the Emperor himself. It is needless to say that these were all fabrications, for Mr. Faulkner did not meet the Confederate Commissioners until two months after he had ceased to be Minister, and left France, and then, by accident, on the Derby race course in England. On that occasion Mr. Yancey never intimated to Mr. Faulkner the nature of his mission abroad, and the relation of the Confederate States to the European Powers was never the subject of discussion between them. When Mr. Faulkner returned to the United States the war had been for some time in progress. He went direct to Washington, to pay his respects to the President and Secretary Seward, and settle his account with the Government. While in France he had been entrusted with a large contingent fund, to meet the expenses of other missions besides his own. He settled all his accounts, received the balance due him from the Government, and having made his final visit to the State Department, was about to leave for his home in Martinsburg, when he was arrested and thrown into prison. He demanded of the Secretary of War, to know upon what charge he had been arrested and detained. He received the following reply:

"You are held as a distinguished citizen of Virginia, as a hostage for James McGraw, State Treasurer of Pennsylvania, who, while searching for the dead body of a friend on the battle-field of Bull Run, was taken and thrown into prison, by the people of your State, now in rebellion against the authority of the Government, and, so help me God, you shall never be relieved until James McGraw and his party are set at liberty and are safe.

"SIMON CAMERON, Secretary of War."

The characteristic answer from Gen. Cameron settled the question in the mind of Mr. Faulkner, and fully contradicted the story that he had been arrested because of infidelity to his trust while Minister to France. After being confined in Washington for a month he was transferred to Fort Lafayette. While imprisoned there he was offered his liberty upon the condition of taking the oath of allegiance to the United States. He refused to accept his liberty upon those terms, for the reason that he had been guilty of no offence, and had been confined without any charge having been made against him, and that he would submit to no conditions for his release. Soon after this he learned that Mr. McGraw, of Pennsylvania, had been set at liberty and was at home. He then addressed a note to Gen. Simon Cameron, Secretary of War, requesting a fulfillment of the promise to release him, when Mr. McGraw should be again safe within the Federal lines. Gen. Cameron promptly replied, saying:

"You are no longer in my custody. You have been transferred to the Secretary of State, as a political prisoner. "SIMON CAMERON, Secretary of War."

Mr. Faulkner's offence against the State was that he had refused to take the oath of allegiance. Soon after this occurred he was removed to Fort Warren, in Boston harbor. While he was in confinement there Mr. Ely, of New York, a Congressman who had been captured while a spectator at the battle of Bull Run, began to press the Government to secure his release. It was proposed to exchange Mr. Faulkner for Mr. Ely, but Jeff Davis, in his annual message, at Richmond, Va., declared he would make no exchange for Mr. Faulkner, but would make his arrest a ground of arraignment before the civilized world. After considerable parleying it was finally decided that Mr. Faulkner should be granted a parole of thirty days, to go to Richmond and effect, if possible, an exchange between himself and Mr. Ely. His arrival in Richmond caused great exceitement.; he was greeted by the Governor, Mayor of the city and a large concourse of people, and called upon to make a public address, which he did. His interview with Jefferson Davis was interesting, as showing the relative position of the two men at that period. During the conversation Mr. Faulkner said: "Mr. Davis, I fear we are just beginning a long and bloody war; a struggle in which, I cannot help thinking, the South will be unsuccessful."

"I agree with you sir," Mr. Davis replied, "that we are at the outset of a protracted and desperate conflict, but I do not agree with you that it will be an unsuccessful one."

This decided difference of opinion did not have the effect of making the interview altogether pleasant, and Mr. Davis did not, at any subsequent period, take kindly to Mr. Faulkner. Finally, but with great reluctance, Mr. Davis consented to the exchange of Mr. Ely for Mr. Faulkner, and when that had been accomplished the latter retired to his home in Berkeley County, but remained there but a few days, he having received a letter from General Stonewall Jackson, who invited him to become a member of his staff. He was accordingly, by Lieut. Gen. Stonewall Jackson, appointed his chief of staff, with the rank, Lieut. Colonel. He wrote all of the official reports of that distinguished soldier, which have always been regarded as models of military literature.

While he was absent from his home, during the war, Martinsburg, near which he lived, was alternately in possession of the Federal and Confederate forces, and although his two sons were in the Confederate army, his property was not seriously injured. His old home, around which clustered the associations of a century, was ordered to be burned, by Gen. David Hunter, and an officer appeared to carry this command into effect. The house was saved by a telegraphic order from Abraham Lincoln, to whom an appeal was made by Mrs. Faulkner' who had resided there during all the war. The close of the war found Mr. Faulkner near Appomattox, where Lee surrendered to Grant. One of the first acts of Mr. Lincoln after the surrender of Gen. Lee, was to request Mr. Faulkner to return home, and he sent Col. Ward Lamon with a message to him, for that purpose. Mr. Faulkner, after the close of hostilities, returned to his home in Berkeley County, the untimely and tragical death of Mr. Lincoln having prevented the conference which the President had intended to have with Mr. Faulkner, when, no doubt, the opinion of the latter on the subject of reconstruction, which had become one of absorbing interest at the close of the war, would have been given due consideration.

VIII.
AFTER THE WAR.

The State of West Virginia had been created out of the Old Dominion when Mr. Faulkner returned to his home. There were new men at the helm, and a new order of things in general. The sting of war had left its rankling in the statutes of the new State, and he found himself not only debarred from the inherrent right of American citizenship, but even of practicing his profession as a lawyer.

At that time this section of the country, almost more than any other along the border, was disturbed by the receding waves of civil war, and the legal, no less than the constitutional, standing of the new State was often called in question. Nothwithstanding the great changes which the war had wrought, and the bitter animosities of the hour, of which at this time there can be but a faint idea, Mr. Faulkner, regarding the separation as irreversible, at once took strong grounds in favor of the new State of Virginia, which was the offspring, not of revolution, but of civil war. He held, and with the spirit of prophecy upon him, that time would soften the asperities of the armed conflict, and that West Virginia, freed from the unjust discriminations of the dominant section east of the Blue Ridge, would speedily become one of the most flourishing commonwealths in the sisterhood of States.

The contest had commenced in 1832, for the overthrow of the unjust discriminations against the section of the State where he had been born, and where were all his interests, social, business and political, had been ended by the sword severing the section west of the Blue Ridge from what was then called, and is yet known, as the Old Dominion.

It is needless to describe in detail his many public acts from 1865 to 1872 in behalf of the New State. Of these the most significant and important was his stand in favor of the two rich counties of Jefferson and Berkeley being attached to West Virginia. The old State of Virginia sued for them as a part of her domain, claiming that they were not legally attached to the new State when created. Mr. Faulkner showed his fidelity to the western section by taking positive grounds in favor of the right of West Virginia to these counties. Virginia instituted her suit in the Supreme Court of the United States, and Hon. Reverdy Johnson was retained as the leading counsel for West Virginia, but he was made Minister to England before the case came on for argument, and Gov. Boreman, at the request of the delegation from those counties, engaged Mr. Faulkner to take Mr. Johnson's place. The case was argued before the Supreme Court of the United States, in February, 1871, The argument of Mr. Faulkner was an exhaustive presentation of the equity of the claim of West Virginia to the two counties, and they were awarded to her by the decision of the Court. In January, 1872, Mr. Faulkner was a member of the Constitutional Convention of West Virginia, which framed the present fundamental law of the State. This was the first even quasi-political office he had held since the war. He was chairman of the Judiciary Committee on Revision, the two most important in the body. It is needless to say that he was one of the leaders in the debates and work of that body.

In June of the same year his political disabilities were removed by special act of Congress, and in the fall of 1874 he was elected to the House of Representatives, by 3,436 majority, in a district until that time doubtful. He served on the important committees of Foreign Relations and Education and labor, and took a leading position in the debates on all important questions. As his term was drawing to a close he declined a re-election, for the purpose of becoming a candidate for United States Senator, and in the contest for that position which followed, in the Legislature, he secured a plurality of the Democratic votes in caucus, but was defeated in the Legislature by a combination of the Republicans with a number of Democrats in favor of his opponent. He was, at a subsequent period, mentioned as a candidate for Governor, but was again defeated by a combination of hostile interests, and then withdrew from public life.

IX.

HOW A LADY SAVED HER HOME FROM THE TORCH.

"Madam, I am ordered to burn this house to the ground. You will have one hour to leave it; you will be permitted to take nothing away except the wearing apparel of yourself and daughters."

Thus spoke General Martindale, an officer of the First New York Cavalry, who was at that time serving as a staff officer to General David S. Hunter, who was in command of the Union forces in the Shenandoah Valley during the eventful years of 1863-64. The house was one of those quaint ancestral mansions seen nowhere but in the South, and there so common as hardly to attract attention. It was odd; it was almost rude in its architecture, but even its rather faded exterior gave evidence of the wealth of hospitality, and accumulations of rare work, both literary and artistic. In its historical treasures it was especially rich, and besides the great array of valuable books it contained many manuscripts even then of great worth, which were to become more valuable with the lapse of time.

This house filled with treasures and crowded with sacred memories, had been the home of the lady addressed, and of her progenitors for generations. To her every room—nay, every corner and part of every room—was peopled by happy, wholesome memories. It is not strange, therefore, that to her the words of the officer which doomed her home to the torch were freighted with no common sorrow.

But she was not a woman to sit down and wait for misfortune to overwhelm her. She had little time to do anything to save her house; little chance that anything she might do would be successful. But she determined to make an effort to save her home, and she did what many others did in these distressful days; she made by telegraph an appeal to the patient, sympathetic, forgiving Abraham Lincoln, President of the United States. A messenger galloped to the town, and the fateful message was instantly flashed to Washington. The distracted lady could only wait and each moment of that hour seemed to her laden with the anxiety of a century. Meanwhile the officer and his soldiers lounged upon the beautiful lawn that stretched out before the old mansion to the main road, fully a quarter of a mile away, waiting for the appointed time to apply the torch. They knew nothing of what the Mistress of the mansion had done, and if they had known would not have been greatly concerned. They were only obeying orders and had so little liking for their work that they would be glad of some excuse for not doing it.

The moments came and went with exasperating speed; the old clock in the hall seemed to count the minutes into the past with malignant and unusual speed. The servants were hastily packing trunks with the few articles to be spared from the flames, but the lady herself seemed to take no notice of what was going on about her. She sat at a window, which commanded a view of the road leading to the town, as if to catch the first glimpse of a horseman flying to her relief.

The three quarters had gone; the lady still strained her eyes at the window, the soldiers still lounged listlessly under the shade trees, but their talk was becoming more subdued and their dislike for the task before them was becoming more apparent.

Suddenly the clatter of the horse's hoofs in full gallop was heard down the road. The lady sprang to her feet with an expression of mingled hope and fear upon her face. The soldiers hardly noticed the rapid approach of the courier, for they could not be aware that the incident had any interest for them. The messenger came into plain view and the lady saw that he was waving a letter in his hand as he urged his horse to greater speed. In an instant more the messenger sprang from his horse and rushed up the broad graveled path to the house. The lady met him at the door. He handed her the telegram. She tore it open. It was a brief message of only a few words, but it had the potency of a kingly command. It said:

"The property of Charles James Faulkner is exempt from the order of General David S. Hunter for the burning of the residences of three prominent citizens of the Shenandoah Valley, in retaliation for the burning of the Governor Bradford's house in Maryland by the Confederate forces."

(Signed) ABRAHAM LINCOLN.

The lady handed the telegram to Captain Grey Martindale. He read it and raised his cap in salutation. Turning to his men he gave the orders which put them in their saddles, and in a moment more he and his small command were clattering down the dusty road toward their camp. Thus was her home saved; thus did Abraham Lincoln add another to the many acts of kindness with which he illumed and softened the rugged road of civil war which it was his hard fate to tread. Thus was the painful duty of Captain Martindale accomplished. The orders to burn houses had not been confined to this single home, and when he appeared on the scene which has been sketched in the above lines the officer and his command had just come from the burning of other residences of other prominent Virginians. General David S. Hunter, who issued these orders, was one of those old-time soldiers who believed that war was not a holiday pastime. Among the homes which had been first burned were those of Hon. Alexander R. Boteler, near Shepherdstown, along the Potomac river, formerly a member of Congress, and who for a time before the war had defeated Mr. Faulkner in one of the most desperate and closely contested Congressional elections which had ever taken place in that section. Another house burned was that of Andrew Hunter, a member of the Confederate Congress and a cousin of General Hunter. He found his consanguinity to the Union commander was no protection for his property. There seemed to be some of the irony of fate in these occurrences of the war.

At that time the rebels held as a prisoner Mr. Ely, a member of Congress from New York, who had been one of the many who had gone down from Washington to see the rebellion crushed at Bull Run. They saw another sort of spectacle and Ely was captured, and the rebels clung to him as a prize of great value. Finally the friends of Mr. Ely hit upon the plan of exchanging him for Faulkner, and by their importunities finally gained the consent of the Government at Washington to their scheme. Mr. Faulkner was to be released upon parole, and went to Richmond to effect the desired exchange. He was successful. Mr. Ely was restored to his home, and he was released and sent within the Confederate lines.

After a short stay in Richmond, where his arrival had caused great excitement, Mr. Faulkner retired to the home of his daughter, near Appomattox, where most of his time during the continuance of the rebellion was spent. He served for a time, however, upon the staff of General Stonewall Jackson, and wrote most of the orders and reports of that officer which received such general praise as models of military literature. After the close of the war he returned to his home near Martinsburg, where he has ever since continued to live. Soon after his return he began to take an active interest in the public affairs of the new State of West Virginia, which was that portion of the Old Dominion which had always enlisted his heartiest sympathies and best efforts.

It is worthy of being added that General Cameron and Mr. Faulkner had broken the bread of reconciliation since the war. Both were far advanced in years, the one having passed four score years, the other fast approaching that advanced age. There was one more incident. Soon after the war Mr. Faulkner and Mr. Magraw, although the lines of their fates had so crossed each other at a stirring period, met for the first time, and their interview was interesting and pleasant to both. It is queer how time softens the asperities of this life and brings together those who were far separated by the circumstance of war. The old mile-posts that tell the story of that conflict are fast falling and crumbling into decay. The history of one is full of interest, but where is there one that furnishes more good thoughts and facts than the one in that old house that Grey Martindale was ordered to burn.

LIFE'S LABORS OVER.

The death of Charles James Faulkner occurred at his residence, Boydville, Martinsburg, at fifty minutes past six o'clock Saturday morning, Nov. 1st, 1884. It was

Life of the late Hon. C. J. Faulkner. 341

the belief of his physicians that he would have passed away several days before but for a restless energy which ever stirred within him, and which he in particular summoned up in the last hours of his life. But his end was come and, surrounded by all the members of his family, he drew his last breath and passed peacefully away. There were present at his death his two sons, Hon. E. Boyd and Judge Chas. James Faulkner and families; his six daughters, Mrs. S. P. F. Pierce, Mrs. Thos, Bocock, Mrs. Jno. P. Campbell, Mrs. Dr. W. S. Love, Mrs. Joel W. Flood and Mrs. Dr. J. W. McSherry; also Dr. W. S. Love and family, Hon. Thos. S. Bocock, Mr. Faulkner Pierce, Mrs. Jas. Booker, Miss Bolling Flood and Miss Ella Bocock. As soon as he was dead the sad news was sent over the wires to his friends around, and many were the words of consolation and sympathy returned to the bereaved family. The services of his funeral took place on Monday following and were largely attended. Among the prominent men present were Judge W. S. Clark, Judge Richard Parker, Hon. Holmes Boyd, attorneys P. H. Boyd, H. H. Boyd, John E. Norris, James E. Norris, Capt. Powell, T. B. Kennedy, President, and Superintendent Boyd, of the Cumberland Valley Railroad; Mr. Gallaher, of the *Free Press*; J. Rufus Smith, Esq., and a large number of others. Nearly a hundred of the Masonic fraternity, of which order he was a member, turned out, and headed by the City Band marched at 3 o'clock, the hour of his funeral, to solemn music to the residence, around which had gathered by this time more than two thousand people. The body of the venerable Chas. James Faulkner lay in the parlor in a handsome casket, decked with wreaths of beautiful flowers; floral crown, cross and inscription of FATHER made of roses and rare flowers were placed upon the casket cover. After all had viewed in procession the honored remains, the Presbyterian choir sang "Rock of ages cleft for me;" prayer was offered by Rev. Pitt, after which Rev. F. M.

Woods delivered a funeral oration on the late deceased, a tribute to his memory. Rev. R. C. Holland followed with prayer, and reading of hymn "Nearer my God to Thee," by Rev. Andrews, which was sung by choir and benediction by Rev. F. M. Woods. After the sermon the funeral cortége marched to the Episcopal Cemetery, next to the lawn, led by the City Band, followed by nearly 100 members of the Masonic fraternity under the auspices of Equality Lodge, the remains carried by the pall bearers, Blackburn Hughes, J. L. W. Baker, P. Showers, C. P. Matthaei, J. W. Pitzer, D. Hedges, A. J. Thomas, C. W. Doll, C. M. Shaffer, Wm. Kilmer, Jacob Miller, J. W. Thatcher, M. S. Grantham, Casper Stump, Col. J. Q. A. Nadenbousch, J. H. Gettinger and J. N. Abell; the ushers, Messrs. E. J. Simpson, H. L. Doll, Stuart W. Walker, G. C. Janney, G. C. Swartz, A. S. Hughes, and D. C. Hunter, who followed bearing floral tribute of FATHER, Grandfather and Rest with cross and crown, the immediate members of the family, two sons, six daughters, thirteen grandchildren—only three absent —the near relatives of the deceased, the bar and officers of the Court, the City Council and corporation officers and over two thousand citizens. The services at the grave were conducted by the Masons with beautiful and impressive ceremony such as is usual on occasions of Masonic burial. Never perhaps in the history of Martinsburg were there so many people gathered together to pay their last tribute of respect to the honored remains of a venerable citizen, one who was successful as a jurist, politician, diplomatist, and statesman, whose life will live after him, and his deeds be recorded on the pages of the world's history.

CHAPTER XIV.
THE CHURCHES—ORGANIZATION AND PRESENT CONDITION.

IT has been stated in a former chapter that the Tuscarora Church, about two miles from the city, was the first place where the gospel was publicly preached and divine service performed west of the Blue Ridge Mountain. This was and still remains a Presbyterian edifice. Among the early settlers a number of Irish Presbyterians, with a few Scotch and English families, removed from Pennsylvania and settled along Back Creek, the North Mountain and Opequon. The Baptists were the next to establish a public worship, which was done about the year 1754. Mr. Stearns, a preacher of this sect, with several others, removed from New England, and under the care of Rev. John Gerard, formed a Baptist Church on the Opequon, the first founded this side of the Blue Ride. The Baptists were not among the earlist emigrants; but in the years 1742 or 1743, about fourteen families of that persuasion migrated from New Jersey and settled in the vicinity of what is now called Gerardstown. From this date other denominations sprang up, and at the present day our entire county is supplied with well regulated and disciplined churches of nearly every sect. The following sketches are given of our churches, that have sown their seed broad-cast and been the means of establishing religion throughout the county:

TUSCARORA CHURCH—THE OLDEST WEST OF THE BLUE RIDGE MOUNTAINS.

On a bright Tuesday morning, April 3d, 1888, I mounted a bicycle and wended my way in the direction of the old Presbyterian Church, situated on Tuscarora. I seated myself on a bench near by, and carefully scanned the small stone building of one story, on which every trace of mortar, between the stone, seemed to speak of the years, yea a century or more, through which it has stood the test of time—the wintry blasts and the rainbeat of bygone days. Then I would pause, upon looking at the wood work, which, when compared with the workmanship of the present day, presents rather a rude appearance, and one can readily imagine that the erection of buildings in those days consisted of hard labor, with poor tools to work with. Next, I directed my attention to the stone steps in front, the weather-beaten doors, and the old shingled roof, which plainly show that by their use they were not over-estimated by the workmen. Sitting beneath a small birch tree, I began to wonder, as if in a dream, whether the early settlers that erected this grand old building, ever gave thought to the fact that their good works and deeds would be handed down to rising generations for centuries to come. But then my dream was interrupted and awakened by the peck of the wood-chuck, the chirp of the sparrow, and the warble of the robin overhead.

I turned my gaze heavenward, then looked around me over the beautiful landscape of improved and cultivated soil, the neat dwellings—and then glancing at a marble slab before me, I thought of His blessed word on high: "Surely their good works do follow them." Interrupted by the warbling notes of the bird overhead, I looked up at it, and with its little throat swelled it seemed to say, that happiness in His sight is the Goddess of all nature divine.

Truly, it was a grand sight—with the bright shining sun above, to announce the coming of spring,—the budding of trees around, stirred now and then by a fresh breeze and sending forth a fragrant odor,—the sod beneath sprouting up, and beginning to don its coat of green—all of which seemed to teach a soul-comforting lesson: "A great and loving Father, creator of heaven and earth, hath endowed us with these blessings of nature." And then upon reading a slab before me, I was again reminded: "According to the manner in which thou hast lived, so shalt thou be judged, at the judgment bar of God, He that hath endowed us with all these blessings." Here I was interrupted and awakened from my reverie by an inquirer, who wanted to know my business at this lone spot, and at such a time. After satisfying him with my object and reason, he walked off; and again I was left alone, save my God, with the tombs of the dead. I raised my eyes, and found myself confronting the tomb of Rev. Louis F. Wilson, on which were these words: "Died March 24th, 1873, in his 64th year —Our Faithful pastor for 37 years." This aroused a deep sense of feeling within me, and I began to wander amongst the tombs, of perhaps, many loved ones, endeared to both God and mankind. I noticed particularly an old slab, rustic and covered with moss, and propped up at each end by small foundations. With a small stick I cleaned it as best could be done, and with a pencil traced the letters in order to make them out. The stone has been washed by the storms, until the letters can hardly be found. It read thus: "Under this marble rests the body of Rev. Hugh Vance, a faithful minister of the Gospel of Christ 26 years. Born in the year 1736. Died in the year 1791. Live the life if U would die the death of the righteous. This stone is erected to preserve and perpetuate the Memory of this Worthy Man by his affectionate friends in Berkeley County, Virginia."

Nearby stood a number of wooden slabs, almost rotted and decayed, and it is to be supposed that at an early day these tombs were enclosed by a fence, as four snags of posts are still standing. I became interested in the names and dates of the slabs, and began to note some of which I thought might prove interesting to the reader. Among them were John Chenowith, died October 8th,

1842, aged 63 years ; Thomas Miller, died November 30th, 1854, aged 64 years ; James Chenowith, did 1836, aged 53 years ; Emily Marker, died 1838, aged 21 years ; Margaret Hull, died August 31st, 1846, aged 57 years ; Wm. Slauter, died April 28th, 1834, aged 52 years ; Robert Lyle, died 1786, aged 34 years ; Robert Brighton, died September 10th, 1797, aged 60 years ; Margaret Brighton, died September 20th, 1786, aged 47 years ; Margaret Herd, died July 26th, 1794, aged 27 years ; David Miller, died September 15th, 1825, aged 51 years ; the next was an old blue lime stone marked : "Here lies the body of Hugh Lyle, who departed this life April 14th, A. D., 1790, aged 84 years." Another was an old sand stone, the letters almost washed away, and bore the name of Hugh Lyle, Jr., died February 27th, 1797, aged 42 years. In a large stone vault were contained Wm. Snodgrass and wife. The date of his death was May 13th, 1836, at an age of 61 years ; and his wife died in 1852, aged 76 years. There was a large marble tomb with the Holy Bible engraved upon it, and the name of Sarah Ireland, who died January 20th, 1857, aged 79 years ; also her son Alexander who died April 29th, 1800, at an age of 9 years. A number of graves were marked with small rocks and wooden slabs—and there was nothing to designate the name of the dead or date of death. Some of the slabs were rustic and almost entirely covered by moss, or washed by the storms until the letters are invisible. In places the grave has been entirely lost by the growth of the monster oak. Near the center stands a large brick enclosure—the wooden roof entirely rotted away, and the walls fast going to ruin. Beneath this, I am informed, a number of persons were buried, but nothing remains to give information as to who they were.

After strolling around to my heart's content, I returned to the church and took my seat in a side door. I looked over the profile of stones and slabs, some of which have fallen down, and others broken and decayed—and then pondered long in meditation, whether the present generation knew who and which of their foreparents might be buried here ; or whether many, perhaps, given up for lost, might be sleeping under this sod. At this moment the sweet notes of a little bird, perched near by, thrilled my soul :

> I looked around, o'er the tombs of the dead,
> And thought their spirits, from overhead,
> Were looking down with earnest eye,
> On tombs in which their bodies lie.
> When lo, the stillness seemed to say,
> Man is mortal—his life a day.

The church is still used for public worship by the Presbyterian denomination, and has a small membership. Interments are still made in the old graveyard, and fine marble stones are taking the place of the old slabs. The present pastor is the Rev. J. H. Gilmore, of Hedgesville, who also has charge of the Falling Waters church, another very old edifice.

This sketch was written by the author of this book especially for the history of the old graveyard. Amongst the dates will be found some who were born nearly two centuries ago, and have been buried on this spot nearly a century. There were others, doubtless older, but no trace could be found to identify them. However, I feel confident that those mentioned will prove of interest and value to the reader.

ST. JOHN'S LUTHERAN CHURCH.

This is one of the oldest congregations in the Valley of Virginia. It was founded and formed here in 1775 by German emigrants from Pennsylvania and Maryland. In 1782 a church record for the exclusive use of the Lutheran congregation was obtained, and still remains in the archives of the church. The first regular pastor was Rev. Christian Streit, who took charge of a Lutheran congregation in Winchester, Va., July 19th, 1785. The circuit over which he had charge embraced the counties of Berkeley, Jefferson and Frederick. He acted in the capacity of Bishop or overseer of the Lutheran interest in these sections, ministering until 1790.

Succeeding Rev. Streit, and the first pastor who resided here, was Rev. J. D. Young, who took charge of the congregation December 12th, 1790, in which position he served until 1800, when after an absence of two years he returned and served it from November 3d, 1802, up to the time of his death, which occurred February 10th, 1804, at an age of 54 years. He was the originator of the first known constitution or form of government for the congregation, which was signed by 103 members. The congregation was next supplied by Rev. F. W. Jazinsky for about one year, and who was succeeded by Rev. John P. Ravenack, the second resident pastor. Rev. John Kackler became pastor December 1st, 1817, and continued until 1819. Rev. C. P. Krauth took charge in the autumn of 1819 and served six years, resigning in 1827. His successor was Rev. Jacob Medtart, who entered upon his pastorate in 1827, which position he filled successfully until 1835, when he resigned. The following is the list of pastors as they succeeded each other, and their terms, to the present date: Rev. Reuben Wiser, from March 1st, 1835, to 1837; Rev. Charles Martin, March 29th, 1837 to 1842; Rev. Samuel Spreecher, Feb. 13th, 1842, to 1843; Rev. Joseph A. Seiss, May 29th, 1843, to to 1846; Rev. John Winter, November 23d, 1845, to 1847; Rev. C. P. Krauth, Jr., November 8th, 1847, to 1848; Rev. B. M. Schmucker, May 21st, 1848, to 1852; Rev. Reuben A. Fink, April 1st, 1852, to 1855; Rev. Wm. Kopp, November 25th, 1855, to 1857; Rev. Edwin Dorsey, April 1st, 1858, to 1860; Rev. Charles Martin, October 21st, 1860, to 1861. Here an interruption was made by the late war, and the pastorate duties again resumed by Rev. J. S. Heilig, August 9th, 1866, to 1868; Rev. M. L. Culler, December 1st, 1869, to July 24th, 1881, and was succeeded by Rev. R. C. Holland, the present pastor, November 23rd, 1881.

The Churches. 349

The first church edifice was the joint property of the Lutheran and Reformed congregations, and was located on the corner of Church and John streets, being built entirely of logs. It was constructed for a tavern by Jacob Shortel, but afterward purchased by the congregations on the 20th of March, 1786, and then completed as a house of God for religious worship. The two lots lying between King and John streets were also purchased at the same time for the same owner, and have since been used as a graveyard. At that time nails were too expensive, and the plastering lathes were fastened by grooves cut into the logs. A pipe organ was afterward purchased, the bellows of which was worked by ropes and weighted down by stones.

Rev. R. C. Holland, the present pastor, is a zealous and earnest worker in the cause of religion. In his intercourse with his members and brethren, in religion, he has won their friendship and esteem, and as a citizen the respect of the people. The present membership of the church is over 300, and the Sunday School numbers over 275 scholars. Mr. Geo. Knapp, for a number of years, has successfully officiated as Sunday School Superintendent. The following is a list of the Deacons and Elders : Deacons—G. S. Hill, D. A. Cline, Geo. D. Whitson, Jas. H. Small and Geo. A. Mason. Elders—H. N. Deatrick, Geo. Knapp, Geo. P. Walters and M. V. Small.

The old graveyard is an object of deep and tender interest to this city and much of the surrounding country, as many have some relative or friend buried there. The first cup of which there is any knowledge, which was used by the congregation in the ministration of the Holy Communion, is still in existence, bearing the date 1791, and the mysterious inscription : "P. K.* B. K. M."

In 1815 a subscription was taken up in the two churches amounting to $3,059.00, for the purpose of building a new church for their joint use. This project, for some cause, had never been carried out. Later on the present site was purchased from Jacob Schoppert, and an edifice erected at a cost of $3,786.50, and was dedicated June 10th, 1832, Rev. Abram Reck officiating. The church was improved again in 1854, and a large bell placed in the tower. During the late war the congregations were considerably scattered, and the church very much injured.

In 1884 the church was remodeled, and extensive and important changes made. The corner stone was laid July 12th, 1884, with impressive services, by Rev. M. L. Culler, the former pastor, and other clergymen assisting the pastor, Rev. R. C. Holland. The cost of this improvement amounted to $10,000.

FIRST BAPTIST CHURCH.

The first Baptist Church of Martinsburg was originally organized in 1858, with ten members. Rev. J. W. Jones was chosen pastor, and, for nearly two years, preached in the stone academy that stood near the Episcopal Cemetery. In 1859 the lot on West King street, where the present building now stands, was bought, with a view of building a church edifice, but soon after the late war between the States came on, and but little was accomplished until after the close of the war. During this time the society had a mere nominal existence, and nothing worthy of note occurred in its history; but preaching was held at intervals in the German Reformed and Lutheran Churches. In the spring of 1869, ground was broken and work commenced for the erection of a church building. The corner stone was laid Aug. 24th, 1869, with imposing Masonic ceremonies. Rev. J. A. Haynes, of Middleburg, was present, and delivered an appropriate and eloquent address. The work was then continued without interruption, until the building was under roof. In the month of May, 1870, the lecture room was completed, and the first sermon was preached in the new house of worship on the third Sunday of that month, by the pastor, Rev. W. S. Penick. At this time the church was reorganized for active work with Rev. W. S. Penick, as pastor, and W. M. Van Cleve and Joseph B. Kearfott as deacons. On the second Sunday in June, 1870, the Sunday School was permanently established. The building was completed in March, 1874, and on the 29th day of that month it was dedicated, with an appropriate sermon by Rev. J. W. M. Williams, D. D., of Baltimore. The total cost of the building, including furniture, etc., was $7,364.43, for which a collection of $656.50 was taken up at the dedication services. The entire indebtedness has since been paid off.

Rev. W. S. Penick served the church as pastor from 1869 to July 1st, 1874. Rev. P. P. Murray, of Buchanan, W. Va., succeeded the former and entered upon his pastorate with the church October 18th, 1874, continuing until November 17th, 1875, when he resigned and was succeeded by Rev. A. E. Rogers, who entered upon his mission work in September, 1876. Since the advent of the latter pastor the church has been constantly increasing. During the fall of 1881, both the interior and exterior of the building have been greatly improved, and the entire front changed, at a cost of over $500.00.

Rev. A. E. Rogers was shortly afterward tendered a call to Missouri, which he accepted. Rev. Rogers was then succeeded by Rev. R. H. Pitt, of Richmond, Va., Nov. 1st, 1883. Rev. Pitt served the church until 1886, when he resigned and returned to his former people. He was succeeded by Rev. F. P. Robertson, of Grafton, (W. Va.,) church, formerly of Virginia, in May, 1886, who has still charge of the church, and is doing a grand and noble work. Rev. Robertson is a kind, courteous and affable gentleman, and has the esteem and love of his entire pastoral charge. He is an excellent preacher, of an intelligent mind, and educated ability. The following names compose the deacons of the church : B. F. Fiery, Samuel Aler, Sr., Jos. West, W. L. Pearl, J. B. Kearfott, T. B. Grove.

F. S. Emmert is the Sunday School Superintendent,

which capacity he has filled for five years. The church membership is 200, and the average Sunday School attendance 112.

TRINITY (EPISCOPAL) CHURCH, AND NORBORNE PARISH.

By an Act of Assembly, in the year 1769, this parish and county were taken from Frederick. The original parish included all the territory now embraced by the counties of Jefferson and Berkeley, and contained within the limits, probably three churches. About the year 1740, one was built at Mill Creek, or Bunker Hill, and founded by Morgan Morgan—the first Episcopal Church erected in the valley. A short time before the parish was formed, a chapel was erected at Hedgesville. The other was erected in Mecklenburg, (now Shepherdstown) and built by Van Swearingen. The original parish contained these three churches. The first Episcopal Church in Martinsburg was built about the close of the war, and was erected by Philip Pendleton, Esq., a zealous churchman. It was built at the entrance to Norborne Cemetery, which was laid out by Adam Stephen, and established by law in 1778. Upon the formation of Jefferson County in 1801, which was taken from Berkeley, that territory was cut off from Norborne Parish. This reduced the latter, and it contained but the three churches.

The old church that stood in the Cemetery became unsafe for use, and in 1835, measures were taken to erect another in the town. The lot was donated, and about 1838 or 1839, the present edifice, on West King street, was commenced. There was no stated place of worship in the town, for eight years or more before its completion. The following memorandum is taken from the old church record: "Trinity Church, Martinsburg, was consecrated by Rt. Rev. William Meade, Bishop of Virginia, on Thursday, August 10th, 1843. Present and assisting, the following of the clergy: Revs. Alexander Jones and J. Chisholm, of Virginia, and Revs. James A. Buck and

Theodore B. Lyman, of Maryland. Sentence of consecration read by the rector of the parish."

The church was badly damaged during the late war, and in 1865 it was found necessary to renovate it before it could be used for divine worship. The present vestibule and iron railing were placed in front of the church in 1869. There are many breaks in the succession, regarding the clergy of the parish, and it is supposed there were no ministers in charge at those times. The parish was organized in 1769, and no indentification of the clergy as its Rector can be found until the year 1771. Rev. Daniel Sturges was then licensed by the Bishop of London as Rector for Norborne Parish. Rev. Mr. Veasey succeeded him in 1786, and was followed by Rev. Mr. Wilson. Rev. Bernard Page was the Rector in 1795, and who, it is said, in his ministerial work, was far beyond the standard of the parish. He was succeeded by Rev. Emanuel Wilmer, about the year 1806. Between the lapse of 1811 and 1813, Rev. Mr. Price was made rector. Here a temporary stop was put to all clerical effort by the war of 1812, and in 1815, Rev. Benjamin Allen took charge of the parish. While in Martinsburg he contributed largely to the *Christian's Magazine* and *Layman's Magazine*, church papers published in the valley. He was also an author of marked ability, having published six volumes of poems, and running through three editions of a history of the Reformation. He was the first to propose a division of the diocese, and the following committee was appointed to confer with the Bishop and standing committee on this subject: Rev. Enoch Love, Edward Colston and Robert Page. He had spent a while afterward in England for the benefit of his health, and on a homeward bound vessel died.

The first confirmation, of which there is any knowledge, was held in the Martinsburg Church by Bishop Meade, in 1830. The number confirmed composed a class of nineteen. West Virginia became a separate diocese in

1878, since which time the church has rapidly increased. In 1848 Norborne Parish was divided and was made to include Mt. Zion Church, Hedgesville, and Calvary Church, Back Creek; the other, Trinity Church, Martinsburg.

After the death of Rev. Allen, this parish was supplied by Rev. Thomas Horrel, in 1816, who remained there years, and from this date was succeeded by ministers as follows: Revs. Enoch Love, Edward R. Lippett, 1823; John T. Brooke, 1826; James H. Lyng, 1830; William P. C. Johnson, 1832; Cyrus H. Jacobs, 1836; Charles C. Taliaferro, 1837; James Chisholm, 1842; D. Francis Sprigg, 1850; Richard T. Davis, 1855; W. D. Harrison, 1860; John W. Lea, 1875; and Robert Douglas Roller, 1879, who served the parish until April 1st, 1888, when he resigned to accept a call at Charleston, W. Va.

The present edifice has been handsomely renovated and refurnished in an artistic manner. The church now has a membership of 170, and an average Sunday School attendance of 85. The Superintendent is Wm. B. Colston; Senior and Junior Wardens, J. T. Young and B. S. Lyeth; Registrar, J. L. W. Baker; Treasurer, J. H. Doll; Vestrymen, J. T. Young, B. S. Lyeth, J. L. W. Baker, Geo. A. Chrisman, W. B. Colston, John M. Howell and J. H. Doll.

PRESBYTERIAN CHURCH.

This church was organized in 1825, and is the daughter of the venerable old church on Tuscarora, about two and a half miles from town. The church was organized in April and seems to have been without a pastor for the first year. But in the year 1826 or 1827, the Rev. John Mathews, who had been serving the churches of Shepherdstown and Charlestown jointly for twenty years, gave up his charge with Shepherdstown and removed to Martinsburg. He divided his time equally between these two churches until he removed to the west in 1831. Mr. Alex. Cooper was the first ruling Elder, who was also an

The Churches. 355

Elder in the old church in the county for some time before the separation. Rev. Wm. C. Mathews became acting pastor in April, 1831, and served the congregation 1835. During the years 1836 and 1837, the pulpit was vacant, and in the spring of 1838, Rev. Peyton Harrison was called to the pastorate of the church, and remained in this city for six years. In April, 1838, the name of Mr. Samuel Baker appears in the records as a Ruling Elder. Rev. John Bogg became pastor in 1845, who, probably remained only a few months, though possibly longer, for there is a blank in the Records from April, 1845, to April 1847. At this latter date Rev. Wm. Love took charge and served as pastor until 1849. During this year he was succeeded by Rev. R. L. Berry, who continued to serve the church for nerly ten years. In August, 1858, Mr. Berry resigned, which was accepted by the church with much regret. During his pastorate the death of Mr. Alex. Cooper occurred, who for forty-five years had held the office of Ruling Elder, and nearly all that time had charge of the sessional records. On the 23rd of the following April, 1853, Mr. James N. Riddle and Mr. John F. Harrison were ordained to the office of Ruling Elders in the church. On the 19th of April, 1855, Mr. Peyton R. Harrison, a son of Dr. Peyton Harrison, the former pastor, was also chosen by the congregation to the same office.

After the resignation of Mr. Berry, the congregation called successively Rev. J. G. Hanner, D. D.; Rev. Lewis C. Baker, of New Jersey, and Rev. M. B. Riddle, then quite a young man. None of these ministers found the way clear to accept the call. In April, 1859, Rev. A. C. Hopkins, was tendered a call, which was accepted, and on the 6th of Dec. following Mr. Hopkins was ordained and installed pastor. At a meeteng held on the 19th of January, 1861, Mr. Geo. Tabb and Mr. John M. Harmon were unanimously elected Ruling Elders. On the 2nd of May, 1866, Mr. G. Boyd Harlan, of Falling Waters

Church, and Mr. Wm. N. Riddle were chosen to the office of Ruling Elders in this church. Rev. Mr. Hopkins resigned this pastoral charge in Aug., 1865, and on the 2nd of June, 1866, a call was accepted by Rev. Jas. E. Hughes, who was afterwards installed by a committee of Winchester Presbytery. On the 23rd of Sept., 1867, he died, and since the birth of this congregation, in 1825, this was the first time God had called them to bury their pastor.

In the following spring, 1868, Rev. Dr. Riddle, of Lebanon, Pa., began his ministry in Martinsburg, in this church, and continued until April, 1877, when he resigned on account of infirmity of health. On the 14th of July, 1879, the congregation for the thirteenth time in its history was called upon to select another shepherd. The lot fell upon the present pastor, Rev. F. M. Woods, who has for the past nine years been endeavoring to realize this responsible trust. Within these nine years there has been an encouraging increase in this church, along with her sister churches, that gives a pleasant prophecy of the future of their active, busy town. The congregation of the church have built a most delightful and commodious manse at a cost of nearly $6,000. The church membership now numbers over 200, with a Sunday School attendance averaging 75. Mr. C. W. Wisner is the present Sunday School Superintendent, with Hugh A. White, as assistant. The Elders are Jacob Miller, Blackburn Hughes and J. L. E. Combs.

CATHOLIC CHURCH.

The first services held by this denomination were in the house of John Timmons, now located on Race Street. Mass was said in this house for a period of nearly nineteen years, from about the year 1810 to 1830. The first church was then built where St. Joseph's Cemetery is now located, by Rev. J. B. Gildea, with a membership consisting of about fifty families. The cost of the building amounted to nearly $4,000 and the ground was given

The Churches.   357

by Richard McSherry. The Sisters of Charity were established here by Father Whelan years ago, but afterwards left, as the congregation was too small to support it.

The stone work of the present church was begun by Father Plunkett, but was suspended for the want of means. Rev. Andrew Talty, his assistant, finished the church to the extent of the funds, and placed a pair of wooden steps in front. Rev. J. J. Kain afterwards replaced them with stone, and also finished the basement.

During the war, the Jessie Scouts used it for a stable in which they kept about 70 horses, and used the Sacristy rooms as prisons. Capt. H. Kyd Douglas was confined here for a period of six months. The wooden steps were very frail and inconvenient, and were only used by the soldiers twice. It is said the erection was commenced about 1845, the subscription paper dating Feb., 17th 1850, in which year the corner stone was laid. At a cost of about $40,000, the church was dedicated by Bishop McGill, Sept. 30th, 1860.

The names of those in charge, from its earliest existence to the present date, are as follows: Rev. Father Cahill, Rev. Readman, Rev. J. B. Gildea, Rev. Whelan, Rev. O'Brien, Rev. J. A. Plunkett. At different times a number of distinguished churchmen had charge, among whom were Bishops Whelan, of Wheeling; Becker, of Wilmington, Del.; and Kain, of Wheeling, each remaining several years. During the early period, at intervals, priests from Hagerstown and Frederick, Maryland, visited the mission. History records no names of the pioneers of Catholicity in this county, and there is no doubt that the communion members of the church of Rome came to this section in the decline of the last century.

The present edifice, situated on South Queen Street, is a strong and substantial building, with a massive stone front. The interior is handsomely frescoed and furnished, and contains a beautiful marble altar. In 1883, the denomination purchased the Judge Hall property at a cost of $5,000, and made improvements to the amount of $2,200. The parochial school was taught in the basement of the church for a long while, but upon the purchase of this property the Sisters of Charity, from Emmittsburg, took charge Sept. 1st, 1883. The school now has an average attendance of over 200 children, and is very successful. The present church membership numbers over 1500, with a large Sunday School attached. Rev. J. McKeefry is the present pastor, with Rev. Fred. J. Lucke, as assistant. Rev. Lucke entered upon his mission here March, 17th, 1887, and continued until April 1st, 1888. At the earnest request of Bishop Keane, Rector of the Catholic Union of America, he was called upon to take charge of the St. Augustine Cathedral, at Florida. He will succeed Rev. Dr. Pace, who takes the chair in the Theological Union. Father Lucke was held in the highest esteem by the people of all denominations.

GERMAN REFORMED CHURCH.

This is one of the oldest congregations in the valley, and was founded by German emigrants, who migrated principally from Pennsylvania. This society, in connection with the Lutherans, worshipped together in a log building, about the year 1776. (See sketch of Lutheran Church.) This church used jointly by the two congregations for many years was found to be too small, and in 1840 the German Reformed congregation, procured a more suitable site on Burke Street, and erected an edifice, the present one, at a cost of about $5,000. The services were formerly conducted in the German language, but have now been supplanted by the English. The old members of the church adhered to the use of their mother tongue in conducting their services, and thereby caused a number of their descendents to connect themselves with the English speaking congregations. The first church bell introduced in this section of country was purchased by this denomination in 1808.

The pastors as they succeeded each other are as follows: Revs. George Adam Geting, Jonathan Rahauser, Lewis Mayer, from 1808 to 1820; Samuel Helfersty, 1820 to 1824; Jacob Beecher, 1826 to 1831; Robert Douglas, 1834 to 1845; Daniel F. Bragunier, 1845 to 1860; William D. Lafever, 1866 to 1869; Stephen K. Kremer, 1870 to 1874, and John A. Hoffheins in 1875, who is now the present pastor. The elders are H. Seibert, John Fitz, Chas. Matthaei, James H. Myers. Deacons, Harry Cushwa, Lewis Bentz, D. M. Kilmer, G. R. Shoafstall and Wm. W. Cushwa. The present church membership now numbers about 250, with D. J. S. Boak as Sunday School Superintendent, and a scholarship of about 100, average attendance.

METHODIST EPISCOPAL CHURCH.

The first Methodist preaching in this State west of the Blue Ridge Mountain was commenced by Bishop Francis Asbury. On the 2nd of June, 1782, he stopped in Martinsburg on his way westward over the mountains, and delivered the first sermon in the Market House. In 1789 the first circuit west of the Blue Ridge was formed with Martinsburg as the centre, and which continued unbroken until the civil war opened in 1861. Shortly after a number of societies were organized in Martinsburg and throughout Berkeley and adjoining counties. The first building occupied by this congregation is still standing, located on John street, south of the jail. The congregations of this society were assembled by blowing a tin horn, as they were bitterly opposed to ringing church bells. The laws of the church were strongly anti-slavery, and on account of which fact they met with much opposition, then universal in the South. A division in the church was caused by this subject, which occurred in 1846, and the society known as the M. E. Church South was afterward organized.

Many were the obstacles and oppositions that encountered this society; but, notwithstanding, it grew and flourished. From the time it became thoroughly established until 1850 its membership numbered nearly a hundred. It became popular on account of making no distinction in its admission and encouragement of members, and was at that time termed the common people.

In 1850 the Martinsburg society became an independent church, and being set off from others in the county, it was known as Martinsburg Station. During this year the Baltimore Conference appointed Rev. Henry Furlong as pastor of the church, who completed the reorganization. He remained with the church nearly eleven years, during which time the membership increased to over two hundred. In 1861 the civil war broke out and the society was completely broken up, causing almost an entire suspension of religious services. In fact, such was the case generally throughout the State. From the Spring of 1861 until 1863 the Methodists held no religious services in the county excepting at irregular intervals, by some itinerant Southern preacher at different places.

The church was again reorganized throughout the county in the latter part of 1863 by Dr. John Lanahan, Presiding Elder for the Virginia portion of the Baltimore Conference. At this time Dr. John M. Green (since deceased) became pastor in charge of Martinsburg, since which time Methodism has rapidly increased throughout the county, and especially in Martinsburg. Since the ruins of the church building from the effects of the war, their property has advanced upwards of $50,000. During 1850 only two Methodist preachers were employed in the county, which so continued until 1861.

The following is a list of the pastors as they succeeded each other: Revs. H. Furlong, 1850; David Thomas, 1851–1852; G. W. Cooper, 1853–1854; J. H. Brown, 1855–1856; J. Landstreet, 1857–1858; S. McMullen, 1859–1860; C. A. Reid, 1861; J. M. Greene, 1862–1863; J. H. Swope, 1864–1865; H. C. McDaniel, 1866–1867; E. D. Owen,

1868-1869 ; S. V. Leech, 1870-1871 ; A. R. Reily, 1872 ; J. F. Ockerman, 1873-1874 ; J. W. Cornelius, 1875-1876 ; J. E. Amos, 1877-1878-1879 ; M. F. B. Rice, 1880-1881; G. V. Leech, 1882-1883; A. S. Hank, 1884-1885-1886 ; John Edwards, present pastor, 1887-1888. The present trustees of the church are Wm. H. Mathews, Henry Crim, Luther Miller, Jacob Eversole, Wm. Westrater, Wm. McElroy and I. L. Bender. The missionary Society is composed of A. D. Darby, President ; F. A. Chambers, Vice-President ; C. David Darby, Secretary ; Miss Lilly Mathews, Treasurer. The present church membership numbers 401, with a Sunday school attendance of 330. Sunday School Superintendent, Lee M. Bender ; Assistant Superintendent, Frank Weaning.

METHODIST EPISCOPAL CHURCH, SOUTH.

This society was organized in December, 1866, by Revs. David Shoat and John A. Kearn, with a membership numbering fifteen. They worshipped in a small school building on King street for nearly a year, and in the fall of 1867 completed an edifice on German street, (now Maple avenue,) at a cost of $3,500, where they worshipped until January, 1886. The demand for a better house of worship had long been felt by those of Southern Methodist persuasion, and the effort to procure one culminated in the "Centenary or thank offering," lifted December 21st, 1884, for the purpose of improving or building a new church. The amount realized was $2,000, which gave such an impetus to the enterprise that those having the matter in charge determined to build a new church that would be an adornment to the town and a credit to the congregation. The present site on West Martin street was purchased from Mr. Fred. Becker in April, 1885, and the work of laying the foundation was immediately commenced after the removal of several old buildings.

The corner-stone was laid with Masonic rites Sept. 19th, 1885, and addresses were delivered in the Presbyterian Church by Grand-Master Shyrock, of Maryland, and others. The Mayor and City Council attended in a body, and the City Band furnished music suitable to the occasion. In the meantime the old church was sold by the trustees, after which the congregation worshipped in the Court House and Feller's Hall, until the opening of the lecture room in the new edifice, March 21st, 1886. This was dedicated by Rev. John L. Clark, of Virginia, the first station preacher this charge ever had, and who was largely instrumental in organizing the society here. On this occasion a collection amounting to $1,700 was taken up.

The new edifice was completed and dedicated Sunday, October 2nd, 1887, and services conducted morning and night by Bishop Alpheus W. Wilson, of Baltimore. Collections were lifted on both occasions amounting to $2,100. The building committee was composed of Rev. J. R. Andrew, pastor, C. M. Shaffer, N. T. Fisher, G. W. Buxton, H. Wilen, G. S. Rousch and J. H. Shaffer.

The first pastor in charge was Rev, John L. Clark, who served from 1869 to 1871, and was succeeded as follows: Thomas B. Sargent, 1871; John S. Maxwell, 1872; Wesley Hammond, 1873; Louis C. Miller, 1874 to 1877; John Poisal, D. D., 1877; Presley B. Smith, 1878; O. C. Beall, 1879; J. H. Davidson, 1880; John Landstreet, 1881 to 1884; J. R. Andrew, 1884 to 1888, with Rev. H. H. Kennedy as the present pastor. The church membership now numbers 211, with a Sabbath School attendance of 200. The Sunday School Superintendent is Mr. R. F. Barr, and the Stewards are G. S. Rousch, N. T. Fisher, H. T. Hopper, John Young, Eugene Newton and Joseph H. Shaffer.

UNITED BRETHREN CHURCH.

The Church of the United Brethren in Christ was founded by William Otterbein and Martin Boehm about the middle of the eighteenth century. The former was a distinguished theologian and minister in the German Reformed Church, and the latter a member of the Mennonite Church. They had grown tired of the cold formalism and inactivity of the churches to which they belonged, and began the work of promoting revivals and insisting upon a spiritual membership. They were eminently successful in their labors. These two devoted christian men were for the first time brought together at a great union meeting which was being held in Isaac Long's barn, at Lancaster County, Pennsylvania. Mr. Boehm preached the first sermon, and one of great power. At the close of his speech Mr. Otterbein arose and, embracing the eloquent speaker, he exclaimed : " We are brethren." The multitude that witnessed it was deeply and favorably impressed at this exhibition of christian fellowship and good will. Here originated the name " United Brethren." The words " In Christ" were afterward added, to distinguish the church from the Moravian United Brethren. In 1774, with Mr. Otterbein as pastor, the first organization occurred in Baltimore, Md., about which time the first church was built, and is used to this day by a German United Brethren congregation. The first conference was held in 1789, and since has made a steady and permanent growth. She has forty-eight annual conferences in the United States and territories, also one in Canada, one in Germany and one in West Africa. They have established at Dayton, Ohio, a printing office worth nearly $250,000, which is clear of debt and annually turns over to the church thousands of dollars. In 1858, with a few hundred members, the West Virginia Conference was organized, and at the close of the late war it was found the number had considerably decreased. The membership in this State now numbers over 7,500, with three presiding elder districts and thirty-six fields of labor.

In 1856, the society in Martinsburg was formed, and in 1857, the present edifice was completed. It is located in "Strinesville," the Northern part of the city, and is well furnished. During the war it was considerably damaged, but since has been put in complete repair. The present membership numbers nearly 150, with a Sabbath School attendance of about 100. Rev. J. R. Ridenour is the present pastor, with Mr. Philip Rimel as Sunday School Superintendent, and Messrs. Joseph Long and James Buchanan as Stewards, John Anderson General Steward.

FREE WILL BAPTIST CHURCH, (COLORED.)

This church was organized shortly after the war by the Home Mission Society, and was built under the supervision of Miss A. S. Dudley, of Maine, who was then engaged in school teaching and general missionary work among the colored people. With the assistance of Revs. N. C. Brackett and A. H. Morril, considerable aid was given the church in its early struggle. The present church was built directly after its organization, at a cost of $2,500, and a parsonage connected at a cost of $800. Its location is on North Raleigh street,—an excellent brick building, with a seating capacity of 400. The present pastor, Rev. A. F. Adams, is a refined and scholarly gentleman, and a graduate of Storer College, Harper's Ferry, W. Va. The membership of the church number 110, and has an average Sabbath School attendance of 97. Mr. G. W. Green is the Sabbath School Superintendent. The church trustees are J. H. Veney, Wm. Marshall, Minor Duval, Henry and J. F. Carter. Deacons, J. R. Veney, Stephen Elam, Thomas Ellis and Brown Freeman.

METHODIST EPISCOPAL CHURCH, (COLORED.)

No records are to be found to show any exact date for the establishment of this denomination in our county, but like the other colored church, it was not founded until after the late war. The first building was erected on West Martin street, (the site of the present edifice,) in which public services were held. It has since been torn completely down, and a large, commodious brick building erected in its stead. The church is very ably supported, and with a present membership of about 125, is doing a grand work. The Sunday School, with Mr. J. W. Corsey, as Superintendent, has an average attendance of nearly 100 scholars. The present pastor is Rev. F. F. Wheeler, who succeeded Rev. J. H. Smith in 1887. Rev. Mr. Wheeler is an earnest worker and possesses marked ability for his ministerial duties. The Stewards are Samuel Hopewell, James Willis, John Shaw, Wm. Ford, Chas. Brooks, Z. Silvers, Henry McGill and John Lowman. Trustees, Samuel Hopewell, James Clayton, Frank Corsey, James Willis and John Shaw.

CHAPTER XV.

BERKELEY COUNTY IN 1810—TOPOGRAPHICAL DESCRIPTION OF BERKELEY COUNTY—NATURAL CURIOSITIES—MINERALOGY AND LITHOLOGY—INHABITANTS, TOWNS, MANUFACTORIES, ETC.

THROUGH the courtesies of Mrs. M. W. Faulkner, the author has been enabled to secure from the memoranda of her husband, the late Hon. C J. Faulkner, a large amount of historical facts. The following sketch of Berkeley County in 1810, was taken from an old printed pamphlet, now in the possession of Mrs. Faulkner. This chapter, when compared with the following one, will give the reader a general idea of our county 78 years ago, and also of the manner in which it has improved.

BERKELEY COUNTY,

Lies between the 39th degree and 18 minutes North latitude, and extends 20 miles in length and about 18½ in breadth, and is bound to the North, inclining to the East, by the river Potomac, which divides the States of Virginia and Maryland; to the East, inclining to the South by said river, and Jefferson County; to the South, inclining to the West, by Frederick County; to the West, inclining to North, by the county of Hampshire, and the river Potomac. Martinsburg is the capital and the seat of justice of this county.

CONTENTS.

It contains 484 square miles, or 319,760 acres.

PRODUCTIONS.

The same as in Frederick County.

POPULATION.

When the last census was taken in 1800, this county and Jefferson were but one; it then contained 15,000 white inhabitants and 3,600 slaves; suppose that ⅓ of the white population has been taken to form the county of Jefferson, 10,000 would still remain to Berkeley. It is supposed that half the above number of blacks fell to Jefferson County, although the division of the whites was not so equal. There is now in this county 2,100 tithables, or males above 16 years of age, paying the poor tax.

THE MOUNTAINS IN THIS COUNTY ARE—

First—The North Mountain; it is remarkable on account of its raising immediately like a wall. It has a summit beautifully undulated in all its length. It might be computed to be about 500 feet perpendicular at its greatest height. It is not cultivated. The East side could be planted with vines. Mr. Edward Tabb, living immediately under that side of the mountain, exhibited an European vine which resisted the coldest winters, and without either pruning or cultivation, afforded large quantities of lucious grapes every year.

Second—The third Hill and Sleepy Creek mountains are nearly joining, and both run parallel to the North Mountain; they are not cultivated, except in the middle of the two, where issues a stream of water, called Meadow Branch, and where the plantation of a huntsman is seen. The heighth of both mountains is about 700 feet from their base.

Third—The Warm Spring ridge, is broken in several places; it is about 300 feet high; it divides Berkeley County from Hampshire. These ridges succeed each other in the above order, running Westerly from the North Mountain.

RIVERS.

The Potomac is the only river in this county; it divides this State from Maryland.

CREEKS.

The creeks are, Opequon, Mill, Middle, Tuscarora, Back, Sleepy, and the Warm Springs. The three first, as well as part of the Warm Spring Creek, are never-failing streams, owing to the springs that feed them being in limestone land, which is deep and spongy, and suffers the rain water to penetrate it. The water is therefore kept there, as it were, for the supply of the springs, while those creeks, which have the head springs, on slate or rocky bottoms that do not permit the water to penetrate their substance become dry in the hot seasons of the year. This circumstance does not, I think, corroborate that system already spoken of respecting the springs receiving their supply from the sea by subterraneous passages.

QUALITY OF THE SOIL.

I have thought that in order to give an accurate idea of the qualities of the soil of this county, I ought to divide it into three parcels or valleys.

First—The first parcel is nearly all limestone, of an excellent quality; except on the ridge, where, I think that a mountain existed, and where the Sulphur Springs are to be found. This ridge continues its course through this county, but it has been washed by the rains more than in Frederick County and lies lower. The quality of the soil is good, and by means of clover and plaster of Paris, I think, will grow more valuable yet.

Second—This parcel contains the valley of Back Creek, and is watered by it. I will observe that there is a tract of land marked on the map with the sign of a hill, on account of being higher than the other part of the valley, and extends from Mr. Gaunt's to Mr. Robertson's mill, on the Warm Spring road, and on a breadth of about two miles, which is of a good limestone land. The remainder of it is slate and Mountain land, except the bottom on the creek, which is a loam. The whole is susceptible

Inhabitants, Towns, &c.

of great improvement, and will become very valuable by attention to agriculture.

Third—Is the valley of Sleepy Creek watered by the said creek. Some part along the Warm Spring is limestone; some bottoms on the creek are loam; the rest is slate and mountain land, which, however, improved by the plaster of Paris and clover, would afford, in my opinion, good crops of small grain.

LITHOLOGY.

As part of this county is limestone, marble will consequently be found in it, sooner or later. "I have seen spars of different kinds in the limestone land, near Martinsburg; there are some in the form of a column, with sides, and truncated, white and transparent. On Apple-pie Ridge, there are masses under ground of these spars, of different forms. The people on whose lands these stone are seen, believing them to be gypsum, (plaster of Paris), had them ground and spread on their lands; indeed, many bushels, they said, had been sold as such. I went to those places and obtained specimens of those stones, and made a trial on them, which is commonly used for detecting the true gypsum from the common stone: I put them in contact with fire, and I found, after several experiments, that the most intense heat had not the least immediate effect on them, in causing them either to lose their transparency or hardness, and consequently, I took them to be rather a carbonate of lime (of the nature of limestone) instead of being the sulphate of it, (of the nature of plaster,) and in order to make the people on whose land these stones are found better acquainted with the nature of the true plaster of Paris, I shall extract part of a chapter of Chaptal's on chemistry. He expresses himself thus: The plaster loses its transparency by calcination, at the same time that it becomes pulverulent, and acquires the property of again seizing the water of which it had been deprived, and resuming its hardness; it does not give fire with the steel, nor effervesce with acids. He says farther, 100 parts of gypsum contains 30 parts of sulphuric acid, 32 calcarius earth, and 38 water; it loses nearly 27 per cent. by calcination. It is soluble in 500 times its weight of water, at the temperature of 60 degrees of Fahrenheit. When it is exposed to heat, its water of crystalization is dissipated; it becomes opaque, loses its consistence, and falls into powder. If it be moistened, it becomes hard again, but does not resume its transparency; a circumstance which appears to prove that its firm state is a state of crystalization; if it be kept in fire of considerable intensity, in contact with powder of charcoal, the acid is decomposed, and the residue is lime, &c."

Upon the principle above stated we learn that plaster and lime are both calcareous earth, and we might draw a conclusion from them, that if any virtue is attributed to the former in promoting the growth of clover and other plants, it is owing to the sulphuric acid that the plaster contains, and that both a pyretous and limestone ground is required for the formation of it.

I will add for information, also, that as the plaster, when calcinated, looks nearly as white as any other calcareous matter, and in order that one might be known from the other, pour some drops of water on both. It will cause an immediate efferverscence on the lime, while the plaster will receive no effect from it. Besides, when the plaster, after calcination, is pounded, pulverized and sifted, it can be formed, with the addition of water, into a paste which will grow solid by drying, while it will not be so with any other calcareous substance.

"Near the mill of Mr. Stephens, on Tullis branch, I found a kind of soft lime-stone, that the people also took for plaster of Paris, which being easily reduced into powder, either by pounding or grinding, or made into lime by fire, may probably answer to improve lands.

"Another kind of lime-stone I found also, at Mr. Samuel

Hedges', in Sleepy Creek Valley, which would perhaps answer the same purpose as the above described."

"I have seen at Mr. Sheerer's mill, on the Potomac, flag stones, that he raised from the bottom of that river, near his house, which surpass in color, beauty and size, any shistus (slate stone) I have ever seen. Those slabs can be polished and sawed easier than marble, and Mr. Sheerer has used them in its stead to embelish his new house. When the navigation of this river shall be improved, no doubt that they will be boated down to the cities below, and will constitute a branch of commerce. Those stones would be of great service in the raising of dams and locks on this river, for the improvement of navigation, in the same manner as spoken of in the article of Rivers in Frederick County."

MINERALOGY.

On the banks of Opequon, near the house of Mr. John Vanmetre, two or three miles from Martinsburg, is found a kind of sulphate of iron, (copperas,) which immediately turns leather black. It is found between the slates, but not in abundance; however, when a diligent search is made much may be found.

Iron, copper, as well as silver ores, are found on Sleepy Creek Mountain, but the last ore is not found in quantities sufficient to be worthy of exploring. No search yet, with a particular view to obtain these ores, has been made by any chemist on those mountains. The waters of Sleepy Creek contain the iron in solution to such a degree that the stones on its bed are covered with the oxide of it.

NATURAL CURIOSITIES.

There is a natural reservoir bearing the name of Swan Pond, in this county, the waters of which run off in a stream for some distance and then sink all at once, and no more is seen of them until near the mouth of Opequon Creek, where, in a hollow or pit of about 100 feet deep and 300 feet in circumference, you hear them pass under the rocks of the bottom of that pit, and going undoubtedly to join Opequon Creek.

MILLS.

There are in this county upwards of 50 grist or merchant mills, as many saw mills, several fulling mills, an oil mill and one paper mill.

MANUFACTORIES.

A large and convenient stone-built merchant mill on Tuscarora and joining Martinsburg has been bought lately from Mrs. Hunter by Messrs. Hibbert and Gibbs for the purpose of establishing a wool and cotton manufactory. Mr. Hibbert is a fuller by trade; he has already erected all the apparatus for fulling, dressing and dying all sorts of cloths on a pretty large scale. Mr. Gibbs is an ingenious mechanic; he has moved from his cotton manufactory at Hagerstown all his machinery for carding and spinning both wool and cotton, to place them in this building.

Mr Jonathan Wickersham, a fuller, the proprietor of a fulling mill and carding machine established on Middle Creek, near the precincts of Bucklestown, has added lately to his factory a jenny of fifty spindles to spin wool, and having at hand a number of capable weavers, he intends to carry on a complete factory of cloth. I hope these two infant manufactories may be encouraged so as to become permanent establishments and add to the stock of wealth of the country.

MINERAL WATERS.

There are several of the sulphur kind on Opequon, in this county, but the most remarkable is the one occupied by Mr. Minghini, about 8 miles from Martinsburg, this house is well fitted for accommodation, and several hundred persons resort there every season.

There is another, also, at two miles distance from Martinsburg, on which the citizens of Martinsburg have bestowed some trouble and expense to render it convenient and useful to visitors. They have put up a shower bath, which is used by the neighbors and townsmen.

The most conspicuous one is at Bath Town, under the Warm Spring Ridge, from the foot of which and by different channels issues a torrent of water capable to turn a mill. Water cannot be more limpid and beautiful than this is. This place, though agreeably ornamented and capable of contributing to the pleasures of the gay and healthy, as well as convenient and salutary to the sick and invalid, might be greatly improved and embellished by taste and liberality if the Legislature of Virginia was disposed to encourage any practicable scheme to raise money for that purpose. Nature has been lavish of her favors to this spot of country, for in addition to those medicinal springs, she has showered her bounties upon the whole neighborhood by spreading over it a magnificent variety of the most finished and grand scenery.

The soil around this place, as a mountainous country, has the appearance of sterility, but by proper attention to culture might be made productive and rich.

I will not attempt to elucidate the properties of these waters; I will only say that the country in this valley looks barren and is uncommonly dry, and as under the surface of the earth there generally exists a hard rock, which prevents the rain water from penetrating so as to produce permanent springs, my curiosity was so much awakened as to induce me to look for the source of this spring, and after much pains, I was informed by the neighbors and hunters living on the Ca-Capon Creek, that the waters of that creek were sinking at about 10 miles from its mouth, and formed a vortex. This spot lies to the South-west of the Warm Springs ridge, and of the Ca-Capon mountain, and at the distance of about 9 miles in a straight line from Bath Town. This seemed to me the more probable, as these springs are never influenced either in their temperature, or quantity, by the warm, or cold, or wet, or dry weather, and probably after having sojourned and passed through the mazes of the subterranean cavities under the Ca-Capon mountain, as well as under the valley which lies between the Ca Capon mountain and the Warm Springs ridge, the soil of which is calcareous and having been in contact with the different pyrites composing their bed, receives by their decomposition, the degree of heat, that those waters contain, as well as the gases with which they are impregnated, and after a due filtration through the sandy rocks, of which the basis of that Warm Spring ridge is composed, they arrive at this spot.

These waters, when boiled, have strong incrustations on the sides of the vessel, which plainly evince that they are highly mineralized, and consequently possessed of the virtues for which they have been so much extolled, in relieving or removing complaints. I took with me, last fall, some of those sediments to Philadelphia, and gave them to Dr. Barton, who, an eminent chemist, will give a full analysis of their contents.

I have inserted this in order to counteract the opinion of those, who, without taking any pains in the investigation or analysis of these waters, have advanced, that they contain no minerals in solution, neither in a state of oxide nor gas, and consequently, are totally destitute of any properties whatever, more than common water.

MARTINSBURG

Is the capital of the County of Berkeley; it contains about 200 houses, and nearly 1,200 inhabitants; it is the seat of justice, and has for that purpose a handsome Court House and Jail of stone, and a Market House, well supplied with the necessaries of life. The situation of this town is remarkably pleasant and healthy, on account of its standing on an elevated spot, and for having the Creek of Tuscarora watering its precincts, which could be carried in pipes through the town for the convenience and comfort of the inhabitants, if desired. The streets are wide, and partly planted with Lombardy poplars, and have a very fine appearance. Eight taverns are kept in this place; one of them has the reputation of being one of the best in the United States, and is well known by those who resort to the Warm Springs. Here is kept a coffee house, where, almost all the papers in the United States are read; 8 large stores, one printing office; there are also five public meeting houses for worship, one English Episcopalian, a Catholic, a German Lutheran, a Presbyterian, a Methodist and a Baptist; three English schools, several manufactories, and every description of artificers and mechanics.

Latitude, North 39 degrees, 32 minutes. It is 22 miles from Winchester, 20 from Hagerstown, 100 from Baltimore, 81 from the Federal City, 117 from Staunton, 171 from Philadelphia, 172 from Richmond, and 16 from Charlestown.

MIDDLETOWN, OR GERARDSTOWN,

Situated on a level soil, partly limestone, one mile and a-half from Mill's Gap, under the North Mountain, to the East side of it, and nearly at the head of Mill Creek. It contains about 40 families; a physician and a Presbyterian clergyman reside here; several large stores are kept in this town, for the supply of the farmers around it; here are also a number of mechanics. There is in this place a handsome brick church, built by the Presbyterians. This town is 10 miles from Martinsburg, and 15 and a-half from Winchester.

DARKESVILLE, OR BUCKLESTOWN,

Lies 7¼ miles from Martinsburg, on the road to Winchester; 15 miles from that place, and on Middle Creek, a never-failing stream, which crosses this place. There are 30 dwelling houses, 4 taverns, 3 stores, 2 blacksmiths, 2 weavers, one tailor, one cabinet maker, one wagon maker, one distillery of whiskey; a Methodist meeting house stands at the North end of this town.

BATH-TOWN, OR WARM SPRINGS,

Situated immediately under the East side of the Warm Spring ridge, 6 miles from the Potomac, in a narrow valley, watered by the stream which runs from the Warm Springs. Several years ago this town was handsome, but the houses, as being built with wood, have decayed, and on account of the celebrity of its waters, was yearly visited by above 1,000 of the *beau monde*. It had lost its reputation on account of some diseases which raged during one season, occasioned by a pond where the waters were stagnating; but, since the cause was removed, it has regained its character. Last year, 1779, it was visited by above 500 people, and no doubt will increase each year. Here are five large, convenient and handsome taverns, or boarding houses, kept for the accommodation of visitors and invalids; 26 families are living in this place; among the number various branches of mechanics. Here are several stores and a manufactory of leather.

I must not omit to mention, for the information of the people, who are to visit this watering place, that besides the above springs, there is a sulphur spring, 4 miles distant from this place, near Sleepy Creek. It is but slightly impregnated with sulphur, and no accommodation near it, and a chalibiate spring on this ridge, about half a mile from this town. It is 25 miles from Martinsburg, 35 from Winchester, 34 from Hagerstown, 106 from the Federal City, 108 from Baltimore, 185 from Richmond, and 196 from Philadelphia.

JAMESBURG

Is situated in Back Creek Valley, and has only the name of a town; for it contains only a few scattering houses, without regularity. It is about 13 miles from Martinsburg.

The larger portion of this chapter was taken from old pamphlets, from which no evidence can be found as to the writer.

CHAPTER XVI.
PRESENT SITUATION OF THE TOWN AND COUNTY—JOURNALISM IN THE COUNTY—COUNTY COURT AND OFFICIALS—MARTINSBURG SCHOOLS—HOME ORGANIZATIONS, LODGES, ETC.—MANUFACTURING ADVANTAGES, RAILROAD FACILITIES AND BUSINESS STANDING.

MARTINSBURG is, geographically, admirably situated as the county seat of Berkeley County, which ranks third in size and amongst the first in number of acres of improved land and value of farm products in the State. Topographically the city lies nestled near the foot of the Little North Mountain, which ever sends fresh, sweet air and clear, pure water to invigorate and strengthen our people. This same mountain stands as a bulwark to the west and north against the rough blasts of winter, and protects the valley from the fury of destructive storms.

The town of Martinsburg is contained within the following boundaries, to wit: Beginning on the middle of the county bridge crossing the Baltimore and Ohio Railroad, south of Green Hill Cemetery and corner to Martinsburg, Arden and Opequon districts; thence with the line of Opequon north 11½ degrees east, 66 poles to a stake at the angle of the fence and in an original line between the land of Ezra Herring and the lot of C. Henry; thence north 5½ degrees east, passing through the lands of E. Herring, A. Quinzel, P. Strine's second addition, and the south-east corner of A. Roth's lot, 253 poles to a stake in the field; thence north 60 degrees west, passing along the line between the additions of James A. Boyd, John Strine and Hockinberry 62 poles to a stake in a stone fence on the west side of the M. & P. turnpike; thence passing through the lands of David Hess, H. S. Hannis & Co., south 88½ degrees west, 162 poles to a stake in the low grounds, on the east side, and about 3 poles from the Baltimore and Ohio Railroad, and on the land of John W. Stewart, and corner of Opequon, Hedgesville and Martinsburg districts; thence with the line of Hedgesville in part, and finally with Arden district, south 36¾ degrees west, 245 three tenths poles to a stake in the grade at the west end of King street; thence south 90 degrees east, 176 poles to a stake about two rods southwest of a stone house on the lands of Hon. C. J. Faulkner; thence south 71¼ degrees east, 84 poles to a stake at the south end of Queen street; thence north 92 degrees east, 224 poles to the beginning, it being the present limits of the town.

The place is just 100 miles from Baltimore, 80 miles from Washington, 22 Winchester, 19 from Harper's Ferry, 70 from Cumberland, on the 1st division of the Baltimore and Ohio Railroad, and is the southern terminus of the Cumberland Valley Railroad. For business and trade it is the centre of a large territory of country. The machine shops of the B. & O. are located in the city, and give employment to several hundred hands. The Tuscarora Creek passes directly through, which furnishes considerable power for manufacturing purposes. The Hannis distillery, one of the largest branches in the country, and the Tuscarora Agricultural Works, owned by John Fitz, are located on this stream, and also employs a large number of hands. Pay is good, and monthly thousands of dollars are expended for labor.

The surface of the western part of the county is mountainous, but is being well cleared and cultivated. The most valuable forests abound, and excellent qualities of coal, iron ore, limestone, etc., are to be found.

Situation of Town and County. 379

The county is divided into seven districts or townships, with assessable buildings and real estate as follows:

Districts.	Value of Buildings.	Value of Land and Buildings.	County Levy.
Martinsburg......	$ 871,142.00	$1,172,727.00	$ 5,277.34
Hedgesville.......	195,782.00	649,523.00	2,922.68
Falling Waters .	162,252.00	606,577.00	2,135.29
Gerardstown.....	117,845.00	426,477.76	2,023.75
Arden	145,967.00	612,240.80	2,814.67
Mill Creek........	92,477.00	418,011.97	1,940.97
Opequon...........	137,817.00	597,174.14	2,700.97
	$1,723,282.00	$4,482,731.61	$19,815.67

The present population of the entire county, as near as can be estimated from the last two censuses, is 19,860. The city district will number nearly 8,000.

There are a number of towns and villages within the districts supplied with well regulated schools, churches, Post Offices, etc., and which contain a number of the usual business places, thereby making a direct communication and the mail facilities very convenient. The places in direct communication with Martinsburg, the county seat, are as follows: Bedington, Hedgesville, Falling Waters, Vanclevesville, Glengary, Darkesville, Bunker Hill, Gerardstown, Shanghai, Jones' Spring, Little Georgetown, Soho, Tomahawk, Ganotown and North Mountain. The roads are in a fine condition and well kept up.

The soils throughout the county are loams and clay, and in the west are thinner and less productive; but in the east there is a large amount of highly productive and improved calcareous lands. The depth of the soil varies from two to four inches on the hills and 12 inches or more on the levels. The grains specially adapted to the lands are wheat, corn, oats and barley. The principal industries are stock farming and grain raising. Principal exports are wheat, corn and stock.

The public buildings and private residences will stand

a favorable comparison with any town of proportionate size, and will far surpass many of the larger cities. The older buildings are fast disappearing, and in a few years our town will be composed entirely of the latest modern structures.

It may be of interest to mention here some of the late improvements to our city. The old Carpenter lot and building on West King street, which had probably stood for centuries, was purchased by Messrs. Dr. J. B. Snodgrass and B. F. Fiery, and two fine large and commodious dwellings erected in its stead. Messrs. Dr. J. W. McSherry, John Fitz, E. Boyd Faulkner, C. W. Doll, Senator C. J. Faulkner, Emmert & Fiery, John Dunn, James H. Walker, E. E. Herring, C. P. Herring, D. W. Shaffer, E. C. Williams, Jr., J. W. Bishop and a number of others have made big improvements. Two large and handsome hotels are well supported in the town; the St. Clair, under the management of Geo. W. Ramer, and the Continental, under the management of Wm. Rutledge. Both are run and furnished in the best of style, with rates from $2.00 per day upwards.

Mr. John Fellers has lately built a large town hall called the "Academy of Music," which is generally well patronized. There is also a City Hall, erected by the corporation for its own use. The town is well graded and the streets kept in an excellent condition.

Two of the largest and finest banks in the State are supported in this city, viz.: The People's National Bank and the National Bank. Both are well managed, and for promptness and dispatch of business cannot be surpassed.

The corporation officers are C. O. Lambert, Mayor; Councilmen, First Ward, Dr. J. W. McSherry and M. W. Martin; Second Ward, A. Staubley and F. C. Williams; Third Ward, W. H. Kaufman and Geo. W. DeGrange; Fourth Ward, G. Wellinger and M. V. Green; Fifth Ward, Arthur Stephens and J. A. Bowers; Clerk,

C. A. Young; Sergeant, Henry Wilen; Policemen, C. R. O'Neal, Thos. F. Ahern and John W. Poisal; Attorney, J. Nelson Wisner; Engineer Water Works, Jacob M. Shaffer.

TOWNS AND VILLAGES IN BERKELEY COUNTY.

Gerardstown.—The town of Middletown was established about the year 1787, and soon afterward its name was changed to Gerardstown in honor of its founder, Rev. David Gerard, who laid it off into one hundred town lots. William Henshaw, James Haw, John Gray, Gilbert McKown and Robert Allen were appointed trustees. The town is located eleven miles southwest of Martinsburg, and one mile east of North Mountain, on Mill Creek. The present population numbers nearly 300, with one free and one high school. There are four churches in the town, owned and occupied by the Presbyterians, Lutherans, Methodist Episcopal and the Methodist Episcopal, South. The town contains a number of stores, a large tannery and other important industries. Two newspapers are published here—the *Times* and the *West Virginia Good Templar*, by J. B. Morgan.

Shanghai.—This village is located one mile west of Back Creek, and contains several stores, blacksmith shops, etc. A large factory is owned and run here by a joint stock company called the Shanghai Manufacturing Association, for the purpose of manufacturing lumber and grinding sumac, tan bark, etc. The Presbyterian Church and one free school are also located in the town.

Ganotown.—This place is situated on Back Creek, three miles south of Shanghai. The Methodist Episcopal Church was built here in 1871, and has a large congregation. This place was originally called Jamestown, the first settlement in the district being made on the site of the present village. Several stores and various other industries are supported.

Jones' Spring.—Located near the north line of the district, at the foot of the ridge, about one mile west of

Back Creek. It contains several blacksmith shops, stores, etc. In 1872 the church edifice of the Episcopal society was purchased by the Calvary Church, United Brethren, and is used by this denomination at the present day.

Darkesville.—This village was laid out in October, 1791, and is situated at the junction of Middle Creek, on the Martinsburg and Winchester turnpike. It was named in honor of General Darke, who was then a resident. The place was formerly known as Bucklestown, named after General Buckles, who resided there. It contains a number of stores, blacksmith shops, etc.

Bunker Hill.—Situated at the junction of Mill Creek and on the Martinsburg and Winchester turnpike. It contains two churches, occupied by the Methodist and Episcopal denominations. During the late war between the States, this locality became a historic spot on account of the many important events that occurred.

Hedgesville.—This town is located seven miles North of Martinsburg, one mile West of the B. &. O. R. R., and is situated in what is now known as Skinner's Gap, in North Mountain. It was laid out in 1830 by Hezekiah Hedges, and named after his family who long resided there. One of the first Episcopal Churches erected in the valley, known as "Hedges' Chapel," was located here. It has been authentically stated, that while on his surveying expeditions in this locality, several years prior to the opening of the Revolutionary War, the illustrious George Washington worshipped here. The town is well laid off and consists of fine dwellings, churches, schools, stores, etc.

Bedington.—This village is located on the C. V. R. R., about four miles North of Martinsburg, and is noted as a resort during the summer months. Near by is a large grove, containing the most valuable mineral waters, among which are the noted Sulphur Springs. The town is composed of several stores, schools, churches, etc.

Falling Waters.—Located about seven miles North of

Situation of Town and County. 383

Martinsburg, on the C. V. R. R., and near the Potomac River. This place was the scene of many important incidents during the late war. One of the oldest churches in the county was erected here by the Presbyterian denomination, which is standing and occupied at the present day. Within its limits are to be found several large flouring mills, stores, churches, schools, etc.

Glengary.—Situated between the North Mountain and dividing line, about sixteen miles Southwest of Martinsburg. It is composed of schools, churches, stores, etc.

Little Georgetown.—This place is noted as a great fishing resort, and is located on the Potomac River, above Dam No. 5, and about nine miles North of Martinsburg. Schools, churches, stores, etc., are to be found within its limits.

Soho.—Situated in the extreme North-west end of the county, about sixteen miles from Martinsburg. It is composed of well-regulated churches and schools, and contains stores, etc.

Tomahawk.—Situated six miles South of Hedgesville, and contains stores, churches, schools, etc.

North Mountain.—Located on the B. & O. R. R., about six miles North-west of Martinsburg, and contains store, churches, schools, etc. This place is also a shipping point for Tomahawk and Hedgesville.

There are a number of smaller villages scattered throughout the districts ; but my object has been to locate those in direct communication with Martinsburg, the county seat, and of greater importance. All are rapidly increasing in size and population, and are inhabited by an industrious and energetic people.

JOURNALISM IN THE COUNTY.

Martinsburg Gazette.

The first newspaper published in Berkeley County was the Martinsburg *Gazette*, which was established in May, 1799, by Nathaniel Willis, father of the renowned poet, Nathaniel Parker Willis. Long before the advent of the telegraph, telephone, railroad and steamship, this paper commenced its publication, and considering this fact, it is astonishing to observe how the columns of the early files are crowded with interesting news. As an evidence of enterprise on the part of the proprietors, it contains the details of many important events that occurred throughout the country but a short time previously. One feature of special importance is the war of 1812, and the stirring events happening on the western border,—the historic achievements on the banks of the historic Maumee, in North-western Ohio, by General Harrison and Anthony Wayne. The publication of these articles were made within twenty days after their occurrence. In January, 1811, John Alburtis became editor and proprietor, and continued its publication until October 25, 1822, when he was succeeded by Washington Evans. In December, 1833, Mr. Alburtis commenced the publication of the *Journal*, at Shepherdstown.

Martinsburg Independent.

At the close of the war of 1861, the first paper published in Martinsburg, was the *Berkeley Union*, an advocate of Republicanism, with Mr. J. Nelson Wisner as its editor until April, 1873. In 1866, the *New Era*, a Democratic paper was started, and closed its career with Messrs. Shaffer & Logan as editors, in April, 1873. From the consolidation of these two papers grew the *Martinsburg Independent*, April 1st, 1873. Until April, 1876, it was published daily and weekly, and since that date it has been published weekly. From the time of its establishment until April, 1876, it was controlled by the Independent Printing Company, when it passed into the hands of Wisner & Logan. This firm continued the publication until March, 1885, when Mr. Logan, on account of illness, was compelled to withdraw from the business, and his entire interest was purchased by Mr. Wisner.

Its name and motto indicates its independence on all

subjects, and its aim to benefit the public welfare. It is useless to comment on its past record, as the fact of its being the oldest established paper in the county and of nearly twenty-five years duration, will speak for itself. Its forty-eight columns are always full to the brim with interesting and important news, live editorials, and wide-awake advertisers. The office and various departments are complete in every detail, and skilled workmen execute every branch of the business. The *Independent* has a very large circulation and controls a vast influence. It is of good clear print, and shows every evidence of marked ability on the part of its present editor and proprietor, Mr. J. Nelson Wisner. Mr. U. S. Grant Pitzer is at present acting in the capacity of assistant editor, and Mr. H. C. Mathews, as foreman, with Edward Wild, C. C. Pitzer and Walter M. Aler as compositors.

As an act of appreciation on the part of the author of this work, he takes this opportunity and pleasure in stating that on this paper he acquired the greater portion of his learning, and served his apprenticeship under the instructions of Mr. H. C. Mathews, a veteran typo of some forty years experience. He was taken from the associations of the average wild boy at an early age, and under Mr. Wisner's training was given every advantage of the art of printing and journalism in general, besides access to libraries of books. Through the care and interest manifested on the part of this gentleman, a deep and lasting impression has been made, which shall ever retain a sacred place to his memory.

Martinsburg Statesman.

This paper is amongst the oldest established in the county, and has been from its infancy a staunch advocate of Democratic principles—in fact the only Democratic paper in the county. It has always been conducted under strict management and party principles, and has been a paper used to the interest of the public of both town and county.

In public affairs it is always ready to take a stand, and has been the means of accomplishing considerable enterprise on the part of the citizens.

This paper originated from the *Valley Star*, which was established by James W. Robinson, in the year ———. It was purchased in 1869 by D. S. Eichelberger, and the name changed to the Martinsburg *Statesman*, under which name it has continued to the present day.

During Mr. Eichelberger's control, the paper was well published, and contained an excellent and large run of advertisements, which it still holds at the present day. Through its columns can be found numerous items, arousing the citizens of the county to a state of enterprise, and industry. The heading of the paper contained a cut of the present Court House, before the late improvements were made.

In 1883, the plant was purchased by Capt. W. B. Colston, who is the present editor and publisher. Since taking charge of the paper, Capt. Colston has improved it considerably, both in print, size and make-up. He has equipped the office with new material, and allowed the cylinder press to take the place of the hand press. The *Statesman* is ably edited, and deserves patronage of the public in general. Job printing of every description is also executed in the most workmanlike manner.

The *Statesman* has the proud distinction of having been the first newspaper, as far as the writer knows, to suggest the name of Grover Cleveland for the Presidency, after his phenominal run for Governor of New York in 1882. To form an idea of the *Statesman's* worth and value to the community, it is only necessary to glance over the file papers of the past, and then compare the improvement of both town and county of the present day. Mr. John S. Robinson, is at present acting in the capacity of local editor and foreman, with Thos. W. Leigh, John V. Sloan and Harry H. Sharffs as compositors.

Martinsburg Herald.

In the year 1881, this valuable paper, commenced publication under the control of Messrs. A. S. Goulden and John T. Riley. This end of the state was for a long time without a Republican paper, and the party was more or less dependent in politics. The *Herald* was continued as a conservative Republican paper, under the above management, until 1885. During this year Mr. Riley purchased the entire interest of Mr. Goulden, and associated with himself Mr. Geo. F. Evans, one the leading Republicans in this end of the State. From that time the *Herald* has gained ground, irrespective of politics, and by prudent, conservative management, has received the support of the best people of the county and State. It has several times been enlarged in size, during its publication, and is a neat and clear print. The present proprietors, Messrs. Riley & Evans, have speared neither pains nor money, to make the *Herald* a newsy and interesting sheet, and under the editorial control of Mr. Riley, it commands considerable influence. Their office, in all its branches, is complete in every detail with material, and they execute job printing in the most artistic manner.

These gentlemen deserve much credit, and the patronage of every Berkeley citizen, for the manner in which they have labored for the interest of both town and county. The paper contains reliable advertisers, and news of interest to all. Like all the county papers, its worth and value can be obtained by judging from its files of the past, the manner in which it has aroused the public industry. The compositors engaged on this paper are George W. Ryneal, W. C. Riddleberger, C. K. Chambers, and A. M. Staubly.

Pioneer Press.

Under the management of J. R. Clifford, (colored,) this paper was established in 1883, with a circulation of 100. The *Press* is a neat, 4-page paper, and is published monthly, but will shortly merge into a weekly journal. From the date of its existence Mr. Clifford has labored hard to make it a newsy and interesting sheet. It is the only journal in the State devoted to the colored race, and now has a large and excellent run of reliable advertisers, with a circulation upwards of 1,000. His energies have been crowned with a marked success, both as an editor and manager. The paper was printed at the *Independent* office until the spring of 1888, when he purchased the entire outfit of the *Hardy Express*, Moorefield, W. Va., and erected a building near his residence on West Martin Street, where he now publishes his paper. Politically, the *Press* is Republican, and commands considerable influence among both races.

Central Methodist.

In 1887 this paper was founded by the Typographical Association, of the colored M. E. Church Corference. It is devoted entirely to the local interests of the District Conference, and has a circulation of nearly 500; which is rapidly increasing. The paper is published at the *Independent* office, under the management of Rev. F. F. Wheeler, pastor in charge at this place. Its editors are John A. Holmes, T. A. White and F. F. Wheeler.

Gerardstown Times.

The *Times* was established in the year 1870, and has been continued to the present day, by J. B. Morgan, proprietor and editor. It is a neatly printed four column quarto, and is well managed and edited. Its politics are neutral, and is devoted principally to home news. This paper is published every Saturday, with an excellent list of subscribers.

West Virginia Good Templar.

This paper is the official organ of the I. O. G. T., and circulates through all parts of the State. It is a four colunm quarto, devoted strictly to the order, and is published every other week by J. B. Morgan, editor and proprietor.

Situation of Town and County.

COUNTY COURT OFFICIALS.

As has been stated in a former chapter the first Court was held at the house of Edward Beeson, situated on the land now owned by Mr. A. J. Thomas. The first Court house was built where the present building now stands. From the old records we obtained the following list of officers as they succeeded each other from its earliest existence:

Judges of Circuit Court:—Robert White, Wm. Brokenbrough, John Scott, Richard E. Parker, Isaac R. Douglass, John W. Kennedy, L. P. W. Balch, Ephriam B. Hall, Joseph Chapman, E. B. Hall, Jno. Blair Hoge, Chas. J. Faulkner, Jr., and Frank Beckwith the present Judge.

Attorneys for the Commonwealth:—Alexander White, Elisha Boyd, David H. Conrad, Edmund P. Hunter, Jno. E. Norris, George W. Murphy, Joseph T. Hoke, J. Nelson Wisner, H. H. Blackburn, Edmund Shaw, Reuben M. Price, Luther M. Shaffer, W. H. H. Flick, Perry A. Rohrbaugh, Wm. S. Henshaw, Alex. S. Hughes and Geo. W. Feidt, present Attorney.

Clerks of Circuit Court:—Obed Waite, John Strother, Israel Robinson, John Dunn, Joseph Burns, John Canby, E. S. Troxell, three successive terms, and S. H. Martin, who is now ably filling the duties of a second term.

"Clerks of County Court:—William Drew, Moses Hunter, John Strother, Harrison Waite, Norman Miller, Jacob Van Doren,—E. G. Alburtis, two terms, and James M. Robinson, Leaman Gerard and Bernard Doll, as Recorders,—and the present Clerk, C. W. Doll, who is now serving his third term.

PRESENT OFFICIALS.

Members of the Legislature:—George M. Bowers and George H. Ropp.

Judge of the Circuit Court—Thirteenth Judicial District, Frank Beckwith. Clerk of the Circuit Court, S. H. Martin. Commonwealth's Attorney, George W.

Feidt. Sheriff, Robert Lamon. Deputy Sheriffs, W. T. Noll, Charles R. Hollis and George L. Sincindiver. Deputy Sheriff and Jailor, John Dumford.

Commencement of Terms of Circuit Court—Second Tuesday in January, April and October.

County Court of Berkeley—Jacob W. Seibert, President; B. Kitchen and Wm. Kilmer, Commissioners. Clerk of Court, C. W. Doll.

Commencement of Terms of County Court—First Monday in March, June, September and December.

Commissioners in Chancery—John T. Picking and C. W. Doll.

Surveyor of Lands—Geo. W. Vanmeter. Deputy Surveyor of Lands, James W. Robinson.

Assessor First District—David Dodd. Second District—Charles H. Miller. Commissioner of School Lands, (vacant). General Receiver, Henry J. Seibert. Coroner, Frank D. Staley. Sealer of Weights and Measures, Geo. W. Swartz.

Resident Attorneys—E. Boyd Faulkner & M. T. Ingles, W. H. H. Flick & D. C. Westenhaver, Chas. J. Faulkner & Stuart W. Walker, J. Nelson Wisner. Geo. W. Feidt, Blackburn Hughes & Hugh A. White, A. C. Nadenbousch and U. S. Grant Pitzer.

Justices of the Peace—Martinsburg, Wm. McKee and Chas. P. Matthaei; Mill Creek, Chas. Stucky, (vacant;) Gerardstown, A. J. Bowers; Arden, James M. Billmyer; Opequon, G. W. M. Tabler and G. W. D. Folk; Hedgesville, R. R. Coffenberger; Falling Waters, S. O. Cunningham and H. Cox.

Constables—Martinsburg, J. D. Turner and C. R. O'Neal; Mill Creek, Wm. Lemon; Gerardstown,(vacant); Arden, T. A. Potts; Opequon, A. H. A. Gardner; Hedgesville, John L. Emerson; Falling Waters, Jacob V. Carney.

Overseers of Poor—Martinsburg, Henry Wilen; Mill Creek, M. L. Payne, Gerardstown, G. W. McKown;

Arden, H. H. Miller ; Opequon, W. H. Myers ; Hedgesville, George T. Kreglow ; Falling Waters ; A. R. Porterfield.

County Superintendent of Free Schools—D. H. Dodd.

Local Board of Health—Dr. J. W. McSherry, M. S. Grantham and E. L. Hoffman.

MARTINSBURG SCHOOLS.

The public schools of the city were first organized in 1865, but were not in full operation as such until 1866, when a part of the old " Kruzen property," located near the centre of the city, was purchased at a cost of $7,500, and started as a grammar school. Dr. Irwin, W. H. Matthews and Geo. R. Wisong were the first commissioners. About 500 pupils were accommodated, taught by a corps of eight teachers. Four grades were taught as a preparatory to the grammar department, which occupied the second story, containing a large school room and two recitation rooms. The grammar department occupied the lower story, which contained two school rooms and a recitation room. As the population increased new houses were erected, as follows : one in the Second Ward at a cost of $6,900 ; one in the Fourth Ward at a cost of $5,200 ; one in the Fifth Ward, cost $4,800 ; and also a property for a High School at a cost of $7,500. Three of the ward buildings are composed of brick and one of stone ; also, a neat brick building for the colored school. The colored schools were simultaneously organized with the other schools, and are governed by the same board. The Legislature passed an Act in 1870, requiring the German language to be taught in the free schools of the city, and that a capable teacher of both languages be employed. In 1875 an Act was passed by the Legislature, making Martinsburg an independent district.

In 1884 the High School building was erected, on a beautiful location, on South Queen street. All the buildings are well furnished, with heating apparatus, modern conveniences, etc. The city educates nearly all its own teachers, and always gives the preference to graduates of the High School, which has resulted in a unity of system and harmony of action, as to place our schools on equal standing and make them as thorough and efficient as any in the State of West Virginia. Twenty-two teachers are employed in all—twenty white and two colored, all of which are zealous, arduous and competent, thereby placing our schools in a more prosperous condition than ever. Martinsburg has every reason to feel proud of her school officers and system, and to effect, in the future, a more rapid advancement than ever experienced in the past.

The present Board of Education is composed of John Grozinger, President; N. T. Fisher, J. H. Whitson, N. H. Snyder and E. S. Barton.

Board of Examiners: J. A. Cox, President; W. A. Pitzer, J. L. E. Combs. City Superintendent, J. A. Cox, A. M.

Faculty of the High School: J. A. Cox, Principal; Jennie L. Ditto, 1st Assistant; Annie O'Neal, 2nd Assistant; Annie E. Hill, 3rd Assistant.

Faculties of the Ward Schools—Second Ward: W. A. Pitzer, Principal; Lillie Mathews, Lula V. Muth, Bettie M. Day, Assistants. Third Ward: O. F. Ryneal, Principal; Jennie Alburtis, Jessie McElroy, Kate M. Bateman, Assistants. Fourth Ward: J. L. E. Combs, Principal; Kate A. Ahern, Lottie V. McKee, Lenora Smurr, Asssistants. Fifth Ward: Alice V. Wilson, Principal; Jennie E. Mann, Ada M. Rodrick, Clara V. Cutting, Assistants. Colored School: J. W. Corsey, (colored) Principal; Geo. W. Green, (colored) Assistant. Number enrolled in the various free schools in the city: High school, 173; Second Ward, 281; Third Ward, 227; Fourth Ward 355; Fifth Ward, 232; colored school, 130; Total, white children, 1,168; Grand total, white and colored, 1,298.

Situation of Town and County. 393

BERKELEY FEMALE SEMINARY.

This school, which has been in successful operation for many years, is located in Martinsburg, West Virginia, and which combines the advantages of accessibility, healthfulness, good society, and general attractiveness, to a degree unsurpassed by any City in the State. The course of instruction embraces all the primary and advanced studies, essential to a thorough and accomplished female education, and such as are taught at similar institutions of the highest grade.

The standard of proficiency is high, and the ambition of pupils is encouraged by means of monthly reports to parents, showing their standing in their various classes. In the department of music no pains are spared to give pupils every advantage necessary to a thorough musical education. A firm and wholesome discipline is maintained, together with a conscientious regard for the moral and religious welfare, the health and comfort, of all pupils entrusted to their care.

A rigid system of marking is adopted in every department, and reports candidly exhibiting the standing and conduct of the pupils, are sent home every month. General averages are obtained by adding together the average for each study, and dividing by the number of studies. This school has been established for quite a lengthy period, and is taught and managed by its very able and efficient principals, Mrs. Peyton R. Harrison and Miss B. J. Hunter. The school and residence is situated on West King street.

HOME ORGANIZATIONS, LODGES, Etc.

Martinsburg Fire Department was organized in 1870. Officers: C. E. Dieffenderfer, Chief Marshal; C. O. Lambert, Assistant; P. C. Curtis, Commander; H. C. McDowell, Treasurer; C. J. Thomas, Secy.; Engineers, J. M. Shaffer and David Westall; Assistants, George T. Shaffer, David Fitz; number of Members, 110. The Company is equipped with a Silsby engine; has four Reels, with 2,000 feet of hose; has recently purchased a new Reel for 4th Ward. Firemen have been recently equipped with fine dress uniforms and belts.

The Farmers' and Mechanics' Mutual Fire Insurance Co. of West Virginia. Officers: James M. Homrich, Pres't; H. N. Deatrick, Vice Pres't; E. S. Troxell, Sec'y; W. A. Cushwa, Treas. Directors, Charles P. Matthaei, Wm. A. Cushwa, Geo. P. Blessing, Geo. W. McKown, Geo. O. Sperow, Joseph H. Shaffer, C. T. Butler, M. V. Small, Geo. P. Riner. Executive Committee, James M. Homrich, Charles P. Matthaei, Joseph H. Shaffer. Surveyors—H. T. Cushwa, Berkeley County; J. B. Kearfott, Albert Diehl, Jefferson County.

This Company was organized Dec. 18th, 1877, and has been in successful operation since that time, being patronized by a large majority of the most substantial citizens of Berkeley County.

Equality Building Association.—Officers, H. T. Cushwa, President; Wm Edwards, Sec'y; W. O. Nicklas, Treas. Meets every Friday night.

Central Building and Loan Association.—Officers, C. O. Lambert, President; F. D. Staley, Vice-Pres't; Ferdinand Gerling, Sec'y; G. W. Feidt, Treasurer; J. N. Wisner, Attorney. Meets every Tuesday night.

Enterprise Building Association.—Officers, H. T. Cushwa, President; Wm. Edwards, Jr., Sec'y; W. O. Nicklas, Treas. Meets every Tuesday night.

Equality Lodge, No. 44, A. F. and A. M., meets 2d and 4th Tuesdays from October 1 to July 1, and second Tuesday from July 1 to October 1, northwest corner Queen and Burke streets; entrance on Burke street.

Robert White Lodge, No. 57, A. F. and A. M., meets 2d and 4th Monday evenings from October 1 to July 1, and 4th Monday from July 1 to October 1, southwest corner Queen and King streets, Grantham Hall.

Berkeley Consistory, No. 21, A. and A. S. R., meets 3d

Tuesday evening of each month in hall of Equality Lodge No. 44, A. F. and A. M.

Palestine Commandery, No. 2, meets 1st Monday of each week in hall of Robert White Lodge No. 57, A. F. and A. M.

Lebanon Royal Arch, chapter No. 2, meets 2d Monday evening of each month in hall of Equality Lodge No. 44, A. F. and A. M.

St. Joseph's Society, President, John Dumford; secretary, John Farrin; treasurer, James Cox.

St. Patrick's, President, W. J. O'Connor; secretary, Thomas O'Brien; treasurer, Joseph E. Ahern.

Tuscarora Lodge, No. 24, I. O. O. F., meets every Saturday evening, northwest corner Queen and Burke streets; entrance on Queen.

Horeb Encampment, No. 12, I. O. O. F., meets 2d and 4th Tuesday evenings of each month in hall of Tuscarora Lodge No. 24, I. O. O. F.

Bethany Lodge, No. 7, D. of R., K. Westrater, N. G.; E. E. Grazer, V. G.; M. A. Rathman, R. S.; G. V. Rathman, F. S.; E. E. Crist, T.

Lincoln Post, No. 1, G. A. R., meets every Thursday evening in G. A. R. Hall, southeast corner Queen and Burke streets; entrance on Burke, People's National Bank Building.

Prosperity Lodge, No. 29, I. O. G. T., meets every Monday evening in G. A. R. hall.

Franklin Assembly, No. 2373 K. L., meets every Saturday night in G. A. R. hall.

Key Council, No. 432, Royal Arcanum, meets 1st and 3d Friday evenings in G. A. R. hall.

Washington Lodge, No. 1, K. of P., meets every Thursday evening in K. of P. hall, southeast corner Queen and Burke streets; entrance on Burke, People's National Bank Building.

Knights of Honor Lodge, No. 62, meets 2d and 4th Friday nights in hall of K. of P.

Branch No. 29, Order Iron Hall, meets 2d and 4th Thursday nights in hall of K. of P.

Berkeley Lodge, No. 173, Order of Tonti, meets 1st and 3d Thursdays of each month in hall of K. of P., People's National Bank Building.

Mt. Pisgah Lodge, No. 3, A. Y. M., (col'd) meets every Thursday evening on South College street.

Federal Lodge, No. 152, K. of W., meets in People's Bank Building 2d Tuesday in each month; Chairman, H. B. Foard; secretary, W. Corsey.

The Martinsburg Gas Company was organized in 1873; President, H. N. Deatrick; Vice-President, J. H. Shaffer; Secretary and Treasurer, F. S. Emmert; Superintendent, D. Rawlinson.

Mechanics' Band.—The High Street Band, W. H. Frankenberry, organizer and leader, was started about 1871, and changed to the Mechanics' Band about 1882; reorganized and incorporated February 6th, 1886.

The Martinsburg City Band was organized on the 18th of December, 1883; Mr. P. C. Curtis is the genial manager, and Prof. Fred. Luscomb, musical director.

COUNTY ORGANIZATIONS.

Pomono Grange No. 2, located in Martinsburg District; meets last Saturday in each month.

Cherry Grove Grange No. 13, located in Opequon District; meets first and third Saturdays of each month.

Tuscarora Grange No. 14, located in Hedgesville District; meets second and fourth Tuesdays of each month.

Swan Pond Grange No. 22, located in Opequon District; meets second and fourth Saturdays of each month.

Mill Creek Grange No. 26, located in Gerardstown District; meets first and third Tuesdays of each month.

CHAPTER XVII.
PERSONAL SKETCHES OF THE ENTERPRISING PUBLIC AND PROFESSIONAL MEN OF THE PRESENT DAY.
SENATOR C. J. FAULKNER.

IN May, 1887, Mr. Faulkner was elected to the United States Senate, at which time he was on the bench, and resigned to accept the honor conferred upon him. As a representative, he has the respect and esteem of the people throughout the State, who feel proud of his marked ability and energy. Among the representatives of the country at the National Capital, he is fast gaining prominence and favor. After his election to the Senate he associated with him, Stuart W. Walker, an able and prominent young lawyer, for the practice of law, which firm now commands a large and excellent practice.

Senator Faulkner is the younger son of the late Hon. C. J. Faulkner, the eminent jurist and statesman, both of whose sons give promise of attaining the legal and political prominence of their father in State and National affairs. Senator Faulkner was born at the ancestral home at Martinsburg, Va., now West Virginia, on the 21st of September, 1847. He accompanied his father, who was Minister to France, in 1859, and had the advantage of attending noted schools in Switzerland and in Paris. He returned to the United States in August, 1861, and was with his father at the time of his arrest, in Washington; the story of which has become a matter of National history familiar to all. When he learned that his father had been arrested, he immediately started South, making his way resolutely and determinedly through all the difficulties incident to those troublous times. In 1862, when a boy of fifteen, he entered the Virginia Military Institute at Lexington. He served with the Cadets in the battle of New Market, where he was distinguished for his ardor and daring. And later, served as aide on the Staff of General J. C. Breckenridge, until he was made Secretary of War. His courageous and resolute bearing, allied to one so young in years, won for him the admiration of officers and soldiers, and made him a general favorite. He was afterward appointed aide to General Henry A. Wise, and surrendered with him at Appomattox, after which he returned home. Then began a course of mental training under his father's direction, and the foundation was there laid for a successful public life. The bent of his instruction and watchful care, was toward the field of law, in which the father occupied through all his life a leading place in the Circuit and Supreme Courts. Thus prepared by so able a preceptor, he entered the University of Virginia, in Oct., 1866, and graduated therefrom in June, 1868. He was admitted to the bar in Sept., 1868, immediately after attaining his majority. His mental endowments were of such high order that he at once became a member of recognized ability, and of such prominence as that led from the bar to the bench. He was elected judge of the 13th Judicial Circuit, composed of the counties of Berkeley, Jefferson and Morgan, in Oct., 1880, at the age of 33 years, being one of the youngest Judges in the State. He has presided over these courts with credit to himself and to the universal satisfaction of the people, by whom he is held in the highest regard and esteem. His judicial record gave assurance of still higher attainments in his chosen profession. His rulings and decisions have evidenced so impartial a sense of justice and so thorough a knowledge of the law, that a distinguished lawyer and political opponent said of him, "I would not hesitate to trust to Judge Faulkner's decision in his legal capacity upon any political question." His prudence and good judgment were not unnoticed in politics, in which, while not taking an active part, he manifested considerable interest. Senator Faulkner was chairman of the Democratic County Committee for a number of years before going on the bench, and is also widely and prominently known and esteemed in the Masonic fraternity, having been Grand Master of the Masonic Grand Lodge of West Virginia during the years 1879-80. By the last will of his father he inherits "Boydville," the old homestead, after the death of his mother, a place full of historical interest to citizens and strangers. He has built for himself a fine residence adjoining "Boydville," the house now occupied by his venerable mother.

HON. W. H. H. FLICK.

Mr. Flick was born in Cuihoga County, Ohio, February 24th, 1841. His youthful days were spent in the common schools, and a term at Garfield School, Hiram, Ohio. After that he worked on a farm until the war broke out, when he entered the army in July, 1861, serving in the 41st Ohio Regiment. He was dangerously wounded at Shiloh, April 7th, 1862, and joined the recruiting service. After his discharge he taught school to earn money enough to take up the practice of law, and then entered the Cleveland Law School, graduating and being admitted to practice in his native county in 1865. Upon his admission he settled in Moorefield, W. Va., for the practice of his profession, which he followed there in 1865 and 1866. In the Spring of 1867 he went to Pendleton County, where he married and has one child. He served two terms in the Legislature as representative in that county. In 1870 he introduced what is known as the "Flick amendment." He was appointed to fill an unexpired term as prosecuting attorney of Grant County in 1872, and elected to the same position in Pendleton County in that year. In 1874 he moved to Martinsburg, and has served in various official capacities since. In 1886, Hon. W. H. H. Flick made a strong run for Congress in the Second West Virginia District, and came within ninety votes of election. Shortly afterward he associated with him in the practice of law Mr. D. C. Westenhaver, one of the shining lights of the Berkeley Bar. Mr. Flick is an able and efficient talker, and enjoys a legal knowledge that but few can surpass. The firm now has an able and extensive practice in the various courts. It is almost needless to speak of Mr. Flick's popularity, as he is generally known throughout this and the surrounding States. He is of a clever and genial disposition, and makes one feel perfectly at home while in his presence.

HON. E. BOYD FAULKNER.

E. Boyd Faulkner was born in July, 1841. He received his early education at Georgetown College, and University of Virginia, and traveled extensively in Switzerland and Italy. He attended lectures upon constitutional law in Paris, and at the age of eighteen was acting as Secretary of the American Legation at Paris—an unusual and complimentary preferment to one so young—and which gave evidence of rare mental attainments, and of that strongly marked mind and character which distinguishes the man of to-day. He returned to the United States in 1861, was appointed aide on Gov. Letcher's Staff, but resigned shortly afterward and became an officer of distinction in the Confederate Army, until his capture at Port Republic, in June, 1864, when he was taken with other prisoners to Johnson's Island, where he was confined a year, being released in June, 1865. In 1867, he went to Hopkinsville, Ky., where he formed a law partnership with Judge Petree, and the firm had an extensive practice. By his energy and talent Mr. Faulkner soon earned for himself a fine reputation as a lawyer and speaker, and in the Seymour Campaign of 1868, was appointed an Elector for the Second Congressional District of Kentucky. In 1872 inducements were offered him to return to his native State, and he located permanently in

Martinsburg. He is well known at home and abroad as a gentleman of unswerving integrity of character, and his splendid abilities as a lawyer and public speaker in his professional and political career, are so well and favorably known to the people of this section and throughout the State as to require no commendation. He was elected to the Legislature in 1876, where he served with distinguished prominence and ability, and with a faithfulness to the interests of the people which will long be remembered, and especially noteworthy was the legislation by him to relieve the bonded indebtedness of Berkeley County. Under the arrangement made by the court and through the legislation of Mr. Faulkner, on the 2d of January, 1881, the 8 per cent. bonds were paid off or exchanged, and the county relieved of an annual drain upon it for interest and commission alone of about $3,465, besides having the bonds bear their just proportion of the taxes which weighed so heavily upon the people. Such was the universal esteem in which Mr. Faulkner was held that he was elected to the Senate in 1873, upon the expiration of his term in the Legislature. He was an eminent member of that body, and held in the highest regard by his fellow Senators. He declined the Presidency of the Senate, and remained where the work was to be done, becoming chairman of important committees, and his record was such as has been referred to with just pride and pleasure, and led to his being urged to become a candidate for the nomination of Governor of West Virginia in 1834.

At the present time his extensive and important law practice occupies all his time and attention. President Cleveland tendered to Mr. Faulkner the office of Consul-General and Agent to Egypt, which, at the earnest solicitation of his friends throughout the State, he decided not to accept. He was then tendered the Mission to Persia, which he likewise declined. For several years friends of Mr. Faulkner in every part of the State have been urging his candidacy for Governor of West Virginia. That he would receive a large vote and discharge the dignity and duty of the position in the most courtly and popular manner, is admitted by all.

HON. GEO. W. FEIDT.

Mr. Feidt was born in Washington County, Md., and came to Martinsburg in 1872. In his younger days he worked on the farm and taught school and studied law. He finished his law course with Blackburn & Lamon, in this place, and was admitted to the bar in 1875. In 1877 he was appointed Register in Bankruptcy on the recommendation of Chief Justice Waite. He occupies various positions in different organizations, and takes an active part in the interests of the town. He is a sound Republican, and no one does more enthusiastic work for the party than Mr. Feidt. He was elected Prosecuting Attorney of Berkeley County in 1886 by 146 majority, and has satisfactorily transacted the business of the office with skill and the best of legal ability. He is a worthy, affable and learned gentleman, and is a credit to his people.

STUART W. WALKER, ESQ.

Mr. Walker, though young in years, is considered very old in experience and legal knowledge. He is now one of the most able and successful practitioners at the West Virginia Bar, and an influential politician. He is of a clever disposition, social and agreeable to all who come in contact with him. Any one having a business connection will not hesitate to speak of him in the best terms. This able and creditable representative of the legal profession is a son of James H. Walker, now a retired farmer. He was raised on the farm with two other brothers. Much to his credit he possessed an ambition for future usefulness with intent to serve his people. He was educated at the Berkeley Academy, formerly in this city, and decided to make law his profession. This he successfully accomplished by taking a two years' course in one year at the Washington and Lee University, Lexington, Va. Upon his arrival home he was given a thorough examination by Judge C. J. Faulkner and Judge Armstrong, of Romney, who were then on the bench. In this he passed with honors, after which he was admitted to practice in the courts of the district. Through his energy and talent he at once became interested in and represented many of the most important civil and criminal cases before the courts. His success in the various courts attracted the attention of Judge Faulkner and led to his rapid advancement. He is an excellent talker, has a fine delivery and a persuasive and argumentative bearing. He is well known all over the State, having delivered speeches and addresses in every county. He is a man of self-confidence, and is always prepared to speak on any topic at a moment's notice. In May, 1887, Mr. Faulkner was elected to the United States Senate, immediately after which he formed a law partnership under the firm name of Faulkner & Walker. This move of business on the part of Judge Faulkner, while adding much labor to the firm by a heavy increase, encouraged Mr. Walker with more than usual zeal. He has since represented the cases and produced the ablest arguments that have ever been laid before our courts. Important cases have taken him to many counties in the State.

Mr. Walker has been identified by birth with the Democratic Party, and has always taken great interest and worked with untiring zeal for its advancement. During the campaign of 1884 he spoke for weeks, daily, and often twice a day, throughout the Thirteenth Senatorial District. His friends, irrespective of party, are urging him to accept positions of responsibility and trust. For him to accept any nomination will insure a victory to his party. The stand he has taken has led the people to believe that he will mete justice fairly and honorably to all. His past career has been a most honorable and successful one, through which he now enjoys the confidence and esteem of his people. Mr. Walker has the vigor and confidence that will achieve the greatest results.

DAVID C. WESTENHAVER, ESQ.

It was when the conflict of contending armies was expending its force during the late civil war that the subject of this sketch was born. He is a native of this county, and has lived here since his birth. His father was a farmer, and consequently his early education was confined to such branches of information as are usually taught in the average country school. His nature was not such to be content with this, and with an innate desire for a higher and more comprehensive knowledge, we find him aiming at and striving for a greater degree of excellence. He taught school, and at the same time pursued a course of instruction in law under private tutors. This merely opened to him a view of the wide field beyond, into which he boldly plunged alone, and, unaided any more by such private instructions as he previously had. We can say nothing better for him than that few persons, through their own personal efforts and ability, have ever raised themselves to such a degree of high public esteem and in so comparatively short a time as has Mr. Westenhaver.

He completed his law course at the Georgetown Law School, taking a two years' course in one and graduating with honor. The thesis upon which his essay for this occasion was written was "Expatriation and Naturalization," and which gained for him the first prize from the above institution.

Upon entering the active duties of his chosen profession he assumed a partnership with Hon. W. H. H. Flick, under the firm name of Flick & Westenhaver, the firm remaining so constituted at the present time. In 1886 he was appointed Prosecuting Attorney of Berkeley County to fill an unexpired term, and fulfilled the trusts of that office with great satisfaction to the people. Mr. Westenhaver's mental attainments are of the highest order, and though a young man, his place is a conspicuous one at the Bar, as well as among recognized leaders of his political school in this county. In politics he is a Democrat. In oratory he can boast of but little excellence ; his persuasive powers in this direction are effective, not because of any brilliancy of speech, but because of clear and unequivocal argument. His past career as a lawyer has been pre-eminently successful. His is an example of a self-made man. His future career cannot but make him a successful leader and an honored and respected citizen.

BLACKBURN HUGES, ESQ.

This able representative of the Berkeley Bar was born in Cumberland County, Va., and educated at Hampden Sidney College, Virginia, graduating from that institution in June, 1859, with the Speaker's medal from the Union Society. He studied law in Judge Brockenborough's Law School, in Lexington, Va., in 1860 and 1861. He first practiced in the courts of his native county, and for a short time in Richmond, but removed to Berkeley in the fall of 1867, and after the repeal of the test oaths he was admitted to the Bar of this county, in which he has ever since occupied a leading place in talent and the regards of his fellow members and the people in general. Personally, he is a very agreeable gentleman, and takes an active interest in all public matters. He has filled several important trusts in church and State conventions. He was elected a member of the County Court in 1880, and on its organization was elected its President, to which position he has been re-elected each succeeding year.

Politically, Mr. Hughes has always been closely identified with the Democratic Party, though conservative in his views and liberal to all men, however widely differing on public questions. His name was prominently mentioned in connection with the State Senatorship from the 13th District in 1886. In 1887 he associated with himself Mr. Hugh A. White, an able and energetic young lawyer, and they are now engaged in a good practice before the courts of this district.

HON. GEO. M. BOWERS

Is a son of the late John S. Bowers, one of the leading citizens of the county. He was born at Gerardstown and received his education at the Martinsburg High School. When but a mere shool boy he showed promising business qualities and made extensive purchases and sales on his own account. Upon the death of his father he administered the estate (which was a very large one) and made a prompt and satisfactory settlement of everything. He took charge of the Eureka Mills, in this city, in 1884, and is yet carrying on the most extensive milling business in the city. He has considerable interest in real property and also in various organizations, manufactories, etc. On the 17th of March, 1888, he was elected a director of the C. V. and M. R. R., and is one of the most prominent directors of the National Bank. In politics he is a Republican and commands a large influence. By his zeal and energy he has won the esteem and respect of the Berkeley people, and in 1884 he was made Chairman of the Berkeley Delegation to the Parkersburg and Grafton Convention. His success and ability in this placed him before the people of the State, and through which he has achieved the loudest praise. In 1886 he was nominated on the Republican ticket for Legislature, and was elected by the largest majority ever given one man in the county. During his term of office he has not once failed or shirked any responsible duty that has fallen his lot. He is now Vice-President of the National Republican League for the State of West Virginia. His name is now being urged for State Auditor, and if nominated, there is but little doubt as to his election being a successful one, and a victory for the party.

Mr. Bowers has a large friendship and acquaintance among the farmers and laboring class of people. His kind, affable manners, and sound reasoning and persuasive powers has endeared him to the hearts of his people. He possesses the ability, and will execute any responsibility thrown upon him in the most successful manner.

PROF. J. A. COX.

Born in Ohio Co., Va., (now W. Va.,) May 30, 1858; graduated at Bethany College, W. Va., in 1882, with the degree A. B., taking the first honor of his class; received the degree A. M. one year later; is now, as Superintendent of the Martinsburg City Schools and Principal of the High School, in his sixth year in the profession of teaching; was two years Principal of the West Liberty State Normal School, at the end of which time the students almost unanimously petitioned the State Superintendent and Board of Regents for his re-appointment; was Principal of Kingwood Academy five months, which position he resigned to take charge of the city schools of Martinsburg; was given a letter of endorsement signed by all his Kingwood students, by his assistant teachers, and by all the trustees of the school; won a first premium in a mathematical contest with 955 competitors, thus becoming one of the authors of "The New Arithmetic," published by Eaton, Gibson & Co., Buffalo, New York; has written considerably on educational and other topics; and is the author of a neat little pamphlet on arithmetic, entitled "Two Hundred Practical Problems." Prof. Cox has given universal satisfaction at Martinsburg, so much so that his salary was raised several hundred dollars by the Board.

CHAS. P. MATTHAEI, ESQ.

Mr. Matthaei, the genial and agreeable Justice, is a native of Germany, and was born in the year 1835. He came to this country in the year 1854, and entered the confectionery business in Baltimore, Md., where he remained about six years. In 1860 he removed to Martinsburg and opened up a confectionery store in the building now occupied by Chas. D. Matthaei, next to Court House. After twenty-three years of business success, he retired, and turned the business over to Charles D., who has continued to the present day.

During his early days, his advantages for an English education were very limited, and Mr. Matthaei may creditably be termed a self-made man. In the fall of 1884 he was elected Justice of the Peace, which office he now holds. During his term of office, he has filled the position ably and creditably, and has given general satisfaction to the public. Mr. Matthaei is a close observer, of sound, practical judgment, and a genial and agreeable gentleman. He has held positions of honor and public trust, and acquitted himself creditably to the satisfaction of his constituents. Mr. Matthaei is considerably interested in the organizations, societies and corporations of the city, and is the owner of a large amount of property. He is well known throughout the State, and a very popular gentleman.

C. O. LAMBERT, ESQ.

Mr. Lambert, the present Mayor of Martinsburg, was born at Frederick City, Md., in 1838, and is a son of Frederick Lambert, Esq. He was educated in the public schools of that city, and at the age of fifteen years, entered the butchering business under Charles D. Schell. Here he served his time as an apprentice, acquiring every art and branch of the business. In 1857 he moved to Shepherdstown, and there carried on business for himself until the commencing of the war in 1861, when he enlisted in the Confederate Calvary, 12th Virginia Regiment. After the close of the war in 1865 he came to Martinsburg and entered business with his brother, George D. Lambert, where he remained until 1869, and then entered business for himself—continuing at the present day. Mr. Lambert was elected Councilman from his ward in 1878, and afterwards served three terms of two years each—five years and a half of which he served as Mayor *pro tem*. In 1884 he was elected Mayor by an excellent majority, and conducted the affairs of the city creditably and with ability. His services in this official capacity were appreciated in such a manner, that in 1886 and 1888, a demand was made by the people for his re-election, which was successfully accomplished. As Mayor of the City, Mr. Lambert has proven himself worthy of the office, and his services are appreciated by the people in general, who hold him in the highest esteem. He is a Democrat in politics, and of a genial and clever disposition. As evidenced by his past career, Mr. Lambert is what may well be termed a self made man. He is also at present carrying on business at his old location, No. 23 N. Queen st., where can be found at all times fresh meats, groceries, provisions, confectioneries, tobaccos, cigars, etc. Mr. Lambert is also considerably interested in farming pursuits, and various other enterprises.

C. W. DOLL, ESQ.

C. W. Doll, Esq., Clerk of the County Court, was born in this city in the year 1820. For nearly thirty years he was engaged in the dry goods business, after which he served six or eight years in the hardware line. He has served the County Court as Clerk since Jan. 1st, 1873, and has done valuable service to the county in the arrangement of the many papers and records on file there. On his election to this office he received almost the entire vote of the Republican and Democrotic parties combined. He is a courteous and obliging gentleman, and is held in the highest esteem by all who know him. As a citizen, he takes a great deal of interest, and is one of the most liberal men in the county.

ROBERT LAMON, ESQ

Mr. Lamon was born in Mill Creek District, Berkeley County, about nine miles from the city of Martinsburg. He was raised on a farm, and at an early age manifested considerable interest and energy in business and public affairs. He is a self-made man, having had advantage of no other education than the common school of his boyhood days. In politics he is a strong and influential Democrat, and under Lincoln's administration he served in the capacity of Deputy Marshal of the District of Columbia. As Secretary and Treasurer, he has been the means, to a considerable extent, of building up the M. & W. Turnpike, which office he fills to the present day. At the election in 1887 he was elected Sheriff of Berkeley County, by a majority of 338, a much larger vote than had been polled previously. He has served his people faithfully in this capacity, and in his accounts is up with the State. He is of a fine manly bearing, and is held in the highest respect. For a number of years he has acted as a Director of the People's National Bank.

S. H. MARTIN, ESQ.

Mr. Martin was born in Pottstown, Montgomery Co., Pa., in 1826, and came to this county in the year 1840. He was a clerk in the store of W. S. Long, at Bunker Hill, for a short while, after which he came to this city and entered the store of Jacob Van Doren. In 1842 he went back to the former place and remained with J. W. Grantham until 1851, when he again returned to town and clerked for B. R. Boyd. In 1857 he formed a partnership with Ezra Herring and continued until 1859, when they dissolved and Mr. Martin continued the store until 1860. Shortly afterward he formed a partnership with George Sherrer, which continued until the breaking out of the late war. In 1861 he went into the employ of the B. & O. R. R. office and remained until 1878. In the fall of '78 he was elected Clerk of the Circuit Court, which capacity he now fills with credit and ability. As a gentleman, he is kind and generous, and is one of Martinsburg's most worthy citizens.

WM. T. STEWART, ESQ.

In the person of Mr. Stewart, is represented one of Martinsburg's most prominent, wealthiest and influential citizens. He was born in this county and raised on a farm, acquiring none other than the common school education. He now holds and ably fills the offices of President of the National Bank, M. & W. Turnpike Company, and is also a Director of the C. V. & M. R. R. Being largely interested in county enterprises, he devotes considerable time and attention to industrial development.

CHAPTER XVIII.
BIOGRAPHY OF MARTINSBURG'S BUSINESS MEN.
THE PEOPLE'S NATIONAL BANK.

THIS institution was established in 1873 as a People's Deposit, with a capital of about $12,000. In 1874 it was re-organized as a National Bank, at which time two competing banks were charging 10 and 12 per cent. interest on money. This bank, after its reorganization, began business by charging 8 per cent., and was the first of the three to fall to 6 per cent. It was a grand success from the day it opened its doors, and has been managed with such financial ability that in fifteen years it has accumulated a very large surplus and dividend. Its line of bank deposits are decidedly larger than those of its competing neighbor. In 1882 the present site, on corner of Queen and Burke Streets was purchased, and has since been improved until it now constitutes one of the finest buildings in the city. The interior is elegantly and conveniently arranged, and handsomely furnished. The vaults are large and secure, and will compare with any in the State. For fifteen years the finances of this bank have been under the management of Jno. B. Wilson, Esq., who has served the institution ably and successfully as cashier. With A. J. Thomas, Esq., as President, it cannot but help insure a successful future. Mr. Thomas is an excellent financier and is largely interested in various enterprises. Through the energy and zeal of Mr. Wilson, cashier, this bank in 1888 gained the topmost round on the ladder of success, by being designated a Depository of the United States. Mr. Wilson is a wide-awake and energetic citizen, popular throughout business circles, and highly esteemed by the people of his county. His assistants are Messrs. Geo. Knapp and Frank Wilson, who efficiently aid in the transaction of affairs, and for a knowledge of general banking business, are unsurpassed. By their liberality, caution and financial ability, the above gentlemen have made it a grand success, and its reputation at home and abroad is established and its business daily growing larger.

JOHN W. WALKER & CO.

Mr. John W. Walker, the efficient manager and head of this firm, is a son of James H. Walker, Esq., and was born in Berkeley County. He was raised on a farm with two other brothers, Hunter and Stuart, all of whom are well-known throughout the county, and are among the enterprising citizens. John W. was given the advantage of the common schools, and later attended an academy taught in Martinsburg by John Sellers, Esq. He next entered the Philadelphia College of Pharmacy, where he remained two years, and afterward started in the drug business in Martinsburg. After a decided success of two years in the latter place, he removed to Baltimore City, and passing a thorough examination before the Board of Pharmacy, he opened up in the drug business. Here he remained two or three years, when he again returned to his native county, and started the present merchandising firm. As a druggist Mr. Walker ranks among the most successful men of the day, having carried off the highest honors of his classes, and passed through the most difficult examinations. Since starting in the merchandise business, he has conducted one of the finest stores in the State. His place is neatly arranged, clean and convenient, and for fresh goods, he is unsurpassed by any in the city. Groceries and provisions of every variety are kept constantly on hand at the lowest possible figures. His present location is on Queen Street, National Bank Building. Mr. Walker is obliging and accommodating, and generally known throughout the county as an industrious and enterprising citizen.

P. A. CUNNINGHAM.

Mr. Cunningham is the eldest son, now living, of Philip S. Cunningham, dec'd., who served in the capacity of 1st Lieutenant under Col. J. Q. A. Nadenbousch, during the late war. P. A. was born in Berkeley County about one mile south of the present city of Martinsburg, in the year 1861. In 1866 the family moved to Fredrick City, Md., and returned to this county again in 1877. His father died before they moved to the former place, in 1865. Patrick A. was given the advantage of the Catholic schools in Frederick City, and at an early age showed considerable energy and enterprise. Like many others, he had the broad world before him, with but little assistance to gain a trade or profession. After their return to this city, he entered the photograph gallery under R. J. Rankin, Esq., where he remained about two years,—serving the required time as an apprentice. He next went with P. C. Hunter, and ably assisted in building up a standard reputation, about the year 1882, and remained for a period of nearly five years. In July, 1886, he purchased the establishment of his former employer, Mr. Rankin, and undertook a business routine, which he has since successfully accomplished and merited. He is a genial and clever young man, and is a great deal thought of by the young people in general. His present place of business is situated over the National Bank, Queen Street, where photography is finely executed in all its branches. He uses the instantaneous process, and guarantees satisfaction. A large and well equipped line of picture frames are always to be found in stock. His studio is well furnished, and everything complete for the trade. He also makes a specialty of copying and enlarging. One will find in Mr. Cunningham a warm friend, and an obliging gentleman.

P. NICKLAS, BRO. & CO.

This firm has been long established in Martinsburg, and has become one of the leading houses in town. The father of the present firm followed carpet manufacturing in the Cumberland Valley from his youth, and the sons have established business houses in several of the leading towns in the Valley. One branch after another has been added, and enlargements made as the business increased, until now they have every convenience for their extensive trade in carpets, furniture, chamber sets, library furniture, wall papers, &c. Fully prepared to do all kinds of upholstering and repairing. Their carpets range from the cheaper goods to the best American and European manufacture. The most obliging attention is given to the trade, and special pains taken to please purchasers. Mr. W. O. Nicklas is the manager of the firm, and is one of our most enterprising citizens. He takes part in various organizations of the town, and has built for himself a neat and attractive home on the corner of Queen and John Streets. The business rooms of the firm are at No. 11 Queen Street.

E. G. BARTLETT.

Mr. Bartlett is a native of Marshal Co., W. Va. He located in Cumberland in 1867, and was engaged in railroading, and removed to Martinsburg in 1866, following the same occupation. He was appointed to a position in the Hannis Distillery under President Arthur, and fulfilled his duties very acceptably, remaining until the new administration came in. He purchased the Book store of A. Oden, No. 17 Queen Street, in 1885, where he set to work to build for himself a permanent business. He deals largely in books, stationery, daily, weekly and monthly papers and magazines, tissue paper, drawing paper, map drawing and sketch books, school supplies, water color paints, steel engravings, autotypes, mottoes, picture frame mouldings; picture frames made to order; albums and scrap books, scrap pictures, music and musical merchandise ; agent for all newspapers and magazines at publishers' prices.

H. L. DOLL & CO.

Mr. Doll, the genial manager and proprietor of the large hardware establishment, situated on the Public Square, was born in Martinsburg in the year 1853, and is a son of C. W. Doll, Esq., Clerk of the County Court. He received a common school education, and afterward entered the hardware business as a clerk with H. A. Riddle, where he remained nearly ten years. In 1879 the firm of H. L. Doll & Co. was formed, and business commenced in the large and commodious building known as "King Street Hall," at which place they have continued till the present day. Mr. Doll has had considerable experience in the business, and has met with a decided success. The firm holds an excellent and most reliable reputation, and their business is conducted on a strict and sound basis. They keep constantly on hand everything connected with the hardware line, and make a specialty of House Paints, Builders Hardware, Farmers' Supplies, etc. They deal largely in Timothy and Clover Seed, and furnish every part of the business at the lowest possible figures. Their store and ware rooms, occupying two large floors, present a neat and clean appearance, and everything is arranged in the most convenient and pleasing manner. Their present location is on the corner of King and Queen Sts., Public Square.

R. FRANK BARR.

Mr. Barr, one of Martinsburg's enterprising young business men, is a son of Robt. Barr, Esq., a native of Virginia, and was born one mile south of Winchester, Va., in 1862. His advantages for an education were like the majority represented in this work—limited to the common school of his day. About the year 1882 he entered the jewelry business under W. L. Jones, where he remained nearly five years; completing his trade and gaining the advantages of the business in all its branches.

He then resigned his position and acted as General Secretary of the Y. M. C. A. After serving this worthy institution creditably and deservingly for a period of eight months, he decided to enter the jewelry business for himself. In May, 1888, he opened up in the J. L. W. Baker Building, North Queen street. Any article not in stock will be furnished within a short time, and everything offered on sale will be at the lowest reasonable figure. He makes a specialty of fine repairing, etc. Mr. Barr has had considerable experience in his business, and any one wishing to purchase will find in him a courteous and accommodating gentleman. He is a young man, energetic and industrious, and Martinsburg can well feel proud of him as a citizen.

BURKHART & CO.

Dr. Wm. D. Burkhart, the leading partner and manager of the above firm, is a native of Berkeley County. In 1852 he graduated in medicine at the University of Maryland, and afterwards practiced in this city for about three years. As a physician he built up a splendid practice and fine reputation. A short while afterward he gave up his practice and became teller in the old Bank of Berkeley. About the year 1865 he organized the present National Bank, and was elected cashier, which position he filled with ability and success. Through his untiring efforts this institution continued to progress, until it had gained a reliable and wide reputation. He continued in the banking business for a period of twenty-five years. In 1879 he established the Glass and China firm, known as Burkhart & Co., which he has successfully managed to the present day, and gained for it an enviable reputation. He is the exclusive dealer in the city, in fine goods of his line. The store is neatly and artistically arranged with beautiful lamps, fancy goods, etc., of every description. Dr. Burkhart is a genial and clever gentleman, and one with whom it is a pleasure to deal. Their present location is on North-east corner of Public Square, adjoining his residence, and near Continental Hotel.

JOHN W. NEER.

Mr. Neer was born in the year 1829, and is a native of Loudon County, Virginia. His boyhood days were spent in farming pursuits, and no other advantages were had for an education, excepting those offered by the common schools. He came to Martinsburg in 1850, and was employed as an engine man on the B. & O. R. R., until 1857. He then returned to Loudon County and engaged in farming until 1863. Shortly afterward he served as sutler in the Fourth Brigade of the 19th Army Corps of the 24th and 28th Indiana, and 26th and 27th Ohio Regiments, commanded by Col. Washburn. About the year 1865 he engaged in the coal, wood and lumber business at Harper's Ferry, where he remained until 1870, when he was washed out by the great flood on the Shenandoah River of that year, and incurred a loss of about $3,000. He then commenced farming in Jefferson County, W. Va., and continued from 1871 until 1873, when he again engaged in the service of the B. & O. R. R., and served the company until 1887. After a service of twenty-one years as engine man on the B. & O., he decided to permanently locate in business. On the 13th of March, 1888, he purchased the entire stock and fixtures of G. A. Smith, and opened up on King street, near St. Clair Hotel, a first-class general merchandise store. Everything in the line is kept always on hand at the lowest possible figures, and his store is neatly arranged and stocked with fresh goods. He makes a specialty of fine cigars, tobaccos and green groceries. Mr. Neer is a pleasing and accommodating gentleman, and the general public will find in him energy and enterprise,—so essential for the requirements of an upright business.

J. P. SWARTZ.

Mr. Swartz was born in the year 1829, and is a native of Berkeley County. During his early days his entire time was given to the milling business, and with a common education, he commenced business in what is now known as the "Swartz" mill, in 1842. Here he continued until 1880, when he established himself permanently in the merchantile business. As a miller, Mr. Swartz has few superiors, and while engaged in the business met with much success. His patronage extended far beyond Berkeley and adjoining counties. In 1880 he opened his store in the room adjoining O'Neal's drug store, but on account of increasing demands in business, was compelled to seek larger quarters. Shortly afterward he moved to Wysong's Hall, where he remained a short while, and then removed to the large and commodious room he occupies at present. His place of business is centrally located, being next door to the Post-office. At all times can be found good, fresh goods, and at reasonable prices. He makes a specialty of flour, feed, grain and groceries, besides a well supplied stock of general merchandise. Mr. Swartz is a genial and clever gentleman, and one with whom it is a pleasure to deal.

LEMEN BROS.

The genial manager of the above firm, Thomas T. Lemen, is a native of Jefferson County, and was born in the year 1863. During his boyhood days his entire attention was given to farming pursuits. In the fall of 1878 he entered Shepherd College, at Shepherdstown, and graduated in 1881. He then resumed farming and continued until July 25th, 1887, when he and his brother entered business in Martinsburg. They purchased the store and fixtures, for many years occupied by J. W. Roberts on Queen street. Thomas T. is yet a young man, and, although young in years he is old in practical business experience. He is a son of M. B. Lemen, Esq., an old, experienced and reputable farmer, yet residing in Jefferson County. During his younger days, Thomas manifested and showed considerable ability for business qualifications, and at an early age became interested in many important matters. With his brother, he is doing a large and successful business on a sound basis, commanding an excellent reputation. Their present location is Queen street, next door to Adams Express Office. They deal in flour, feed, coal, wood, etc., at the lowest possible figures. Mr. Lemen is an obliging and accommodating gentleman, and deserves the patronage of the general public.

M. L. DORN, JR.

Mr. Dorn, the young and energetic tailor, situated on East Martin street, is a son of Martin L. Dorn, Sr., and was born in Martinsburg in the year 1861. He was given the advantages of the common schools for an education, and at an early age entered the tailoring business under his father. He applied himself to every branch of the trade, and after several years service attended a cutting school in New York, under the well-known firm of John J. Mitchell & Co. After acquiring the art and its advantages, he returned to Martinsburg, and in 1883 established himself permanently in business. Mr. Dorn has devoted his entire attention to the trade, and as a cutter, he is unsurpassed by any in the State. He is yet a young man, energetic and industrious, and is held in the highest esteem by all his acquaintances. His place of business is located on East Martin street, where can be found at all times the latest styles and best qualities of Cassimeres, fancy suitings and pantaloonings. At his place will be furnished the lowest prices, with a full line of goods always open for inspection. Mr. Dorn is genial and courteous, and guarantees satisfaction to all his patrons.

I. L. BENDER & BRO.

Messrs. I. L. Bender & Bro. engaged in the lumber business about twelve years ago, succeeding H. L. Clippinger & Co., for whom I. L. was book-keeper. Their yard at that time occupied a small leased lot on corner of East Race and Spring streets. They have since, by purchase, obtained possession of this and adjoining lots, thus extending their yard from a front on East Race along Spring, with rear on John street. They have also added large buildings and sheds for shops and the storage of an ample supply of lumber, doors, sash, blinds, flooring, siding, etc., for the demands of their trade. Their own railroad siding for loading bark, loading and unloading lumber, and their central location and convenience to the railroad shops, makes their place of business one of the most desirable in the city. In 1881 they added the coal and wood business to their already large trade. In this they have enjoyed a marked success, owing to their well deserved reputation for furnishing the best coal in good condition, good weight and prompt delivery. Messrs. Bender are among our substantial and reliable business men, who have added by their own energy and kind indulgence much to our city's appearance, as well as to the comfort of not a few of our people.

Lee M. Bender, of the above firm, was born in Pennsylvania, raised on a farm, and attended public day schools during the winters. Later he attended a private school at Greencastle, Pa., where he stood among the highest in his class in Latin and the higher mathematics. From here, in 1875, he went to the Williamsport Commercial College. After graduating he took the position of head book-keeper for the firm of Rowley & Hermance, now the largest manufacturers of machinery in the State. During the winter of 1876 he was emplyed as Professor in the theoretical department of the College High School. Coming to Martinsburg in 1878, he entered the lumber business in which he is still engaged.

J. WM. HILL.

The above name represents one of Berkeley County's most energetic and enterprising young men. Mr. Hill was born in the year 1859, in Martinsburg, and is a son of James E. Hill, an old established and reputable shoemaker, situated on West John Street. He obtained no other advantages for an education than those offered by the common schools of his day. At the early age of fourteen years he entered the shoe business with his father, and served five years. Leaving this he acted in the capacity of a clerk from 1879 until 1882, when he entered the Post Office as delivery clerk under the efficient Post-master, J. Nelson Wisner. He remained here about fifteen months, and then went to Baltimore, where he completed a practical clerkship under the reputable firm of Geo. K. McGraw & Co., one of the finest retail stores in that city. He afterward returned to Martinsburg and resumed a clerkship until 1888. Having obtained a complete and practical idea of the grocery business, he established himself on Queen Street, and opened up a first-class store. Mr. Hill is well known throughout the town and county, and is a popular young man. He possesses a kind and courteous disposition, is honest and upright in his dealings, and is agreeable to all. His place of business is located on Queen Street, next door to Crump's hardware store. At all times can be found a fresh and well supplied stock of groceries, provisions, etc., at reasonable prices.

HYDE'S JEWELRY STORE.

A short sketch of the jewelry establishment of Mr. H. S. Hyde, its past history, and present dimensions, may be of interest to the reader.

Vast contrasts are presented as between the jewelry house of H. S. Hyde as it is now and as it was in 1823, when Jas. Hutchison, a practical silversmith, established it. It was then the first enterprise of its kind in the Valley; its patronage was but limited, and its trade came from a sparsely settled country, whose inhabitants had little use for jewelry, and whose possessions of silver plate were usually limited to a modest array of articles that now-a-days would seem primitive enough. The premises occupied by Mr. Hutchison were small—only about 12x15 feet, but for a long series of years they afforded ample room. In 1854 a son, Samuel Hutchison, succeeded to the business, and in 1870 he remodeled the building and enlarged the salesroom to 17x24 feet. Upon Mr. Hutchinson's death Mr. Hyde purchased the business, the stock then invoicing about $1,500. Mr. H., by the way, is a native of Strasburg, Va., (on the Shenandoah.) Working on his father's farm until he was 20 years of age, he determined upon another field of labor and so entered the jewelry business. In 1872 he went to Springfield, Ohio, where he completed his trade under the instruction of Benj. Allen, a leading jeweler in that city. In 1874 we find Mr. Hyde in Martinsburg connected with the firm of Welland & Hyde, and in 1877 he purchased the pioneer jewelry store of this section—a house whose trade has wonderfully developed under his management.

Upon entering the store (which was recently enlarged, so that now the salesroom is upward of fifty feet deep) one's eyes are greeted with the glitter of gold and the sheen of silver, while one's second self is reflected from numerous mirrors adorning the walls. The contents of the numerous show cases naturally arrest attention; in one case we see gold and silver watches, and precious stones; the contents of the adjoining case are in part a duplicate of the first—here also are gold pens, pencils and other articles. Case No. 3 is chiefly devoted to jet and initial jewelry; No. 4 to fine silver ware; No. 5 to flat ware; Nos. 6 and 7 to granite ware, statues and toilet sets; No. 8 to French clocks; No. 9 to American clocks; No. 10 to novelties of various kinds. We also notice one of Lillie's improved safes, a massive iron and steel affair, weighing 3,900 pounds—a fire and burglar proof receptacle for valuables.

Another thing we notice is the "Regulator," over 7 feet high, its huge pendulum swinging to and fro as it slowly and solemnly ticks out the moments. The room is handsomely finished and painted; the ceiling is especially noteworthy, with its centre pieces of inlaid wood from which depend globed chandeliers; in brief, the apartment is a model of good taste.

In addition to the local trade and the large repair business that is had—this latter department receiving Mr. Hyde's careful attention—the house controls a considerable jobbing business, filling orders in widely different parts of the country, and we fancy that Mr. Hyde has every reason to be satisfied with the aggregates of his business.

Mr. Hyde is still a young man, being only 33 years old. He is what may be styled a "self-made" man. Of the three jewelers who were carrying on business here in 1876 he alone remains. He has certainly accomplished a decided success thus far, and four young jewelers growing up insure success in business. His present establishment is said to be the largest between Baltimore and Wheeling, and is known as Hyde's Building, Nos. 48, 50 and 52 Queen street.

C. E. LAMAR.

Mr. Lamar, the genial and popular livery-man, is a native of Maryland, and was born in Frederick County in 1857. During his early days he was given no other advantages for an education excepting those offered by the schools of Frederick. His life during his younger days was given to business pursuits of various kinds, and in this way he obtained an education and idea of general business affairs. In 1882 he engaged in general merchandising near Shepherdstown, Jefferson County, W. Va., and continued about three years. Disposing of his mercantile business, and about a year later, he opened up a livery and sale stable at Charlestown, in 1884. He contined here about two years, and taking advantage of the opportunity, he decided to move to Martinsburg, where the trade was completely monopolized by one livery-man. In 1886 he announced his opening at the St. Clair Hotel stables, where he has continued to the present day.

Since opening a first-class livery, Mr. Lamar has had the general run of patronage, which is well evidenced by his fine turnouts of horses and vehicles. Mr. Lamar is a genial and agreeable gentleman, and is a very popular man. He can be found at the St. Clair Hotel, where he makes his office, at all times ; and for a fine turnout, at the lowest figure, he can accommodate all.

GEORGE E. KERSHNER.

The above name represents one of Martinsburg's energetic and industrious young men. Mr. Kershner was born in Hedgesville, this county, about the year 1853, and is a son of George M. Kershner, Esq. His advantages for an education were limited to that of the common school. At an early age he apprenticed himself at the plastering business, under his father's instructions, and applied himself to the trade in all its branches. A few years later he entered business for himself, and has succeeded in establishing a reliable business. His present location is on Williamsport Pike, near Moler Avenue. Mr. Kershner is prompt, energetic and industrious, and fair in all his dealings.

JOSEPH STEWART.

Mr. Stewart is a son of J. W. Stewart, Esq., and was born in Martinsburg in 1865. His education was limited to the common schools of his early days, and as a pupil he ranked among the highest of his classes. He apprenticed himself at an early age to the butchering business, under William R. Kline. After remaining with Mr. Kline for some years, and obtaining the advantages of the trade, he opened up business for himself. His present place of business is located on Queen street, North B. & O. R. R. crossing, where fresh meats of all kinds are kept constantly on hand. Mr. Stewart is yet a young man—energetic, genial and industrious, and will give general satisfaction to all who may favor him with their patronage.

EMMERT & FIERY.

Mr. B. F. Fiery, the senior member of this firm, is a native of Washington County, Md., and was born in 1830. He commenced business at Funkstown, Md., in 1864, where for nearly eight years he was engaged in merchandizing. About the year 1872 he came to Martinsburg and enaged in business with Samuel Emmert, father of the present F. S. Emmert. The firm continued a successful business for nearly six years, when F. S. purchased his father's interest.

Mr. F. S. Emmert, of the present firm, is also a native of Washington County, Md., and was born about the year 1852. He came to Martinsburg in 1872, and remained under the old firm until 1878, when he purchased his father's entire interest.

Since the present firm has been constituted it has enjoyed a reputable and successful business. From 1878 they occupied, for a period of nearly nine years, the room now used by Frank Doll & Co., and on account of the increasing demands of their trade they were compelled to secure larger quarters. In the spring of 1887 they purchased the site adjoining the Market House, and in the fall moved into one of the largest and finest buildings in the State. Through their untiring energy and business zeal they now own and occupy the most creditable building in the city. It is a handsome brick structure of three stories, modern plan, and conveniently arranged with steam, gas, lights and many other improvements. The dimensions of their store room are 100 feet deep by 23 feet wide, and is elegantly finished. Their specialties consist in part of dry goods, ladies' wraps, dress goods, carpets, &c. Everything in this line can be had at their place, and with their motto, "good goods and low prices," they will guarantee satisfaction to the trade. This firm is an old established one of an excellent reputation, and their past record will insure a successful future. Both gentlemen are among the popular, enterprising citizens of the county, and are interested in various enterprises.

J. H. MILLER & SONS.

Messrs. J. William and C. A. Miller, the enterprising managers of this firm, are sons of J. H. Miller, Esq., and were born respectively in the years 1858 and 1863, in Hedgesville, Berkeley County. The common school of their day was the only advantage obtained for an education. The greater portion of their time was given to mercantile pursuits, and under their father's instruction they received a general and thorough business knowledge. In 1886 they entered the mercantile business, purchasing the large warehouse they now occupy, and supplying it with a large stock of agricultural implements. Through a well deserved integrity they have succeeded in establishing one of the most reputable and successful houses in the city. Their trade daily increased until now, by additions to their stock, they are handling a large line of improved agricultural implements, fertilizers, buggies, phætons, sulkies, harness, coal, wood, feed, etc. Their location is on North Queen street, at B. & O. R. R. crossing, where the lowest possible figures and reasonable inducements are offered to purchasers. These gentlemen are energetic and abreast of the times, and by their perseverance will push their trade to the highest degree of success, which they justly merit and deserve. Both are popular in the county, courteous and obliging, and are held in the highest esteem by their people.

A. M. GILBERT.

Mr. Gilbert represents one of Martinsburg's industrious and enterprising young men. He is a native of Middleway, W. Va., and was born in 1859. His father, John Gilbert, Esq., is among the successful farmers of Jefferson County. Arthur was given the advantage of a good education, and at an early age entered the drug business under Wm. Dorsey, Esq., where he remained several years. Here he applied himself to every branch of the business, gaining a thorough knowledge of pharmacy and business tact. In April, 1883, he entered business for himself, at his present location, on corner of Queen and Race streets, where he has built up an extensive trade. By steady application to business he has made a grand success and gained an excellent and wide reputation. Mr. Gilbert is yet a young man, sociable and agreeable, and one with whom it is a pleasure to deal. He possesses the necessary energy and vim so essential for a successful business, and from present prospects he is destined to make his mark in the drug business. At his place can be found at all times and at reasonable figures everything kept in a first-class drug store. For compounding prescriptions he has but few, if any, susuperiors.

P. C. HUNTER.

Mr. Hunter, well-known throughout business circles, is a native of White Hall, Baltimore County, Md., and was born in 1844. He received his education in the public schools of that county, and was raised on a farm. Hardly had he arrived at the age of 16 years when his father, P. G. Hunter, Esq., died. This threw a great responsibility upon the young man—managing the affairs of a large farm and family of younger children. Possessing self-confidence and vim, he heeded it not, and in a short while found himself at the helm of success. At the age of 28 years he went under the instructions of Mr. Henry Pollock, the leading photographer of Baltimore city. After mastering his chosen profession in its various branches, he launched out for himself, and entered business in Baltimore in 1872. In April, 1881, he moved to Martinsburg, and opened up a first-class photograph gallery, where he now enjoys the success of a reliable and wide reputation. His past business career has been a grand success, and by steady application he intends to surpass his rivals in the future. Mr. Hunter is agreeable, sociable, and an industrious gentleman. He is an adapt in portraiture in all its branches, such as oil, pastel, crayon, India ink and water colors, in various styles and sizes. His present location is on Queen street, three doors South of Market House.

JOHN FELLER.

Mr. Feller, the genial and clever proprietor of the "Academy of Music" and an energetic citizen, is a native of Hessen, Germany, and was born in 1820. He was educated in the schools of that place, and emigrated to America in 1844. In 1855 he located at Martinsburg, and entered the mercantile business. In this he was very successful for a number of years, when he disposed of his business and built the hotel, known as the Shenandoah House, corner Race and Queen streets. He continued in the hotel business for a period of about 16 years, gaining a popular and well-deserved reputation. About the year 1858 he built the large and commodious hall, known as "Feller's Hall," on the same site. In 1879 the hall was burned down, and afterwards rebuilt. However, at this time, Martinsburg contained no public hall or building of any importance, and consequently Mr. Feller, in erecting a building of this kind, met with the approval of the general public. In 1887 the increasing demands for a larger and better hall, caused him to enlarge and remodel the building in elegant style. An addition of 40 feet was added, making it 100x44 feet in dimension. The building is of two large stories, with a double entrance, and contains all the modern conveniences and improvements. It is handsomely frescoed, well ventilated, elegantly lighted with gas, heated by steam, and comfortably furnished. It contains a stage 22x37 feet, arranged with fine scenery, and well lighted. The name of the hall has since been changed, and now enjoys a wide and established reputation, known as the "Academy of Music." This hall is conceded to be one of the finest in the State, and is ably supported by the general public. Mr. Feller is well known as an energetic, clever and obliging gentleman, and is very popular among the people of his county especially.

L. A. L. DAY, M. D.,

Homœopathist, Martinsburg, W. Va.—Office near the Presbyterian Church, makes the treatment of Chronic Diseases a specialty.

Doctor Day is a graduate of Pulte Homœopathic Medical College, Cincinnati, Ohio, graduating first in his class, receiving the Faculty Prize, a gold medal, and also the first Clinical Prize for passing the best clinical examination.

In 1797 Hahnemann, the founder of Homœopathy, announced the principle which has made him famous. Although it has been received with derision by a vast majority of the medical world, it has steadily progressed in favor, overcoming obstacle after obstacle, until to-day the system of medicine founded upon it, numbers among its patrons and steadfast friends a large proportion of the more intelligent and cultivated of each community. It is recognized in some of our universities. Our State Boards of Health are in part composed of Homœopathists. Some of our state institutions are controlled by them.

Homœopathy is the system of medicine in unison with *Nature's Law,* based on the law of similars, indicating that the drug to be curative must be given to the sick for symptoms *similar* to those produced by the drug on the healthy person, the motto of which is *Similia Similibus Curantur.* The progress of Homœopathy has been very rapid considering the prejudice with which it has had to battle. Ninety-one years have elapsed since Hahnemann promulgated his discovery, that which has made him so honored by the millions of suffering humanity. A law that has caused the greatest revolution ever before or since in the history of medicine. The progress has been so rapid that it is practiced in every portion of the civilized world, and at home here in the

United States. Although it is but about sixty-five years since Dr. Gramm, the first Homœopathic Physician, first settled in New York—and to-day we have eleven Homœopathic medical colleges, one Ophthalmic and Otological college, 17 Periodicals, 43 Homœopathic Hospitals, 26 State Medical Societies, 99 county societies, 43 free dispensaries, probably 10,000 Homœopathic Physicians, and patronized by the hundreds of thousands. The printed literature of the Homœopathic school is numbered by the millions of pages.

Isopathy is a system of medicine, the law of which is often mistaken by many as being the *Homœopathic law*. The Isopathic law is the prescribing of a medicine for the cure of a disease that was caused by the same medicine. For example, if a man is poisoned by *arsenic* he will be given more *arsenic* to cure him. The homœopathist, in treating such conditions will give an emetic and proper antidotes. This is based on chemistry and can only be treated chemically.

Accessory treatment is that branch of therapeutics which is not medicinal, and people must not think that this treatment belongs to any school of medicine, for they are based on chemistry, physiology, hygiene and mechanics. Mechanical or operative surgery and obstetrics are the same and do not belong to any system. Let this fact be remembered, that homœopathy differs only from other systems of medicine in *medicinal treatment*. Many have the small dose of homœopathy as an objection to the system, which varying from drop doses of the pure tincture to portions of a drop or grain at frequent intervals, thus avoiding the sickening, weakening and grave physiological effects produced by medicine when given in large doses: "How does so small a dose act?" it is asked. "How does a large dose act?" Neither can be explained, for it cannot be told how they act. Who can tell how the miasm, an unseen influence, the product of decay, or putrefaction of animal or vegetable substance produces intermittent fever, (the so called malaria,) or the infinitesimal germs too small to be seen with the microscope, yet a fruitful source of disease; or who can tell how the child inherits the much-to-be-dreaded scrofula, or the tendency for consumption from a parent? Yet such is known to be the fact in many instances, but it cannot be explained like the first question, How does the small dose act? or many other facts in science. The small dose has cured and is curing where the large one utterly fails. Under the observation of a conscientious, intelligent and devoted class of physicians, the dose needs no defense, for it is established beyond contradiction both in theory and practice.

In disease the small dose of medicine will assist nature, because nature is trying to remove the cause of disease from the system, therefore the homœopathic remedy, by assisting her efforts, removes the disease, where the larger dose of medicine will weaken the system and thus retard recovery. The healthy eye can endure a very bright light, while the diseased eye will have to be protected, showing that it takes a far less quantity of medicine to have an effect on the diseased body than on the healthy, because the one acts in unison with nature's law, while the other acts contrary.

THOMPSON & TABLER.

Mr. James F. Thompson, senior member of the above well-known firm, was born in Martinsburg, W. Va., (then Virginia,) September 15th, 1859. He is the eldest of the thirteen children of Samuel J. and Sallie Thompson—a quiet, industrious couple. When the war closed and the school system was in its incipiency, James entered the old Third Ward School, on John street, and began to drink deep at the fountain of knowledge. He was naturally a bright boy, but his father's family was a large one, and rather than throw the entire burthen of its support upon him, James worked hard during the summer months and studied earnestly and late during the long winter nights,—laying the foundation of a good business and general education. He was ambitious, however, and soon left Martinsburg to work with his uncle, Jno. W. Dalgarn, in the office of the *Spirit of Jefferson*, at Charlestown. Here, for over three years he worked at odds, steadily advancing from "devil" to compositor and assistant editor, and winning a splendid reputation for business qualities, earnestness and sobriety, and making numerous influential friends. But he loved old Martinsburg—the scene of his boyhood, the hope of his future. Once more, working hard and persistingly for a livelihood in the humblest spheres of labor, (but still attending the Grammar School during the winter,) he won the commendation and esteem of the watchful public of his native town. His energy and determination were not lost sight of by business men. When Louis Bouton opened his large store at the now Berry stand, young Thompson was employed by him. A hard man with whom to get along, James retained his position, while old clerks went out and new ones came in every month. He remained with Mr. Bouton about two years and a-half. Then Mr. H. N. Deatrick obtained his services. "Jim" stood up to his new avocation, and soon became the leading salesman in town. Persons knew he would not deceive them. He remained with Mr. Deatrick until he closed out his stock, after which he sought more suitable quarters and went in with Mr. David Weil, in the clothing business, occupying the confidential position of manager of the store in the Staley Building. By dint of carefulness and push, he advanced in the estimation of Mr. Weil to such an extent, that in one year he held a partnership in the business. His success was phenominal. Soon afterwards Mr. Weil retired, and James, or "Jim" as the boys familiarly call him, continued the business, taking in as a partner Mr. M. G. Tabler, a clerk under the old firm, and a pushing, watchful young gentleman. These two worked up an enormous trade. Their quarters grew too small, and the stocks was removed to their present handsome location in the Homrich building, on Queen street, where prosperity has followed them. Mr. Thompson is a self-made man—the success he enjoys is the result of years of attentiveness and toil. No man in Martinsburg has an equal knowledge of all the details of the clothing business. He seems to be a part of the business. He is a good judge of material; has a quick insight into the markets,—knows when to recommend,—keeps the best makes of clothing, and treats poor and rich with equal courtesy and attention. "Can't" is a word not to be found in his dictionary; and business tact is a family trait. With the spheres of his usefulness ever widening, he enjoys the confidence of the entire community, and lends a helping hand to every laudable enterprise. He was mainly instrumental in establishing the celebrated See Chair Factory here, and when the company went out of organization, in company with Messrs. H. C. Berry and Dr. L. A. L. Day, he purchased the business, and will spare no means or time to push it to activity and paying advantage. Mr. Thompson was married to Miss Minnie S. Ray, of Shepherdstown, on February 28th, 1888, and now resides on West King street, in one of the DeGrange buildings.

Mr. M. G. Tabler, the junior member of the firm of Thompson & Tabler, is the eldest son of James W. and Amelia Tabler, of Berkeley County. His father is an enterprising and thrifty farmer, and instilled within the very being of his son, the essence of thrift and push that made his own life so successful. Mayberry was born November 8th, 1862, in the neighborhood of Darkesville, and spent the days of his early manhood on his father's farm But he felt that his sphere of usefulness was too limited on the farm, and when eighteen years old, came to Martinsburg and entered the Berkeley Academy. Here he applied himself diligently for two years, winning the esteem of Prof. Dieffenderfer, and going to the front in his class. His teacher said: "Tabler had an originality of conception, an acute insight, was energetic and attentive, and had every indication of possessing the essentials going to make up a good business man." He was quiet and industrious, watchful of the small things, and thorough in his work. After leaving the Academy, he entered the services of Mr. D. Weil, then conducting a flourishing clothing business in the Staley building. Here he met Mr. Jas. F. Thompson, and formed those mutual ties of confidence and friendship which finally united the two young men in the business they now so successfully pursue. Mr. Tabler is careful and honest. His face is an index of his character, and a warrant from him, as to the quality of goods, is as good as gold. Being a young man and possessing a large circle of acquaintances, he has done much to make the business of the firm stable and permanent. The country people feel that in him they can depend. Under the careful training of his more experienced partner, and possessing natural qualifications for the business, he has developed into a safe and careful salesman, and an efficient business man. None complain of his dealings. Having made, moulded and fashioned his own character, winning his deservedly popular name of "fair dealer," he goes on quietly in the even tenor of his way, contented to see his patronage increasing and his customers satisfied.

The business of the firm is steadily increasing. The store room is one mass of handsome novelties, fine suits, and the general concomitants of the business. Conducting a large "made to order" feature with the well-known firm of M. Friedman & Sons, of Baltimore, Md., the suits they turn out are perfect in fit and material. Theirs is undoubtedly the soundest and best trade in town. Satisfaction always follows the sales, and their patronage is not limited to counties, states or ages. The growth of the business is the result of the old saying : "By industry, true worth thrives."

CHARLES H. BOWERS.

Mr. Bowers, one of Martinsburg's enterprizing citizens and business men, is a son of Jno. A. Bowers, Esq., and was born in Martinsburg in 1857. He received his education at the common schools of his day, and in 1872 entered the B. & O. R. R. machine shops as an apprentice, where he remained four years—serving the required time and acquitting himself creditably. Shortly afterward he was called to Garrett City, Indiana, where he commanded an excellent position in the B. & O. shops. After remaining about one year, he was compelled to leave on account of ill health, and returned to the shops at this city. In 1885 he established himself in the merchandise business on North Queen Street, and has continued to the present day. His store occupies the entire floors of a two-story building, wherein an enormous stock of goods is kept and a successfull business transacted. His stock consists of staple and fancy goods, groceries, canned meats, fish, fruit, vegetables, imported and domestic pickles, sauces, choice teas, coffees and spices, relishes and other condiments and delicacies, in fact all the necessaries and luxuries of the table, as well as the latest novilties in the dry goods line, including the most popular dress patterns, imported and domestic hosiery, underwear, ladies and gentlemen's furnishings, trimmings, embroideries, sewing materials, white goods and notions. His present location is on North Queen Street, near B. & O. R. R. crossing. Mr. Bowers is a shrewd business man, energetic and industrious, and of a genial and clever disposition. He takes considerable interest in various enterprises, and has won the respect and esteem of his people.

HANSON T. MORROW.

Mr. Morrow, one of Hedgesville's enterprising and energetic business men, is a native of Jefferson County, is a son of James W. Morrow, Esq., and was born in the year 1846. His advantages for an education were those offered by the common school of his day. At an early age he entered the milling business under his father, and remained for a period of about seven years. Afterward he returned to school, attending during the winter season and milling during the summer months. In 1864 he entered the military company under Captain Robt. Baylor, in Company "B," 12th Regiment, Virginia Cavalry, and served until the close of the war, a period of about one year. After the war he followed the pursuit of farming for about two years, when he entered the silversmith business under Wm. Johnson, of Frederick, Md. Here he remained two years and gained every advantage offered in the business. In the spring of 1887 he opened up in Hedgesville, and from that date has continued until the present day in a successful business. His present location is on Main street, and conveniently arranged for the benefit of the general public. Mr. Morrow first opened in the silversmith business and afterwards added the saddler business, repairing of machinery and sale of flour and feed. In his trades he is a skilled workman of talent and energy, and is doing a thriving business. Considerable amount of repairing on jewelry, watches, etc., is sent him from the larger cities. Mr. Morrow can well be termed a self-made man, and as an industrious and clever gentleman, holds the highest respect and esteem of his people.

SAMUEL W. HOPEWELL, (COL.)

Mr. Hopewell represents one of the energetic, clever and industrious colored citizens of Martinsburg. He is a native of Jefferson County, W. Va., and was born at Shepherdstown, December, 17th, 1826. He was a son of Henry Hopewell, Esq., who was well known throughout Jefferson County for his sobriety and uprightness. During Samuel's early days the advantage for an education was very limited with his race, and consequently he obtained no other learning than that given him by his friends. He was employed on a farm, where he remained for nearly twenty years, and made many warm friends. He afterward acted as a caterer and carried on barbering for a number of years. During the late war, in 1863, he was conscripted by the Eastern Maryland Regiment. However he served but a short while, and was exempted from service on account of ill health. He then returned to Martinsburg, from which place he went to St. Louis, Mo., and remained until after the surrender at Richmond. Mr. Hopewell is well known throughout the community, and takes an active part in business affairs. With his race he stands high in their estimation, and has won the respect of a large circle of acquaintances. During the past twenty years he has successfully followed barbering, and continues at the present day on East Martin Street. As a tonsorial artist he cannot be surpassed in hair cutting, shampooning, dying and shaving. He employs two skilled workmen regularly, and has his shop conveniently arranged.

APPENDIX.

SKETCH OF

◁ HENRY SHEPHERD, ESQ., ▷

— OF —

SHEPHERDSTOWN, JEFFERSON COUNTY, WEST VA.,

WITH THE HISTORY OF

✻ WILD GOOSE FARM. ✻

HENRY SHEPHERD, ESQ.

THE REWARD OF ENERGY AND INDUSTRY A GRAND SUCCESS.

A MAGNIFICENT COUNTRY SEAT.

WILD GOOSE FARM.

AN ELEGANT RESIDENCE, SURROUNDED BY WELL CULTIVATED AND IMPROVED LANDS AND MODERN STRUCTURES.

ONE of the most attractive country seats in the Eastern portion of our Mountain State, is the time honored manor of the well-known Shepherd Estate, four miles North of Shepherdstown, in Jefferson County.

Looking out from a gently reclining hill, on the picturesque Potomac, with its varied and beautiful scenery, this old Virginia Homestead is one of those well remembered resorts, which in ante-bellum days were the pride and boast of the people of the South.

This part was then owned by the late Mr. R. D. Shepherd, a wealthy and distinguished member of the family, by whom it was christened "Wild Goose Farm."

This magnificent estate, which altogether embraces about a thousand acres of the most fertile and productive land in this section of the country, has since been purchased by Mr. Henry Shepherd, who is its present owner, and by whom it has been greatly improved, especially that portion upon which he and his family reside, and which he calls his *Upper* Farm.

Passing up a long avenue of well grown and carefully

selected forest trees—beech, linden, maple and others—we approach the mansion. Here on a knoll, embowered 'mid a profusion of waving willows, stately poplars, and quaking aspens, stands the residence, built in a quadrangular shape, with two extended wings—a pretentious frame structure of a comparatively modern architecture.

To some it may not seem effectively grand, but around it is woven a web of early family history, of intense interest to the living representatives of an aristocratic ancestry, long since passed away.

We enter through a Gothic porch, a spacious hall, leading to the parlors, which are simply but richly furnished—skillfully reflecting mirrors and choice paintings adding to the pleasing effect.

The library, adjoining, is a most unique and handsomely furnished room, and the dining and bed-rooms in elegance and taste correspond with the parlor and library.

From a wide piazza, in a lovely window in front, we look down upon a miniature lake, on which sport the graceful swan, lordly geese and countless Muscovies.

A view of the garden presents a happy blending of the useful and ornamental—real vegetable gardening decorated. In fact, an observing eye will see at a glance over the surrounding grounds, beds, mounds and terraces, vines, shrubbery and arbors, that Mr. Shepherd exhibits the same fondness for embellishment, garden, park and landscape, as do the English people of fortune and culture.

From the dwelling a fine gravelly walk leads down to the dairy and spring, while northward two white shelly roadways wind around a diamond-shaped centre plat, converging at the barn.

The stables, in which the well-bred driving horses stand, are constructed after the best models, and the mangers furnished with the latest contrivances for safe feeding.

The carriage room, with oiled floor, is equipped with

barouches, phætons, falling tops and village carts, while the room connecting exhibits a fine display of harness, most admirably arranged,—altogether affording the material for several handsome turnouts.

Around the stables are a number of fox and rabbit cages, while near by howl a pack of anxious hounds, ready for the chase—sport in which Mr. S. sometimes indulges.

Across from the stables is an octagon Japanese Pagoda, tastefully designed and painted, and surmounted by a gilt ball, weather cock and wild goose. Here stands the morning sentinel, who at appointed hours strikes the bell, giving signal and summons for all the workmen to repair to labor.

The barn and extended range of stables are planned and equipped with a view to the greatest convenience and usefulness.

A long row of painted shedding contains and shelters the various agricultural implements, all assorted and kept with the same system and care which mark everything about the premises.

Hostlers and watchmen are constantly on duty about the barn and stables, taking care of the property and the large herds of valuable cattle, sheep and hogs—all in quality and condition in keeping with the fine order of things so plainly visible wherever you turn.

Passing down the avenue from Wild Goose you behold dotted here and there over the farm, a number of modern style cottages where dwell the workmen in plenty, comfort and contentment.

Leaving the avenue and entering upon the well known Shepherd Grade, a mile drive over a fine stretch of wide level road, long famous as the course upon which the speed of many a steed was tried in other days, and you arrive at another branch of the Shepherd Homestead, now known as the *Lower* Farm.

This was the life-long residence of Mr. Henry Shepherd, Sr., the father of the present owner and proprietor, as also that of the grandfather, Capt. Abram Shepherd, who, in the language of a memorial by an eminent divine of Virginia, "served with distinction in the Revolutionary War under Col. Hugh Stephenson. He marched with his company from Shepherdstown to Boston, in July, 1775, and in March, 1776, returned to New York. He was in the celebrated battle of King's Bridge, Nov. 16th, 1776, and after Col. Rawlings and Major Otho H. Williams, of Maryland, were wounded, he commanded the Rifle Regiment of Maryland and Virginia during the remainder of the action. He received a letter from Gen. Washington but two months before the General's death, speaking of him as a valuable officer in the Revolutionary War."

Here is a unique and queerly constructed large stone mansion, built more than a century ago, and while Mr. S. is making many improvements in the surroundings, including barns, stables and other buildings, yet the main dwelling itself is preserved, unoccupied by any one, in its original state, and its internal arrangement and much of the old time furniture still kept intact, even the old desk and arm chair and huge inkstand remain as left by his father, in marked contrast with the too common spirit of the day, which soon loses attachment for old landmarks, and in the desire for change entirely obliterates them.

Situated on a beautiful incline, shaded by tall oaks and hardy locusts, its white walls look out in their virgin purity from amid the drooping foliage, giving an air and appearance of some ancient castle, but its chief glory is storied rather in traditions and memory of a venerated ancestry than in the architectural beauty or symmetry of the structure.

Such is a fair, modest description of the Shepherd estates, as will be fully realized by any one visiting this beautiful country seat, in which is centered the most hallowed associations and cherished recollections of a historic family.

But this sketch would be incomplete without at least a brief notice of the individual characteristics of both the founder of Wild Goose Farm, the late Mr. R. D. Shepherd, and the present owner of the combined estates described, Mr. Henry Shepherd.

The former, Mr. R. D. Shepherd, was one of those remarkable characters, embodying in one individual to a rare degree a number of those positive qualities that make men great. He was strong in intellect, rigid in system, firm and inflexible in conviction, of uncompromising integrity and extraordinary executive ability. Still, he was generous and kind-hearted, distributing large sums of money among those of his kin whom he deemed worthy, and hardly any of them can be named who have not at some time or some way shared his beneficence and gratuities. As a friend and adviser he was frank, honest and valued, and this reputation is not merely local. Residing at different periods of his life in Baltimore, Boston and New Orleans, his record is everywhere the same, and the implicit confidence he enjoyed and universal respect he commanded, wherever known, will long remain as the indisputable evidence of a pure and unimpeachable character. He retired in the later years of his life, after an active, useful and successful career, to the place of his nativity, Wild Goose Farm, where he died in November, 1865.

The present Mr. Shepherd possesses, in large degree, the qualities and characteristics which distinguished his uncle, R. D. Shepherd, with the advantage in his favor of the many advances of the age in which he lives.

He is a gentleman of culture and refinement, recognized public spirit and generosity, strict system and order at the same time, liberal and kind, and especially so to the poor.

Like hosts of Southerners, he was crushed financially

by the war, but with a business capacity that rebounds from reverses and overcomes them unaided, and by the force alone of his own energies, he has recuperated his fortunes and risen again to the comforts of plenty.

A recent business incident well deserves special mention. Instances are rare where men who once completely failed ever afterwards pay their creditors anything. Such cases, when they do occur, afford the highest standard of personal credit. Mr. Shepherd is one of the very few entitled to this honorable rank. Although his own failure was entirely caused by that of others—purely wrecks of the war—yet after the years of earnest effort by which he regained means, as soon as able and without realizing anything from those who are still largely indebted to him, and though his debts were long since legally barred, he voluntarily, and at a cost of a large sum—many thousands of dollars—paid and settled to the entire satisfaction of all his creditors. To-day he stands fully acquitted and discharged of all financial obligations whatever, a promised source of much future comfort and satisfaction amid the reflections of his retired life.

The true measure of the man in character and capacity, in heart and intellect, is best shown by his career in life—the struggles he has survived, the success attained, and the position of prominence and influence and respect which he still enjoys in the community in which he lives.

The past prestige and memory of the Shepherd family and estates are being well preserved and maintained, and will be creditably and honorably perpetuated and transmitted to posterity by the present worthy representative and proprietor, Mr. Henry Shepherd.

THE SHEPHERD FAMILY.

Mr. Henry Shepherd, the subject of this sketch, married Miss Azemia McLean, a daughter of Mr. Wm. James McLean, one of the most prominent and successful merchants in the city of New Orleans. As a result of this union they have been blessed with four sons, bearing the names of R. D. Shepherd, Henry Shepherd, Jr., Wm. J. and Augustus M. The two eldest were educated at the leading schools in this country, and have chosen occupations suitable to their refined and cultivated tastes; and the two youngest, Wm. J. and Augustus M., are now at college.

MR. R. D. SHEPHERD.

Has adopted the stage profession, under the *nom de plume* of "R. D. McLean," in honor of his accomplished and singularly gifted mother. The press pronounces the highest encomiums upon his theatrical talent, and predicts for him the brightest future. He has already been classed among the leading tragedians, and in proof of this we append the following criticism from the New Orleans *Democrat*, one of the leading journals of the South, which is complimentary in the highest degree. Mr. R. D. McLean has accomplishments rarely found, which fit him for the stage, and he voluntarily left his magnificent home in order that he might gratify this laudible ambition. He is possessed of a splendid physique and is a superb gentleman in the full sense of the term.

Thus it will be seen that the members of this historic family are aspiring to and filling positions of honor and trust, which is a source of unaffected consolation to their father, Mr. Henry Shepherd, who has stimulated his children by example and precept to honorable endeavor, and has been in a position to gratify their every wish. Such in brief is the history of this remarkable family and of their vast estate, known as Wild Goose Farm. The New Orleans *Democrat* says of R. D. McLean:

"It has given great satisfaction to our whole community, who take a natural and justifiable pride in the achievements of our native sons, to read the many eloquent encomiums of the dramatic art and accomplishment of our young tragedian, R. D. McLean, which have appeared in the newspapers of all the cities and towns in which he has filled engagements.

His dramatic tour, beginning August 15th, last, has embraced the states of Louisiana, Texas, Georgia, Alabama and Mississippi. In the principal towns in these States there has been one uniform concurrence of opinion and criticism in assigning to him the leading position on the American stage as a tragedian and artist.

With his remarkable natural endowments, physical and mental, and an innate histrionic tendency, all that was needed to develop in him all the qualities of a histrion of the highest class was the practice and training through which he has just passed, in the two years during which he has so zealously pursued his onward and upward course in the profession which he adopted with great personal sacrifice, but with an unextinguished affection and inexhaustible devotion.

Even in straight-laced Philadelphia, the tributes everywhere paid to Mr. McLean's achievements in his art throughout the South have been fully indorsed and confirmed by the able and appreciative journals of that city.

Thus, that most sedate and conservative of journals, the Philadelphia *Inquirer*, of May 8th, describes our young tragedian's appearance in that refined and cultured city :

The Philadelphia *Inquirer* of May 8th says : "The production of 'Ingomar' at the Arch Street Theatre last evening was the opening of the engagement of the two eminent artists, Miss Marie Prescott and R. D. McLean. Unusual interest was centered in the performance owing to the fact that it was the first opportunity which the Philadelphia dramatic public has had of seeing the latter of the two stars, and Miss Prescott had not been seen here for an unfortunately long time. In selecting 'Ingomar' for the initial performance the stars were happy in the choice of a drama in which they made a thoroughly enjoyable and strong dramatic representation. Mr. McLean is an actor of the most robust and manly pattern, of commanding physique and natural grace. His voice is powerful, deep-toned, resonant, and musical, and capable of every modulation and inflection with which to add strength to the romantic impersonation of the love-tamed, love-civilized barbarian, Ingomar. In voice and bearing he has every natural fundamental qualification for a tragedian, and his attainments show such a cultivation of the powers in his command as to leave no doubt about his possession of dramatic talent of the highest order. It would be vain to personify hypercriticism to attempt to find fault with a characterization which in every respect received such careful and pains-taking treatment as that which Mr. McLean has bestowed upon his romantic role. In every line and action he portrayed the true disposition of the barbarian, whose coarse nature underwent the rapid process of civilization through the influence of his hostage."

Another leading journal of the same city thus speaks of Mr. McLean's masterly delineation of Shylock:

"The delineation of Shylock by Mr. R. D. McLean last night at the Arch Street Theatre was especially powerful and impressive. He invested the character with new and telling points and became most intense at times in the representation. Instead of the beetle-browed, common, tricky and abhorrent Israelite of the slums, Mr. McLean's Shylock was a Jew of intellectuality, bitter and intense in his hatred of Antonio, not as a personality, but as the representative of Christian sects, who had stolen his daughter and his ducats and from time immemorial had persecuted his forefathers, stigmatized and scorned them. Mr. McLean was especially powerful in the scene which finds its climax in the words. "But I will not eat with you, drink with you or pray with you." His glorification when he learns of Bessanio's misfortune, finding expression in the sentence, "I thank

God for this news," was followed by a paroxysm of exultant laughter, intense in its hatred and bitterness. He clutches the air in his wild glee as he bade Tubal "Go and meet me at the synagogue" to thank God that the pound of flesh was to be his. He was called several times before the curtain. Miss Prescott made an impressive Portia, but her modulations often led to inaudibility, and she should tone her voice on a higher plane. All the other characters were well taken. This evening "Pygmalion" and "Galatea" and "Taming of the Shrew."

In a lighter and more graphic style the *Sunday News* gives the following sketch of our young tragedian:

"Jumping from a real estate office to depicting *Brutus* and his stentorian dialogue on a professional stage, isn't much of a jump for R. D. McLean. The rest of us, I opine, may not be able to so successfully and similarly jump.

It was from pleasant H. Grattan Donnelly that I first had the idea that the mantle of a great artist and actor is pretty certain to fall upon the broad shoulders of young McLean. Then I witnessed his *Ingomar* and *Brutus* and I fell into Donnelly's way of thinking.

The career of this new comer—for his is that to a certainty—is full of interest. Two years ago he made his initial bow on a professional stage at Kingston, N. Y. Three years ago and he did not know a professional actor. First the leading support to Miss Marie Prescott, and this year staring equally with her and coming an entire stranger to Philadelphia, he meets with remarkable press notice and cordial receptions. It is small cause for wonder if the prognostications of enthusiastic, kindly H. Grattan Donnelly should come true.

I was ushered into the room of the young Roman at the Continental one day last week, and there had a pleasant chat. He was the manager of a leading real estate firm in New Orleans early in 1887, when Miss Marie

Prescott came to the Crescent City by invitation of the Crescent City Shakspeare Club, to give a performance of "Hamlet." McLean was a member of the club, and played Horatio, this being his first appearance with a professional. Miss Prescott put on "Pygmalion and Galatea," by request, and Mr. McLean was asked to play Pygmalion. This he did for seven performances. Later he received a proposition from Miss Prescott to come to New York as her leading man, and after many inward debates and much hesitancy, the young man, then twenty-seven years of age, accepted.

The study that Mr. McLean has put in can scarcely be comprehended by the Prompter's readers, but it is a fact that he had never seen *Romeo*, *Ingomar*, *Malovlio*, *Fetruchio* or similar parts played, and his acting was therefore his own and based upon ardent study and many sleepless nights. Once only had he seen Salvini play *Ingomar*. Once only he saw McCullough play in "Virginius." He has been on the stage for two years, knows the parts of Shakspearean plays, and that too, thoroughly. He loves Roman characters, and will devote his best years only to such parts.

Mr. McLean was born in New Orleans, his father being Henry Shepherd, Esq., a Virginian, and his mother's name being McLean. He took the latter name for the stage. He is a nearer resemblance in physique to John McCullough than any actor living, and he has an arm like a village smithy. He is a trained athlete, can box like Billy Madden, went for years through regular gymnastic training, and he is more often boisterous than some critics like.

"When does the season close?" queried the prompter as he was taking his departure.

"At Chicago, two weeks from now, and I will not be sorry. We opened the season August 15th, and have been at it steadily every since, playing South—Texas, Mississippi, Georgia, Alabama and Louisiana. We have our coming season laid out to cover the very same places. Where do we rusticate? I go to Shepherdstown, W. Va., where my father still resides, and I shall study and yell amid the rocks and woods on the farm to my heart's content. Miss Prescott, I presume, remains in Chicago. Good day."

HENRY SHEPHERD, JR.

An able assistant and counterpart of his father, in all that appertains to the successful management of this vast estate, is the youngest son, Henry Shepherd, Jr. He is nearing the age of twenty-one years, and has already developed marked business capacity. His father, after whom he was named, has given him the general supervision of his extensive farming operations, and he has given evidence of his ability to carry out the wishes and desires of this ideal farmer, Henry Shepherd, Sr.

As a very necessary qualification to the successful prosecution of his chosen occupation, Henry Shepherd, Jr., has familiarized himself with farm work in every department, and has a thorough knowledge of the best methods of raising and developing thorough-breds of all kinds.

Having at this early age exhibited such marked business capacity, we confidently predict for this young husbandman an honorable and prosperous future—and that he will prove a worthy successor to his illustrious father.

www.ingramcontent.com/pod-product-compliance
Lightning Source LLC
Chambersburg PA
CBHW050324230426
43663CB00010B/1731